Suspicious Praise for *The United States of Paranoia*

"A superb analysis of American paranoia. . . . Ingenious . . . terrific, measured, objective." —*Publishers Weekly* (starred review)

"A remarkably comprehensive, wide-ranging look at the way American culture, politics, religion, and social structure have been affected by conspiracy stories. . . . Walker's intent is neither to ridicule nor debunk but simply to explore. . . . A lively, extremely interesting, and occasionally more than slightly scary book." —*Booklist*

"An insightful and entertaining look at the demons and devils that haunt the American imagination." —*Kirkus*

"Walker is able to convincingly illustrate how conspiracy narratives that may appear at first glance to be isolated, episodic interludes specific to the idiosyncratic circumstances of a particular era or social sphere, though distortions, are also real manifestations of enduring facets of a national consciousness. . . . *The United States of Paranoia* [is] a work of moral instruction." —*Los Angeles Review of Books*

"Free-floating fear and half-baked ideas about what's really going on have been a more significant part of American history than is generally accepted, according to Jesse Walker's thorough, meticulously researched book." —*Vice*

"Thoroughly researched and completely readable . . . engrossing . . . plays to the conspiracy theorist in all of us." —*New York Daily News*

"Oddly entertaining. . . . Walker quickly demolishes [Richard Hofstadter's "The Paranoid Style in American Politics"]. It's all too rare to come upon a writer willing to attack the sacred cows of the right and left with equal amounts of intelligence and flair."

—*Los Angeles Times*

"First there was *A People's History of the United States*. Now there's a paranoid's history, with Jesse Walker revealing that normal, sensible citizens have been conspiracy nuts ever since our nation's beginning." —Debbie Nathan, author of *Sybil Exposed*

"Prepare to be amazed." —Jeet Heer, author of *In Love with Art*

THE UNITED STATES OF PARANOIA

THE UNITED STATES OF PARANOIA

A CONSPIRACY THEORY

JESSE WALKER

NEW YORK • LONDON • TORONTO • SYDNEY • NEW DELHI • AUCKLAND

HARPER PERENNIAL

 For information, address HarperCollins Publishers, 195 Broadway, New York, NY 10007.

HarperCollins books may be purchased for educational, business, or sales promotional use. For information, please e-mail the Special Markets Department at SPsales@harpercollins.com.

All illustrations are courtesy of the author except where noted otherwise. Frontispiece: detail from front cover of *They Knew Too Much About Flying Saucers*, courtesy of the author.

FIRST HARPER PERENNIAL EDITION PUBLISHED 2014

Designed by Michael Correy

The Library of Congress has catalogued the hardcover edition as follows:

Walker, Jesse, [date]
The United States of paranoia : a conspiracy theory / Jesse Walker.—First edition.
pages cm
Includes bibliographical references and index.
ISBN 978-0-06-213555-1
1. United States—Politics and government. 2. United States—Civilization. 3. National characteristics, American. 4. Paranoia—Political aspects—United States. 5. Paranoia—Social aspects—United States. 6. Conspiracy theories—United States. 7. Political culture—United States. I. Title.
E183.W18 2013
973—dc23 2013011426

ISBN 978-0-06-213556-8 (pbk.)

14 15 16 17 18 OV/RRD 10 9 8 7 6 5 4 3 2 1

For Maya and Lila,

live fearlessly

Can't you see, he'd said, the truth is so much more interesting: secret societies have not had power in history, but the *notion* that secret societies have had power in history *has* had power in history.

—John Crowley, *Ægypt*

CONTENTS

THE UNITED STATES OF PARANOIA

S COMINTERN ENEMY WITHIN KU KLUX KLAN MIND C
ATAN ASSASSINS 9/11 ANGELS THE MATRIX ENEMY AB
GHOST DANCE "BOB" MYSTIC CLAN ENEMY OUTSIDE BA
ER OF THE QUEST HIDDEN PERSUADERS FREEMASO
ECRET CHIEFS JONESTOWN DANITES ILLUMINATI CIA Z
AN MIND CONTROL FEMA COINTELPRO BENEVOLENT C
NEMY ABOVE OPERATION CHAOS MEN IN BLACK ELDERS
TSIDE BACKMASKING NIGHT DOCTORS WATERGATE CU
MASONRY TRYSTERO SLAVE POWER MKULTRA ENEMY
NATI CIA ZOMBIES GENEVA CLUB

PART I

ROSICRUC
BENEVOLENT CONSPIRACY DISCORDIAN SOCIETY SA
N BLACK ELDERS OF ZION POD PEOPLE HOMINTERN GH
VATERGATE CULTS MANCHURIAN CANDIDATE ORDER OF
A ENEMY BELOW VATICAN FLYING SAUCERS SECRET CH
COMINTERN ENEMY WITHIN KU KLUX KLAN MIND CONT
SASSINS 9/11 ANGELS THE MATRIX ENEMY ABOVE OP
T DANCE "BOB" MYSTIC CLAN ENEMY OUTSIDE BACKMA
HE QUEST HIDDEN PERSUADERS FREEMASONRY TRYST
ECRET CHIEFS

PRIMAL MYTHS

JONESTOWN D
EMY WITHIN KU KLUX KLAN MIND CONTROL FEMA COIN
ANGELS THE MATRIX ENEMY ABOVE OPERATION CHAOS
TIC CLAN ENEMY OUTSIDE BACKMASKING NIGHT DOCT
RSUADERS FREEMASONRY TRYSTERO SLAVE POWER M
ANITES ILLUMINATI CIA ZOMBIES GENEVA CLUB ROSIC
TELPRO BENEVOLENT CONSPIRACY DISCORDIAN SOC
S MEN IN BLACK ELDERS OF ZION POD PEOPLE HOMINT
OCTORS WATERGATE CULTS MANCHURIAN CANDIDATE
POWER MKULTRA ENEMY BELOW VATICAN FLYING SAUC
LUB ROSICRUCIANS COMINTERN ENEMY WITHIN KU K
AN SOCIETY SATAN ILLUMINATI ASSASSINS 9/11 ANG
ION POD PEOPLE HOMINTERN GHOST DANCE "BOB" M
S MANCHURIAN CANDIDATE ORDER OF THE QUEST HID
W VATICAN FLYING SAUCERS SECRET CHIEFS JONEST
ENEMY WITHIN KU KLUX KLAN MIND CONTROL FEMA C
/11 ANGELS THE MATRIX ENEMY ABOVE OPERATION CH
MYSTIC CLAN ENEMY OUTSIDE BACKMASKING NIGHT D

1

THE PARANOID STYLE *IS* AMERICAN POLITICS

If men define situations as real, they are real in their consequences.

—*William and Dorothy Thomas*[1]

On January 30, 1835, as Andrew Jackson exited a congressman's funeral, an assassin drew a weapon and pointed it at the president. The pistol misfired. The gunman pulled a second weapon from his cloak. Though loaded, it too failed to fire. The cane-wielding Jackson and several bystanders subdued the would-be killer, an unemployed housepainter named Richard Lawrence. Lawrence later informed interrogators that he was King Richard III, that Jackson had killed his father, and that with Jackson dead "money would be more plenty."[2] He was judged insane and committed to an asylum, where he died three decades later. Lawrence was a lone nut.

Or at least that was the official story. It wasn't long before two witnesses filed affidavits claiming to have seen Lawrence at the home of the Mississippi senator George Poindexter shortly before the attack. Poindexter was a noisy opponent of the Jackson administration, and pro-Jackson newspapers accused the senator of plotting the president's murder. So did Jackson's allies in Congress, who quickly convened an investigation. Jackson himself told bystanders after the assault that the shooter had "been hired by that damned rascal Poindexter to assassinate me."[3]

Some of Jackson's critics countered by suggesting that the president had staged the assault to gain public support, and that this explained why both weapons had failed. And many Jacksonians pointed their finger at John Calhoun, the South Carolina senator and former vice president, arguing that if he had not been directly involved in the assassination attempt, he had at the very least incited it with a speech denouncing Jackson as an American Caesar.[4]

When the Republican writer John Smith Dye described the crime twenty-nine years later, he saw an even more devilish plot at work. Calhoun might not have been directly involved in the assault, Dye conceded: "Whether this man was induced to attempt to murder the President by listening to his defamer making speeches in the Senate . . . or whether he was secretly hired to assassinate him, God alone can determine."[5] But Dye believed that Calhoun had been a part of a larger force, the Slave Power, that would have benefited if Jackson had been put in the ground. And the Slave Power, Dye informed his readers, was more than willing to kill a powerful man to get its way.

In 1841, for example, President William Henry Harrison told Calhoun he wasn't sure he was willing to annex Texas, which southerners wanted to add to the union as a slave state. Harrison promptly died. Officially the cause of death was pneumonia, but Dye was sure that arsenic was to blame. Nine years later, Dye continued, President Zachary Taylor opposed the Slave Power's agenda in Cuba and the Southwest, and so he was killed by the same poison. And when President-elect James Buchanan prepared to make some appointments of which the slaveocrats disapproved, Dye declared, he narrowly survived one of the most elaborate assassination plots ever conceived.

On February 23, 1857, according to Dye, southern agents poisoned all the bowls containing lump sugar at the National Hotel in Washington, D.C. Southerners, he explained, drink coffee; coffee drinkers use pulverized sugar; so the southern diners would be spared and the tea-drinking northern diners, including Buchanan, would be wiped out. The future president barely survived the illness that followed. "Intimidated by the attempted assassination," Dye wrote, Buchanan "became more than ever the tool of the slave power."[6]

There is little evidence for Dye's explosive charges. You can make a case that Harrison's doctors did more to hurt than to help the ailing president, but no more than conjecture supports the idea that anyone deliberately killed him.[7] Coroners debunked the belief that Zachary Taylor had been poisoned when his body was exhumed in 1991. And Buchanan was not even present in Washington on February 23, 1857, though dysentery did break out at the hotel when Buchanan stayed there a month earlier and again when he returned for his inauguration. Today the outbreaks are usually attributed to a sewage backup that contaminated the inn's food and water, but at the time several stories circulated blaming poisoners for the illnesses, with the suspects ranging from a Chinese cabal to a band of homicidal abolitionists. Inconveniently for Dye's tea-and-coffee thesis, the dead included a southern congressman, John Quitman of Mississippi.

But when Dye's book *The Adder's Den* was published in 1864, the country was at war with the South, and when a new edition appeared two years later, under the title *History of the Plots and Crimes of the Great Conspiracy to Overthrow Liberty in America*, the nation was still reeling from the assassination of Abraham Lincoln.[8] In that atmosphere, a book that feels like a 1970s conspiracy movie set in the antebellum era received a respectful notice in *The New York Times* and was excerpted in the *Chicago Tribune*;[9] Republican papers praised it in Philadelphia, Harrisburg, Trenton, and New York City, and in

Richard Lawrence attempts to kill Andrew Jackson, National Archives

Pennsylvania even the Democratic *Easton Express* proclaimed it "the most powerful book of this century."[10]

Nor did Dye invent his theories from nothing: He drew on rumors that had been floating through Whig and Republican circles for years. After Lincoln was elected—well before Dye's book appeared—several supporters of the incoming president sent letters warning him to watch out for the plotters who had killed two of his predecessors. "General Harrison livd but a Short time after he was Installd in office," one concerned citizen pointed out, and "General Taylor livd but a short time after he took his seat. . . . You Sir be careful at the Kings table what meat and drink you take."[11] Another letter informed Lincoln that "I have often heard it stated by Physicians, that it was an undoubted fact, that our two last Whig Presidents, Gen's Harrison & Taylor, came to their sudden and lamentable ends, by subtle poisons, administered in their food at the White House."[12]

After Lincoln died, at least two prominent ministers—George Duffield of Detroit and William Goodwin of Connecticut—worked the supposed murders of Harrison and Taylor into their sermons.

Reverend Henry Ward Beecher not only invoked their alleged assassinations in an article for *The New York Ledger* but added the anti-secessionist Democrat Stephen Douglas to the list of victims, writing that he had been killed because his position in the party "made him one of the most efficient champions against the Rebellion."[13] During the effort to impeach Lincoln's southern successor, President Andrew Johnson, Representative James Mitchell Ashley of Ohio brought up the same old accusations, declaring that Harrison, Taylor, and Buchanan had been "poisoned for the express purpose of putting the vice presidents in the presidential office."[14]

And in May 1868, an extraordinary article in the *New-York Tribune* managed to out-Dye Dye, accusing a Democratic conspiracy of engineering the city's malaria outbreaks. After commenting that Zachary Taylor "fell under the malarious vapors of Washington and died" because he was prone to "acting honestly and straightforward," the *Tribune* writer claimed that Washington in subsequent years "was free of malaria—that is, for Democrats; but when the new Republican party began to gain strength, and it was possible that they might become the ruling power in Congress, the water of Washington suddenly grew dangerous, the hotels (particularly the National) became pest-houses, and dozens of heretics from the Democratic faith grew sick almost unto death." The contagions continued until Lincoln put "the walls and springs of the Capital" under "the care of loyal soldiers," ending the outbreaks. But after Lincoln was deposed, the pattern returned: Right before the vote to impeach Johnson, "we had a return of that bad water, and two or three Senators—Republicans, mind you—are prostrated with sudden illness. What does it mean? Why does it happen that whenever the current sets against the Master Demon of Slavery (*and never at any other time*), we find the air, and the water, and the whisky of Washington full of poison?"[15]

The assassination theorists weren't the only Americans worried about conspiracies of slaveholders. Dye didn't coin the phrase "Slave Power." The term was common currency in the North, where it was used to describe the political influence of the planter elite. This was not in itself a conspiracy theory, but it often adopted a conspiratorial coloring. In the words of the historian Russel B. Nye, the Slave Power had an alleged agenda to extend slavery "to the territories and free states (possibly to whites)" and "to destroy civil liberties, control the policies of the Federal government, and complete the formation of a nationwide ruling aristocracy based on a slave economy."[16] Lincoln himself believed that he could "clearly see" a "powerful plot to make slavery universal and perpetual,"[17] and in his famous House Divided speech he engaged freely in conspiratorial speculation.[18]

Senator Henry Wilson, later to serve as Ulysses S. Grant's vice president, put the idea bluntly: "Slavery organized conspiracies in the Cabinet, conspiracies in Congress, conspiracies in the States, conspiracies in the Army, conspiracies in the Navy, conspiracies everywhere for the overthrow of the Government and the disruption of the Republic."[19] Meanwhile, southerners had elaborate conspiracy theories of their own, blaming slave revolts, both real and imagined, on the machinations of rebellion-stoking abolitionists, treacherous land pirates, and other outside agitators.

It was a paranoid time. In America, it is always a paranoid time.

Pundits tend to write off political paranoia as a feature of the fringe, a disorder that occasionally flares up until the sober center can put out the flames. They're wrong. The fear of conspiracies has been a potent force across the political spectrum, from the colonial era to the present, in the establishment as well as at the extremes. Conspiracy theories played major roles in conflicts from the Indian wars of the seventeenth century to the labor battles of the Gilded Age, from the Civil War to the Cold War, from the American Revolution to the War on Terror. They have flourished not just in times of great division but in eras of relative comity. They have been popular not just with dissenters and nonconformists but with individuals and institutions at the center of power. They are not simply a colorful historical byway. They are at the country's core.

Unfortunately, much of the public perception of political paranoia seems frozen in 1964, when the historian Richard Hofstadter published "The Paranoid Style in American Politics."[20] Hofstadter set out to describe a "style of mind" marked by "heated exaggeration, suspiciousness, and conspiratorial fantasy," detecting it in movements ranging from the anti-Masonic and anti-Catholic crusades of the nineteenth century to the "popular left-wing press" and "contemporary right wing" of his time. A flawed but fascinating essay, "The Paranoid Style" is still quoted frequently today. Half a century of scholarship has built on, rebutted, or otherwise amended Hofstadter's ideas, but that work rarely gets the attention that "The Paranoid Style" does.

That's too bad. The essay does contain some real insights, and if nothing else it can remind readers that conspiracy theories are not a recent invention. But it also declares that political paranoia is "the preferred style only of *minority* movements"—and, just to marginalize that minority some more, that it has "a greater affinity for bad causes than good."[21] In an earlier version of his article,[22] Hofstadter went further, claiming that the paranoid style usually affects only a "modest minority of the population," even if, under certain circumstances, it "can more readily be built into mass movements or political parties."

Hofstadter did not provide numbers to back up those conclusions. We do have some data on the popularity of well-known conspiracy theories, though, and the results do not support his sweeping claims. In 2006, a nationwide Scripps Howard survey indicated that 36 percent of the people polled—a minority but hardly a modest one—believed it "very" or "somewhat" likely that U.S. leaders had either allowed 9/11 to happen or actively plotted the attacks.[23] Theories about JFK's assassination aren't a minority taste at all: Forty years after John F. Kennedy was shot, an ABC News poll showed

70 percent of the country believing a conspiracy was behind the president's death. (In 1983, the number of believers was an even higher 80 percent.)[24] A 1996 Gallup Poll had 71 percent of the country thinking that the government is hiding something about UFOs.[25]

To be sure, there is more to Hofstadter's paranoid style than a mere belief in a conspiracy theory. And there's a risk of reading too much into those answers: You can believe the government has covered up information related to UFOs without believing it's hiding alien bodies in New Mexico. (You might, for example, think that some UFO witnesses encountered weapons tests that the government would prefer not to acknowledge.) There is also a revised version of Hofstadter's argument that you sometimes hear, one that accepts that conspiracies are more popular than the historian suggested but that still draws a line between the paranoia of the disreputable fringes and the sobriety of the educated establishment. It's just that the "fringe," in this telling, turns out to be larger than the word implies.

But educated elites have conspiracy theories too. By that I do not mean that members of the establishment sometimes embrace a disreputable theory—though that does happen. When White House deputy counsel Vince Foster turned up dead during Bill Clinton's term in office, sparking an assortment of conspiracy tales, former president Richard Nixon told his personal assistant that the "Foster suicide smells to high heaven."[26] Clinton himself, on being elected, asked his old friend and future aide Webster Hubbell, "Hubb, if I put you over at Justice, I want you to find the answers to two questions for me. One, Who killed JFK? And two, Are there UFOs?"[27] But I mean something far broader than that. You wouldn't guess it from reading "The Paranoid Style," but the center sometimes embraces en masse ideas that are no less paranoid than the views of the fringe.

Consider the phenomenon of the *moral panic*, a time when fear and hysteria are magnified, distorted, and perhaps even created by influential social institutions. Though he didn't coin the phrase, the sociologist Stanley Cohen was the first to use it systematically, sketching the standard progression of a moral panic in 1972: "A condition, episode, person or group of persons emerges to become defined as a threat to societal values and interests; its nature is presented in a stylized and stereotypical fashion by the mass media; the moral barricades are manned by editors, bishops, politicians and other right-thinking people; socially accredited experts pronounce their diagnoses and solutions; ways of coping are evolved or (more often) resorted to; the condition then disappears, submerges or deteriorates and becomes more visible."[28] To illustrate the idea, Cohen examined the uproar over two teen subcultures of early 1960s Britain, the rockers and the mods, and their sometimes violent rivalry. In press accounts of the time, seaside towns were destroyed by warring gangs, with pitched battles fought in the streets. But the kids had actually stuck to insults and minor vandalism until the media trumpeted their distorted account, inspiring an intense public concern, an increased police presence, and, ironically, a new willingness among the mods and rockers to behave the way they'd been described.

An essential feature of a moral panic is a folk devil, a figure the sociologist Erich Goode has defined as "an evil agent responsible for the threatening condition"[29]—typically a scapegoat who is not, in fact, responsible for the threat. The folk devil often takes the form of a conspiracy: a Satanic cult, a powerful gang, a backwoods militia, a white-slavery ring. (In the case of the rockers and mods, Cohen writes, the press sometimes claimed that their battles "were masterminded, perhaps by a super gang.")[30] Cohen's case study is British, but there are plenty of American equivalents. One is the antiprostitution panic of the early twentieth century, which featured lurid tales of a vast international white-slavery syndicate conscripting thousands of innocent girls each year into sexual service. An influential book by a former Chicago prosecutor claimed, in the space of three paragraphs, that the syndicate amounted to an "invisible government," a "hidden hand," and a "secret power," and that "behind our city and state governments there is an unseen power which controls them."[31]

Coerced prostitution really did exist, but it was neither as prevalent nor as organized as the era's wild rhetoric suggested. Yet far from being consigned to a marginal minority movement, the scare led to a major piece of national legislation, the Mann Act of 1910, and gave the first major boost in power to the agency that would later be known as the Federal Bureau of Investigation. Within a decade, the Bureau would be extending its purview from alleged conspiracies of pimps to alleged conspiracies of Communists, getting another boost in power in the process.[32]

Such stories are missing from Hofstadter's account, which drew almost all of its examples from movements opposed to the "right-thinking people" Cohen described. The result was a distorted picture in which the country's outsiders are possessed by fear and its establishment usually is not. The essay had room, for example, for "Greenback and Populist writers who constructed a great conspiracy of international bankers,"[33] but it said nothing about the elites of the era who perceived Populism as the product of a conspiracy. Hofstadter did not mention the assistant secretary of agriculture, Charles W. Dabney, who denounced William Jennings Bryan's Populist-endorsed presidential campaign of 1896 as a "cunningly devised and powerfully organized cabal."[34] Nor did he cite the respectable Republican paper that reacted to the rise of the Union Labor Party, a proto-Populist group, with a series of bizarre exposés claiming that an anarchist secret society controlled the party. "We have in our midst a secret band who are pledged on oath to 'sacrifice their bodies to the just vengeance of their comrades' should they fail to obey the commands or keep the secrets of the order," warned one article in 1888.[35] "How shall we maintain our honored form of government, or protect life and property from assassination at the hands of these conspirators, if their dark and damning deeds are allowed to continue and be perfected?" asked another.[36] The paper kept up the drumbeat till election day.

Or consider this passage from Hofstadter:

> This enemy seems to be on many counts a projection of the self: both the ideal and the unacceptable aspects of the self are attributed to him. A fundamental paradox of the paranoid style is the imitation of the enemy. The enemy, for example, may be the cosmopolitan intellectual, but the paranoid will outdo him in the apparatus of scholarship, even of pedantry. . . . Secret organizations set up to combat secret organizations give the same flattery. The Ku Klux Klan imitated Catholicism to the point of donning priestly vestments, developing an elaborate ritual and an equally elaborate hierarchy. The John Birch Society emulates Communist cells and quasi-secret operation through "front" groups, and preaches a ruthless prosecution of the ideological war along lines very similar to those it finds in the Communist enemy. Spokesmen of the various Christian anti-Communist "crusades" openly express their admiration for the dedication, discipline, and strategic ingenuity the Communist cause calls forth.[37]

It is the most astute argument in the essay. But it never acknowledged that the same point applies to much of Hofstadter's elite audience.

There is a reason, after all, that Hofstadter's article begins with a reference to "the extreme right wing." In the early 1960s, the United States experienced a wave of alarm about the radical Right. This dread had been building throughout the Kennedy years and exploded after the president's assassination, which many people either blamed directly on the far Right or attributed to an atmosphere of fear and division fed by right-wing rhetoric. By the time Hofstadter's essay appeared, the "projection of the self" that he described was in full effect. Just as anti-Communists had mimicked the Communists, anti-anti-Communists were emulating the Red-hunters.

In 1961, for example, Walter and Victor Reuther of the United Auto Workers wrote a twenty-four-page memo urging Attorney General Robert Kennedy to join "the struggle against the radical right."[38] The letter, coauthored by the liberal attorney Joseph Rauh, called for Kennedy to deploy the Federal Bureau of Investigation, the

Internal Revenue Service, and the Federal Communications Commission against the enemy. By "the radical right," the Reuthers and Rauh meant not just the Birchers and the fundamentalist Christian Crusade but Senator Barry Goldwater and the libertarian William Volker Fund. In *Before the Storm*, his study of Goldwater's presidential campaign, the historian Rick Perlstein described Group Research Incorporated, an operation funded by the Reuthers' union, as "the mirror image of the political intelligence businesses that monitored left-wingers in the 1950s, identifying fellow-traveling organizations by counting the number of members and officers shared with purported Communist Party fronts. Group Research did the same thing, substituting the John Birch Society for the reds."[39]

Interestingly, the phrases that sounded so dangerous on the lips of the Right weren't always so different from the rhetoric of the Cold War liberals. Robert DePugh—the founder of the Minutemen, a paramilitary anti-Communist group of the 1960s—claimed to have been inspired by JFK's own words: "We need a nation of Minutemen, citizens who are not only prepared to take up arms, but citizens who regard the preservation of freedom as a basic purpose of their daily life." In *Before the Storm*, Perlstein noted that Kennedy "spoke often in these absolutist, apocalyptic terms."[40] When Hofstadter sketched out the paranoid style, he listed an "apocalyptic and absolutistic framework" as one of its characteristics. But he didn't have the thirty-fifth president of the United States in mind.

When scholars and pundits aren't claiming that paranoia is limited to the political extremes, they sometimes claim that it's a product of particularly harsh times—that a conspiracy panic might leave the fringe and seize a large portion of the population, but only when the country is in turmoil. In 2009, the conservative writer David Frum offered that explanation for the popularity of Glenn Beck, a right-wing broadcaster with a fondness for conspiracy stories. "Conspiracy theories," Frum wrote, "always flourish during economic downturns."[41]

He's right: They *do* flourish during economic downturns. But they also flourish during economic upturns. Frum was specifically attacking Beck for his interest in the idea that the Federal Emergency Management Agency (FEMA) was building secret concentration camps, so it's worth noting that the very same fear was previously popular on the left during the booming eighties and on the right during the booming nineties. For the last few decades, elements of whatever party is out of power have worried that the party in power would turn fascist; the FEMA story was easily adapted to fit the new conditions. (Beck, I should note, wound up rejecting the FEMA theory.)

Even if you set aside purely partisan fears, the 1990s, a time of relative peace and prosperity, were also a golden age of both frankly fictional and allegedly true tales of conspiracy. There are many reasons for this, including the not unsubstantial fact that even at its most peaceful, the United States is riven by conflicts. But there is also the possibility that peace breeds nightmares just as surely as strife does. The anthropologist David Graeber has argued that "it's the most peaceful societies which are also the most haunted, in their imaginative constructions of the cosmos, by constant specters of perennial war."[42] The Piaroa Indians of Venezuela, he wrote, "are famous for their peaceableness," but "they inhabit a cosmos of endless invisible war, in which wizards are engaged in fending off the attacks of insane, predatory gods and all deaths are caused by spiritual murder and have to be avenged by the magical massacre of whole (distant, unknown) communities."[43] Many middle-class bloggers leading comfortable lives spend their spare time in a similar subterranean universe.

This is a book about America's demons. Many of those demons are imaginary, but all of them have truths to tell us. A conspiracy story that catches on becomes a form of folklore. It says something true about the anxieties and experiences of the people who believe and repeat it, even if it says nothing true about the objects of the theory itself.

Just as an animist treats natural forces as conscious spirits, many conspiracists treat social forces as conscious cabals. Real restraints on national sovereignty become a pending UN occupation. Lousy conditions in the ghetto become a genocidal plot against blacks. An ongoing increase in executive power becomes an imminent dictatorial coup. Even a less elaborate theory can play this allegorical role. Take the idea that the football star O. J. Simpson was framed for the murder of his wife. Simpson was probably guilty, but sometimes the police do frame suspects, and few would claim that innocent black men never run into trouble with racist cops. For many African Americans, the Simpson case became more than one man's encounter with the law. As the journalist Sam Smith wrote during the trial, Simpson's defense served "as the mythic translation of stories never allowed to be told. The stories that should have been on CNN but weren't. Everything is true except the names, times and places."[44]

In the next few chapters I will lay out five primal myths that underlie America's conspiracy folklore. By using the word *myths*, I don't mean to suggest that these stories are never true. I mean that they're culturally resonant ideas that appear again and again when Americans communicate with one another: archetypes that can absorb all kinds of allegations, true or not, and arrange them into a familiar form. One is the Enemy Outside, who plots outside the community's gates, and one is the Enemy Within, comprising villainous neighbors who can't easily be distinguished from friends. There is the Enemy Above, hiding at the top of the social pyramid, and there is the Enemy Below, lurking at the bottom. And then there is the Benevolent Conspiracy, which isn't an enemy at all: a secret force working behind the scenes to improve people's lives.[45]

Because these are tales of masks and puppeteers and events that are not what they initially seem, the cabals can shift their shapes over time. Plotters at the bottom of the social hierarchy are suddenly discovered to be manipulated by plotters at the top; or the plotters at the top turn out to be agents of a foreign conspiracy; or, conversely, it's the foreign conspirators who are controlled by plotters at home.

In the 1960s, the John Birch Society, which had attracted notoriety by accusing eminent Americans of being agents of international communism, changed course and started arguing that international communism was controlled by powerful U.S. capitalists. The society also suggested that black and student protesters in the United Sates were pawns of the same cabal, a setup the Birchers described as "pressure from above and pressure from below."[46] And those shifts took place within the worldview of a single organization. Conspiracy tales can change even more dramatically when a story leaks from one social group to another. Different people adopt and adapt these myths for their own needs, keeping the scaffolding of a story line in place while changing the content.[47]

There are few pure examples of those five core myths. But there are prototypical tales that tell us a lot about how each category functions. In the first half of the book, we will watch those stories take hold in early American history, and we will see some of the ways they have echoed through the centuries that followed. In the second half, we'll move from the deep end of history into the more recent past, watching those primal tales in action as Americans react to events from Watergate to Waco to today. Throughout the book, we will also see the myths manifest themselves in stories that do not pretend to be true—in fiction, film, television, songs, comics, games—and watch as those overtly imaginary tales influence accounts that are supposed to be accurate. We will also observe the rise of an ironic style of American paranoia, a mind-set that is less interested in believing conspiracy theories than in playing with them.

But before we do any of that, I should make three things clear, both to prevent misunderstandings and to distinguish my project from some of the other conspiracy books that are out there.

First: *I'm not out to espouse or debunk any particular conspiracy theories.* It would be absurd to deny that conspiracies can be real. Spies, terrorists, and mafias all exist. Alger Hiss really did engage in espionage for the Soviet Union. The Central Intelligence Agency really did plan a series of coups and assassinations. At the very moment that you're reading this, someone somewhere is probably trying to bribe a politician. The world is filled with plots both petty and grand, though never as enormous as the ancient cabals described in the most baroque conspiracy literature.

It will sometimes be obvious, as with John Smith Dye's yarn about the plan to poison James Buchanan, that I think a conspiracy story is untrue. There will also be times, particularly in chapter 7, when I discuss conspiracy stories that clearly *were* true. Often a theory will have elements of truth and elements that are more fanciful. But this is ultimately a history of the things people believe, not an assessment of whether those beliefs are accurate. This book has nothing to say about who killed the Kennedys or what UFOs might be. It has plenty to say about the stories we tell about assassins and aliens.

Second: *This book isn't exhaustive.* Every significant event in U.S. history has inspired at least one conspiracy theory, and plenty of insignificant events have done the same. I will describe a lot of them, but it would be impossible to cover them all. Still, if I've done my job, you will not simply come away from this book having learned about the stories I've told. You'll come away with a tool kit that will help you make sense of the stories I *didn't* tell, including the yarns that have yet to emerge.

Similarly, I will generally ignore the political paranoia found in the rest of the world, though I will occasionally cover a foreign story if it has had an influence on these shores. I do not believe that the United States is unusually paranoid in comparison with other countries, and I'm sure a fine book could be written comparing and contrasting the conspiracy theories that flourish in America with the tales told elsewhere. But this is not that book.

Finally: *When I say* paranoia, *I'm not making a psychiatric diagnosis.* I hope it's obvious that I'm using the word *paranoia* colloquially, not clinically. But it's worth stressing the point, because there's a long history of people using psychiatric terms to stigmatize political positions they oppose. I wish a better word than *paranoia* were available, but I don't think such a term exists. (*Conspiracism* comes close, but it doesn't quite cut it, since political paranoia can take the form of a dread that is broader than the fear of a cabal.)

To his credit, Hofstadter insisted that he had "neither the competence nor the desire to classify any figures of the past or present as certifiable lunatics," adding that "the idea of the paranoid style would have little contemporary relevance or historical value if it were applied only to people with profoundly disturbed minds. It is the use of paranoid modes of expression by more or less normal people that makes the phenomenon significant."[48] But you still can come away from his article with the sense that large swaths of the American past have just been put on the psychoanalyst's couch. And not every writer in his tradition has been as careful with his caveats as Hofstadter was. The same fall that *Harper's* published "The Paranoid Style," with its opening declaration that "the Goldwater movement" showed "how much political leverage can be got out of the animosities and passions of a small minority," *Fact* magazine announced that "1,189 Psychiatrists Say Goldwater Is Psychologically Unfit to Be President!"[49] Naturally, those irresponsible diagnoses from afar included the claim that the candidate had "a paranoid personality."

Like Hofstadter, I'm not limiting my scope to certifiable lunatics. Unlike Hofstadter, I'm not limiting my scope to minority movements either. By the time this book is over, I should hope it will be clear that when I say virtually everyone is capable of paranoid thinking, I really do mean virtually everyone, including you, me, and the founding fathers. As the sixties scare about the radical Right demonstrates, it is even possible to be paranoid about paranoids.

And to illustrate that last possibility, I'll tell one more story before we plunge into those primal myths.

On October 30, 1938, at 8 P.M., the CBS radio network transmitted "The War of the Worlds," a special Halloween edition of *The Mercury Theatre on the Air*. The broadcast, directed and narrated by Orson Welles, was based on H. G. Wells's famous novel about a Martian invasion of Earth, but the action was moved from Victorian England to contemporary New Jersey. The first half of the story jettisoned the usual format of a radio play and adopted a more adventurous form: a live concert interrupted by ever more frightening bulletins. It was and is a brilliant and effective drama, but the broadcast is famous today for reasons that go well beyond its artistic quality.

You might think you know this story. In popular memory, hordes of listeners mistook a science fiction play for an actual alien invasion, setting off a mass panic. That's the tale told in one of the most frequently cited accounts of the evening, a 1940 study by the social psychologist Hadley Cantril. "For a few horrible hours," Cantril wrote, "people from Maine to California thought that hideous monsters armed with death rays were destroying all armed resistance sent against them; that there was simply no escape from danger; that the end of the world was near. . . . Long before the broadcast had ended, people all over the United States were praying, crying, fleeing frantically to escape death from the Martians. Some ran to rescue loved ones. Others telephoned farewells or warnings, hurried to inform neighbors, sought information from newspapers or radio stations, summoned ambulances and police cars." At least six million people heard the broadcast, Cantril claimed, and "at least a million of them were frightened or disturbed."[50]

The truth was more mundane but also more interesting. There were indeed listeners who, apparently missing the initial announcement that the story was fiction, took the show at face value and believed a real invasion was under way. It is not clear, though, that they were any more common than the people today who mistake satires in *The Onion* for real newspaper reports. Cantril's numbers are dubious, and the people interviewed in his book were not a representative sample of the population. "Nobody died of fright or was killed in the panic, nor could any suicides be traced to the broadcast," the media scholar Michael Socolow noted. "Hospital emergency-room visits did not spike, nor, surprisingly, did calls to the police outside of a select few jurisdictions. The streets were never flooded with a terrified citizenry. . . . Telephone lines in New York City and a few other cities were jammed, as the primitive infrastructure of the era couldn't handle the load, but it appears that almost all the panic that evening was as ephemeral as the nationwide broadcast itself, and not nearly as widespread. That iconic image of the farmer with a gun, ready to shoot the aliens? It was staged for *Life* magazine."[51]

Of the people who *did* mistake the fictional news bulletins for real reports, a portion were under the impression that the invaders were not extraterrestrials but Germans, a less implausible scenario. Even the spikes in telephone calls didn't necessarily represent public panic. The press critic W. Joseph Campbell has pointed out that the calls could be "an altogether *rational* response of people who neither panicked nor became hysterical, but sought confirmation or clarification from external sources generally known to be reliable." Campbell added that the call volume must also have included "people who telephoned friends and relatives to talk about the unusual and clever program they had just heard."[52]

If Welles's broadcast derived some of its impact from Americans' anxieties about international tensions, the exaggerated reports about the response have persisted because they speak to another set of fears. After the play aired, the prominent political commentator Walter Lippmann took the opportunity to warn against "crowds that drift with all the winds that blow, and are caught up at last in the great hurricanes," adding that those "masses without roots" and their "volcanic and hysterical energy" are "the chaos in which the new Caesars are born."[53] As Socolow put it, the legend of the Mars panic "cemented a growing suspicion that skillful artists—or incendiary demagogues—could use communications technology to capture the consciousness of the nation."[54]

To *capture consciousness*: what a chilling image. It's an idea that appears when dissidents warn that our leaders are using the mass media to brainwash us. But you can also find the fear among those leaders themselves, who have a long history of fretting over the influence of any new medium of communication. If Orson Welles was cast as a wizard with the power to cloud men's minds, his listeners were imagined as a mindless mob easily misled by a master manipulator. The social order is disrupted; riots are sparked from afar.

The "War of the Worlds" story is usually told as a parable about popular hysteria—of a sudden spike in the sort of fear that Hofstadter's essay decried. But at least as much, it is a parable about elite hysteria—of the antipopulist anxiety that Hofstadter's essay exemplifies. No history of American paranoia can be complete unless it includes the latter.

2

THE DEVIL IN THE WILDERNESS

Indians were the first people to stand in American history as emblems of disorder, civilized breakdown, and alien control. . . . The series of Red scares that have swept the country since the 1870s have roots in the original red scares.

—*Michael Paul Rogin*[1]

Here's the story:

Satan got here first. He knew he was losing ground to God as the Gospel spread through the Old World, so he "drew a Colony out of some of those barbarous Nations dwelling upon the Northern Ocean" and promised the pagans "a Countrey far better than their own."[2] Those disciples became the Indians, and with those savages as his servants Satan established an empire in the American wilderness. And there, "like a *dragon*," the dark lord waited, "keeping a guard upon the spacious and mighty *orchards* of America."[3]

When Christian settlers eventually arrived, they found "a World in every Nook whereof, the devil is encamped," his "*Bands of Robbers*" ready to menace the European arrivals. The American air was "fill'd with *Fiery flying serpents*," and there were "incredible Droves of Devils in our way";[4] hostile Indian tribes were led by "ministers of Satan," all "actuated by the Angel of the bottomless pit."[5] The Puritans established their colonies, and they did all they could to keep Satan beyond their walls. But the Devil's Indians constantly conspired against them.

Some Indians were more than the Devil's pawns: They were devils in disguise. After one clash with the natives and their French Catholic allies, the influential minister Cotton Mather suggested that some of the shadowy figures firing on his countrymen were not men but "daemons in the shape of armed Indians and Frenchmen."[6] You thought you were watching a western, but that was just a mask: It was a horror movie all along.

You're never quite safe from the Enemy Outside, even when you're at home. And when you *leave* your home, you take your life and soul into your hands. From 1682 onward, the American colonies saw a flood of captivity narratives, printed accounts by settlers who had been held prisoner by the natives. In the archetypal captivity story, as the literary historian Richard Slotkin described it,

> a single individual, usually a woman, stands passively under the strokes of evil, awaiting rescue by the grace of God. . . . In the Indian's devilish clutches, the captive had to meet and reject the temptation of Indian marriage and/or the Indian's "cannibal" Eucharist. To partake of the Indian's love or his equivalent of bread and wine was to debase, to un-English the very soul.[7]

To be un-Englished: to be made alien. The Devil built his New World, Mather said, by "seducing the first inhabitants of America into it."[8] Given a chance, he would seduce the new Americans as well.

The Puritans were aware of those dangers when John Sassamon

arrived in the New England town of Marshfield one December day in 1674. Sassamon was no stranger to the colonists. He was a Christian convert from the Massachuset tribe, and he had served the English as an interpreter. He had even attended Harvard for a spell in the 1650s. But this wasn't a social call. He had grave news for Josiah Winslow, the governor of Plymouth Colony.

Sassamon had just been to the camp of the Wampanoag leader known as Philip, he told the governor. He had heard something terrible: Philip was plotting to combine his forces with the other tribes in the area and to lead an assault on the English. The colonists were in danger, and so, Sassamon added, was he.

It wasn't the first time such a story had circulated about Philip. In 1667, some members of his tribe had informed the English that he was plotting an attack. He had defended himself by claiming that their story was itself an Indian conspiracy, aimed at undermining Philip's power and manipulating the colonists. The Puritan authorities had accepted his explanation that time. They were less trusting in 1671, when they again heard that Philip was planning for war. That time, Philip was forced to surrender his weapons and pay a fine.

But in 1675, Winslow dismissed Sassamon's story. Increase Mather—Cotton's father—would later offer an explanation for why the warning had been disregarded: It had come from an Indian, "and one can hardly believe them," even "when they speak truth."[9] Sassamon was sent on his way.

It was the last time any Englishman would see him alive. Sassamon disappeared that day, setting off for the village of Namasket but never arriving. On January 29, 1675, his body was found under the ice of Assawompset Pond. The colonists concluded that he had been murdered, noting that his neck had been broken in a way that suggested someone had deliberately twisted it. An Indian witness came forward to swear that he had seen three Wampanoag assassins killing the informer and concealing his body under the ice.

Or that's the story, anyway.

The allegations in that tale operate on two different scales. At one end you have the mysterious death of John Sassamon, which may well have been a genuine murder committed by a genuine conspiracy. At the other end there is the legend of Satan and the Indians, a story that is larger, more mythic, and to modern eyes offensive and absurd.

This distinction will become familiar as we move through American history. There are conspiracy theories about particular crimes, many of which are plausible and some of which are true, and there are grander visions of long cosmic struggles, which might resonate on a metaphoric level but do not have much empirical grounding. It will always be possible to accept one of the smaller theories while rejecting a larger theory associated with it, and it will usually be possible to do the reverse. Believing that Philip was behind the death of John Sassamon did not require you to believe that Satan was behind the activities of Philip, and believing that Satan was directing Indian conspiracies did not require you to believe in any particular plot by the Indians.

Let's start with the smaller allegations. In this case, that means starting with uncertainty. To this day, it is unclear whether Sassamon's death was an accident or an assassination. If it was an assassination, it is unclear whether the three Indians accused of the crime were guilty. If they were guilty, it is unclear whether Philip, who denied all involvement, was a party to the crime. "After years of Philip's appearing relatively ineffectual in controlling the English," the historian James David Drake pointed out, "some Wampanoags, especially male youths, undoubtedly would have been tempted to take matters into their own hands."[10]

Today a Kennedy assassination theorist can spend a lifetime poring over autopsy photos of the president's head wounds. In 1675, Sassamon did not receive an autopsy at all, and no official record of the inquest into his death was made; if you have questions about, say, the condition of his broken neck, you're out of luck.[11] Meanwhile, the prosecution's star witness, a Christian Indian, owed money to the three men he fingered as the culprits—a fact leading some historians, though hardly all, to doubt his testimony.

Nor is it clear what to make of the plot that Sassamon allegedly uncovered at Philip's camp. Was he telling the truth about what he had heard, or was he spreading false reports for his own reasons? Sassamon was a former aide to Philip who had established a power base of his own, and even before his mission to Marshfield some of the Wampanoag considered him disloyal and deceitful. And it was not unprecedented for an Indian to extract assistance from the English by dishonestly accusing other natives of plots against the colonists.[12]

A reasonable person can read the surviving evidence and conclude that John Sassamon was probably the victim of a conspiracy. Another reasonable person can read the same evidence and conclude that he probably wasn't. In 1675, a New England jury concluded that he was. The alleged assassins were executed. Within three days there were rumors of Philip's men taking up arms, and within three weeks the Wampanoag were battling settlers in the town of Swansea. It was the beginning of King Philip's War, one of the bloodiest chapters in American history—a war more lethal, in proportion to population, than any other conflict involving either the English colonies or the independent United States.

In wartime, the fear of conspiracy grew still stronger. On September 11, a Rhode Island settler relayed a rumor that "all the Indians were in combination and confederacie to exterpate and root out the English."[13] This was surely untrue, given that many tribes, having their own differences with the Wampanoag, took the colonists' side in the war. But with such suspicions we have started our transit out of the territory of ordinary empirical claims and into the realm of cultural myth, where the competing interests of real-world Indians are obscured by the image of "all the Indians."

It's just a short jump from there to that larger scale of cosmic conflict. At one point in the war, one New England writer claimed that the Indian enemy, by "worshipping the Devil," had been able to conjure "a most violent Storm of Wind and Rain, the like was never known before."[14] The vestiges of such folk beliefs persisted for longer than you might expect. Nearly a century later, the Congregationalist minister Ezra Stiles—a cofounder of Brown University and later the president of Yale—casually included this detail in a description of Philip's attack on the town of Bridgewater: "[T]he Devil appeared in the Shape of a Bear walking on his 2 hind feet; the Indians all followed him & drew off. The Indians said if the Appearance had been a Deer they would have destroyed the whole Town & all the English."[15]

The idea that Indians were Devil worshippers was common among the settlers, and not just in the English colonies. In sixteenth-century Chiapas, ruled by Spain, when the local bishop learned that some of the area's Indians had maintained elements of their old religion, he construed the worshippers as a clandestine coven of witches, writing that they were "giving cult to the Devil and plotting against our Christian religion."[16] (The secret sect's beliefs, he added, resembled those of the Spanish heretics known as the *Alumbrados*, or Illuminati.) The notion that Satan had brought the Indians to America was advanced by the English theologian Joseph Mede, and in New England it was repeated by two of the most important figures in Puritan politics: William Hubbard, who found "the greatest probability of truth"[17] in Mede's account; and Cotton Mather, whose history of New England included his own version of the story.

Not everyone agreed. Some settlers even thought that the Indians were the lost tribes of Israel, giving them godly rather than demonic origins. But that relatively benign theory still made the mistake of looking to the legends of the Old World to explain the people of the New. Europeans, having landed on strange shores, viewed what they found through the lenses of the worldviews they imported, and that sometimes led to deep misunderstandings of the cultures they encountered. The New England Indians' tales of a Creator were often seen, the anthropologist William Simmons wrote, "as mistaken, confused, and desiccated vestiges of the Christian God." Other spirits were believed to be the Devil, and powwows were perceived as Satanic ceremonies.[18] Some colonists managed to mistake puberty rites for ritual child sacrifice.[19]

Such cultural projection wasn't limited to the religious realm. The settlers tended to imagine their own social structures among the natives, mistaking decentralized networks for centralized states, loose alliances for empires, an influential Indian for a grand conspirator. The fighting that broke out in 1675 is called "King Philip's War," but Philip was actually a *sachem*, not a king; the Europeans had no exact counterpart of that position, and they didn't always understand that the person who held it did not have anything akin to absolute authority in his own village, let alone outside it. Because colonists "feared organized Indian conspiracies," Drake argued, they "probably attributed greater unity to the Wampanoags than the circumstances warranted. The label 'King Philip's War' suggests an organization and structure for the conflict that is unsupported by evidence." Philip the purported puppeteer "had quite possibly lost control by 1675," Drake added. And even if he really was behind Sassamon's death, "much of what ensued over the next fourteen months was out of his control."[20] The war itself dragged on in some places for a year after Philip died.

When the English exaggerated Philip's power, they were enacting another familiar pattern, one that the historian Jeffrey Pasley has called "the myth of the superchief." From the first English colony at Roanoke to the closing of the frontier, Pasley wrote, "serious or widespread Indian resistance was usually attributed by Europeans and later chroniclers to the machinations of some preternaturally brilliant, all-powerful" leader. Often, "a widespread conflict was blamed on someone who was really only a major figure in some critical early encounter, or promoted himself as the primary conspirator in a later treaty with the white authorities."[21]

But even imaginary cabals can have real effects. In the early 1640s, in the wake of the Pequot War, dubious rumors of Indian plots helped inspire the creation of the New England Confederation, the first union of English colonies in the New World. The resulting regime remained in place for four decades.[22] And while King Philip's War raged, the fear of a vast Indian conspiracy—in one colonist's words, a "universall Combination of the Indians"[23]—had dreadful consequences for those natives who thought they had joined the colonists' community. In August 1675, the Massachusetts Council confined all Christian natives to "praying towns," fourteen villages of Indian converts that had been set up over the previous two and a half decades. In October, the government rounded up at least five hundred Christian Indians and interned them on Deer Island in Boston Harbor.

More than half of the Deer Island prisoners died that winter. Several of the remainder were enslaved. And still that wasn't enough for certain settlers, so convinced were they that all the Indians were in league with one another. After some Nipmuc warriors burned the town of Medfield, the magistrate Daniel Gookin reported sadly, it "gave opportunity to the vulgar to cry out, 'Oh, come, let us go down to Deer Island, and kill all the praying Indians.' They could not come at the enemy Indians, for they were too crafty and subtle for the English; therefore they would have wreaked their rage upon the poor unarmed Indians our friends."[24]

The fact that whole towns could be filled with native converts to Christianity cuts against the idea that the Indians and the English lived in diametrically opposed worlds. So does the fact that several unconverted tribes took the colonists' side in the war. So does the fact that Harvard allowed John Sassamon to study there, and that Harvard's 1650 charter described it as a place for "the education of English and Indian youth."[25] So does the fact that an Indian known to his people as Wassausmon would answer to the name "John Sassamon" in the first place; and, for that matter, that a sachem called Metacom would adopt the name "Philip." Behind those black-and-white tales of the Enemy Outside lay a much messier reality, one where English and Indian worlds overlapped, settlers and natives found common ground, and there was an ongoing process of assimilation and exchange.

When I use the word *assimilation*, I don't simply mean that Indians adopted European ways. The colonists absorbed a lot from the

Indians too. When the men who built the colonies feared the frontier, they were afraid of more than just Indian attacks. They knew that frontier life lured people away from the discipline of life in a Puritan town, and they were concerned that men and women of European descent might feel the pull of the Indian's ways, which they associated with sexual license and spiritual degeneration.

Thanks to the land available in the wilderness, Increase Mather complained, people "that profess themselves Christians have forsaken Churches, and Ordinances." Away from strong social controls, frontiersmen put worldly self-interest above their devotion to God, trading arms with the Indians without any thought for the greater good. "[W]ould ever men have sold Guns, and Powder, and Shot, to such faithless and bloody creatures, if a lust of Covetousness had not too far prevailed with them?" Mather asked.[26] "How many that although they are *Christians* in name, are no better then *Heathens* in heart, and in Conversation? How many Families that live like profane Indians without any *Family prayer*?" Whole towns, he declared, "have lived from year to year, without any publick Invocation of the Name of God, and without his Word."[27]

Those anxieties were fuel for the Puritans' paranoia. When societies are still acquiring a sense of identity, Slotkin suggests, "the simplest means of defining or expressing the sense of such a norm is by rejecting some other group whose character is deemed to be the opposite."[28] For many New Englanders, the Indians filled that role, with the undisciplined, Indianized frontiersmen forming a potential fifth column. The temptations of native culture had to be resisted, and clear lines were needed between the community of the devout and the hostile outer world.[29]

The Puritans weren't the only colonists struggling with the Enemy Outside. The fear of unlikely Indian conspiracies flared up in settlements ranging from Quaker Pennsylvania to Anglican Virginia. In 1689, it sparked a revolution in Maryland.

A Protestant rebellion in England had deposed the Catholic king James II just a year before. In Maryland—the only colony in

English America to be ruled by Catholics, though it had a predominantly Protestant population—a rumor started to circulate that "the great men of Maryland hath hired the Seneca Indians to kill the protestants."[30] Ten thousand Seneca Indians were said to be gathering at the head of the Patuxent River; when that army turned out to be a fiction, a new report claimed that nine thousand were gathered at the mouth of the river and another nine hundred had already invaded a settlement. One man swore that he had overheard some drunken Eastern Shore Indians blabbing that a man on the Provincial Council had hired them to attack the colonists. The rumors cooled down for a spell when the invasion didn't materialize, only to flare up again when the colony's government failed to recognize the new king and queen of England. A Protestant agitator named John Coode raised an army, seized the State House, and installed himself as the new governor of Maryland.[31] The colony then banned Catholic worship, a restriction that would not be lifted until after the American Revolution.

As with the French soldiers who bedeviled Cotton Mather, this was a case of an alleged alliance between the Indians and a white foe. Usually such alliances involved one Enemy Outside joining forces with another. The Maryland rumors were different in that they combined the Enemy Outside with a cabal in the highest reaches of the government—in our terms, the Enemy Above. The fear of the Indian/Catholic conspiracy had at least as much to do with resentment of Maryland's autocratic regime as it did with the fear of an external attack. A similar tale took hold around the same time in the Dominion of New England: An unpopular governor, Edmund Andros, was accused of conspiring with the Wabanaki, deliberately sending white troops to be slaughtered by the Indians. (In one soldier's words, his comrades wondered whether Andros had "brought them theither to be a sacrifice to their heathen Adversaries.")[32] As in Maryland, such reports fed a revolt, and in 1689 Andros was deposed.

But the Indians' alleged allies were usually based outside the community's gates. At different moments, Philip was said to be a

THE AIM OF POPE PIUS IX.

“BEWARE, THERE IS DANGER IN THE DARK!”

From Isaac Kelso, *Danger in the Dark*, 1855

pawn or partner of an Old World power, of a Catholic conspiracy, or of a Quaker conspiracy. He was hardly the only Indian whose purported plots were supposedly linked to the machinations of white allies. In 1653, while England and the Netherlands were at war in Europe, the colonists of New England looked suspiciously at the colonists in New Netherland. A belief took hold that, in Increase Mather's words, "there was an horrid Conspiracy amongst the Indians throughout this Land to cut off all the English, and that they were animated thereto by the Dutch." (The evidence for the plot, Mather conceded, was "vague and uncertain.")[33] In 1700, in turn, the former New Netherland—now controlled by the English and known as New York—barred all Catholic clergy from the colony, citing among its reasons the Church's alleged efforts "to Debauch, Seduce and Withdraw the *Indians* from their due Obedience unto His Majesty; and to excite and stir them up to Sedition, Rebellion and Open Hostility."[34] In 1736, the founder of Georgia claimed casually that "the French and Spaniards" were "labouring to debauch [the Indians] from us."[35] In 1755, part of Pennsylvania went into an uproar after news spread that a "parsell of Indians" had gathered a few miles from the local Catholic chapel.[36] The fretful colonists didn't worry that the Indians were about to attack the building. They worried that the Indians and the Church were in cahoots.

Catholic conspiracies are, in fact, the second most significant form taken by the Enemy Outside. The pope was perceived as a master manipulator; priests and nuns were seen as his corrupt and licentious lieutenants. Anti-Catholic sentiment has deep European roots, but it found a new shape in North America, particularly after independence. Nineteenth-century nativists believed that the Church was plotting to impose its hierarchy on an egalitarian American republic. If Indian conspiracies embodied the settlers' fear of the anarchic New World, papal conspiracies embodied their fears of the aristocratic Old World they had left behind.

Yet both Enemies Outside were closely linked to anxieties about Satan, sexuality, and ethnic impurity, and the two were often imagined as allied. There was even an anti-Catholic equivalent of the Indian captivity story, with books like Maria Monk's *Awful Disclosures* (1836) claiming that convents were prisons filled with sex slaves. Under the influence of such tracts, Protestant Americans sometimes invaded the institutions and attempted to free the nuns.[37]

So not every Enemy Outside had red skin. The Enemy Outside isn't defined by any particular origin; he's defined by the fact that you think he's out there trying to come in. The details vary at different times and places, but several characteristics recur. There is the image of the world outside your gates as an unfriendly wilderness where evil forces dwell. There is the proclivity to see those forces as a centralized conspiracy guided by a puppet master or a small cabal. There is the fear of the border zone where cultures mix, the suspicion that aliens at home are agents of a foreign power, and the fear that your community might be remade in the enemy's image. And there is the tendency to see this conflict in terms of a grand, apocalyptic struggle—if not literally against Satan, then against something deeply evil.[38]

If you didn't have to be a Native American to be seen as the Enemy Outside, you didn't have to be a colonist to suspect the Enemy Outside was on the prowl. Some Indians of colonial New England believed in a malevolent creature they called Cheepie, a spirit whose apparitions were thought to bring disease and death. According to one tribesman, Cheepie resembled an "Englishman, clothed with hat and coat, shoes and stockings." When the folklorist Richard Dorson repeated that statement, he found a lesson in it: Perhaps the Indians, like the white man, "equated the Devil with their enemy."[39]

For the United States, the Indian wars effectively ended in 1877, when U.S. forces fought several Sioux tribes, seized the gold-rich Black Hills, and completed the conquest of the Plains Indians. Over the previous two centuries, the colonies and then the independent United States had subdued a series of tribes—or, if you were tuned more closely to cultural myths than to the facts, a series of superchiefs, from Philip of the Wampanoag to Geronimo of the Apache. The end of the Black Hills War didn't put an end to the fighting between the white man and the red, but from that point forward the battles would consist of rebellions by the natives and crackdowns by the government, not clashes between independent nations.

But the fact that the most notorious Enemy Outside was no longer actually outside the country's borders didn't mean the whites were ready to retire their Indian conspiracy stories. When a millennial faith called the Ghost Dance started sweeping through Native America in 1889, many officials and reporters were already primed to perceive it as a sign of trouble. And when the Ghost Dance was embraced by Sitting Bull, a Hunkpapa Sioux leader who had fought in the Black Hills War, the conspiracy story took over: Out in the wilderness, in strange ceremonies, the aliens were plotting an attack.

Sitting Bull had already been cast in the role of superchief, literally playing the part when he went on tour with Buffalo Bill Cody's Wild West troupe. (The show touted the Indian as the man behind the death of General George Armstrong Custer at the Battle of the Little Bighorn. In fact, he probably wasn't present at the battle at all.) It is true that in 1867, Sitting Bull had been anointed the supreme chief of the seven Lakota tribes. But though that sounded impressive, several important tribes that he allegedly led—and even some of Sitting Bull's own Hunkpapa people—had never recognized his authority.

Still, even as late as 1890, if there was any area where Sitting Bull and his Caucasian foes agreed, it was, in the words of the historian Rex Alan Smith, that both "believed Sitting Bull to be the most important and powerful Sioux alive."[40] He was charismatic, mysterious, and intransigent, an imposing figure with an even more imposing reputation. When the children's writer Elbridge Streeter Brooks described Sitting Bull in a novel about Little Bighorn, he presented the old Indian as a manipulator operating behind the scenes, with the Midnight Strong Hearts, a prestigious order of Sioux warriors, recast in conspiratorial terms:

> "Why, Sitting Bull is the Master of the Strong Hearts; and they don't give in, I can tell you."
>
> "The Master of the Strong Hearts?" Jack was certainly learning many new things, and each one only increased his curiosity. "What's that?" he queried; "some sort of a secret society?"
>
> "That's just where you're right, sonny," the squaw-man assented with an emphatic nod. "The Strong Hearts are just the biggest, secretest, most consarnedly bravest and determined of all the Sioux societies. And their main point, in all their doings is just this: never to back down, back out, or give up, when once they've determined to do anything. And that's what the Bull meant. . . . I never knew him to lead on the war-path never. He leaves the real fighting to some of the other big chiefs—like Red Cloud, or Gall, or Iron Hawk, or Rain-in-the-Face. The Bull, he just makes medicine for the boys, and they pitch in and fight, while he dreams things out for 'em and eggs 'em on. . . ."[41]

The Ghost Dance, meanwhile, was a messianic movement centered on a Northern Paiute Indian named Wovoka. Around 1869, Wovoka's father, Tavibo, claimed that the Great Spirit had told him a new world was coming, one where the whites would all be swallowed by the earth, the ghosts of dead Indians would return, and everyone would be immortal. To bring this day, Indians needed to perform a sacred ritual called the Ghost Dance, which Tavibo began to teach.

Tavibo's movement faded fairly rapidly, and he died when Wovoka was in his teens. His son was adopted by a white family, who renamed him Jack Wilson and gave him a conventional Christian upbringing. He took in other Christian ideas as well, studying the tenets of groups ranging from the Shakers to the Mormons. In the late 1880s, he announced that he too had encountered the Great Spirit, and he started preaching doctrines that drew at least as much on Christianity as they did on traditional Indian spirituality. The son of God would usher in the new age, Wovoka promised. Many of his followers decided that the son of God was Wovoka himself.

There were other differences between Wovoka's vision and his father's. Most notably, Wovoka did not teach that the white people were all to die. But he still saw the end of the familiar world and the arrival of a new one, the return of the dead and the immortality of the living. To bring that day, he proclaimed, Indians of all tribes must set aside their differences, give up guns and alcohol and idleness, dance the Ghost Dance, and spread the good news.

Since the new faith was transmitted orally, it mutated and adapted rapidly, absorbing different attributes in different places as different tribes encountered it. Among the recently defeated Sioux, living hungry and resentful lives in the Dakotas, the religion took on a militant flavor. The idea that the whites were to be wiped out crept back into the creed, and the notion took hold that special ghost shirts would make the wearers impervious to bullets.[42]

All the same, it remained an explicitly nonviolent religion. Indeed, it may well have tamped down the impulse to attack the whites, since it allowed angry Indians to believe that the intruders would soon be removed by supernatural means. Nonetheless, when Sitting Bull endorsed the Ghost Dance he broke a peace pipe in public and announced that he was ready to fight and die for the faith. And with the old chief's reputation, that was enough for the local Indian agent, Major James McLaughlin, to fire off a letter to the commissioner of Indian affairs. After insisting that he was not "an alarmist" and did not expect an "immediate" Indian attack, McLaughlin went on to describe

> the excitement existing among the Sitting Bull faction of Indians over the expected Indian millennium, the annihilation of the white men and supremacy of the Indian, which is looked for in the near

> future and promised by the Indian Medicine men as not later than next spring. . . .
>
> Sitting Bull is high priest and leading apostle of this latest Indian absurdity; in a word, he is the chief mischief-maker at this agency, and if he were not here this craze, so general among the Sioux, would never have gotten a foothold at this agency. Sitting Bull is a man of low cunning, devoid of a single manly principle in his nature or an honorable trait of character, but on the contrary, is capable of instigating and inciting others (those who believe in his powers) to do any amount of mischief. He is a coward and lacks moral courage; he will never lead where there is danger, but is an adept in influencing his ignorant henchmen and followers, and there is no knowing what he may direct them to attempt.[43]

The McLaughlin letter leaked to the papers, which couldn't resist the combination of a mysterious ritual and an infamous superchief. The *Chicago Daily Tribune* published a version of the document under the headline "TO WIPE OUT THE WHITES: What the Indians Expect of the Coming Messiah."[44] The Philadelphia *Evening Telegraph* fretted that "Army officers may be perfectly well informed of Sitting Bull's intrigues, but they can do nothing until he deliberately perfects his rascally plans and gets ready to start his young bucks on a raid."[45] *The New York Times* announced that "the redskins are dancing in circles," then quoted a "half-breed" courier as to what such symbolism must mean: "The Sioux never dance that dance except for one purpose, and that is for war."[46] At one point the *Tribune* reported that a battle with the Indians had already left sixty people dead or wounded. In fact the clash had never occurred.

By that time the more nervous whites were begging the government for greater protection, steeling themselves for a fight of their own, or in some cases simply fleeing. More responsible papers attempted to debunk the rumors. (The *Aberdeen Saturday Pioneer* editor L. Frank Baum, later to become famous as the author of *The Wonderful Wizard of Oz*, wrote that "the Indian scare" was "a great injustice" fanned by "sensational newspaper articles."[47] Baum was no friend of the Indians—he would soon call for their extermination—so you can't accuse the man of special pleading.) But fear carried the day, particularly after President Benjamin Harrison sent the military to suppress the dancing. On December 15, 1890, a botched attempt to arrest Sitting Bull ended with the chief, several of his supporters, and some of the arresting officers dead. Fearing retaliation, hundreds of the Hunkpapa fled. The Seventh Cavalry caught up to them and took them to Wounded Knee Creek on December 28. The soldiers ended up killing between 170 and 190 of the Indians, including at least 18 children. More than two dozen whites died too, largely from friendly fire. And with that the great dancing conspiracy was eliminated.

When Elbridge Streeter Brooks's book describes the death of Sitting Bull, there is no reference to the massacre at Wounded Knee. Wovoka's religion rates only a passing allusion, when an Indian character mentions that he had caught "the Messiah craze and the ghost-dance fever." The explanation for the superchief's death is much simpler: "Sitting Bull had stirred up his followers—Strong Hearts, most of them, you know."[48]

Once the Enemy Outside story line was established, it could be applied to all kinds of alleged villains, not just popes and superchiefs. When the United States entered the First World War in April 1917, joining the alliance against Germany and Austria-Hungary, its battles were fought far away in Europe, but much of the country was seized by a fear that the enemy's long tentacles had entered the U.S. heartland.

The domestic struggle against the alien octopus was sometimes horrifying, sometimes comic, sometimes a bit of both. Some towns prohibited performances of German music. Pittsburgh banned Beethoven. There was a vigorous crackdown on German-owned breweries. The comic strip *The Katzenjammer Kids* retconned the title characters' national origins, reassuring readers that the boys were really Dutch.

Harold H. Knerr, the Katzenjammer family revises its origins

German books were burned at rallies around the country. Vigilantes seized and tortured German immigrants and vandalized their property. In Collinsville, Illinois, a mob lynched a German-American miner on a groundless suspicion that he was a spy. A jury quickly acquitted the killers, following a trial in which the defense attorney described the crime as a "patriotic murder."[49] The town's mayor argued that the whole episode could have been avoided if only Congress had done more to prevent disloyalty.

Some of this was simply traditional ethnic bigotry brought to new heights by war fever. But the hysteria represented paranoia as well as prejudice. Germany's head of state, Kaiser Wilhelm II, was imagined as the monstrous Beast of Berlin, and every adult American with German blood was suspected of being a spy in his employ. "On the assumption that all were potential enemy agents," the historian Frederick Luebke wrote, German Americans "were barred from the vicinity of places deemed to have military importance, such as wharves, canals, and railroad depots. Moreover, they were expelled from the District of Columbia, required to get permission to travel within the country or to change their place of residence, and forbidden access to all ships and boats except public ferries. . . . Subsequently several thousand were interned in concentration camps as minor infractions of the rules were exaggerated into major offenses."[50] Shades of Deer Island.

Lutheran parochial schools, with their overwhelmingly German-American student bodies, were rumored to be hotbeds of subversion. Several states banned the schools from using the German language, and many states and cities ordered their public schools to stop teaching German too. (If you were eager to stop espionage, you'd think you'd want *more* Americans to understand the spies' language. Evidently not.) Three states established committees to probe for German propaganda in textbooks. When a flu pandemic swept the country, killing approximately 675,000 Americans, a story spread that the outbreak had been caused by Bayer—a German company—contaminating its aspirin.

The fountainhead of paranoid literature was the Committee on Public Information, a propaganda agency created by President Woodrow Wilson. Along with traditional agitprop painting the German soldier as a savage—"the Hun"—who committed terrible atrocities abroad, the committee brought the war home with literature that reimagined ordinary American environments as a domestic battleground haunted by the enemy. "German agents are everywhere, eager to gather scraps of news about our men, our ships, our munitions," warned one advertisement. "It is still possible to get such information through to Germany, where thousands of these fragments—often individually harmless—are patiently pieced together into a whole which spells death to American soldiers and danger to American homes."

Vigilance, the ad continued, didn't merely mean maintaining discretion:

> [D]o not wait until you catch someone putting a bomb under a factory. Report the man who spreads pessimistic stories, divulges—or seeks—confidential military information, cries for peace, or belittles our efforts to win the war.

Send the names of such persons, even if they are in uniform, to the Department of Justice, Washington. Give all the details you can, with names of witnesses if possible—show the Hun that we can beat him at his own game of collecting scattered information and putting it to work. The fact that you made the report will not become public.

You are in contact with the enemy *today*, just as truly as if you faced him across No Man's Land.[51]

Spies *and* Lies

German agents are everywhere, eager to gather scraps of news about our men, our ships, our munitions. It is still possible to get such information through to Germany, where thousands of these fragments—often individually harmless—are patiently pieced together into a whole which spells death to American soldiers and danger to American homes.

But while the enemy is most industrious in trying to collect information, and his systems elaborate, he is ***not*** superhuman—indeed he is often very stupid, and would fail to get what he wants were it not deliberately handed to him by the carelessness of loyal Americans.

Do not discuss in public, or with strangers, any news of troop and transport movements, or bits of gossip as to our military preparations, which come into your possession.

Do not permit your friends in service to tell you—or write you—"inside" facts about where they are, what they are doing and seeing.

Do not become a tool of the Hun by passing on the malicious, disheartening rumors which he so eagerly sows. Remember he asks no better service than to have you spread his lies of disasters to our soldiers and sailors, gross scandals in the Red Cross, cruelties, neglect and wholesale executions in our camps, drunkenness and vice in the Expeditionary Force, and other tales certain to disturb American patriots and to bring anxiety and grief to American parents.

And do not wait until you catch someone putting a bomb under a factory. Report the man who spreads pessimistic stories, divulges—or seeks—confidential military information, cries for peace, or belittles our efforts to win the war.

Send the names of such persons, even if they are in uniform, to the Department of Justice, Washington. Give all the details you can, with names of witnesses if possible—show the Hun that we can beat him at his own game of collecting scattered information and putting it to work. The fact that you made the report will not become public.

You are in contact with the enemy *today*, just as truly as if you faced him across No Man's Land. In your hands are two powerful weapons with which to meet him—discretion and vigilance. *Use them.*

COMMITTEE ON PUBLIC INFORMATION
8 JACKSON PLACE, WASHINGTON, D. C.

Contributed through Division of Advertising *United States Gov't Comm. on Public Information*

Committee on Public Information, National Archives

At this point you might be thinking of Hofstadter's remarks about the paranoiac's "projection of the self" and "imitation of the enemy." You should also note that, contra Hofstadter, the Committee on Public Information was anything but a "minority movement." Not only was it run by the federal government, but it helped inspire a host of public and private vigilance efforts on the local level. And those, in turn, had the blessing of the country's establishment. *The Washington Post* spoke for much of the American elite when it editorialized, "In spite of excesses such as lynching, it is a healthful and wholesome awakening in the interior of the country."[52]

The committee's efforts didn't net many actual spies. But the authorities did do a capable job of rounding up people who cried for peace, for an end to conscription, or for anything else that might be construed as undermining the war effort. (A German-American filmmaker, Robert Goldstein, was imprisoned under the Espionage Act because he included scenes of English atrocities in a picture about the American Revolution. The government argued that the movie might undercut audiences' support for Great Britain, our wartime ally.) In *Words That Won the War*, a sympathetic account of the committee's work, James R. Mock and Cedric Larson acknowledged that the spy hunt could get out of hand. "Captain Henry T. Hunt, head of the Military Intelligence counterespionage section during the war, has told the authors that in addition to unfounded spy stories innocently launched there were many started with the apparent object of removing or inconveniencing political, business, or social rivals," they reported. At one point "two of his own men were taken into custody by the Department of Justice, while seeking to determine the loyalty of the headwaiter in a Washington hotel."[53]

Here the search for diabolical immigrants and other clearly foreign figures—for enemies easily identified as aliens—shifts into something else: a search for enemies who, on the surface at least, can't be distinguished from "normal" Americans. In other words, the story of the Enemy Outside yields to the story of the Enemy Within. We'll take a closer look at that second archetypal foe in the next chapter. But before we get there, let's allow the tale of the Enemy Outside to reverberate one more time.

May 2, 2011. Navy SEALs storm a mansion in Abbottabad, Pakistan. The compound is the home of Osama bin Laden, the Saudi-born jihadist at the top of the terror network known as Al Qaeda.

In the popular imagination, Al Qaeda is a tightly disciplined, globe-spanning hierarchy, with bin Laden serving, as *The Washington Post* put it, as a "terrorist CEO in an isolated compound."[54] In practice, the group has never managed to be both large and centralized at the same time. In the decade before the Abbottabad attack, it became an increasingly loose network, an organization with "no single center of gravity, but multiple ones," according to George Michael, a professor at the Air War College. Al Qaeda cells, Michael has explained, "can act on their own initiative when the opportunity presents itself"; they don't depend on a central authority for direction. Since 2002, nearly every Islamist terror attack around the world has been conducted either by one of those peripheral franchises or by a group whose only link to bin Laden is ideological.[55] By the time the raid was planned, Al Qaeda was urging independent "lone wolf" terrorists to carry out attacks on their own.

In other words, when the *Post* uses phrases such as "terrorist CEO," it falls into the same sort of conspiracy thinking that attributed dispersed Indian raids to a single superchief. And the *Post*'s words weren't an isolated lapse. Even when Osama's group was more centralized, it was often conflated with the larger Islamist movement of which Al Qaeda was merely the most notorious part.[56]

All the same, bin Laden and his lieutenants have plenty of blood on their hands. They have been responsible for several lethal operations, most infamously the assaults on the Pentagon and World Trade Center that killed nearly three thousand people on September 11, 2001. Because of those massacres, armed Americans have arrived in Abbottabad.

There is a firefight at the compound. Bin Laden is killed. The SEALs relay the news to Washington with a code word: *Geronimo*.

3

THE DEVIL NEXT DOOR

They're here already! You're next!

—*Invasion of the Body Snatchers*[1]

Here's the story:

Night falls in Salem Village. Leaving his wife at home, a Puritan called Goodman Brown walks into the wilderness, fretting that devilish Indians might be lurking behind the trees. Instead he encounters the actual Devil, a worldly, well-dressed man who bears a distinct resemblance to Brown himself.

As the two walk together, Brown suggests nervously that he should return home. "My father never went into the woods on such an errand, nor his father before him," he protests. "We have been a race of honest men and good Christians since the days of the martyrs."

Don't worry, says Satan:

> I helped your grandfather, the constable, when he lashed the Quaker woman so smartly through the streets of Salem; and it was I that

> brought your father a pitch-pine knot, kindled at my own hearth, to set fire to an Indian village, in King Philip's war. They were my good friends, both; and many a pleasant walk have we had along this path, and returned merrily after midnight. . . .
>
> I have a very general acquaintance here in New England. The deacons of many a church have drunk the communion wine with me; the selectmen of divers towns make me their chairman; and a majority of the Great and General Court are firm supporters of my interest. The governor and I, too— But these are state secrets.[2]

The pair encounter one of Salem's respectable citizens, the woman who taught Brown his catechism; she reveals that she is a witch and that she is heading to a mysterious meeting. The deacon and the minister pass by, riding to the same night gathering. Then Brown thinks he hears his wife in the woods, and when he calls out her name her voice replies with a scream.

In a space in the forest, Brown finds a Black Mass in progress. Virtually all of Salem is present:

> Among them, quivering to and fro between gloom and splendor, appeared faces that would be seen next day at the council board of the province, and others which, Sabbath after Sabbath, looked devoutly heavenward, and benignantly over the crowded pews, from the holiest pulpits in the land. Some affirm that the lady of the governor was there. At least there were high dames well known to her, and wives of honored husbands, and widows, a great multitude, and ancient maidens, all of excellent repute, and fair young girls, who trembled lest their mothers should espy them. Either the sudden gleams of light flashing over the obscure field bedazzled Goodman Brown, or he recognized a score of the church members of Salem village famous for their especial sanctity. Good old Deacon Gookin had arrived, and waited at the skirts of that venerable saint, his revered pastor. But, irreverently consorting with these grave, reputable, and pious people, these elders of the church, these chaste dames and dewy virgins, there were men

> of dissolute lives and women of spotted fame, wretches given over to all mean and filthy vice, and suspected even of horrid crimes. It was strange to see that the good shrank not from the wicked, nor were the sinners abashed by the saints. Scattered also among their pale-faced enemies were the Indian priests, or powwows, who had often scared their native forest with more hideous incantations than any known to English witchcraft.[3]

Brown learns that he and his wife are to be initiated at the witches' Sabbath that night. As the man and his bride stand before an altar, the Devil outlines his creed: "Now are ye undeceived. Evil is the nature of mankind. Evil must be your only happiness. Welcome again, my children, to the communion of your race."[4]

At the last moment, Brown calls out to his wife to look upward to heaven and resist the Devil. Suddenly everyone vanishes, and Brown is alone in the woods; he does not know whether his wife succumbed, or even whether he witnessed a ritual or merely dreamed it.

Either way, he is scarred for life. From that night till his death, he is a gloomy, distrustful man who sees wickedness in everyone around him.

Or that's the story, anyway.

I've just laid out the bare bones of Nathaniel Hawthorne's "Young Goodman Brown," an enigmatic short story published in 1835. It imagines a conspiracy in colonial Massachusetts, but this is not the kind of cabal we encountered the last time we discussed the Puritans. The Indians have been reduced to a cameo role. The chief conspirators don't live outside the village gates anymore, and they aren't easily identified as aliens. Anyone might be a part of the plot. Even the investigator who discovers the secret circle is in danger of being absorbed by it. Goodman Brown has met the Enemy Within.

The story's obvious inspiration is the witch fever of 1692 and 1693, in which a wave of witchcraft accusations swept through Salem and the surrounding area. One of the judges in those trials was Hawthorne's great-great-grandfather John Hathorne. Judge Hathorne's father, William Hathorne, was responsible for an act attributed to Goodman Brown's ancestor: He ordered a Quaker woman whipped through the streets of town. Hawthorne felt considerable guilt for this family history, and it's easy to read his story as a critique of a society that set out to destroy monsters but ended up becoming monstrous itself. Acts done in the name of fighting the Devil, from persecuting Quakers to slaughtering Indians, appear in the text as crimes committed with Satan's blessing.

The critique applies not just to the woman-whipping, village-burning citizens of Salem but to Goodman Brown himself. Though he intended to resist the Devil, he ended up living his life as though he accepted the doctrine the Devil preached: "Now are ye undeceived. Evil is the nature of mankind." And it is Brown who adopts the mind-set of a witch finder, always suspecting that Satanists are everywhere. Indeed, one reading of the story suggests that Brown's vision in the forest was itself the Devil's work and that by accepting it as valid Brown fell into the Devil's trap.[5]

The trials that inspired Hawthorne's story weren't the first witch-finding expedition in New England, but they were both larger and more lethal than the others. If you set aside the Salem saga, ninety-three accusations of witchcraft are known to have hit the colonies' courts in the whole seventeenth century, of which sixteen led to executions.[6] In the Salem episode, by contrast, at least 144 people went on trial in a little more than a year, and many others were accused without landing in court. Fourteen women and six men were executed, mostly by hanging; even a couple of dogs were sent to the gallows. Another man and three women died in jail, as did several babies.[7] The defendants came from a much wider spectrum of ages, occupations, and social ranks than the typical docket of witches. The trials cast an unusually wide geographic net, too: The accused hailed from more than twenty locations, not just Salem Village and the adjoining Salem Town.[8]

By European standards, on the other hand, the trials were small potatoes. English America was less witch-obsessed than England, and England in turn was less witch-obsessed than Scotland or the Continent. From 1623 to 1631, the German bishopric of Würzburg burned an estimated nine hundred people for their ostensible dealings with demons. If that body count is accurate, one tiny principality killed more supposed Satanists in an eight-year period than were executed in all of New England in the entire seventeenth century.[9] That didn't satisfy the authorities' appetite for blood: European witch hunts continued to erupt for decades after the Würzburg carnage. The trials of 1692, by contrast, disgusted so many people that they effectively ended witchcraft prosecutions in Massachusetts.

The Salem saga began two and a half years into King William's War, a bloody conflict that pitted the English colonies against the French and their Wabanaki Indian allies. In January 1692, a pastor's daughter, age nine, and her cousin, age eleven or twelve, suddenly began to suffer wild and inexplicable fits. They "were bitten and pinched by invisible agents," wrote Reverend John Hale, who witnessed the girls' spasms; "their arms, necks, and backs turned this way and that way, and returned back again, so as it was impossible for them to do of themselves, and beyond the power of Epileptick Fits, or natural Disease to effect. Sometimes they were taken dumb, their mouths stopped, their throats choaked, their limbs wracked and tormented."[10] As weeks went by and the children's condition grew worse, the local experts suspected witchcraft.

Following a traditional (and rather witchy) ritual to discern the source of the sorcery, the girls accused Tituba, an Indian slave in their household, of being their tormenter.[11] Tituba denied the accusation. Then some older neighbors declared that they too had suffered fits and that Tituba and two other women were responsible. At that point Tituba confessed. She would later report that her confession had been extracted only after her owner had beaten her.

"Young Goodman Brown" begins with an excursion into the external wilderness, where there "may be a devilish Indian behind every tree,"[12] and then unexpectedly turns inward, imagining a plot at the heart of Salem society. The real-life Salem story followed the same pattern. When the witch hunt began, the first accusation was directed against an Indian woman, and the Indians never disappeared entirely as the episode unfolded. The purported witnesses to witchcraft frequently described Satan or his emissary as "a black man," which in the local context was more likely to suggest an Indian than an African. One alleged witch, Reverend George Burroughs, was accused of "bewitch[ing] a great many soldiers to death" in the Indian wars.[13] Cotton Mather even suggested that the attacks "by the *spirits* of the *invisible world*" originated "among the Indians, whose chief sagamores are well known unto some of our captives to have been horrid *sorcerers*, and hellish *conjurers*, and such as conversed with *dæmons*."[14] In one essay he announced that "at their Cheef Witch-meetings, there has been present some French canadians, and some Indian Sagamores, to concert the methods of ruining New England."[15]

But the movement that began with an accusation against an Indian quickly expanded to include the white townspeople, and when that happened a different set of fears and feuds came to the fore. In their 1974 book *Salem Possessed*, the social historians Paul Boyer and Stephen Nissenbaum made a strong case that the initial wave of accusations was closely correlated with long-standing local disputes over land, church politics, and the tensions between the agrarian Salem Village and the more mercantile Salem Town. Meanwhile, many accusations came wrapped in a long history of gossip, as old chatter about who might be a sorceress, a wife beater, or a whore made it easier for certain citizens to fall under suspicion.

From there the circle widened. More purported witches were accused, and many of them confessed, sparking still more accusations. The recriminations extended into areas far removed from the local dynamics discussed by Boyer and Nissenbaum, and the ranks of the purported Devil worshippers increasingly included people who defied the standard profile of a witch: ministers, wealthy merchants, the governor's wife. When Hawthorne wrote that "the lady of the governor" had been at the Black Sabbath—or at least that "some affirm" that she had been there—he was reciting the historical record. "The afflicted," one prosecutor wrote, "spare no person of what quality so ever."[16]

Along with the other forces fueling the inquisition, from small-town gossip to an especially nasty war, the accused had an incentive to admit or invent spiritual crimes: It soon became clear that a purported witch who confessed would not be executed. There is even the possibility, suggested by the historian Chadwick Hansen, that some of the defendants really were witches—not that they actually wielded supernatural powers, of course, but that they attempted to do so.[17]

There was also, as the sociologist Richard Weisman has pointed out, a change in the role of the government. The typical New England witchcraft accusation involved townspeople blaming their neighbors for various mundane misfortunes. If you look past the fact that the charges involved the use of magical powers, you'll find that the conflicts weren't so different from the disputes that modern people have over rat-attracting junk piles, dogs that dig up gardens, or tree branches that extend into an adjoining yard. Even by the legal standards of the time, the use of malevolent magic was difficult to prove, so the New England courts were ordinarily reluctant to take on such cases.

But now the state was throwing itself into the conflict, creating a situation closer in spirit to Europe's persecutions than to traditional tiffs between neighbors. An ordinary citizen of Salem might worry that the witches next door were poisoning his cow or making his children sick. The authorities had a grander fear: in Weisman's words, that "an organized plot to subvert the Puritan mission had successfully infiltrated the core of the church."[18] Tales of vast conspiracies began to appear in the confessions. In August, when one William Barker confessed to witchcraft, he reported that "Satans design was to set up his own worship, abolish all the churches in the land, to fall next upon Salem and soe goe through the countrey."

In the new Satanic society, he continued, "all persones should be equall . . . there should be no day of resurection or judgement, and neither punishment nor shame for sin."[19]

The accusers eventually overreached, and the furor abated. By May 1693, when the final hearings were held, several witch finders were having second thoughts about the process, not least when they found themselves or their loved ones in the crosshairs. (Reverend John Hale lost his enthusiasm for the trials when his wife was accused.) In 1697, Massachusetts recognized a day of repentance for the prosecution of innocent people. One magistrate announced that he accepted "the blame and shame" for his role in the affair, and a dozen Salem jurors signed a formal declaration of regret.[20]

The witch hunt encapsulated the most essential element of the Enemy Within: *Anyone could conceivably be—or become—a part of the conspiracy*. With the Enemy Outside, the conspirators are conspicuously alien. The Enemy Below and the Enemy Above have well-defined positions in the social hierarchy. But in Salem the alleged plot permeated ordinary society. As one minister summed up the situation, superficially Christian men and women who seemed to be "real members of [Christ's] mystical body" could instead be "instruments" of Satan's "malice against their friends and neighbors."[21] When the Enemy Within is at work, ordinary life is a masquerade.

During the Salem witch hunt, the ranks of the conspirators were constantly expanding. If you believed the testimony of the afflicted, the specters would offer to end their torments if they would sign the Devil's book; once they signed it, specters in the signers' shape would torture another person and present that person with the same bargain. So the Enemy Within could be more than just a plot among your neighbors. It could be a plot to take your children and other loved ones away from you, to add them to the conspiracy's growing circle.

When the fear of the Enemy Within is at its strongest, even the physical world might feel inauthentic, like a fragile shell obscuring a hidden realm. In Salem, spectral evidence became admissible in court; the boundary between the waking world and the land of dreams broke down. That deep uncertainty is dramatized in "Young Goodman Brown" and is part of what makes it such a powerful incarnation of the Enemy Within story. The Black Mass that Brown attends might be a real meeting and thus a sign that the everyday world conceals terrible truths. It might itself be a false reality projected by the Devil. And it might merely be a dream.

If the Enemy Within is the most dreamlike and fantastic of America's primal conspiracy myths, it is also the most homely and prosaic. The suspicions that haunt our day-to-day lives usually feature our families, neighbors, and coworkers, even if we don't believe they're puppets of a Satanic cabal. Think back to New England's earlier witchcraft cases, before the frenzy of 1692 broke out: petty feuds fueled by gossip and bad blood. A large-scale, Salem-style mania may seem bizarre to us, but the day-to-day misgivings that led Americans to cry witch shouldn't seem so strange at all.

There were whispers that Ann Lee was a witch too, but she had the good fortune to live in New York at the end of the eighteenth century rather than New England at the end of the seventeenth. So there never was a risk that she'd be hanged. Not for witchcraft, anyway.

Lee was born in England in 1736, the daughter of a Manchester blacksmith. At age twenty-two she fell in with the Shakers, a sect that had been born about a decade before. The Shakers believed that the end of the world was close. They also believed, more unusually for the time, that women could be leaders in the church, and Lee quickly rose in the ranks, eventually becoming the head of the organization. Along the way she started proclaiming her own revelations from God, and with time her followers began to describe her as the second coming of the Christ spirit. Lee put her personal stamp on the group's beliefs, not least when her revulsion toward sex became a full-fledged doctrine of Shaker celibacy.

In 1774, Lee came to America with a handful of followers. As pacifists, the Shakers refused to fight in the revolution, and that led to rumors of subversion; Lee was jailed for a spell as a suspected British spy. The first wave of American anti-Shaker literature appeared in this period, and it often took the form of a jeremiad against the Enemy Outside. One pamphlet described the religion as "a body of more than two thousand people, having no will of their own, but governed by a few Europeans."[22] If you think that sounds like the charges Protestants liked to levy against Catholics, you're right. Indeed, apostate Shakers were known to claim that the young faith's doctrines "exactly agree with the doctrines of the church of Rome."[23] There were rumors that the movement was a front for the pope.

Such sentiments died down somewhat as the revolution receded into the past. When anti-Shaker fears flared up again a decade or so into the nineteenth century, the group's foreign origins were no longer a concern. The Shakers had become an Enemy Within.

A religious revival swept the United States in the early nineteenth century, a spiritually rambunctious period now known as the Second Great Awakening. On the outskirts of the excitement, unusual sects were finding new followers: not just Shakers but Adventists, Mormons, Oneidans. With the new wave of worship came a new wave of paranoia. The idea of a Catholic conspiracy, a fear that had been relatively quiet in the wake of the revolution, came roaring back to life. And just as the Salem inquisitors slid easily from a fear of Indian conspiracies to a fear of homegrown witches, nineteenth-century Americans surrounded by fears of that other traditional Enemy Outside, the Vatican, adapted those anti-Catholic myths into tales of domestic conspiracies.

You can see that process at work in *Protestant Jesuitism*, a remarkable volume published a year after "Young Goodman Brown." Written by Reverend Calvin Colton, a Presbyterian, the book began in a familiar anti-Catholic manner. Colton condemned the Jesuits, informing us that the order "controlled the power of princes; absorbed the chief sources and principal ramifications of social and political influence; and while professing obedience to Rome, like the janizaries of the Sublime Porte, it held the staff in its own hand, and thus had nearly brought the world in subjection to its sway, and threatened to bind it in perpetual chains."[24] But Colton endorsed immigration from Catholic countries, arguing that the Europeans' arrival would make it easier to convert Catholics to "pure Christianity."[25] And he denounced nativist fantasies such as Maria Monk's *Awful Disclosures*, calling them a "false alarm."[26] Colton's target didn't dwell in the Vatican. The "Jesuitism of Popery," he told us, had been joined by a domestic force operating "under the Protestant name."[27]

The force in question consisted of groups that had appeared during the Second Great Awakening, voluntary associations devoted to moral reform and missionary work. A handful of people "who stand at the head of moral and religious organizations" aimed to impose "a new structure" on "the whole frame of society," Colton warned, putting "the great mass in subjection to the will and control of select, and often self-elected, individuals."[28] No one "can openly oppose them without the risk of being crushed by their influence," he added.[29] "Their agents swarm over the land in clouds, like the locusts of Egypt."[30]

The Second Great Awakening was well under way when Hawthorne composed "Young Goodman Brown," and it is entirely possible that as he wrote it he was thinking about the America he lived in as well as the America of the past. The Satanic night meeting in the story does resemble the big camp meetings of the revival circuit. As the literary scholar Robert S. Levine has pointed out, Hawthorne's

> frenzied meeting is presided over by "some grave divine of the New-England churches" in search of new enthusiasts. "Bring forth the converts!" the minister thunders; and Brown responds to the summons by emerging from the shadows and approaching "the proselytes, beneath the canopy of fire."[31]

Traditional religious leaders often denounced revival preachers as puppet masters engaged in a sort of mass hypnosis. The same year that Colton published *Protestant Jesuitism*, he attacked the revivals as events at which minds were "*compelled*, in a moment of the greatest possible excitement, to yield themselves entirely—their intellect, their reason, their imagination, their belief, their feelings, their passions, their whole souls—to a single and new position, that is prescribed to them. . . . The mind, reduced to such a bondage, can never afterward be free."[32]

Other critics compared the revival style to mesmerism. A former revivalist, La Roy Sunderland, gave up preaching and devoted his career to investigating and demonstrating hypnosis (or "Pathetism," as he called his philosophy), arguing that the techniques with which he put people into trances were essentially the same methods he had used in his ministry days. (Sunderland also thought that his theory would "explain all the mysteries of witchcraft.")[33]

The camp meetings and moral reform groups were mainstream movements. If *they* could inspire such reactions, imagine the horrified responses the more unusual offshoots of the Awakening inspired. The Shakers, who by now had set up several enclaves where they could live according to their principles, rejected both the familiar family structure and the sexual intercourse that makes a family possible. Their prophet was a woman, and they frequently put other women into leadership roles. To a certain mind-set, the sect was a standing threat to the traditional household: a domestic menace in more ways than one.

The biggest difference between the witch fear and the Shaker fear was that you knew whether someone was a Shaker. Shakers didn't live normal lives by day and meet in secret spectral sessions at night. They lived in communes, refused to have sex, and engaged in ecstatic trance dancing, by some accounts in the nude. They stood out precisely because they were different. That's one reason it was so easy to transform tales of alien Catholic conspiracies into stories about domestic "cult" conspiracies: The new religious movements made themselves alien.

What made them an Enemy Within was that they threatened to

make ordinary white Protestants into aliens too. The captivity narrative was frightening enough when the captors were imagined as Indians. The fear took on a new dimension when the enemy looked and sounded like your neighbors and kids. Outsiders accused the Shakers of drawing in new recruits with mesmerism and keeping them in line with intense physical violence. When one parent left the Shakers and the other stayed put, the sect sometimes found itself charged with keeping the children prisoner.

Some Shaker children really did want to leave the colonies, just as boys and girls raised in traditional families sometimes want to run away from home. At other times there were episodes such as the "rescue" of Ithamar Johnson from a colony in Ohio: The rescuers held the teenager overnight, and on his release the next morning he promptly returned to the Shakers. In 1825, a boy ran away from a Shaker settlement in Kentucky, then helped raise an armed posse to free his sister. They took the girl, but unlike her brother she didn't want to go; a year later, her relatives were still attempting "to re-create her mind" along the lines they preferred.[34] (Who exactly are the body snatchers here?) Other mobs broke into Shaker buildings, burned Shaker churches, and assaulted the Shakers themselves, all in the name of what were basically custody disputes.

But for all the vitriol and paranoia among the Shakers' critics, there was at least one rising religious movement that attracted even more opposition. It was born in upstate New York in 1830, and it is still with us today. It calls itself the Church of Jesus Christ of Latter-day Saints, and its members are better known as Mormons.

Mormonism began after Joseph Smith, a failed farmer and part-time treasure hunter, claimed to have found a holy book engraved on golden plates. The plates contained a host of revelations, he reported, including the old idea that the Indians were descended from Israelites and the new idea that Christ had visited their ancient American civilization. On a more paranoid note, Smith's Book of Mormon, allegedly transcribed from the plates, describes a criminal "secret society of Gadianton" that was based in the wilderness and whose leader had sworn "secret oaths and covenants" to the Devil.[35] (In Mormon folklore the Gadianton robbers still haunt the American West.)[36]

"Mormonism in Utah—The Cave of Despair," February 4, 1882, *Frank Leslie's Illustrated Newspaper*

As Smith attracted followers, he moved his church's base to Ohio and then to the Missouri frontier, where its adherents faced heavy harassment from their non-Mormon neighbors. (*Gentiles*, the Mormons called them.) The church tried to establish a town of its own in Illinois, and it was in that state that an angry mob killed Smith while he was confined to a jail. Control of the movement shifted to a Vermont-born tradesman named Brigham Young, who led the Mormons west to establish a kingdom in the desert.

Smith's religion was a product of the Second Great Awakening yet stood apart from it, a faith capable of alarming both the old Protestants and the new. Almost from the beginning, there were rumors of Mormon conspiracies.

Some of those tales featured the sorts of suspicions that had befallen the broader religious resurgence. Critics of Mormonism, like critics of Shakerism, took old anti-Catholic themes and retrofitted them for a younger faith: Smith and then Young were imagined as the all-powerful popes of a cult, their followers as docile sheep. There was the predictable suggestion that their allegiance was achieved through a sort of mind control, and Mormonism was mistaken for mesmerism.

A rich example appears in the best-selling *Female Life Among the Mormons* (1855), which presented itself as the memoir of a woman hypnotized into marrying a Mormon elder. (A more accurate description was offered by the historian David Brion Davis, who called the book a "ridiculous fantasy.")[37] At one point in the narrative the author asks another ex-Mormon how Joseph Smith had managed to master Franz Mesmer's mind-control method before "its general circulation throughout the country." Her informant, Anna Bradish, replies that "Smith obtained his information, and learned all the strokes, and passes, and manipulations, from a German peddler, who, notwithstanding his reduced circumstances, was a man of distinguished intellect and extensive erudition. Smith paid him handsomely, and the German promised to keep the secret." What's more,

"You, madam, were subjected to its influence. So have ten thousand others been, who never dreamed of it. Those most expert in it, are generally sent out to preach among unbelievers."[38]

The church started promoting polygamy privately in 1843, and it acknowledged the practice to the outside world in 1852. That heightened the sexual dimension of *Female Life Among the Mormons* and stories like it. In the popular imagination, Mormon men were out to add Gentile women to their harems, by hypnotic seduction if possible and by force if necessary. Like Shaker celibacy, plural marriage was perceived as a threat to the traditional family, and the anxieties it inspired unleashed a flood of fantasies about the other sorts of sexual nonconformity that the Latter-day Saints might be up to. The excommunicated Mormon John C. Bennett spread stories of a "secret lodge of women" who serviced church officials, going into great detail about the orders within the lodge and the duties and depravations identified with each. The Consecrates of the Cloister, for example, was an order "composed of females, whether married or unmarried, who, by an express grant and gift of God, through his Prophet the Holy Joe, are set apart and consecrated to the use and benefit of particular individuals, as *secret, spiritual wives*. They are the *Saints of the Black Veil*, and are accounted the special favorites of Heaven."[39]

As with the anti-Catholic tracts, there's a lot of projection involved here. In Davis's words, readers "took pleasure in imagining the variety of sexual experiences supposedly available to their enemies. By picturing themselves exposed to similar temptations, they assumed they could know how priests and Mormons actually sinned." Bennett, he added, had been "expelled from the Church as a result of his flagrant sexual immorality."[40]

When Mormons clustered in a single location, the fear that they might steal Christian bodies and souls through kidnapping and conversion was joined by another anxiety: the fear that Mormons would steal American institutions by voting en masse, installing a government that would replace the republic with a theocracy. And since you couldn't expect such a subversive menace to limit its efforts to the ballot box, another story began to take hold: that the church commanded an army of assassins, dubbed the Danites, to inflict its will by force.

The historical Danites were a vigilante group created in 1838 to compel dissenting Mormons to exit the area and, subsequently, to protect Missouri Mormons from their neighbors' attacks. It has never been proved that the organization lasted longer than a year, but it became a central part of anti-Mormon rhetoric for decades afterward, its reputation growing ever more fearsome with time. When Brigham Young set up a group of minutemen in Utah, saying that they were to battle rustlers and hostile Indians and the like, the group was quickly nicknamed the Destroying Angels, conflated with the old Danites, and feared as a secret squad of hit men. In 1859, the frontiersman John Young Nelson could casually (and inaccurately) assume, on meeting a Mormon painted like an Indian, that the latter was one of the church's "fanatical renegade-destroying angels, whose mission was to kill every white man not belonging to the sect, and particularly those who were apostates."[41]

Those whose fears of the Danites were grounded in more than mere rumors could point to a memoir written by the outlaw William "Wild Bill" Hickman after he was arrested for murder in 1871. Hickman, who had been excommunicated from the Latter-day Saints a few years earlier, claimed to have carried out several murders on Young's orders. There's no consensus on how much of what he wrote was accurate and how much was blame shifting or braggadocio, but all of it was incorporated into the anti-Mormon lore.

To see the hold that lore had on the American imagination, read Mark Twain's 1872 account of an evening supposedly spent with a Mormon assassin, a tale calculated to puncture the minutemen's image as a sinister elite. "'Destroying Angels,' as I understand it, are Latter-day Saints who are set apart by the Church to conduct permanent disappearances of obnoxious citizens," Twain wrote in *Roughing It*. "I had heard a deal about these Mormon Destroying Angels and the dark and bloody deeds they had done, and when I entered this one's house I had my shudder all ready. But alas for all our romances, he was nothing but a loud, profane, offensive old blackguard! He was murderous enough, possibly, to fill the bill of a Destroyer, but would you have *any* kind of an Angel devoid of dignity? Could you abide an Angel in an unclean shirt and no suspenders?"[42]

The Mormons might not have maintained an order of covert killers, but they did build their own institutions: schools, temples, courts of arbitration, an elaborate private welfare system, a network of cooperatives. Those were the sorts of voluntary organizations that Americans often celebrate, but they appeared to be entwined with civil government in predominantly Mormon areas out west, with the same figures dominating both church and state. Sometimes they were more influential than the formal institutions of government.

This stoked still more fears of subversion, and it led to some stunning restrictions on the Saints' civil liberties. In 1884, the Idaho territory made it illegal for Latter-day Saints to vote, hold office, or serve on a jury. Legislators invoked the standard anti-Mormon conspiracy theories, but lurking behind those exotic charges were more ordinary resentments: opposition to plural marriage, jealousy of the Mormon co-ops' economic clout,[43] and, above all, Republicans' eagerness to disenfranchise a group that in Idaho voted overwhelmingly for the Democrats.

There were fears as well that Mormon practices—and Mormon weapons—were finding their way to the local Native Americans.[44] Meanwhile, in the face of Gentile harassment, many Mormons started to identify with the Indians. But that had its limits, as one group of natives learned on September 11, 1857.

It was the middle of the conflict called the Utah War. The federal government thought the Latter-day Saints were plotting a rebellion. The Mormons thought the feds, who had dispatched more than 2,500 troops to the region, were plotting to eliminate them. In that tense atmosphere of mutual distrust, a group of Mormons—it is not known whether they were following Brigham Young's wishes or acting on their own—combined forces with a group of Paiute Indians (or, by some accounts, simply posed as Paiutes) and slaughtered around 120 unarmed emigrants passing through Mountain Meadows, Utah, including about 50 children. Afterward the Mormon hierarchy tried to scapegoat the natives, claiming that the assault had been committed by the Paiutes acting alone. Evidently, a church that identified with the persecuted red man wasn't above appealing to anti-Indian prejudice.

By that time Mormon conspiracies were a staple of popular culture. Dozens of lurid novels depicted Danite assassinations, church-sanctioned white slavery, and other alleged LDS crimes. On the other side of the Atlantic, the first Sherlock Holmes story, Arthur Conan Doyle's *A Study in Scarlet* (1887), featured a Danite plot to force a woman into an unwanted marriage. The most famous American yarn about Mormon conspirators is probably Zane Grey's *Riders of the Purple Sage* (1912), a book often credited with setting the mold of the formula western.

Grey's story is set in the devilish wilderness: the "wild country"[45] of Utah in 1871, in a Mormon town afflicted by rustlers. The book is built around a captivity plot, with Mormons and outlaws in the captor role filled elsewhere by Indians and white-slavery rings. Indeed, the tale contains several captives. There is Milly Erne, an eastern woman abducted and forced to marry a Mormon elder; there is Fay, a little Gentile girl the Mormons kidnap near the end of the novel; there is Milly's daughter, Bess, raised in captivity by the rustlers (who are secretly in cahoots with the church elders). But the book's most important captivity involves no imprisonment at all. Jane Withersteen has been enmeshed in Mormon society since her birth. In theory, she occupies a high place in the community: Her father founded the settlement, and she is one of the town's wealthiest citizens. But she refuses to marry an elder who wants her, and the consequences of that decision demonstrate just how little autonomy she has.

Since a Mormon hierarchy controls every community institution, this may sound like an Enemy Above story. And indeed there are elements of that here. From Withersteen's perspective, the conspiracy represents the eldritch forces of social control: "Above her hovered the shadow of grim, hidden, secret power."[46]

But the conspiracy doesn't just lurk *above* her. Like Goodman Brown at the witches' Sabbath, Withersteen soon finds traces of the secret power at every level of the social hierarchy; it isn't an authority bearing down on her so much as an all-enveloping system that's almost impossible to escape. Her friends and servants inform on her, and her ranch is haunted by spies and assassins. Everyone in her Mormon community is a potential betrayer. Lassiter—Milly Erne's brother, who rode west seeking revenge on the cabal that captured his sister—tells Withersteen just how few people she can trust:

> " . . . An', Jane," he went on, almost in a whisper, "I reckon it'd be a good idea for us to talk low. You're spied on here by your women."
>
> "Lassiter!" she whispered in turn. "That's hard to believe. My women love me."
>
> "What of that?" he asked. "Of course they love you. But they're Mormon women." . . .
>
> There came a time when no words passed between Jane and her women. Silently they went about their household duties, and secretly they went about the underhand work to which they had been bidden. . . . They spied and listened; they received and sent secret messengers; and they stole Jane's books and records, and finally the papers that were deeds of her possessions. Through it all they were silent, rapt in a kind of trance. Then one by one, without leave or explanation or farewell, they left Withersteen House, and never returned.[47]

Even apparently empty spaces are haunted. "There's no single move of yours, except when you're hid in your house, that ain't seen by sharp eyes," Lassiter tells Withersteen. "The cottonwood grove's full of creepin', crawlin' men. Like Indians in the grass. When you rode, which wasn't often lately, the sage was full of sneakin' men. At night they crawl under your windows into the court, an' I reckon into the house."[48]

Worse yet: Because Withersteen occupies such an important position in the community, she herself is implicated in its conspiracies. Milly Erne was forced to marry Jane's father, and even after she grows fond of Lassiter she refuses to tell him the identity of the man he's after. She may recognize some of the rot at the core of her world, but she also feels compelled to defend it. Indeed, though her affection for Lassiter is real—and eventually blossoms into a sincere romance—she also befriends and flirts with him for the express purpose of dissuading him from carrying out his revenge. Jane isn't just confined by the cabal that rules the region; she's a volunteer agent of the same conspiracy that harasses her.

So *Riders* isn't ultimately about Gentiles being seized and enslaved by Mormons. That *happens* in the story, but Withersteen, born Mormon, faces the same pressure—not to join the church but to submit to it sexually by becoming an elder's wife. The woman-snatching conspiracy is willing to take Jane by force if it has to. "Your body's to be held, given to some man, made, if possible, to bring children into the world," Lassiter tells her. "But your soul? . . . What do they care for your soul?"[49]

Forty-four years after Grey's book appeared, the question was easily answered: When the enemy takes our bodies, it will dispose of our souls altogether. Or at least that's the premise in *Invasion of the Body Snatchers*, a low-budget 1956 film that was released to little fanfare but would eventually establish itself as one of the most enduring artifacts of its era.

The story begins with Dr. Miles Bennell returning home from a conference to Santa Mira, California. Almost immediately, he encounters two people convinced that close relatives—an uncle, a mother—are imposters. Bennell's secretary tells him that his office has been crowded with people desperate to see him, but when he arrives at work the patients have canceled their appointments. Miles and his girlfriend, Becky, run into Danny Kauffman, the local psychiatrist. He tells them that a mass hysteria has hit the town: A dozen people have told him the same story about imposters. It's "a strange neurosis, evidently contagious," he says.

A shadow does seem to have fallen over Santa Mira. Family members don't trust one another. Formerly convivial public places have been deserted. A restaurant has had to lay off its house band and replace it with an emotionless invader: a jukebox. Eventually we learn that those patients weren't neurotic at all: Extraterrestrial seeds have fallen to Earth, where they are growing into enormous pods with the power to adopt the form and engorge the minds of the creatures near them—including, as it happens, Danny Kauffman. "There's no pain," the doctor tells Miles after his alien identity is revealed. "Suddenly, while you're asleep, they'll absorb your minds, your memories, and you're reborn into an untroubled world." Your replacement may have your memories, but its personality will be only a facsimile: Under the skin, everyone will be identical.

As Miles and Becky watch in horror, the invaders gather in the center of town and plot to bring more pods to more cities. After Becky falls asleep and is replaced by a pod person, the distressed Miles runs out onto the highway and tries to warn the drivers about the invasion. They whiz past, doing their best to ignore him. Miles climbs onto the back of a truck and realizes with horror that it's full of pods. Turning to the camera, he shouts a final warning to the audience: "You're next!"

The studio deemed that ending too frightening, and it insisted that director Don Siegel add a prologue and epilogue implying that the invasion would be defeated. Siegel reluctantly agreed, grumbling that pod people had taken over the film industry. The change blunts the picture's paranoid vision: Though the director's cut shows us a world where the agents of psychiatry and law enforcement are completely malevolent and untrustworthy, the studio version ends with Miles breathing a sigh of relief as a psychiatrist alerts the FBI to the invasion. But in either incarnation, it is a harrowing and disturbing film. The story may be science fiction, but it's rooted in a familiar experience. "I've seen how people have allowed their humanity to drain away," Miles mulls to Becky in one scene. "Only it happens slowly instead of all at once." The film's star, Kevin McCarthy, proposed an alternative title for the film, which Siegel liked but the studio rejected: *Sleep No More*.[50]

So while middlebrow America was taking in tales such as Arthur Miller's play *The Crucible*, a heavy-handed allegory in which the Salem trials stand in for McCarthyism, you could find much more potent visions of the Enemy Within in disreputable genre fare. *Invasion of the Body Snatchers* is the most memorable example, but it was hardly the only movie engaging those anxieties. It wasn't even the only movie about extraterrestrials disguised as human beings.

It Came from Outer Space, for example, subverts the formula by making the aliens benign: They don't intend to invade Earth; they crashed here by accident, and they plan to leave as soon as they've repaired their spacecraft. They have adopted the forms of the people they've encountered not because they planned to replace them but because they didn't want to alarm anyone by appearing inhuman. "We cannot, we would not, take your souls or minds or bodies," one of the intruders informs us. "Don't be afraid."[51]

In this film, fear itself is the Enemy Within, possessing people and leading them to do destructive things. "How do we know they're not taking over?" a paranoid sheriff exclaims. "They could be all around us and I wouldn't know it!" Moments later, he's raising a posse and chasing the alien into the Arizona desert. (You thought you were watching a science fiction flick, but that was just a mask: It was a western all along.)

The movie sounds like a response to *Invasion of the Body Snatchers*, but it came out in 1953, three years before *Body Snatchers* was released. Let me repeat that: Three years before *Invasion of the Body Snatchers* appeared in theaters, stories about aliens possessing or impersonating Earth people were familiar enough that a movie could play with viewers' expectations by presenting extraterrestrial imposters who turn out not to be invaders at all. *Invasion* may be the best of the body-snatching stories, but it wasn't the first.

Tales about possession and imposture have been around for centuries, of course. In a science fiction context, the trail goes at least as far back as Harl Vincent's "Parasite," published in 1935, in which invaders from a doomed world transform themselves into "microscopic energy charges" that can reproduce their minds in the bodies of their human victims.[52] *Astounding Stories* published H. P. Lovecraft's novella *The Shadow Out of Time* a year later, though it was written before Vincent's story appeared; it too dealt with inhuman beings possessing human bodies. In England, H. G. Wells's 1937 novel *Star Begotten* toyed with the idea that extraterrestrials are manipulating us via cosmic rays, so that new babies who appear to be Terran would actually have Martian minds. Back in the United States, John W. Campbell, Jr.'s, influential 1938 novella *Who Goes There?* featured an alien with the ability to adopt the appearance of the people it consumes.[53] A variation of the idea even appeared in the ongoing series of sequels to *The Wonderful Wizard of Oz*, which continued to be produced by other hands after L. Frank Baum died. In *The Magical Mimics in Oz* (1946)—written by Jack Snow, who cut his teeth in the Lovecraftian pages of *Weird Tales*—supernatural creatures capture Dorothy and the Wizard, adopt their physical forms, and take the opportunity to engage in espionage within the Emerald City, searching for the spell that will allow their race of monsters to invade Oz and subject the rest of its people to the same fate.

Some of those stories are close to the *Body Snatchers* model. Others are more distant. Lovecraft's intruders are more interested in exploration than invasion. The tone of the Wells book is more ironic than paranoid, with a narrator who's clearly dubious about the alien force that the characters think they perceive. (Nor do all of those characters imagine the incursion as a body-snatchers scenario. Some see something closer to those Coming Race stories where we've got to make way for the *Homo superior*.) But all those tales established a set of plot devices that invaded Hollywood in the middle of the twentieth century. Besides *Body Snatchers* and *It Came from Outer Space*, fifties films that feature aliens impersonating or controlling human beings include *Invaders from Mars* (1953), *Killers from Space*

(1954), *It Conquered the World* (1956), *I Married a Monster from Outer Space* (1958), and *The Brain Eaters* (1958). Body snatchers continued to appear on the printed page as well, the most notable examples being Robert Heinlein's *The Puppet Masters* (1951) and Jack Finney's *The Body Snatchers* (1954). Finney's novel was the direct inspiration for Siegel's film.

Since these stories involve extraterrestrial invaders, they may sound more like tales of the Enemy Outside than the Enemy Within. But although that's arguably true of a few of them—*The Puppet Masters*, for example, is obviously an allegory for the Cold War—most of them locate their horror not in the skies but in the suspicion that anyone you encounter, even your own spouse or parent or child, might secretly be something else, and in the possibility that you too might be made alien. In *The Brain Eaters*, outer space is a red herring: The invader turns out to come from the interior of the earth. In *Invasion of the Body Snatchers*, the invading seeds may have drifted to our planet from space, but they took root and grew on Earth's own soil. In several other films, the aliens set up their base in a cave or under the earth's surface. The most famous British version of the story, the 1955 TV serial *Quatermass II*, ends with the hero defeating the enemy by riding a rocket to an asteroid. But in Hollywood, meeting the monster behind the invasion is more likely to require a trip underground. To encounter this enemy, you don't aim for the stars; you descend into Hell.[54]

It is often said that *Invasion of the Body Snatchers* can be read as a critique of either communism or McCarthyism. The flip side is that the opposition to both communism and McCarthyism fed on the same dread that animated the movie, a horror at the thought of being swallowed by the conformist collective. That was one of the core fears of the 1950s. It surfaced in the work of writers as diverse as William Burroughs, Ayn Rand, and Jean-Paul Sartre; it appeared in intellectual critiques of "mass man," in uneasiness about subliminal advertising, in worries that suburbia would become a ticky-tacky nightmare.

It was especially visible when the topic was mass culture. When the leftist psychiatrist Fredric Wertham testified to Congress in 1954 about the alleged evils of comic books, he warned that "the sinister hand of these corrupters of children, of this comic-book industry" might prevent the distribution of his book *Seduction of the Innocent*.[55] (The book was distributed without incident.) Television was seen as an instrument of thought control, the means by which the next "War of the Worlds" panic might be incited. Conservatives, such as the ex–FBI men who published the 1950 report *Red Channels*, probed TV for Communist propaganda. Liberals, such as the filmmakers behind the 1957 feature *A Face in the Crowd*, fretted that far-right demagogues might broadcast their way into power.

If mass culture was supposed to be a potential prelude to fascism, advertising was imagined as mass-market mesmerism. In his 1957 best seller *The Hidden Persuaders*, Vance Packard warned that "many of the nation's leading public-relations experts have been indoctrinating themselves in the lore of psychiatry and the social sciences in order to increase their skill at 'engineering' our consent to their propositions."[56] There's an echo here of the nineteenth-century critics who saw religious revivals as episodes of mass hypnosis. (Indeed, Packard added, "Public-relations experts are advising churchmen how they can become more effective manipulators of their congregations.")[57] In *A Face in the Crowd*, a villain who uses his powers to sell mattresses and energy supplements then goes to work for an ultraconservative senator.

The persuaders' power was expected to grow. "Eventually—say by A.D. 2000—perhaps all this depth manipulation of the psychological variety will seem amusingly old-fashioned," Packard wrote. "By then perhaps the biophysicists will take over with 'biocontrol,' which is depth persuasion carried to its ultimate. Biocontrol is the new science of controlling mental processes, emotional reactions, and sense perceptions by bioelectrical signals."[58]

When Packard described the effects of ads, he used such words as "we" and "ourselves," but the impression left by most anti-ad rhetoric (and by films such as *A Face in the Crowd*) drew a line separating the dupes from the elect. *You* might not have been brainwashed by those Madison Avenue Mesmers, but the pod people around you aren't so strong.[59]

Body Snatchers wasn't the only fifties film open to both left-wing and right-wing readings. To see how easy it was to reimagine a rightist conspiracy as a leftist conspiracy, watch the 1951 picture *The Whip Hand*. The movie was originally going to tell the tale of a reporter stumbling on a Nazi plot in an isolated Minnesota town. After the film wrapped, studio chief Howard Hughes decided that the bad guys ought to be Communists instead, and with a little rewriting, a little redubbing, and a few brief additions and subtractions, the switch was made. The central villain was still a Nazi scientist, but now he had disappeared behind the Iron Curtain after the war and offered his services to the Reds. It's a funny sort of communism that he's embraced: The first time we encounter one of his goons, the guy warns the reporter that he's "on private property."[60] But communism isn't the point here, any more than Nazism was; they're just convenient costumes.

More subtly—and more strangely—there is *I Led 3 Lives*, a TV drama that ran from 1953 to 1956. Inspired by the experiences of Herbert Philbrick, an advertising salesman who had infiltrated the Communist movement for the FBI, the series was a vivid example of anti-Communist popular culture. It was also sometimes scripted by the victims of the Red Scare.

The show, the historian Thomas Doherty has pointed out,

> speaks to the blacklist with suspicious frequency: to the moral dilemma of the informer, to the problems of the prodigal politico, and to the plight of the duped liberal smeared by his past associations. As Philbrick's party comrades might put it, this is no accident. According to producer Frederick Ziv, blacklisted screenwriters wrote for the show under assumed names. Likes moles burrowing from within, they commented on their own dilemma, doubtless savoring the irony

> of using the premiere anti-communist series on television to critique anti-communist paranoia. In another episode, when Philbrick is assigned responsibility for party security, his lesbian-coded cell leader, Comrade Jenny, orders him to hunt for subversive elements. "I needn't remind you that one of the greatest threats to communism is internal—from the party itself. Diversionists, traitors, opportunists, social patriots, reformers—you'll make every effort to discover these enemies and report them to me." The camera holds tight on her severe face as she tells him to name names: "And should you fail to report them—I'll be forced to conclude that you're one of them yourself!"[61]

In another episode, the Communists quiz Philbrick "about his pre-'communist' anticommunist past. What about the anticommunist rallies he attended? The anticommunist petitions he signed?"[62]

The line between Left and Right is even blurrier in Richard Condon's 1959 novel *The Manchurian Candidate*, a satiric thriller in which the Communist conspiracy and a Joseph McCarthy–like senator are secretly on the same side. The story turns on the idea of brainwashing, a word that entered the language after U.S. POWs broadcast propaganda messages for the Communists during the Korean War. The soldiers had been subjected to intense indoctrination sessions, and the idea took hold in Washington that their captors had reprogrammed their minds.[63] The term might have been new, but the animating anxiety goes at least as far back as the Indian captivity narratives, stories that drew much of their power from the possibility that an enemy could remake Americans as something alien.

In Condon's book, the brainwashed soldier becomes an unwitting assassin, an Enemy Within manipulated by an Enemy Outside who, by the end, is revealed to have been manipulated in turn by an another Enemy Within. Condon clearly despises both the Communists and the McCarthyists, but his book is ultimately more about the evils of manipulation than the evils of any particular gang of manipulators. The author was a former public relations man with a cynical view of his old job, and his book gleefully draws parallels between brainwashing and advertising; at one point his Communists condition their captives "to enjoy all the Coca-Cola they could drink, which was, in actuality, Chinese Army issue tea served in tin cups."[64] Later the chief brainwasher in Korea casually informs an audience that "any of you who are interested in massive negative conditioning" should read "Frederic [*sic*] Wertham's *The Seduction of the Innocent*, which demonstrates how thousands have been brought to antisocial actions through children's cartoon books."[65] Condon's chronology is skewed—Wertham's book wasn't published until after the Korean conflict ended—but, as is often the case with conspiracy stories, the impossible connection makes a poetic sort of sense.

While anti-Communists and anti-McCarthyists worried about enforced conformity, the Communists and McCarthyists themselves sometimes felt the same fear. A Soviet-style dictatorship is no place for a nonconformist, but the average American Marxist was deeply aware that he was out of step with society. And though the Red Scare made it harder to express unorthodox opinions, the era's most infamous scaremonger was, in the words of his biographer Richard Rovere, "closer to the hipster than to the Organization Man." Senator Joseph McCarthy, Rovere wrote, "denounced the very institutions that are customarily thought of as the fortresses of American conformity: the Army, the Protestant clergy, the press, the two major parties, the civil service. And of course he attacked by his very existence the conformities of U.S. politicians. He never affected the pieties of a Dwight Eisenhower. He made little pretense to religiosity or to any species of moral rectitude. . . . He didn't want the world to think of him as respectable."[66] Jack Kerouac spoke favorably of McCarthy, and his fellow Beat scribe William Burroughs's favorite columnist was the pro-McCarthy pundit Westbrook Pegler.[67]

If it's odd to see Communists and McCarthyists concerned about conformity, it should be odder still to see the professed enemies of totalitarianism endorsing authoritarian measures. Instead it is common, and it has been for as long as totalitarianism has existed. The historian Leo Ribuffo coined the term *Brown Scare* to describe a wave of countersubversive activity in the 1930s and '40s, when an understandable fear of Nazis unleashed some much less defensible calls for restrictions on the far Right's freedoms of speech and assembly. In the process the authorities conflated very different people, leading to surveillance not just of people who sympathized with Germany but of reputable conservatives.[68] Like the better-known Red Scares but pointing rightward rather than leftward, a Brown Scare both exaggerates the threats at hand and obscures the distinctions between genuinely violent plotters, radical but peaceful activists, and members of the mainstream.

The Brown Scare of the Roosevelt years didn't just resemble the Red Scare of the late 1940s and the '50s; it paved the way for it. In the aftermath of World War II, having expanded its surveillance powers, the FBI didn't find it hard to shift the focus of its spying from the Right to the Left. Likewise, when Congress voted in 1938 to recharter the House Committee on Un-American Activities, many liberals voted with the ayes because they wanted to investigate fascists. Later, the committee would take the lead in the anti-Left crusades of the Cold War.

Something similar happened with the Alien Registration Act of 1940, better known as the Smith Act, which criminalized advocating the overthrow of the U.S. government. Passed with liberal support, the law was quickly used against alleged fascists, most infamously in the great sedition trial of 1944, an ill-fated effort to imprison thirty antiwar writers and speakers as the pawns of a Nazi conspiracy. The law was also used against antiwar Trotskyists, with the Communist Party supporting the prosecution. Just a few years later, the Communists would become the act's chief victims.

The fear of mass culture had an authoritarian side too. It was shot through with distrust of ordinary people, who were often described in terms that suggested they weren't fully human. Erich Fromm's influential *Escape from Freedom* (1941) argued that while some of us had achieved a "genuine individuality," monopoly capitalism had created a "compulsive conforming" in which "the individual becomes an automaton, loses his self, and yet at the same time consciously conceives of himself as free and subject only to himself."[69] Not every critic of mass culture would go that far, but they all contrasted the individual man with the amorphous mass.

Such ideas don't *have* to lead to authoritarian conclusions. But if you see the average voter as an automaton, it's obviously easier to support laws that might otherwise seem like restrictions on his freedom. And if you think he's being manipulated by occult forces—advertisers, broadcasters, comic book publishers—it's easier to rationalize those restrictions as an act of liberation.

That brings us to our final entry in the Eisenhower-era body-snatching cycle. "The Monsters Are Due on Maple Street" is an episode of *The Twilight Zone* that first aired on March 4, 1960. Written by Rod Serling, the tale is set on the deliberately generic "Maple Street, USA." It begins with a mysterious roar and a flashing light passing overhead. Then the street loses power. The residents are mystified, particularly since it's not just a grid failure—cars and portable radios have stopped working too. But a boy feels confident about what's going on: The outage was caused by monsters from space, he says. After all, that's how it always happens in science fiction. "He's been reading too many comic books or seeing too many movies," a woman declares.[70]

The boy persists. In the story he read, the aliens sent an advance party who "looked just like humans." The crowd pooh-poohs the idea, but then someone's car starts by itself. One of the neighbors notes that its owner didn't seem concerned with "that thing that flew overhead." Someone else says, "He always was an oddball. Him and his whole family." A woman recalls that she's seen him looking up at the sky at night.

One man tries to stop the panic, mocking the idea of "fifth columnists from the Great Beyond." It's no use: The suspicions just start to fall on him too. Then a mysterious entity starts to approach from the distance. "It's the monster!" cries the boy.

The leader of the mob fires a gun, and the approaching figure falls dead. It turns out to be a neighbor who had gone to the next block to see if the power had failed there too. The lights come on in the shooter's house, and then the mob turns on him: Maybe *he's* the monster. Soon everyone is accusing everyone else, and the streets are filled with shouts and gunfire as the camera pulls back on the scene.

The story ends with one of *The Twilight Zone*'s trademark twists. Two aliens have been watching the entire time. "Understand the procedure now?" one asks. "Just stop a few of their machines and radios and telephones and lawn mowers. Throw them into darkness for a few hours, and then sit back and watch the pattern."

"And this pattern is always the same?" his companion asks.

"With few variations," the first invader answers. "They pick the most dangerous enemy they can find, and it's themselves. All we need do is sit back and watch." As the aliens return to their spaceship, one describes their plan: "Their world is full of Maple Streets. And we'll go from one to the other and let them destroy themselves."

Like *It Came from Outer Space*, "The Monsters Are Due on Maple Street" subverts the body-snatchers formula, but it does so in a very different way and with very different results. In *It Came from Outer Space*, extraterrestrials pose as human beings but are not actually plotting against us. In "Monsters," the aliens *aren't* posing as human beings but *are* planning to conquer us. "Monsters" is a critique of paranoia, but it is also extremely paranoid; and the paranoid vision it adopts should seem familiar. The setting is suburban. The boy who sets off the hysteria has been reading comic books. The neighbors are quick to shed their individuality and form a mob. And an alien cabal is able to guide their behavior with a few remote signals. In real-world America, sociologists have shown that it's rare for people to panic or riot in a disaster, particularly in a community with few serious social divisions.[71] In "Monsters," all it takes to induce the collapse of civilization is to arrange a few inexplicable mechanical failures.

Yes, it's an allegory; you shouldn't expect *The Twilight Zone* to give you a sociologically sound portrait of a community in distress, any more than you'd expect the pod people in *Body Snatchers* to follow the laws of botany. But it's an allegory that reflects a particular vision of society: one where people are easily maneuvered from afar, individuals lose their identities in crowds, and mass culture is a stepping-stone to fascism. A vision, in other words, where the pod people are already here.

It was an outlook that the Jungian psychologist Erich Neumann managed both to explain and to exemplify when he offered a theory of where scapegoating comes from. When people can't accept the corruption within themselves, he argued in 1949, they project it instead onto others. So "evil is invariably experienced by mass man as something alien, and the victims of shadow projection are therefore, always and everywhere, the aliens."[72] For Neumann, presumably, the aliens were "mass man," onto whom he could project his own propensity for scapegoating.

If we're looking at supposed subversives who can't easily be distinguished from other Americans, who are rumored to recruit young people into an underground society, who gather in forbidden places and communicate through code, there's one more subculture we should discuss before leaving the Enemy Within behind. Even its members have been known to describe their lives with metaphors of conspiracy. "Occasionally two homosexuals might meet in the great world," Gore Vidal wrote in *The City and the Pillar*. "When they did, by a quick glance they acknowledged one another and, like amused conspirators, observed the effect each was having. It was a form of freemasonry."[73]

In the early 1940s, people sometimes joked about the "Homintern," or Homosexual International—a play on the Comintern, a global network of Communist parties commanded from Moscow. It isn't clear who coined the word, which has been attributed at different times to W. H. Auden, Maurice Bowra, Jocelyn Brooke, Cyril Connolly, Harold Norse, and no doubt others. The joke was probably obvious enough to be invented independently by several different people. But it didn't take long for the idea to take hold among men and women who didn't see it as a gag at all.

In 1952, the conservative weekly *Human Events* ran an article by Rose Waldeck headlined "Homosexual International." Gay people, Waldeck argued, belong "by the very nature of their vice" to "a world-wide conspiracy against society." This hydra "has spread all over the globe; has penetrated all classes; operates in armies and in prisons; has infiltrated into the press, the movies, and the cabinets; and it all but dominates the arts, literature, theater, music, and TV." The threat it poses, she added, should be "evident to anyone who had an opportunity to observe the mysterious manner in which homosexuals recognize each other—by a glance, a gesture, an indefinable pitch of voice—and the astonishing understanding which this recognition creates between men who seem to be socially or politically at opposite poles."[74]

Fear of homosexuality has always been an element of American culture, but it went into overdrive after World War II, when the country entered a period the historian David K. Johnson has labeled the Lavender Scare. Thanks to a wave of anxiety about sexual predators, twenty-one states and the District of Columbia adopted "sexual psychopath" laws in the decade after the war. These measures were promoted as a way to protect children from sexual assault, but they were almost immediately used in cases involving no one but consenting adults. Meanwhile in Washington, the sex scare was intersecting with the Cold War: When Waldeck warned that "the homosexual international has become a sort of auxiliary of the Communist International," officials took the idea seriously. Representative Katharine St. George (R–N.Y.), best known today as an early advocate of laws against sexual discrimination, had Waldeck's article entered into the *Congressional Record*.[75] And the director of the Central Intelligence Agency, Roscoe Hillenkoetter, warned a House committee that "perverts in key positions" formed "a government within a government." In a darker version of Vidal's line about a gay freemasonry, Hillenkoetter testified that civil service homosexuals "belong to the lodge, the fraternity. One pervert brings other perverts into an agency, they move from position to position, and advance them usually in the interest of furthering the romance of the moment."[76] Gays and lesbians were presumed to be security risks, though the evidence for that assumption was slight.

The result was a great purge. Bureaucrats informed investigators that they suspected coworkers of being homosexual; interrogators pressured suspects into naming other gays and lesbians in the workforce. Many private companies imitated the crackdown in D.C., particularly when they had government contracts that required security clearances. By at least one measure, the Lavender Scare had a larger effect than the Red Scare. Johnson has estimated that the State Department fired about a thousand employees believed to be homosexuals in the 1950s and '60s, far more than the number of alleged Reds who got the ax.[77] That shouldn't be surprising: the United States has always been home to far more gays than Communists.

Fear of fictional homosexual conspiracies led the government to conspire against homosexuals; fear of real repression led gay organizations to adopt the trappings of a conspiracy. In one such group, the Mattachine Society of Washington, Johnson wrote, "The secretary could only keep two sets of membership records and they were only open to MSW officers. Anyone who 'breached the security' of the organization could be expelled by a two-thirds vote of the membership. Pseudonyms were the norm, not only in meeting minutes and publications, but also in conversations at meetings."[78] All this in turn inspired yet more paranoia among the gay-hunters. When the Mattachine Society of Washington's founder, Frank Kameny, testified to a congressional committee in 1962, he informed his interrogators that the group's mailing list had only about a hundred names on it. That was inconceivable to congressmen such as John Dowdy, a Texas Democrat who had assumed that the society was an arm of a "national and international organization" with "up in the millions" of members.[79] The committee was puzzled further by the fact that Kameny believed that there were a quarter-million homosexuals in the city—not because they doubted that there were so many, but because he didn't have each one's contact information. The investigators assumed, Johnson wrote, "that homosexuals were inherently drawn to the same clique and would somehow all be on the same mailing list."[80]

Antigay paranoia isn't as widespread now as it was then, but it has hardly disappeared. In 2012, a bishop in Maryland's Hope Christian Church called same-sex marriage "a Satanic plot to destroy our seed."[81] In the same state, the antigay activist Michael Peroutka raised the specter of body snatchers. "You see, homosexuals can't reproduce," he explained. "So they must recruit. The best place to recruit is in schools where they can have unfettered access to children. . . . [W]hat is being pushed is nothing short of government-authorized perversion of Maryland children."[82]

The great gay conspiracy never existed: Sexual subcultures may resemble secret societies in some ways, but they have no cell structure, no hierarchy, no Homintern. But gay *people* are very real, and they often have had good reasons to conduct their love lives covertly. Imagine a descendant of Goodman Brown working in Washington in 1945—perhaps he's lending a hand with the war effort—and wandering one warm night into the same-sex pickup spot that was Lafayette Park. He has left his wife at home, naturally. A devilish older gentleman strikes up a conversation, and the longer it goes on, the more guilt Brown feels. He spots some seemingly respectable people that he knows, en route to some private revelry in the bushes. He tells himself nervously that he has entered a hidden world with its own secret signs. And he's absolutely right.

4

THE BEAST BELOW

Rumors flew about that black bands, numbering in the scores, even hundreds, were fanning out in all directions. Messengers galloped hither and yon to warn villages of approaching rebels. Invariably the rumors proved false—but no matter, an explanation was ready to hand. Black informers, it always turned out, had luckily alerted the white people to their impending doom, days or just hours beforehand, and the ringleaders were now safely in jail, the others having melted into the shadows. Yet everyone was warned to stay vigilant, no matter how normally the slaves were behaving in the quarters and fields.

—*Bertram Wyatt-Brown*[1]

Here's the story:

It wasn't a long walk from the respectable neighborhoods of New York City to the grimier world of the waterfront, where sailors, slaves, and thieves gathered in taverns to drink, dance, roll dice, and draw up plans for revolutionary terror. The plotters were members of the Geneva Club, a secret society modeled on the Masonic orders of the gentlemen the Genevans were pledged to destroy. There were at least two lodges within the club: Smith's Fly Boys, who met at John Hughson's pub by the North River; and the Long Bridge Boys, who met at John Romme's place by the Battery.[2] There were other meeting spots too, such as Gerardus Comfort's house near the docks, where more than twenty seditious slaves assembled one Sunday in 1741. They "whetted their knives on a stone," one woman later recalled, "some complaining, that their knives were rusty and blunt, and some said, that their knives were sharp enough to cut off a white man's head: That they would kill the white Men, and have the white Women for their Wives."[3]

Then there was the winter bacchanal hosted by Hughson, a white cobbler and barkeep who trafficked in stolen goods on the side. It was against the law to entertain slaves without their owners' permission or for more than three slaves to meet after dark, but Hughson regularly opened his doors to far more slaves than that, at all hours and without bothering to ask their masters' consent. On that day he laid out a banquet for the conspirators: a goose, a fowl, a quarter of mutton, two loaves of bread, two bowls of rum punch. As they feasted, a slave named Ben announced that he had the run of his master's house and that when it was time to rise up he could easily steal a gun. Then Ben asked another slave, called Quash, what role he'd take in the rebellion. Quash replied that he didn't care, but he could kill three, four, five white men before the day ended.

One by one, the others declared their plans for the revolution. One slave said he would kill his mistress first and then go out to the streets to fight. Another pledged to burn his master's stables. Many men promised to steal weapons or to set their masters' houses on fire. And then they all swore themselves to a pact. The next evening they gathered again, and while Ben played the fiddle they danced and drank deep into the night.

There were many meetings, many oaths, many plans. Romme knew some black men in the countryside who could read; he would write to them about the plot, he promised, and they would recruit a horde to descend on the city. There was talk that the Spanish were planning an invasion of New York. The rebels agreed that if the Spaniards came they would combine forces with the invaders, timing their uprising to coincide with the attack.

After the revolt, they whispered, Manhattan would be turned upside down. Hughson would be king, a slave named Caesar would be governor, and the insurgents would divide the city's wealth. A "great many people had too much, and others too little," a slave called Cuffee liked to say. His "master had a great deal of money," Cuffee continued, "but in a short time, he should have less."[4]

They set the first fire at Fort George on March 18, 1741, and it left the governor's mansion in cinders. The second came on March 25 at the home of a prominent naval officer. There was a fire at a storehouse on April 1, and April 4 brought two more fires in two separate structures. On April 5, someone found some coals under a haystack, and a woman overheard three slaves talking on the street. "*Fire, fire, scorch, scorch*, A LITTLE, *goddamn it*, BY-AND-BY," one of them said, and then he laughed.[5]

There were four more fires the next day. As citizens scrambled to suppress the flames, someone spotted Cuffee leaping from the window of a burning storehouse. The witness called out, *"A negro, a negro!"* As the cry spread, it became a general alarm: *The Negroes were rising*.[6]

People started remembering something they'd seen on the first day of the fires, as Fort George burned. New Yorkers, both black and white, had formed bucket lines from the port to the blaze. But when the buckets came to Cuffee, he dumped them on the ground rather than passing them along. And as the flames burned high, the defiant slave started to dance with joy, whistling and singing and shouting *"Huzzah!"*

Or that's the story, anyway.

There really was a wave of fires in New York in early 1741. There may well have been a revolutionary conspiracy behind them, though there isn't a consensus on that. But there's no disputing the colonial government's reaction to the blazes. At least thirty-four people—thirty black, four white—were executed for their purported parts in the plot, with thirteen burned at the stake. Another ninety-one were exiled from the city. One committed suicide behind bars.[7]

It was a bloody exorcism, and the exorcists were deeply frightened men. About 20 percent of Manhattan was black in 1741, far more than any city in Europe. The specter of a slave revolt haunted the city fathers, and they were even more terrified by the thought of a slave revolt aided by the sort of lowlife whites they associated with places like Hughson's pub. You can get a sense of the fear that seized the city from the title of a book published three years later by Daniel Horsmanden, a judge at the trials: *A Journal of the Proceedings In the Detection of the Conspiracy Formed by some White People, in conjunction with Negro and other Slaves, for burning the City of New-York in America and murdering the Inhabitants.*

A
JOURNAL
OF THE
PROCEEDINGS
In the Detection of the
CONSPIRACY
Formed by ſome White People, in conjunction with Negro and other Slaves, for burning the City of NEW-YORK in AMERICA and murdering the Inhabitants.

Which conſpiracy was partly put in execution, by burning his Majeſty's houſe in fort George, within the ſaid city, on Wedneſday the 18th of *March*, 1741, and ſetting fire to ſeveral dwelling and other houſes there, within a few days ſucceeding. And by another attempt made in proſecution of the ſame infernal ſcheme, by putting fire between two other dwelling-houſes within the ſaid city, on the 15th day of *February*, 1742; which was accidentally and timely diſcovered and extinguiſhed.

CONTAINING,

I. A narrative of the trials, condemnations, executions, and behaviour of the ſeveral criminals, at the gallows and ſtake, with their ſpeeches and confeſſions; with notes, obſervations and reflections occaſionally interſperſed throughout the whole.
II. An appendix, wherein is ſet forth ſome additional evidence concerning the ſaid conſpiracy and conſpirators, which has come to light ſince their trials and executions.
III. Liſts of the ſeveral perſons (whites and blacks) committed on account of the conſpiracy; and of the ſeveral criminals executed; and of thoſe tranſported, with the places whereto.

By the Recorder of the City of NEW-YORK.

Quid facient Domini, audent cum talia Fures? Virg. Ecl.

Printed at NEW-YORK:
LONDON, Reprinted and Sold by JOHN CLARKE under the Royal Exchange, Cornhill. MDCCXLVII.

It didn't take long for second thoughts to sink in, and skeptics were soon comparing the prosecutions to the Salem witch trials. But the crackdown's defenders had comparisons of their own to offer. Slaves had already rioted in New York in 1712. Just two years before the Manhattan fires, in the Stono Rebellion of 1739, South Carolina slaves had used both arms and arson against the whites. Several rebellions had broken out in Britain's Caribbean possessions, and many more had been either detected in advance or imagined by nervous members of the planter class. In Barbados, where five-sixths of the population was enslaved, the authorities executed thirty-six Africans in 1675 for purportedly planning to burn the plantations and exterminate the white men. By some accounts the rebels intended to kill the white women too, while others believed, in the words of one anonymous pamphleteer, that "they intended to spare the lives of the Fairest and Handsomest Women . . . to be Converted to their own use."[8]

The Barbados crackdown took place while King Philip's War was raging in New England, and the two events were soon linked in the public mind. One early account of the Barbados conspiracy declared matter-of-factly that New Englanders had "tasted of the same Cup" when Philip "Revolted without Cause."[9] But as the real and imaginary slave conspiracies kept coming, a more distinct tale coalesced: the myth of the Enemy Below. In this story, as with the Enemy Within, the community's foe is found inside the city's gates. But these conspirators are not indistinguishable from everyone else. They hold a distinct position at the bottom of the social pyramid, which they aim to overturn. They are alien but familiar, with a well-defined place in society, perhaps even an essential role in the economy. If the Enemy Within can be imagined as a mob whose members have been seduced or conned into losing their individuality, the Enemy Below is presumed to be not quite human in the first place. It is a bestial force with monstrous appetites: a collective id eager to rape, burn, loot, and massacre.

Needless to say, the fact that the accusations in New York conformed to a formula doesn't mean that the charges were all false.

There are good reasons to expect some similarities among uprisings. It's natural, for example, for slaves to turn to fire as a weapon, since it is both extremely destructive and easy to acquire. But because the story formula was well known, it was also natural for the authorities to interpret the evidence to fit the well-worn tale. Once the investigators decided they were seeing a slave insurrection, they knew what to look for, and once the prisoners understood what was expected in their confessions, they provided the necessary details.

The result in Manhattan was as good a distillation of the Enemy Below myth as you'll find—or at least it was until June 1741. Then it became a case study in how a conspiracy narrative can suddenly shift shape, as prosecutors convinced themselves that the real power behind the slaves was that familiar Enemy Outside, the Catholic Church.

The Manhattan story begins with a much smaller conspiracy: not to burn down the city but to rob a shop. A teenage sailor named Christopher Wilson had spotted some valuable pieces of eight in a store as the merchant's wife made change. Wilson mentioned the money to some of the drinkers at Hughson's pub, and a group of them then burglarized the place.

One of the most distinctive coins was subsequently spotted in the possession of the slave Caesar, a Hughson's regular. Soon several members of the tavern crowd were arrested, and others were hauled in for questioning. One of the people questioned was Hughson's disgruntled indentured servant, sixteen-year-old Mary Burton, who charged her white master and various black confederates with complicity in the burglary.

Meanwhile, the fires had started. Officials took the first blaze for an accident, but with each structure that caught fire their suspicions grew. There were suggestions that burglars had been burning buildings to distract people while they stole from their houses. (And indeed, some robberies did take place while homeowners were occupied with firefighting.) Then rumors of a grander plot started circulating. Remember the woman who thought she overheard three slaves on the street speaking suspiciously about the fires. Remember the fear that took hold when Cuffee was spotted jumping from a burning storehouse, the cry that the slaves were rising. A crowd chased Cuffee to his master's house and then dragged him off to jail. By the end of the night, several more black men had been arrested.

On April 8, according to Horsmanden's book, the city council concluded that there was a "villainous confederacy of latent enemies amongst us"[10] and ordered a general search of all the houses in Manhattan. The governor had the militia "dispersed through the city, and sentries of them posted at the ends of the streets to guard all avenues, with orders to stop all suspected persons that should be observed carrying bags or bundles, or removing goods from house to house, in order for their examination."[11] He also offered a reward to anyone able to furnish information about the plot.

Two weeks later, Burton was brought in for more questioning about the robbery. She informed her interrogators that she would talk about the larceny case but would say nothing at all about the fires. That implied, of course, that she knew something about the fires, and a fierce series of questions about the blazes followed. Burton's declarations of reluctance faded away, and soon she was recounting a vast plot to burn down the city, overthrow the government, and install her boss as king.

As all that was going on, Great Britain and Spain were in the second year of the conflict known today as the War of Jenkins' Ear, and Britain's New York colony was rife with rumors that the Spanish were going to attack. Manhattan, meanwhile, had just been through a period of deep political division, including mass opposition to the rule of Governor William Cosby and continued partisan sniping in the wake of Cosby's death. The specter of a revolt allowed the political class both to overcome those divisions and to find a focus for their fears. That consensus would not last forever. But as the grand jury began to try the accused, who had no attorneys and did not enjoy the legal rights that Americans expect to enjoy today, the elites of New York were set on suppressing a domestic threat.

It was under such circumstances, with a war at the colony's doors and suspicions of subversion within, that the Salem authorities had thrown themselves into a witch hunt. And it was at that moment that events in Manhattan started to resemble the Salem trials. Several prisoners were quickly condemned to death. It became clear that the best way to avoid the same fate was to confess, and it became clear that one way to impress the authorities with your sincerity was to name some more conspirators. So even the innocent had an incentive to declare themselves guilty, to offer a story that fit the prosecutors' preconceptions, and, by fingering others, to inflate the size of the purported plot.

Were any of those people guilty? Well, *someone* was setting fires. But if it's reasonable to conclude that the confessions contained some truth, there are also good reasons not to take them entirely at face value. In addition to the credibility issues already mentioned, there was the questionable testimony of jailhouse informants, who repeatedly announced that one prisoner or another had confided the criminal details that he or she would not admit to the authorities. Such witnesses may have been telling the truth, but they also wanted their own punishments lessened, and they had an obvious incentive to say whatever officials wanted to hear.

There is also the possibility that testimony was extracted with torture, making the search for truth even cloudier. Several prisoners recanted their confessions, adding yet more doubt. The confessions weren't always consistent with one another either, and some of the details weren't very plausible. Could Hughson really afford to repeatedly provide the conspirators with free feasts? How credible is it that Cuffee could have sabotaged a fire line and danced a gleeful jig on the first day of the blazes, yet not attract the authorities' attention till nearly three weeks later? The Geneva Club probably existed, and it may well have engaged in the quasi-Masonic rituals attributed to it, though not necessarily with a straight face. But was it really a centralized conspiracy with dozens of members organized into multiple lodges? Or had some petty crooks simply decided to give their little gang a name?

The official story became even less believable when the state fingered a tutor named John Ury as a Spanish spy, a clandestine Catholic priest, and the ringmaster of the terror. Ury steadfastly denied that he was Catholic—at that point in New York history, Catholicism was illegal—but several witnesses insisted that he was. One claimed that he and other rebels would "pray in private after the popish fashion; and that he used to forgive them their sins for burning the town, and destroying and cutting of the people's throats."[12] Ury gradually replaced Hughson (who by then had been executed) as the chief white villain in the plot, and the prosecution reoriented its rhetoric toward the evils of the Enemy Outside in the Vatican. For Catholics, prosecutor William Smith announced, "the most unnatural crimes, such as treason and murder, when done in obedience to the Pope . . . will merit heaven."[13]

It wasn't implausible to suggest that the Spanish would want to encourage a slave rebellion in New York. Spain did have a history of enticing slaves to its side with promises of liberation. But the evidence against Ury was weak, and the accusers' account of his alleged activities was drenched in anti-Catholic fantasies. The purported priest put up a serious defense, and public opinion was not nearly as united against him as it was against the other defendants. Still, it took the jury only about fifteen minutes to find him guilty. Then Ury too was put to death.

What really caused the fires that burned Manhattan in 1741? Many historians over the years have dismissed the entire conspiracy as a fiction or reduced it to a more modest attempt (or several scattered attempts) to use the fires as a cover for burglaries.[14] More recently, some scholars have taken the confessions as largely accurate but have transferred their sympathies to the rebels.[15] What's clear is that prosecutors came to the trials with a preestablished framework for their fears and that they worked hard to fit the evidence to the story they imagined. The only thing that managed to seriously shake up the narrative was Ury, and that was possible because they had easy access to another preestablished framework, one built around long-standing worries about Vatican conspiracies and bolstered by the fact that England was at war with a Catholic power.

Today the trials look like a cautionary tale about unchecked authority and the need for basic legal rights. But for the authorities in 1741, the lesson to be learned was that slaves had too much freedom. When Horsmanden produced his book-length defense of the crackdown, he declared up front that his chief motive for writing was to persuade "every one that has negroes, to keep a very watchful eye over them, and not to indulge them with too great liberties, which we find they make use of to the worst purposes, caballing and confederating together in mischief."[16] During the trials, the grand jury was urged to "make diligent enquiry into the œconomy and behaviour of all the mean ale-houses and tipling-houses within this city; and to mark out all such to this court, who make it a practice (and a most wicked and pernicious one it is) of entertaining negroes, and the scum and dregs of white people in conjunction."[17]

That wasn't unusual. Insurrection panics were usually followed by calls for new restrictions on slaves' ability to meet, move freely, educate themselves, and bear arms; by demands for similar restrictions on free blacks or even for their deportation; by proposals to pump up the powers of the slave patrols; and by cries against the places, such as Hughson's tavern, where black Americans might plot in secret.

White fears intensified after the Western Hemisphere's one successful slave rebellion, the Haitian Revolution of 1791 to 1804. After the revolt, every single slave state in the United States passed legislation to prevent Haitian immigration. The federal government imposed an embargo on trade with the black republic. In Virginia, a printer who had published the island nation's declaration of independence was charged with inciting an insurrection and imprisoned for eight months. In the same state, Gabriel's Rebellion of 1800 was rumored to have been led by Haitian agitators. One Virginia town petitioned the legislature for action after grumblings among the city's free blacks reached officials' ears: In Haiti, they said, "such language among the free people of colour" had led to the revolt "that totally annihilated the whites."[18]

You didn't need an actual revolution to set off an insurrection panic. You didn't even need a series of crimes, such as the Manhattan fires, that could plausibly be blamed on revolutionaries. There doesn't seem to have been a good reason to suspect that a real revolt was imminent in Augusta, Georgia, in 1810 (or possibly 1811) when a cavalry trumpeter reportedly set off an uproar by drunkenly sounding his horn. According to the U.S. Supreme Court Justice William Johnson, who wrote about the event a decade later, the other militiamen thought they'd heard a signal for the slaves to rise, so they captured a black man, whipped him severely, and threatened to kill him, at which point the prisoner identified another slave as the owner of a horn. The instrument in question was covered with cobwebs, Johnson reported, but the slave was nonetheless arrested and quickly condemned to death.[19]

Even an actual insurgency wasn't necessarily all that it seemed to be. The legal historian Peter Hoffer has made a reasonable case that the Stono revolt in South Carolina was not a preplanned uprising but a break-in that evolved into a rebellion after the burglars killed two white men they encountered along the way.[20] In other words, it might not have been the product of a conspiracy at all, or at least not a conspiracy to do more than to take some goods from a storehouse.

Rebellion scares broke out during economic downturns, during fears of foreign invasion, and during times of intensified abolitionist agitation; rumbles about a coming Christmas uprising swept the South from Delaware to Texas in 1856, when the new Republican Party, founded in part on opposition to slavery, ran its first presidential campaign. In general, the anthropologist George Baca has commented, it was "during moments of conflict between white political factions" that "rumors of conspiracy seem to have been more likely to be accepted as true."[21] Spiritual upheaval unleashed some of the same anxieties. The Second Great Awakening didn't merely inspire fears of the Enemy Within; when the excitement caught on among American blacks, whites worried that camp meetings could be a cover for plotting revolts. The authorities sometimes suppressed independent black churches with the same vigor that the New York government brought to suppressing places such as Hughson's tavern. In Booker's Ferry, Virginia, in 1802, suspicion fell on the Catawba Meeting House, a Baptist church; false reports circulated that "quantities of arms and ammunition" had been "found concealed" in the church building and that therefore the worshippers were plotting a "horrid massacre of the whites."[22]

The typical insurrection panic was not induced by a ruling-class conspiracy any more than it was a reaction to a real conspiracy of slaves. Rebellion scares helped the governing caste by fostering white solidarity and discouraging intrawhite conflict; but it was also important, from the rulers' point of view, that this solidarity be channeled into legal repression rather than riotous violence that the authorities couldn't control. Sometimes such channeling took a while.

When Harriet Jacobs, a slave who escaped to the North, recalled the aftermath of a genuine conspiracy—Nat Turner's 1831 rebellion in Virginia—she described the ensuing search of the slaves' homes as "a grand opportunity for the low whites, who had no negroes of their own to scourge."[23] By Jacobs's account, the investigators went on a rampage: "All day long these unfeeling wretches went round, like a troop of demons, terrifying and tormenting the helpless. At night, they formed themselves into patrol bands, and went wherever they chose among the colored people, acting out their brutal will. Many women hid themselves in woods and swamps, to keep out of their way. If any of the husbands or fathers told of these outrages, they were tied up to the public whipping post, and cruelly scourged for telling lies about white men. The consternation was universal. No two people that had the slightest tinge of color in their faces dared to be seen talking together."[24] It didn't end until "the white citizens found that their own property was not safe from the lawless rabble they had summoned to protect them."[25]

In Baca's words, "the widening sense of panic gave poor whites license to harm or even kill slaves, inflicting real property damage on the planter class."[26] Even a slave owner could be charged with complicity in the plot if, out of caution, sympathy, or just a desire to protect his property, he defended an accused slave. Poor whites were, in their way, viewed as another beast below.

"Conspiracy" itself, as a criminal charge, was shaped by the fear of insurrection. The colonies expanded the concept, Hoffer wrote, applying it to any "gatherings of slaves at which a crime was discussed. No attempt to carry out the deed by any of the slaves was necessary to institute the prosecution. All the slaves present (passive as well as active participants in the conversation) were equally liable under the law." If the patrons at Hughson's tavern engaged in some loose talk about killing their masters and overthrowing the government, they were guilty of conspiracy as far as the law was concerned, whether or not they progressed past the talking stage. "Conspiracy prosecutions," Hoffer concluded, "turned crimes merely imagined or anticipated by the master class into opportunities to punish those slaves who dared to speak aloud of resistance to slavery."[27] As more plots were discovered or imagined, the law continued to evolve: North Carolina, for example, responded to the insurrection panics of 1802 by tightening the definition of "conspiracy" to cover plots with as few as two participants.

As in the trial of John Ury, anxious whites imagined alliances between the Enemy Below and the Enemy Outside. Since blacks were widely presumed to be stupid, whites found it useful to portray them as the puppets of wily northern abolitionists or some other alien force; since blacks were widely presumed to be content with their lot, whites found it useful to accuse those aliens of transforming happy workers into a bestial mob. The archetypal figure was John Brown, an abolitionist who really did attempt to lead a slave rebellion; when Brown raided Harpers Ferry in 1859, the revolt panics that ensued often included a hunt for subversive outsiders. (In Jefferson County, Virginia, the government announced that any "strangers" who could not "give a satisfactory account of themselves" would be arrested.)[28] But abolitionists had been playing the Devil role long before Brown came around. By 1859, they had already been blamed for everything from the Haitian Revolution to the fact that plantation slaves sometimes ran away.

Mark Twain spoofed southerners' fears in *Tom Sawyer's Conspiracy*, a novel he never completed, in which Tom persuades Huck and Jim that forming a secret society would be a great prank. Recounts Huck:

> [H]e had struck a splendid idea. It was to get the people in a sweat about the ablitionists. It was the very time for it. We knowed that for more than two weeks past there was whispers going around about strangers being seen in the woods over on the Illinois side, and then disappearing, and then seen again; and everybody reckoned it was ablitionists laying for a chance to run off some of our niggers to freedom. They hadn't run off any yet, and most likely they warn't even thinking about it and warn't abolitionists anyway; but in them days a stranger couldn't show himself and not start an uneasiness unless he told all about his business straight off and proved it hadn't any harm in it.[29]

Before long Tom Sawyer is forging messages for the fictional Sons of Freedom and donning blackface to pose as a runaway. Antebellum wackiness ensues.

Back in the real world, more or less, one of the most memorable panics starred an outsider who *wasn't* an abolitionist, though abolitionists were alleged to be a part of his plot. In that case the purported mastermind was John Murrell, a man known as the Great Western Land Pirate and widely believed to be the head of the Mystic Clan, a network of criminals that Twain later described as a "majestic following of ten hundred men, sworn to do his evil will."[30] The Clan was believed to hatch its conspiracies in—of course—the wilderness. "They held their 'Grand Council' in the deep, dark woods of the Mississippi bottom," one writer later recalled. There was said to be a vast tree in that swamp, seventy-five feet around and capable of holding twenty-four horses within it; and it was there, "in its great hollow, that John A. Murrell and his Clansmen met in grand council, and formed their dark plots, and concocted their hellish plans."[31] You thought you were reading a crime story, but that was just a mask: It was a fairy tale all along.

Murrell really was a criminal, even if he didn't hold court like the King of the Elves in a hidden hollow in the woods; and he really did have an organization, even if Twain exaggerated the size and loyalty of its membership. In 1834, an independent investigator, Virgil Stewart, infiltrated Murrell's gang and helped capture its chief, who was subsequently convicted of slave stealing and sentenced to ten years in prison. Someone called Augustus Q. Walton—probably a pseudonym for Stewart—then wrote a book laying out the secrets Stewart had supposedly uncovered as a member of the Mystic Clan. By Walton's wild account, Murrell had agents everywhere from Maryland to Texas and they had been stirring discontent among the slaves. The grand plan, the bandit had allegedly told Stewart, was to strike the South with a great Christmas rebellion at the end of 1835:

> We design having our companies so stationed over the country, in the vicinity of the banks and the large cities, that when the negroes commence their carnage and slaughter, we will have detachments to fire the towns, and rob the banks, while all is confusion and dismay. The rebellion taking place every where at the same time, every part of the country will be engaged in its own defence; and one part of the country can afford no relief to another, until many places will be entirely overrun by the negroes, and our pockets replenished from the banks, and the desks of rich merchants' houses. . . .

> We find the most vicious and wicked disposed ones, on large farms: and poison their minds by telling them how they are mistreated, and that they are entitled to their freedom as much as their masters, and that all the wealth of the country is the proceeds of the black people's labor; we remind them of the pomp and splendor of their masters, and then refer them to their own degraded situation, and tell them that it is power and tyranny which rivets their chains of bondage, and not because they are an inferior race of people. We tell them that all Europe has abandoned slavery, and that the West Indies are all free; and that they got their freedom by rebelling a few times and slaughtering the whites, and convince them, that if they will follow the example of the West India negroes, that they will obtain their liberty, and become as much respected as if they were white, and that they can marry white women when they are all put on a level.[32]

It was the perfect story for nervous whites, particularly so soon after Nat Turner's rebellion. It presented disgruntled slaves as the puppets of rapacious white people, abolitionism as a cynical tool for manipulating the field hands. And of course it included the traditional threat to white womanhood.

The book was a sensation. Even though Murrell was now in prison, fears of a coming uprising started to spread. They caught fire in June, when some slaves in Madison County, Mississippi, were overheard grumbling about their lot. Worried whites seized the suspects, and under torture the prisoners told their captors what they wanted to hear: On July 4, under cover of celebrating Independence Day, the slaves would gather together to attack the whites.

Vigilantes promptly lynched the captives, then went searching for the rest of the conspiracy. An alleged member of the Murrell gang was compelled to confess that the plot was real, explaining that it had been moved from Christmas to Independence Day because Walton's book had blown their cover. He also laid out more details of the purported plan, which were then reported in the Clinton *Gazette*: After launching the rebellion in remote Madison County, the slaves and gangsters intended "to proceed thence, through the principal towns to Natchez, and then on to New Orleans—murdering all the white men and ugly women—sparing the handsome ones and making wives of them—and plundering and burning as they went."[33] To prevent this reenactment of the Manhattan plot, nervous whites reenacted the Manhattan crackdown, lynching dozens.[34] For years afterward, Americans along the Mississippi attributed all kinds of crimes to the Mystic Clan.

Long after slavery was abolished, the outside agitator stirring up rebellions would be a key villain in southern white demonology. During Reconstruction, conservatives claimed that northern carpetbaggers were conspiring to empower the newly freed slaves at the expense of ordinary whites. (Such fears fed the rise of a real conspiratorial secret society, the Ku Klux Klan.) A century later, southern leaders were telling the same stories about the civil rights movement.

Haiti made another contribution to the idea of the Enemy Below in the early twentieth century, when a distorted version of a voodoo legend started shambling into American pop culture. The *zombie* was a human body that no longer contained a human mind. A zombie was in the deepest trance possible, a creature completely subservient to its master's will; it was also a violent subhuman threat.[35]

Early zombie stories stressed the power of the monsters' masters. There is a scene in Victor Halperin's 1932 film *White Zombie* where a white man's mill is run entirely by a black zombie workforce; the sequence was enough for a later critic to declare forthrightly that "Zombies are black slaves."[36] Later zombie pictures, from George Romero's *Night of the Living Dead* (1968) on, usually dropped the master from the equation. These movies' monsters are appetites on autopilot, released from all control—cannibal corpses devouring everyone in sight. The idea of the Enemy Below rests on two great fears: that a subversive force could somehow step into the role of the mesmerizing master, and that the master might disappear altogether, transforming zombie slaves into an unrestrainable zombie rampage.[37]

D. W. Griffith's *The Birth of a Nation* (1915), an enormously influential movie set during the Civil War and Reconstruction, exalts the Klan and denounces northern carpetbaggers. It climaxes with a mob of former slaves attacking whites who have holed up in a cabin. If you've seen Romero's zombie movies, you've seen an afterimage of the cabin scene: In Griffith's eyes, the black figures outside that little house are the Living Dead, their monstrous arms reaching through the doors and windows while our heroes try desperately to fend them off. (In *Night of the Living Dead*, Romero subverts that subtext: His hero is black; his zombies are white.)

As wild as these stories could get, there were two kernels of truth to them. Angry African Americans did resist white supremacy, and they did have Caucasian allies in the North, both in the battle against slavery and in the battle against segregation. The myth of the Enemy Below distorted their dissent into something feral and demonic, and the myth of the Enemy Outside gave whites credit for a movement launched and led by blacks. But the threat to the racial power structure was real, even if the tales told about the threat were drenched in fantasy.

You didn't have to be black to be cast as the Enemy Below. In the 1870s, while a six-year depression ravaged the country, a Tramp Scare swept the press, as papers filled their columns with accounts of crimes by unemployed wanderers. Some of the stories strained the reader's credulity, and even the plausible ones were often soaked in fearmongering rhetoric. A typical report, published in the New York *World*, listed a series of unconnected "outrages by tramps"—a burglary in one town, a stickup in another—culminating with the comment that a "number of fires have occurred within the past two weeks, presumably set by tramps."[38] (Presumably!) Later that month, after some hoboes were shot while resisting arrest, the same paper called the killings a "partial solution of the tramp question"; "some more shooting," it suggested, "might be wholesome for the community."[39] In the academic world, Yale Law School dean Francis Wayland wrote a paper describing the tramp as "a lazy, shiftless, sauntering or swaggering, ill-conditioned, irreclaimable, incorrigible, cowardly, utterly depraved savage."[40] Several states passed anti-tramp statutes, which allowed the authorities to arrest and imprison vagabonds essentially at will.

As is often the case with moral panics, conspiracy theories followed. In 1878 Horatio Seymour, a former governor of New York and former Democratic presidential nominee, argued in *Harper's* that vagabonds were "rapidly gaining a kind of organization" that was "growing into a system of brigandage" with "systems of communication and intercourse, which are made more perfect each year."[41] A Texas paper informed its readers that undercover Massachusetts detectives had discovered a "perfectly organized brotherhood" in which "each tramp has a special duty assigned to him. Some of them beg and some of them steal, and they are even instructed what to steal and whom to steal it from."[42]

While the army of tramps crisscrossed the country, a more settled Enemy Below was haunting the Pennsylvania coal country. When mine owners, foremen, and superintendents started turning up dead in the 1860s and '70s, word spread that they'd been killed by a secret society of Irish-American workers called the Molly Maguires. Back in Ireland, the story went, the Molly men would dress as women, blacken their faces, and assassinate the landlords' agents and other enemies. In the United States the Irish continued to conspire against the social order, applying blackface and murdering men in the night. There were thousands of Molly terrorists, with lodges that held their conclaves in Irish saloons. Or so said the local authorities, who convicted twenty miners of murder after James McParlan of the Pinkerton Detective Agency testified that he had infiltrated the Mollies and learned their secrets.

No one doubts that the area's Irish laborers sometimes beat and even killed people perceived as enemies of their communities. There is considerable doubt, on the other hand, about the tale of a far-reaching Molly conspiracy, a story that relies heavily on the word of a detective who was never a neutral party. There has also been a reaction against any history of the coal industry that stresses workers' violence while playing down the considerable violence brought down on the miners, including vigilante killings of suspected Molly Maguires.

The war between the Mollies and the Pinkertons is usually framed as a battle between workers and employers: The Pinkertons were brought in by the president of the Philadelphia & Reading Coal & Iron Company, and one of the crackdown's goals was to prevent *any* sort of labor organizing, not just the kind that ended with a foreman dead.[43] But the tale of Molly terrorism reflected ethnic enmity as well as class conflict. As early as the 1850s, the historian Kevin Kenny noted, "the term *Molly Maguires* was being used in the anthracite region as a synonym for Irish social depravity."[44] The authorities attempted to link the Mollies not just to the budding union movement but to the Ancient Order of Hibernians, an Irish fraternal association that McParlan believed was a Molly front.

That didn't make the Mollies an Enemy Outside. Just as slave conspiracies were not believed to be based in Africa, the Mollies were not, by and large, accused of being manipulated from abroad. While other Irish immigrants were denounced as pawns of the pope, prosecutor Franklin B. Gowen, an Irish Protestant, struck a different note during the Molly trial, pointing out that the Vatican had condemned the Maguires and calling on his ethnic brethren to reject the Maguires as "not true Irishmen."[45] Think of it as the paranoid underside of assimilation: As the Irish became American, alleged Irish conspiracies evolved from a foreign to a domestic threat, from an Enemy Outside to an Enemy Below.

Alleged leftist conspiracies evolved in the other direction. America's first Red Scare began with the brief reign of the revolutionary Paris Commune in 1871. It gradually grew as the depression set off labor unrest at home, including much of the activity attributed to the Mollies, and it peaked with the railroad strike that swept several states in 1877.[46] The strikers were imagined as a classic Enemy Below, but they were frequently tied to an Enemy Outside as well. After the Tompkins Square Riot of 1874, in which New York police beat thousands of demonstrators who had gathered without a permit, the *New York Herald* did not merely blame the rally on "dangerous conspirators against society." The paper suggested that the protesters had received "the material aid to carry on these nefarious projects" from "the booty of the plundered churches of Paris," the Commune's tendrils apparently extending into the United States three years after the French revolutionaries had been defeated.[47] After the Russian Revolution, the focus shifted further. The popular image of the domestic Communist enemy looked less like a union organizer and more like a spy, and the spy in turn was less likely to be imagined as an immigrant. The Red foe was now conceived as an imperial Enemy Outside allied with a subversive Enemy Within.

But the older narrative wasn't forgotten. As in the antebellum days, the black underclass could be cast as the beast below. Sometimes its supposed plots were small-scale affairs. During World War II, black "Bump Clubs" were rumored to be organizing covert carnivals of aggression, specially designated days on which black women would deliberately bump into white women who were shopping. "Because of the tensions of the war," one study of racial rumors later reported, "both the Federal Bureau of Investigation and local police departments felt it necessary to investigate these white beliefs." Not surprisingly, they didn't find any evidence that the tales were true.[48]

Other black threats that haunted the white imagination were much larger. And in the absence of John Murrell and John Brown, new outside agitators were tapped to fill their shoes.

In 1919, *The New York Times* blamed race riots in Chicago and Washington on an organized campaign of "Bolshevist agitation . . . among the negroes," even though the violence in both cities had been launched by whites against blacks, not the other way around.[49] In 1943, Texas Congressman Martin Dies reacted to a race riot in Detroit by suggesting that Japanese Americans released from internment camps had made their way to Michigan and fomented the disorder. Meanwhile, across the South, blacks were rumored to be covertly aligned with the Japanese, perhaps via a secret organization called the Black Dragon Society, or with the Germans, perhaps via a secret organization called the Swastika Club. "Hitler has told the Negroes he will give them the South for their help," one informant told the sociologist Howard Odum, who collected rumors in the southern states during World War II. "Hitler will make the white people slaves and the Negroes the leaders," declared another. One person claimed that black churches were "receiving Nazi propaganda. They can arise and attack the whites whenever they want."[50]

By the 1960s, the Axis powers were no longer in a position to be charged with kindling racial violence. But the Communists were still available.

On August 11, 1965, in the Los Angeles neighborhood of Watts, the California Highway Patrol pulled over a young black man named Marquette Frye on suspicion of drunk driving. A brawl broke out between the cops and some of the locals, and the fighting grew worse when a rumor radiated through the crowd that the police had beaten a pregnant woman. Soon Watts was engulfed in a full-scale, five-day riot. Residents burned entire blocks, fired guns, hurled bricks, looted stores. It was the first of many riots that would shake America's cities in the sixties.

While Watts burned, rumors circulated that the violence had been planned by street gangs, Communists, the Nation of Islam, or some other ghetto menace. In 1965, unlike in 1741, some people in positions of authority tried to tamp down the fears: In December the governor's commission on the riot rejected the idea that there had been "outside leadership or pre-established plans for the rioting."[51] Two years later, nonetheless, a widely distributed tract described Watts as a subversive "Plan to Burn Los Angeles."

The pamphlet, which had originally appeared as an article in the John Birch Society journal *American Opinion*, claimed that the riot had been "a rehearsal for a nationwide revolution."[52] According to the author, Gary Allen, the

> board of revolutionary strategy which planned, engineered, and instigated the Watts Rebellion was composed of some forty to fifty Negroes sent by the Communists in the Los Angeles area from all over the United States. Included in the group were Black Muslims, Black Nationalists, representatives from the paramilitary Deacons of Defense, the Communist Revolutionary Action Movement

> (R.A.M.), and professionals from other such militant and Marxist groups. These men are not hoodlums or criminals in the ordinary sense, but are drawn from among an intellectual elite of the Negro community. . . . This small revolutionary group, which is referred to in Watts and by the Intelligence Division of the Los Angeles Police Department simply as "The Organization," has three common denominators among its members: high intelligence, hatred of "The Man" (Caucasians), and a disciplined commitment to the interests of the International Communist Conspiracy.

This curious coalition of Muslims and Marxists had picked Watts, Allen wrote, because blacks were actually rather well off there: "[I]f Watts could be exploded they could do it anywhere else in America." So they had flooded the area with propaganda, most notably a "publicity campaign rivaling the Advertising Council's promotion of Smokey the Bear" aimed at "the construction of the myth of *police brutality*." With that meme installed, the conspiracy's agents had been able to spread the rumors that had set off the riot, which the mesmerized locals embraced uncritically: "The denizens of the area had been conditioned by the years of prior propaganda to accept such fairy tales without question."

The Organization had incited teenagers to throw bottles and burn cars, Allen continued, and over the next few days had been seen "directing the chaos [while] wearing red armbands and using electric megaphones." They had made a special effort to loot and burn liquor stores ("keeping the mob intoxicated so it could be more easily led"), supermarkets (so residents would "suffer a lack of food" and blame the authorities), pawnshops ("to acquire large supplies of firearms"), and department stores (so the Organization could get more "guns, ammunition, merchandise, and money"). Gullible outsiders might have assumed the looting was unorganized, but Allen assured us that "as much as 90 percent" of the stolen guns and money found its way to the Organization, with Organization snipers covering Organization looters as they stole the goods, which they would use "NEXT TIME."

When NEXT TIME comes, Allen warned, the Organization will begin with a mass assassination of police officers. Then it'll launch the campaign it calls "Burn Los Angeles, Burn." It'll start fires in the oil fields near the harbor and the foothills that surround the city; then it'll set the Civic Center ablaze and put a torch to the Wilshire neighborhood. After that, "'The Organization' hopes to herd its 'ghetto' mobs into Beverly Hills." As simultaneous riots break out in San Diego, Long Beach, Compton, Pasadena, Bakersfield, Fresno, San Francisco, Oakland, Richmond, and Sacramento, the National Guard will be unable to contain all the revolts at once. The plotters hope that whites will be roused to "invade Negro neighborhoods in retaliation," thus forcing "the ninety percent of the Negroes who want no part of the revolution" to join the fighting in self defense.[53]

The John Birch Society's account, unlike the rumors that had seized Manhattan in 1741, came from a group outside the political mainstream. But the mode of thinking that Allen's article represented wasn't confined to the outer circles of politics. In 1966, it was possible for an Iowa congressman to go to a Farm Bureau meeting expecting queries about agriculture policy and instead be grilled about the waves of black Chicago rioters that his constituents were convinced were planning to invade the state "on motorcycles."[54] A year later, when the Lemberg Center for the Study of Violence surveyed seven northern cities, 77 percent of the whites interviewed believed that outside agitators were at least partly responsible for the riots.[55]

Some officials believed the same thing. LAPD Chief William Parker spouted some of the same theories as Gary Allen (attributing them, as Allen did, to the force's Red squad). The mayor of Los Angeles, Sam Yorty—a man with more direct authority over Watts than anyone involved with the governor's commission on the riots—shared Parker's take on the era's urban violence. Testifying before the House Committee on Un-American Activities on November 28, 1967, Yorty warned that "subversive elements" liked to "plan incidents that they would hope would spark a riot." Even when a disturbance was apparently unplanned, he added, the radicals' "broad propaganda campaign" had created "an atmosphere where a riot may break out spontaneously, in appearance, but actually where there has been a great groundwork laid for it."[56] For Yorty, as for Allen, the chief aim of the propaganda was to spread the idea of police brutality, a social problem that by Yorty's account barely existed at all.

Yorty and Parker were not the only influential figures who saw a hidden hand behind the riots of the 1960s. The Peace Officers Research Association of California, one of the country's biggest law enforcement lobbies, released a film denouncing a pair of black politicians as "the two leading Communists in the state and the instigators of the Watts riot."[57] The popular evangelist Billy Graham declared that "a small hard core of leftists" were using the fires as "a dress rehearsal for a revolution."[58] When riots hit San Francisco in 1966, Mayor John Shelley told the press that he suspected "outside agitators" might have been responsible.[59] (According to one of Shelley's aides, the agitators were rumored to have come from—where else?—Watts.)

And in 1967, President Lyndon Johnson asked his cabinet if the Communists were behind the country's riots. Attorney General Ramsey Clark replied that there wasn't any evidence of that, but Johnson wasn't convinced. "I have a very deep feeling that there is more to that than we see at the moment," the president commented. He pushed the FBI for evidence that the Reds were behind the turbulence, and when the Bureau came up empty-handed, he just pushed harder.[60]

Allen's article did include one note that was missing from the more mainstream accounts of a riot conspiracy, an especially incendiary echo of the antebellum insurrection scares. When NEXT TIME rolls around, he told us, the conspiracy plans "the shooting on sight of all white men and children." But not the women. "The women," Allen explained, "are to be utilized as a reward for the insurrectionists."

5

PUPPETEERS

. . . a deep-laid and desperate plan of imperial despotism has been laid, and partly executed, for the extinction of all civil liberty.

—*Boston Town Meeting, 1770*[1]

Here's the story:

The conspiracy against America began as a conspiracy against England. A faction had formed in the back rooms of the British government, a "junto of courtiers and state-jobbers" who would "sculk behind the king's authority,"[2] amplifying their influence by bribing legislators and spreading self-serving lies. They aimed not just to enrich themselves but to destroy the freedoms won in the Glorious Revolution of 1688. To that end, this "set of intriguing men," as the polemicist and philosopher Edmund Burke called them, decided to create a secret government. Now "two systems of administration were to be formed," Burke wrote: "one which should be in the real secret and confidence; the other merely ostensible."[3]

The power of the state would be extended over the country, and the power of the puppet masters would be extended over the state.

They were wildly successful. By the 1760s, the cabal controlled Parliament, and the king was either their ally or their dupe. But the Western Hemisphere was a threat to the would-be tyrants' schemes: Their subjects could always flee across the Atlantic, leaving the rulers with no one to obey their commands. If the colonies could be subdued, one pamphleteer warned, the plotters "might open their batteries with safety against British Liberty; and *Britons* be made to feel the same oppressive hand of despotic Power." The alarm was sounded: "a PLAN has been *systematically* laid, and persued by the British *ministry* . . . for enslaving *America*; as the STIRRUP by which they design to *mount* the RED HORSE of TYRANNY and DESPOTISM at home."[4]

Alert Americans found the conspirators' fingerprints everywhere. In 1762, when Anglican missionaries created a Society for Propagating Christian Knowledge Among the Indians of North America, the colonists understood that the evangelists' real target wasn't the natives; it was the rival faiths that had taken root in the colonies. The secret plan, John Adams explained, was to "establish the Church of England, with all its creeds, articles, tests, ceremonies, and tithes, and prohibit all other churches."[5] When the Stamp Act of 1765 imposed a tax on printed paper, Joseph Warren of Massachusetts announced that the law had been "designed . . . to force the colonies into a rebellion, and from thence to take occasion to treat them with severity, and, by military power, to reduce them to servitude."[6] The Boston Massacre of 1770, the Tea Act of 1773, the Intolerable Acts of 1774: All were evidence of the dark design. One isolated act of oppression "may be ascribed to the accidental opinion of a day," Thomas Jefferson acknowledged, but America was undergoing "a series of oppressions, begun at a distinguished period and pursued unalterably through every change of ministers." And that meant it faced "a deliberate and systematical plan of reducing us to slavery."[7]

If you were to poll the founding fathers, you would hear slightly different accounts of who was a part of this conspiracy and what exactly the conspirators were up to. But when it came to where the enemy was taking them, they agreed with Jefferson. George Washington wrote that "a regular Systematick Plan" threatened to reduce the colonists to "tame, & abject Slaves, as the Blacks we Rule over with such arbitrary Sway."[8] Alexander Hamilton concurred: A "system of slavery," he said, was being "fabricated against America."[9] When the revolutionaries formed a Continental Congress, the body denounced the "ministerial plan for enslaving us" and issued a warning to the people of Great Britain: "May not a ministry, with the same armies, enslave you?"[10]

When the colonies declared independence, the plot against America was detailed in the new country's founding document. The Declaration of Independence did not merely describe "a long train of abuses and usurpations." It argued that those abuses added up to "a design" to bring the colonists "under absolute Despotism."[11]

After the Americans defeated the puppet masters in London, they had to contend with like-minded marionetteers at home. A cabal of nationalists were dissatisfied with the young country's constitution, called the Articles of Confederation, with its limits on the central government's powers; they wanted to bring the country under more centralized control, replicating the old order in the now independent United States. They saw an opportunity in 1783, when Congress was unwilling to impose an import duty to fund a standing army. With one hand the cabal encouraged officers to plot a military coup; with the other they counseled the country's leaders "to keep a *complaining* and *suffering* army within the bounds of moderation" by adopting Alexander Hamilton's economic agenda.[12]

The plot, known as the Newburgh Conspiracy, fell apart after George Washington intervened to stop it, but the nationalists merely moved on to new schemes. The soldiers among them created the Society of the Cincinnati, an aristocratic military order that hoped to establish itself as a parallel government in each state, eventually superseding the elected legislatures. The society had "a fiery, hot ambition and thirst for power," one patriot warned, and America's government "will be in a few years as fierce and oppressive an aristocracy as that of Poland or Venice, if the Order of Cincinnati be suffered to take root and spread."[13]

When the conspirators finally struck, though, the blow came from a different direction. In 1787, they persuaded twelve of the thirteen states to hold a constitutional convention. In theory the conclave was merely going to propose some revisions to the Articles, fixing some widely acknowledged defects in the document. Instead, the nationalists "turned a *Convention* into a *Conspiracy*."[14] Behind closed doors, the delegates ignored their assignment and instead set to work replacing the Articles with an entirely new constitution, one that would concentrate far more power in the national government. Of the fifty-five people participating in the meeting, twenty-one belonged to the Society of the Cincinnati.

The extent of the new design did not become clear until a dissenting delegate, Luther Martin of Maryland, broke the convention's code of silence and revealed the coming new order in a long address to his state's House of Delegates. The nationalists, he warned, were "covertly endeavouring to carry into effect what they well knew openly and avowedly could not be accomplished": a plan "to abolish and annihilate all State governments, and to bring forward one general government, over this extensive continent, of a monarchical nature." Allying themselves with figures from the larger states, who didn't share the conspirators' grand design but did share their interest in reducing the smaller states' power, the delegates had dreamed up a document that would enact the oppressions the colonists had fought a revolution to prevent: the power to impose direct taxes, the power to raise a standing army, and, in general, "the most complete, most abject system of *slavery* that the wit of man ever devised, under the *pretence* of forming a government for free States."[15]

Other Anti-Federalists, as the foes of the new Constitution were called, praised the speech. A Pennsylvania writer exulted that Martin had braved "the rage of the conspirators" and "laid open the conclave, exposed the dark scene within, developed the mystery of the proceedings, and illustrated the machinations of ambition."[16] But the exposé wasn't enough: Running roughshod over normal legal procedures, the conspirators rammed through the Constitution in what amounted to an illegal coup d'état. Revising the Articles was supposed to require the thirteen states' unanimous consent, but the nationalists invented a rule allowing the document to be replaced entirely with the backing of only nine states. Even so, the Constitution still had to attract public support, so the nationalists appeased the Anti-Federalists by adding a Bill of Rights to the document.

And then those rights fell under attack as the same gang of nationalists, now headquartered in the Federalist Party, took power. Patriotic printers warned the public: A "detestable and nefarious conspiracy" in the government aimed to undo the revolution and make the president a king.[17] The Federalist president began to surround himself with pomp and ceremony, as though the office were more royalist than republican—an insidious scheme "to familiarise us with the forms of monarchy."[18] Congress began to impose internal taxes, and when frontiersmen protested a particularly onerous whiskey levee, the government smashed their rebellion. John Adams's administration pushed through the speech-squelching Sedition Act, and under the new law's powers it rounded up some of the government's most vocal opponents. Then the original English monster reentered the picture as word spread that Adams planned to "unite his family with the Royal House of Great Britain, the bridegroom to be King of America."[19]

Or that's the story, anyway.

If you take words such as *design* and *plan* and *plot* as metaphors, a great deal of that story is accurate. As Bernard Bailyn pointed out in a widely cited 1967 study, *The Ideological Origins of the American Revolution*, the revolutionary generation tended to see the world as an ongoing conflict between Liberty and Power. "'Power,'" he wrote, "to them meant the dominion of some men over others, the human control of human life: ultimately force, compulsion."[20] When revolutionary pamphleteers discussed Power, they liked to personify it: It would creep and encroach, grasp like a hand and consume like a cancer. That is a literary device, and there is nothing innately conspiracist about it.

But *design* and *plan* and *plot* were not metaphors. They were concrete charges against the colonists' foes in the ministry, in Parliament, and eventually on the throne. Such charges, the intellectual historian George H. Smith has explained, played "a key part of the Whig theory of revolution: Before revolution can be justified, it must be shown that the injustices of a government are not merely isolated and unrelated events but are part of an overall *plan* to establish despotism."[21] Combine encroaching Power with a plan, and you get the fourth of our archetypes, the manipulative and privileged Enemy Above: to borrow a phrase from the founders' day, "the silent, powerful, and ever active conspiracy of those who govern."[22]

The revolutionaries believed that when power is unchecked, the powerful will conspire to expand their wealth and influence. As political philosophy, this is a perfectly defensible position: If power can corrupt, it isn't unreasonable to expect corruption from powerful people. The theories go wrong only when the accusations leap beyond the evidence—a leap that, alas, was a little too easy to make. At the time it was widely believed, as the historian Gordon Wood has summarized it, that since "no one could ever actually penetrate into the inner hearts of men, true motives had to be discovered indirectly, had to be deduced from actions. That is, the causes had to be inferred from the effects."[23] Since the effect of British policy was to reduce the colonies' liberty and self-government, the cause was presumed to be a plot to reduce the colonies' liberty and self-government. Under modern standards of evidence, that isn't enough.

But if the story at the beginning of this chapter isn't always an accurate account of what America was undergoing, it's a good guide to how a lot of Americans felt. England really was extending its power over the colonies in ways that interfered with the colonists' autonomy. The Constitution really did concentrate more power in the central government. The Federalists really did have authoritarian inclinations. There is truth in those stories, even when they're false.

It is undeniable, for example, that some American Anglicans wanted their faith to be the officially established religion. Some of them dreamed of more than that: At one point the president of King's College, Cambridge, complained to the archbishop of Canterbury that Americans "are nearly rampant in their high notions of liberty," suggesting that if the colonies' "charters were demolished and they could be reduced under the management of a wise and good governor and council appointed by the King, I believe they would in a little time grow a good sort of people."[24] But such skylarking hardly proves that the king's ministry and the Anglican ministry were in cahoots, and there are good reasons to believe that the state's attempts to extend its power over the colonies and the church's attempts to extend its reach among the colonists were pursued independently.[25]

Similarly, it's easy to see why men who had just fought a revolution would be alarmed by the Society of the Cincinnati, with its aristocratic trappings and its tendency to support nationalist policies. Jefferson himself distrusted the order and urged General Washington to "stand on ground separated from it."[26] But even if the society had, as the *Boston Gazette* put it, "all the formal parade and arrangement of a *separate government*,"[27] it never did *act* as a shadow government; it was a gathering spot and pressure group for the young country's nationalists, but it was not an instrument through which they governed. It even included a few figures who wound up rejecting the Federalists and joining the party of Jefferson.[28]

On the other hand, the Newburgh Conspiracy really happened, though historians don't agree about the extent to which the soldiers were manipulated by the nationalists. And the part of our opening narrative that is most likely to strike modern ears as odd—the conspiratorial account of the Constitution—is actually the most defensible segment of the tale. It is undeniably true that the Constitutional Convention met in secret, refusing even to publicize the minutes of its debates; that it exceeded its original mission, which was merely to reform the Articles; that some of the delegates intended from the beginning to overshoot those instructions; and that there was no legal basis for allowing the Constitution to take effect with only nine states ratifying it.[29] If the ratification of the Constitution is not usually described in conspiratorial terms today, it isn't because there is any serious dispute over those facts. It's because most people are glad the Constitution became law and thus are less likely to dwell on any irregularities in its birth.[30]

One sign that the English, and later the Federalists, did not perceive themselves as plotters is the ease with which they persuaded themselves that they were the *victims* of conspiracies, falling frequently into Enemy Below and Enemy Outside theories about their foes. Some Englishmen argued that the Revolution was all a French scheme, with Paris employing "secret emissaries" to spread "dissatisfaction among the British colonists."[31] Even without dragging France into it, Tories such as Massachusetts governor Thomas Hutchinson believed, in Bailyn's words, that "the root of all the trouble in the colonies was the maneuvering of a secret, power-hungry cabal that professed loyalty to England while assiduously working to destroy the bonds of authority."[32]

Similarly, the Federalists were filled with fears of revolutionary conspiracies. They looked at Jeffersonian political clubs and saw Jacobins plotting an insurrection, probably under the direction of French foreign agents. The Whiskey Rebellion was taken to be their handiwork, and more revolts were presumed to be on their way. In the last year of the Washington administration, future president John Quincy Adams fretted to his father that the French and their domestic allies were planning the "removal of the President," which would "be followed by a plan for introducing into the American Constitution a Directory instead of a President, and for taking from the supreme Executive the command of the armed forces."[33] (The Directory was the name of France's ruling committee.) With the XYZ Affair of 1798, in which French diplomats demanded a bribe from their American counterparts, and the Quasi-War of 1798 to 1800, in which French and American ships skirmished at sea, the fear of foreign subversion reached new heights. In that soil there sprouted the most infamous of the Federalist conspiracy theories, in which the country was allegedly threatened by a secret society called the Bavarian Illuminati.

The actual Illuminati had been founded on May 1, 1776, by Adam Weishaupt, a professor at the University of Ingolstadt in Bavaria; he was motivated mostly by a desire to undermine the influence of the Jesuits. His followers weren't the first people to call themselves Illuminati: The Spanish *Alumbrados*, French *Illuminés*, and Afghan *Roshaniyya* of the fifteenth and sixteenth centuries had used the label for their religious movements, as had some eighteenth-century French followers of the Swedish spiritualist Emanuel Swedenborg. (Naturally, conspiracy theorists have attempted to link those older sects to the Bavarian order.) Weishaupt's Illuminati were antiauthoritarian in theory and elaborately hierarchical in practice, with a baroque series of degrees and a careful system of secrecy. Recall Richard Hofstadter's remark that the John Birch Society adopted a structure similar to the one it imputed to the Communist enemy. Weishaupt did the same thing, establishing a chain of command that outdid the most intricate image of the Jesuits' secret machinations.

Weishaupt's group took hold within Freemasonry—a secret society inside a secret society—attracting at least two thousand members before the Bavarian authorities started cracking down. The biggest blow came in 1786, when the police raided the home of Francis Xaver von Zwack, an Illuminatus who had recently held a post in the government. The search turned up a large cache of the order's papers, including not just its secret symbols and a partial membership roster but a letter in which Weishaupt wrote that he had impregnated his sister-in-law and then procured an abortion. The papers were published, and the group fell into disgrace. Soon Bavaria's duke declared that anyone caught recruiting new members into the order would be put to death.

That seemed to be the end of it. But rumors continued to circulate that the higher ranks of the Illuminati were still active, and a former member of the organization made a well-publicized though ill-fated effort to launch a similar group under a new name.[34] Continental conservatives whispered that the illuminated underground had infiltrated French Freemasonry and sparked the French revolution of 1789.[35] This idea reached the English-speaking world when the Edinburgh physicist John Robison promoted it in his 1797 book *Proofs of a Conspiracy*. According to Robison, the bloodshed in France was only the beginning: "AN ASSOCIATION HAS BEEN FORMED for the express purpose of ROOTING OUT ALL THE RELIGIOUS ESTABLISHMENTS, AND OVERTURNING ALL THE EXISTING GOVERNMENTS OF EUROPE."[36] At about the same time Augustin Barruel, a French Jesuit exiled to England, offered a more elaborate version of the story in his four-volume *Memoirs Illustrating the History of Jacobinism*. And from Robison and Barruel the theory filtered to the United States, where Federalists afraid of Jacobin subversion found a new basis for their fears.

One of the first to spread the word was the New England geographer and minister Jedidiah Morse, who proclaimed from the pulpit that a global conspiracy was trying to "subvert and overturn our holy religion and our free and excellent government."[37] Morse's sermons laid out the enemy's plans, including a scheme "to invade the southern states from [Haiti] with an army of blacks . . . to excite an insurrection among the negroes."[38] But Morse was ready to expose the conspirators before they could destroy the social order: "I have, my brethren, an official, authenticated list of the names, ages, places of nativity, professions, &c. of the officers and members of a Society of *Illuminati* . . . consisting of *one hundred* members."[39] Prominent figures joined the warnings, notably Yale president Timothy Dwight, who denounced the Illuminati as a threat to chastity, faith, and the family. Eventually, predictably, the scare seeped into partisan politics, as when a Connecticut Federalist attacked Thomas Jefferson as "the very child of *modern illumination*."[40]

The order began to appear in popular culture, too. In 1800, the Maine writer Sally Wood published *Julia and the Illuminated Baron*, a Gothic melodrama set in prerevolutionary France, featuring an Illuminatus who holds a young woman captive and plots against her virtue. Combining anxieties, the book's villain is both an aristocrat and a Jacobin: "He hated royalty, yet was sometimes so vain as to aspire at the possession of a scepter. He laughed at religion, and he trembled at its power and wished to present it."[41] Wood's Illuminati are a depraved band of nature worshippers, seizing pleasures for themselves as they prepare for the coming uprising. At one point in the tale a woman describes their initiation ceremony: "[D]isrobed of all coverings except a vest of silver gauze, I am to be exposed to the homage of all the society present upon a marble pedestal placed behind which sacrifices are to be offered." She adds, "This sect increases daily. They will in a few years overturn Europe and lay France in ruins."[42]

Julia,

AND THE

ILLUMINATED BARON.

A NOVEL :

FOUNDED ON RECENT FACTS,

WHICH

HAVE TRANSPIRED IN THE COURSE

OF

The late Revolution of Moral Principles

IN

FRANCE.

BY A LADY OF MASSACHUSETTS.

"This volume, to the reader's eye displays
Th' infernal conduct of abandon'd man ;
When French Philosophy infects his ways,
And pours contempt on Heav'n's eternal plan ;
Reversing order, truth, and ev'ry good,
And whelming worlds, with ruin's awful flood."

PORTSMOUTH, NEW-HAMPSHIRE,
PRINTED AT THE UNITED STATES' ORACLE PRESS,
BY CHARLES PEIRCE, (*Proprietor of the work.*)
JUNE, 1800.

An important shift happened as the country's republican institutions matured, particularly once the Federalist Party began its decline in 1801. Before then, Federalist conspiracy theorists generally complained about a Jeffersonian Enemy Below (in collaboration, perhaps, with an Enemy Outside based in France), while Jeffersonian conspiracy theorists generally complained about a Federalist Enemy Above (in collaboration, perhaps, with an Enemy Outside based in England). It was a natural sequel to the revolution-era battle between Enemy Above–fearing insurrectionists and Enemy Below–fearing loyalists. When there were exceptions to the pattern, they usually involved white revolutionaries casting a nervous eye at the people below them in the social hierarchy. (Along with its complaints of kingly oppression, the Declaration of Independence charged London with fomenting "domestic insurrections amongst us." Pressure from above, pressure from below.)[43]

But with Jefferson's party in power, it was possible for Federalists to see their rivals as an Enemy Above as well. In 1804, a Federalist paper in Virginia, the *Norfolk Gazette and Public Ledger*, complained that a "club in Richmond" intended to impose the "dominion of an unacknowledged aristocracy."[44] On a national scale, one Massachusetts Federalist protested, "Instead of free republicks united by solemn compact, under a federal government with limited powers, we have become a consolidated empire under the absolute controul of a few men."[45] Across the ocean, a revolutionary republic in France had decayed into the dictatorship of Napoleon Bonaparte; now the Federalists believed they were watching a revolutionary republic in America decay into the dictatorship of Thomas Jefferson. The alleged entente between the Jeffersonians and the Paris-based Enemy Outside still played a prominent role in Federalist thinking; it's just that the nature of their American and French foes evolved as each consolidated power. Even the Constitution, once the great Federalist hope, had "under the hands of its enemies, its present masters, been converted as if it were by magic into a formidable engine of tyranny, adapted to carry into effect the cruel system of the French ruler."[46]

That was a fantasy, but it was a fantasy provoked by real events. By buying the Louisiana territory from France, Jefferson had more than doubled the country's size, leaving Federalists concerned that the nation had grown too large to govern itself; and by imposing an embargo on trade with the British, he had interfered with Americans' economic freedom in a way that fell especially hard on New England cities, where the Federalists were concentrated. Jefferson was, in other words, working at least part of the time for the expansion of Power. It was natural for his critics to denounce him with the language of Liberty. And it was natural for some of those denunciations to take the form of conspiracy theories.

"These purported conspiracies had no fixed origin and no single aim," James Banner wrote in his history of the Massachusetts Federalists. "Plots were laid within the cabinet, in midnight caucuses of 'Jacobin' malcontents, in Napoleon's carriage somewhere in Europe. There were conspiracies of 'internal foes' and of 'external enemies.' There were small conspiracies to seize elections and larger 'secret and systemic' foreign intrigues 'by wicked and artful men, in foreign countries' to 'undermine the foundation of [Christian] Religion, and to overthrow its Altars.'"[47] Outside and Within, Above and Below: Federalists found something to fear from every direction.

Secret societies play a protean role in the paranoid imagination, their secrecy a mask that might conceal anything. In the Illuminati panic, Masonic orders were cast as an Enemy Outside. After Gabriel's Rebellion of 1800, on the other hand, Masons were linked to an Enemy Below: Slaves were said to have planned the insurrection under cover of organizing a Masonic lodge.[48] In 1826, thanks to a high-profile crime in Canandaigua, New York, Masons became a symbol of the Enemy Above. The precipitating event was the apparent murder of William Morgan, an itinerant stonemason and former Freemason who had announced his plans to expose the order's secrets. Morgan subsequently suffered several months of harassment, which culminated when he was abducted and never seen again.

The uproar that followed Morgan's disappearance included several high-profile trials and grand jury investigations, and the testimony aired in those forums convinced many onlookers that Masonic vigilantes had murdered Morgan, that many Masons had perjured themselves to protect the assassins, and that highly placed Masons had abused their power in an attempt to cover up the crime. In 1828, those onlookers formed an Anti-Masonic Party. When it competed in the presidential election four years later, the party garnered nearly 8 percent of the popular vote and carried the state of Vermont.[49] Former president John Quincy Adams joined the movement, commenting privately in the early stages of the 1832 campaign that the "dissolution of the Masonic institution in the United States" was "really more important to us and our posterity than the question whether [Henry] Clay or [Andrew] Jackson shall be the president."[50] Anti-Masonic governors were elected in Vermont and Pennsylvania, and many Anti-Masonic activists would later become important figures in Whig and Republican politics, including future secretary of state William Seward, future senator Charles Sumner, future congressman Thaddeus Stevens, and future Whig party boss Thurlow Weed.

Some Anti-Masons were fairly levelheaded investigators. Others, particularly later on, were given to wild, over-the-top charges. Either way, they were not simply reacting to a probable murder and a suspicion that a larger criminal conspiracy was at work.[51] They were channeling resentment of genuinely powerful institutions. In the upstate New York cradle of Anti-Masonry, the historian Kathleen Smith Kutolowski has noted, Masons held a "disproportionate share of influential public positions." By Kutolowski's estimate, Freemasons made up no more than 5 percent of the voting population in Genesee County. Yet

> half of the county's pre-1822 office holders (including fourteen of seventeen assemblymen and senators) belonged to lodges. In the five years following enactment of the liberalized Constitution of 1821, fifty-five percent of all county political leaders—candidates and party

> committeemen alike—were Masons. A step below, at the town level, Masons dominated officeholding no less. Lodge brothers supplied three-fourths of Warsaw's supervisors and justices and the town's only postmaster, and over half of Le Roy's supervisors, town clerks, and assessors. . . . From 1803 to 1827 two-thirds of the eighty-five known candidates for political office at the county level were Masons, including three-quarters of the Assembly candidates before 1822.[52]

Men attending Masonic meetings were supposed to leave politics at the door, and it is certainly possible that they did. But it's not hard to understand why the Anti-Masons were suspicious. And if those suspicions didn't amount to much before 1826, the Morgan affair magnified them into a movement. (It helped that Andrew Jackson belonged to the secret society. As the movement grew, many critics of the Mason in the White House opportunistically attached themselves to a party opposed to Masonry in general.)

The most obvious place to look for a "silent, powerful, and ever active conspiracy of those who govern" is, naturally, the government. But the fears that attached themselves to the Masons in the 1820s and '30s—and to the Society of the Cincinnati in the 1780s—show that private organizations can fill the same shoes. The state may be the prize sought or tool used by the Enemy Above, but the conspirators themselves might prefer to prepare their plans elsewhere.[53]

With the Bank War of the 1830s, a different sort of private organization was cast as the Enemy Above. President Jackson vetoed a bill to recharter the country's central bank in 1831 and then withdrew the Treasury's deposits from the institution in 1833, reducing the once-mighty Second Bank of the United States to an ordinary state bank, which finally closed its doors a few years later. Throughout the conflict, the president and his supporters denounced the bank as a monster, a dragon, a hydra, an octopus. That populist rhetoric sometimes took on a conspiratorial tone. Jackson described the bank as a shadow state: "a Government which has gradually increased in strength from the day of its establishment."[54] The bank's president, he later added, "rules the Senate, as a showman does his puppets."[55] Such language wasn't so different from the anti-Power rhetoric we've seen before, but rather than being directed at a government or a secret society, it was pointed at a nominally private corporation.

The Second Bank, to be sure, had been created by the U.S. government, and it was from the U.S. government that the bank derived its power. It was in no sense a break with the antistatist past to find an Enemy Above in an institution like this one, a fact the bank's critics made very clear. "The aristocracy of our country . . . continually contrive to change their party name," the Massachusetts Jacksonian Frederick Robinson explained in a Fourth of July address in 1834. "It was first Tory, then Federalist, then no party, then amalgamation, then National Republican, now Whig, and the next name they assume perhaps will be republican or democrat." Those aristocrats, Robinson said, form "societies and incorporations for the enjoyment of exclusive privileges," and the bank was the "most potent and deadly" of those privileged enterprises.[56] To Robinson and those he spoke for, Washington's battle against the British and Jackson's battle against the bank were separate stages of the same long fight.

Still, the Bank War was a step toward a world where puppeteers are perceived in the corporate sector as frequently as they're found in the halls of state. It was also a step toward a world where a populist might turn to the executive branch, traditionally a habitat of the Enemy Above, to find a champion against the elite. That was true whether or not the populist in question was a conspiracy theorist. But as the chief targets of protest changed, so too did the suspicions of the protesters. The next step in that journey came in the wake of the Civil War, as national markets developed and the "octopus" label once attached to the central bank was now affixed to the railroads.

The rail companies, like the Second Bank, were heavily subsidized by the government. Corporations such as Union Pacific would not have existed without government support—or, at least, would not have existed in the form that raised such ire. But though some of the industry's opponents would have been happy merely to cut off its subsidies and legal privileges, a new generation of populists preferred the idea of using the state to take on the rails—and not the way that Jackson had taken on the bank, an approach that had aggrandized the executive's authority but ultimately left the federal government smaller. They called for the government to regulate or even nationalize the railroads. A century earlier, someone who set out to fight the Enemy Above would have wanted to limit the state. Now he might instead intend to bend the state to his ends.

By the time you get to the corporate combinations of the late nineteenth and early twentieth centuries, the octopus metaphor was ubiquitous enough to be spoofed in one of L. Frank Baum's fantasy novels for children. In *The Sea Fairies* (1911), a little girl traveling through an underwater world has to explain to a sea creature why she assumed he was a villain:

> "Why, ev'rybody knows that octopuses are jus' wicked an' deceitful," she said. "Up on the earth, where I live, we call the Stannerd Oil Company an octopus, an' the Coal Trust an octopus, an'—"
>
> "Stop, stop!" cried the monster in a pleading voice. "Do you mean to tell me that the earth people whom I have always respected compare me to the Stannerd Oil Company? . . . Just because we have several long arms and take whatever we can reach, they accuse us of being like— like— oh, I cannot say it! It is too shameful, too humiliating."[57]

There never was a complete split between the anticorporate and antistatist strains of the antioctopus tradition. It was still possible to argue, as many do on the libertarian Right and the antiauthoritarian Left, that big business derives its power from big government and that opposing one therefore entails opposing the other as well. Even those who prefer to focus on either Wall Street or Washington usually find it impossible to entirely ignore the other. Neither the Yippies nor the Birchers trusted the CIA, and neither was fond of the big banks either.

And both antistatist and anticorporate crusaders love the image of the octopus. He does make an excellent puppeteer: He can manipulate eight arms at once.[58]

"A Horrible Monster," July 19, 1880, *The Daily Graphic*

• • •

So the Enemy Above conspires to take people's liberties, reducing them to slaves. But what if you already *are* a slave? There's another tradition of Enemy Above stories in the United States, one that dates back to the days when blacks were held in bondage. Those tales have often involved threats to precariously won freedoms, but they were also present when there weren't any liberties left to steal. In those cases, the conspiracies coveted their victims' bodies.

The fear appeared when Africans first encountered the European slave trade, as captured blacks worried that the Caucasian invaders intended to eat them. As with many conspiracy theories, the captives came to that conclusion through a combination of empirical observation and frightened guesswork. One prisoner remembered seeing "parts of a hog hanging, the skin of which was white—a thing which we never saw before; for a hog was always roasting on a fire, to clear it of the hair, in my country; and a number of cannonshots were arranged on the deck. The former we supposed to be flesh, and the latter the heads of the individuals who had been killed for meat."[59] (You thought you were reading *Roots*, but that was just a mask: It was *The Silence of the Lambs* all along.) Another slave recalled his fellow captives jumping overboard "for fear that they were being fattened to be eaten."[60] Africans arriving in Louisiana and Haiti reportedly mistook their masters' red wine for blood.

As it turned out, the slavers really were conspiring against their prisoners; it was just the nature of the conspiracy that was misunderstood. The captives were to be consumed by the white economy, not by white mouths. If American slave owners had reasons to be afraid of their slaves, the slaves in turn had many more reasons to be afraid of their owners. Some whites resented that dread. Others figured that stoking those fears might help keep the laborers in line.[61] That deliberate fearmongering continued after emancipation, as whites spread scary stories about the perils of urban life to discourage black workers from venturing north.

That might be the origin of one conspiracy story that circulated in the late nineteenth and early twentieth centuries, a rumor in which "night doctors" allegedly captured blacks, killed them, and dissected their corpses. "There was a scarcity of black bodies," one African-American informant recalled to the folklorist Gladys-Marie Fry, and "in order to get one for dissection [the night doctors] would sometimes kidnap people."[62] The earliest versions of the idea date back to slave times, when southern whites tried to discourage blacks from going out after dark by donning Klanlike night doctor disguises. After the Civil War, by some accounts, whites spread word that night doctors awaited any free blacks foolish enough to settle in the cities.

When former slaves moved to the city anyway, they carried those stories with them. "Have you ever heard talk of the old Naval Hospital on E Street?" a black woman from Washington, D.C., told Fry in 1964. "Well, the doctors, the student doctors used to go there, you know, and most of these people were so scared, scared to go out at night. Afraid the doctors might catch them."[63] Some rumors had it that the kidnappers were after any black body, while others asserted that the doctors were interested only in people who were unusual or deformed. ("That's the reason I stayed off from New York so long," another woman told Fry. "I weighed 200 pounds.")[64] Just as black middlemen were complicit in the African slave trade, there were tales of black body snatchers who worked for the whites.

Sometimes the scientists were said to use the bodies' blood to make medicine, a sort of institutionalized cannibalism. A gruesome version of that tale reappeared in Atlanta during the child murders of 1979 to 1981, when at least twenty-one black children and teenagers (and a handful of young adults) were kidnapped and killed. According to one rumor, the government was harvesting the kids' genitals to make aphrodisiacs.

There was more at work here than an old planter disinformation campaign that refused to die. Black people had good reasons to fear white institutions, even those, such as hospitals, that theoretically were devoted to helping people. In the antebellum South, the medical historian Todd Savitt has reported, scientists "took advantage of the slaves' helplessness to utilize them in demonstrations, autopsies, dissections, and experiments."[65] The abolition of slavery did not end the abuses. In the Tuskegee experiment of 1932 to 1972, for example, the federal Public Health Service offered free medical care to several hundred black sharecroppers. It didn't tell the patients that they had syphilis, which the doctors deliberately left untreated in order to study whether the disease affects blacks and whites in different ways.

Beyond that, on a simple day-to-day, nonconspiratorial level, blacks had plenty of firsthand familiarity with high-handed mistreatment at the hands of white doctors. In that context, it shouldn't be surprising that the tale of the night doctors could take hold, or that later generations would find it easy to believe rumors that doctors were injecting black babies with AIDS.

The face of the Enemy Above is usually either a large institution—a hospital, a government, a powerful corporation—or a secret society. In black America, the secret society that has traditionally loomed largest is the Ku Klux Klan. The real-world Klan hasn't been a unified organization since the 1940s, and it was only barely united then. But the Klan of legend is a mighty empire that includes everyone who has ever described himself as a part of the KKK, plus quite a few who never did. As late as 1993, when the Klan had been reduced to a bundle of tiny squabbling splinter groups, the folklorist Patricia Turner found that many blacks were willing to blame pretty much any racially tinged crime on Klansmen. Various businesses have been rumored to be affiliated with the Klan, notably Church's Chicken, said not just to be a Klan front but to be preparing its food in a way that will make black men sterile. "When I asked one black female student if she didn't think the Food and Drug Administration (FDA) would have tried to stop the Klan from doctoring the chicken," Turner recalls, "she speculated that, on the contrary, the KKK would have had no problem gaining control of the FDA."[66]

The rumor about Church's is absurd, and so are some of the other conspiracy tales that have floated through black America. (In one version of the night doctor story, manholes were "a design, you see, to capture persons," opening and swallowing pedestrians at night.)[67] But even ridiculous stories can be rooted in real experiences. Just as the night doctor legend reflected actual medical misbehavior, the chicken legend took hold in a world where, not so many decades before, many states had sterilized low-income blacks without their consent, sometimes without even informing them. (In one infamous case, doctors cauterized a mother's fallopian tubes after she gave birth. She didn't discover till years later that the extra procedure had been performed.)[68] North Carolina social workers were still strong-arming African Americans into vasectomies or tubal ligations as recently as 1973; Virginia and California didn't repeal their sterilization laws until 1979. True stories of abuse make the false tales more tenacious.

The race riots of the sixties are especially interesting in this light, because they allow us to compare the paranoid stories told by blacks and by whites. "During a riot in Boston in June 1967," the media scholar Terry Ann Knopf noted, "local black self-help organizations distributed mimeographed 'survival kits' throughout the community. The kits came complete with instructions for preserving water and keeping rations, all in the belief that the police were determined to 'exterminate' the black community."[69] Notice the mutual reinforcement at work here. A Bircher would look at those handouts and see a plot to inflame suspicions of the police, just as Gary Allen and Sam Yorty were warning people. A Black Panther would listen to Mayor Yorty downplaying reports of police brutality and hear a clumsy attempt to conceal the war on the ghetto.

Knopf and her colleagues compiled a collection of riot rumors from the 1960s and early '70s, with a total of 181 from black sources and 178 from whites. Thirty-three of the black rumors and 48 of the white ones involved conspiracies. "Whites were extremely afraid that the existing order was in danger," Knopf noted, so "various plots were attributed to blacks involving plans to destroy downtown business areas; ransack suburban shopping centers; invade white neighborhoods; do away with vital services (electricity, gas[,] telephone, etc.); even burn entire cities." Blacks, by contrast, centered their attention on brutal, insulting, or otherwise unjust behavior. Before a Pennsylvania riot, for example, "black students were angered by a report that some young whites had gathered together to form an organization called the ANA—Anti-Negro Association." And in Louisville, when the militant leader Stokely Carmichael didn't appear at a rally, "Many blacks were convinced that whites were preventing his airplane from landing, an unverified rumor which helped set off a disturbance."[70]

Two groups glare at each other, frightened and bewildered, one seeing the Enemy Above, the other the Enemy Below. A city is consumed by flames.

Enemy Above theories are the underground literature of power: lurid, often distorted, and inevitable as long as imperious institutions exist. The larger, more powerful, and more opaque those institutions are, the more common Enemy Above stories will be.

These are the most disreputable sort of conspiracy narrative, since they challenge rather than reinforce the social order. In the media, the phrase "conspiracy theory" is often used as though it refers *only* to Enemy Above stories. You needn't even invoke a conspiracy to earn the conspiracy-theorist tag, as long as you entertain suspicions about the people in charge. In one book about political paranoia, the neoconservative historian Daniel Pipes essentially treated any critique of U.S. power as an allegation of conspiracy. At one point he took a swipe at a foreign policy analyst for writing that "today's proponents of global leadership envision a role for the United States that resembles that of a global hegemon."[71] For Pipes, this mild comment constituted a conspiracy theory.

Yet the same mainstream that maligns Enemy Above stories sometimes trumpets them too. It is a long-standing American tradition to imagine yourself as the scrappy rebel and your enemies as the establishment. Hence the standoff between the Jeffersonians and the Federalists, each side casting the other as an aristocratic foe of freedom. Something similar happened while Andrew Jackson was denouncing the Second Bank as a monster: His critics argued that his war on the bank was a pretext to concentrate more power in the presidency. Jackson, declared Senator Henry Clay, sought "a power which was greater than that possessed by any king in Europe."[72]

(Some of his critics preferred to blame a conspiracy of courtiers—in Clay's phrase, "a deep and dark, and irresponsible cabal composed of individuals lean, lank, lantern-jawed, hollow-hearted, and with empty purses, who, to the exclusion of his best and wisest friends, have surrounded and taken possession of the President."[73] Like King George before him, King Andrew was viewed alternately as an ally or a dupe of a shadow government.)

The same thing happened during the Civil War. Republican rhetoric about the Slave Power, with its theme that whites too could be reduced to bondage, certainly owed a lot to the idea of the Enemy Above. Yet northern Democrats drew on the same tradition when they condemned the draft, the suspension of habeas corpus, and military interference in Maryland and Kentucky elections, seeing not just encroachments on American freedoms but a systematic plot to erase the country's liberties. "What is the purpose of this?" the *Chicago Times* asked. "Can any man doubt it for a moment? Look at Maryland and Kentucky. Let your readers contemplate in those states the despotism to which all the states are hastening."[74]

In the twenty-first century, rank-and-file Republicans attack their enemies as the puppets of the billionaire George Soros while rank-and-file Democrats attack their enemies as the puppets of the billionaires Charles and David Koch. We're told that only the fringe believes in the Enemy Above, yet tales of his machinations have become a routine part of partisan politics. The Devil's cleverest trick is to persuade you that hardly anyone believes he exists.

6

CONSPIRACIES OF ANGELS

I'm a kind of paranoiac in reverse. I suspect people of plotting to make me happy.

—*J. D. Salinger*[1]

Here's the story:

An ancient brotherhood of wise men got here first. They knew they were losing ground to savagery as selfishness and superstition spread through the Old World, so they hatched a plan to build an enlightened empire in the West, a new nation devoted to the pursuit of the common good.

For centuries the adepts had been founding esoteric orders—Rosicrucians, Illuminati, Knights of the Holy Grail—and inserting their agents into the halls of power. "All the petty princes of Europe in medieval times had their Merlins, wise old men who in many instances were the actual rulers of the State," all "bound together, in the secret society of unknown philosophers, moving the crowns of Europe as on a mighty chessboard."[2] Behind those alchemists and cabalists and seers and spies stood the Order of the Quest, the grandest secret society of them all, keeping the flame of wisdom alive and preparing the world for "a perfected social order . . . the government of the philosopher-king."[3] Periodically they published hints about their designs. Plato's *Republic*, Thomas More's *Utopia*, Francis Bacon's *The New Atlantis*: All anticipated the coming society.

But dark forces were at work as well, undermining the adepts' efforts. Ambassadors of the order had visited the Americas in the golden age of Greece, and their successors had kept in contact with the secret societies that governed the Indians. Now they cast their eyes westward again, aware that they needed space to create their perfect state and from there to build the world commonwealth of their dreams.

So the order guided Christopher Columbus, sending a mysterious counselor to join him on his first voyage to America. The explorers who charted the new land were also assisted by initiates of the order or sometimes were members of the secret society themselves; they "operated from a master plan and were agents of *re*discovery rather than discoveries."[4] Francis Bacon, a leader of the order, directed the English settlement of America. "Word was passed about through secret channels that here in the Western Hemisphere was the promised land of the future," and settlers from secret societies ensured that America was "conditioned for its destiny—leadership in a free world."[5] When the time was right, the order's agents unleashed the revolution against England. Some of the initiates who battled the British were well known, among them Benjamin Franklin and Thomas Paine. But more often they acted anonymously, dropping in at just the right moment to influence events and then disappearing into the void.

That's what happened on July 4, 1776, when the patriots assembled in Philadelphia began to have doubts about signing the

Declaration of Independence, knowing full well that if their fight for freedom was unsuccessful they could be executed for treason. There was fearful talk of scaffolds, of axes, of the gibbet. Suddenly a stranger started speaking.

"Gibbet!" he cried:

> They may stretch our necks on all the gibbets in the land; they may turn every rock into a scaffold; every tree into a gallows; every home into a grave, and yet the words of that parchment can never die! . . . Sign that parchment! Sign, if the next moment the gibbet's rope is about your neck! Sign, if the next minute this hall rings with the clash of falling axes! Sign, by all your hopes in life or death, as men, as husbands, as fathers, brothers, sign your names to the parchment, or be accursed forever! Sign, and not only for yourselves, but for all ages, for that parchment will be the textbook of freedom, the bible of the rights of man forever. . . .
>
> Methinks I see the recording Angel come trembling up to that throne and speak his dread message. "Father, the old world is baptized in blood. Father, look with one glance of Thine eternal eye, and behold evermore that terrible sight, man trodden beneath the oppressor's feet, nations lost in blood, murder, and superstition, walking hand in hand over the graves of the victims, and not a single voice of hope to man!"
>
> He stands there, the Angel, trembling with the record of human guilt. But hark! The voice of God speaks from out the awful cloud: "Let there be light again! Tell my people, the poor and oppressed, to go out from the old world, from oppression and blood, and build My altar in the new."[6]

When the speech was over, the delegates rushed to sign the Declaration. But when they turned to thank the speaker for his stirring words, the mysterious man had disappeared. No one knew who he was, and no one knew how he had entered and departed the locked and guarded room.

The order steered us through the Civil War and the fight against fascism, and it is still at work today, guiding the world from behind the scenes: an Invisible Government whose powers can only be described as magic. Some say this Great White Brotherhood is headquartered here on Earth—in the mountains of Tibet, in the barren Gobi Desert, or perhaps beneath the slopes of Mount Shasta in California. Others say it has a more ethereal home. Any stranger you encounter might be a member of the order, subtly intervening in our lives, perhaps keeping a protective eye on you.

Or that's the story, anyway.

It isn't always terrifying to see yourself as a pawn in a grand design. Sometimes it's a comfort. People say, "This was meant to be" or "Everything happens for a reason" or "It's all God's plan" to soothe you, not to scare you. It can be calming to think that all the setbacks in your life are more than mistakes and bad breaks, that a divine purpose will someday reveal itself.

It's just a small step from there to a worldview where the grand design is executed not by God Himself but by a Benevolent Conspiracy. In some tellings the cabal is in league with the Lord, and in some it takes the Almighty's place. But it's the same essential story: a small group of highly evolved beings intervening to improve our earthly affairs. It is an especially advanced example of *pronoia*, a condition the Grateful Dead lyricist and Internet guru John Perry Barlow defines as "the suspicion the universe is a conspiracy on your behalf."[7]

As with many stories one hears in the United States, the tale has Old World roots. In Kassel, Germany, in 1614, an anonymous pamphlet titled "Fama fraternitatis" appeared. A follow-up booklet surfaced a year later, and a third, not necessarily from the same source, was published a year after that. The series told the story of the Rosicrucians, an invisible college of alchemists and philosophers working quietly to bring on a new age of enlightenment. The order's founder, Christian Rosenkreuz, was said to have gone two centuries before on a pilgrimage to the East, where adepts imparted occult wisdom to their visitor. He then allegedly lived to the ripe age of 106; and when his tomb was opened twelve decades after his death, his body was supposedly discovered "whole and unconsumed."[8] The pamphlets were an evocative mix of home-brewed legends and hints of great secrets, and they set the European intelligentsia aflame. Many readers tried to find and join the Rosicrucians, while others waited eagerly for the fraternity to reveal itself.

It never did, and most historians doubt that the order existed. With the horrors of the witch hunts and the Thirty Years' War, stories started circulating that the Rosicrucians had retreated from Europe, regrouping in India or Tibet. Other rumors linked the Rosicrucians to Freemasonry. In 1795, another variation on the archetype appeared in the work of Karl von Eckartshausen, a German mystic who has the distinction of having joined the actual historical Bavarian Illuminati, though he later left the group. Eckartshausen described "a hidden assembly, a society of the Elect," that operated not as a secret society but as an "interior illuminated circle" that preceded all secret societies.[9]

In both Europe and the United States, various visionaries and/or con men claimed to be initiates of the Rosy Cross.[10] The Utica-bred medium P. B. Randolph, who advertised himself as a Rosicrucian miracle worker in the years following the Civil War, later wrote frankly about why he had worn that particular mask. Randolph, who was part black, knew that his ancestry hindered his "usefulness and influence," so he "called myself The Rosicrucian, and gave my thought to the world as Rosicrucian thought; and lo! the world greeted with loud applause what it supposed had its origin and birth elsewhere than in the soul of P. B. Randolph."[11]

All those tales and trends combined in the mythos of the Russian-born globe-trotting occultist Helena Petrovna Blavatsky. Blavatsky moved to New York at age forty-two, in 1873, and founded the Theosophical Society there two years later. America was in the throes of the spiritualism fad, and Theosophy drew on that milieu, along with Eastern philosophy, Rosicrucianism, a peculiar take on evolution, the science fiction novels of Edward George Bulwer-Lytton, and much else. The resulting worldview was influential in the late nineteenth and early twentieth centuries, attracting figures ranging from L. Frank Baum to Vice President Henry Wallace,[12] and its ideas continue to echo in the New Age philosophies of today. One of Theosophy's core doctrines held that Blavatsky had spent seven years in Tibet, where she had encountered a powerful lodge of adepts hidden in the Himalayas.

Theosophists described this Great White Brotherhood as the Inner Government of the World. Its members were said to have amazing powers, including the ability to materialize and dematerialize wherever they pleased. Blavatsky claimed that they continued to communicate with her through supernatural means, including letters that appeared unexpectedly in her cabinet. As Theosophy evolved, the list of the Brotherhood's members came to include the Buddha, Jesus, Moses, Plato, Cagliostro, and the mysterious Count of Saint Germain, an eighteenth-century musician and magician who enjoyed fanning rumors that he was immortal. Blavatsky's followers decided that he really *was* immortal, and various Theosophist writers claimed that the identities he had adopted over the years included St. Alban, Christian Rosenkreuz, and both Roger and Francis Bacon.

Skeptical investigators would later show that it was extremely unlikely that Blavatsky had ever had a seven-year stay in Tibet, let alone encountered any Secret Chiefs there. It is possible, as the historian K. Paul Johnson has suggested, that Blavatsky's stories of the Masters were inspired by real people around the world whose identities she wanted to conceal—normal flesh-and-blood human beings, not astral immortals. There certainly are signs that she regretted the fantastic mythology that grew up around her stories. "I saw with terror and anger the false track they were all pursuing," she wrote to an associate in 1886. "The 'Masters,' as all thought, must be omniscient, omnipresent, omnipotent. . . . The idea that the Masters were mortal men, limited even in their great powers, never crossed anyone's mind, though they wrote this themselves repeatedly."[13]

In any event, Hidden Masters based in a remote location became an evergreen theme for mystics. Theosophical lore identified the head of the lodge as the Lord of the World, an eternally sixteen-year-old superman who lives in the Gobi Desert, in Shambhala, the secret city of the Gods.[14] In Britain, one of the best-known occult groups of the day, the Hermetic Order of the Golden Dawn, claimed to have contacted the Secret Chiefs (and soon splintered as different members announced their own lines to the divine). In the United States, various esotericists published their own contact stories. Alice Bailey referred to the Benevolent Conspiracy as the Masters of the Ancient Wisdom. Max Heindel called them the Elder Brothers of the Rosicrucian Order; when he launched a group called the Rosicrucian Fellowship, he said he was spreading their teachings.[15]

H. Spencer Lewis—the founder of another fauxsicrucian operation, the Ancient Mystical Order Rosae Crucis—found a way to lay claim to a popular occultist while denigrating the group she had founded when he wrote that avatars "under the observation of the Great White Brotherhood" were allowed "to organize movements of their own befitting the time and development of the people with whom they were dealing." Blavatsky, he suggested, was one of those avatars, and her "writings and teachings will remain as a monument to her contact with the Brotherhood." But her organization had "accomplished its definite mission, and there seemed to be no need for its continuance under the name and form used by her."[16] Message: Please join Lewis's order instead.

The Theosophists themselves soldiered on, not at all convinced that their mission was complete. A Los Angeles Theosophist, Manly Palmer Hall, gave the legend of the Benevolent Conspiracy its most thoroughly American form. In two books, *The Secret Destiny of America* (1944) and *America's Assignment with Destiny* (1951), he laid out the story I outlined at the beginning of this chapter: that the United

States had been designed to be an enlightened empire and was being guided to this destiny by an ancient Order of the Quest. Columbus's counselor, Bacon's grand design, the speech that swayed the signers of the Declaration of Independence—Hall covered them all.[17]

Hall's books oscillate between paeans to liberty and suggestions that the ideal form of government is an enlightened oligarchy; he repeatedly calls for a "world democracy," but the reader is left wondering just how democratic, let alone free, his world state would really be. He doesn't help matters with his interpretation of Plato's *Republic*, in which Hall describes rule by a wise elite as a "philosophic democracy," since "all men had the right to become wise through self-discipline and self-improvement."[18]

Many figures claimed by students of the supposed Rosicrucian tradition, from Plato to Francis Bacon, espoused authoritarian ideas.[19] And though the sects inspired by the tradition bubble over with individualist exhortations to find your inner light, they are also frequently filled with the idea that the enlightened should govern the unenlightened. The groups often ran themselves in a rather authoritarian manner as well. Call it the Curse of Weishaupt: when organizations allegedly dedicated to liberating minds find themselves embracing hierarchies even more elaborate than those of the old order they aim to replace.

We've seen how easy it is for one myth to melt into another: the Enemy Below unmasked as a tool of the Enemy Outside, the Enemy Outside revealed as a front for the Enemy Above. The Benevolent Conspiracy can change forms too. It was an easy leap from imagining a friendly secret government to imagining an evil one. There was a Theosophical presence in the Populist Party of the 1890s, allowing a belief in a benign lodge of Masters to exist alongside complaints about cabals of eastern bankers.[20] Blavatsky herself said that the Great White Brotherhood was locked in a long war with the evil Lords of the Dark Face. Many of her followers adopted anti-Jesuit or anti-Jewish conspiracy theories, and the Russian Theosophist Yuliana Glinka may have been responsible for bringing *The Protocols of the Learned Elders of Zion*, a notorious anti-Semitic forgery, from France, where it was composed, to Russia, where it was published.[21]

The Silver Shirts, a paramilitary group organized in 1933, offered a particularly tangled mishmash of ideas taken from Christianity, Theosophy, Rosicrucianism, spiritualism, and Nazism. The group's founder, a Massachusetts-born novelist and screenwriter named William Dudley Pelley, claimed to have had an out-of-body experience in 1928, slipping somehow from the physical world to a "sort of marble-tiled portico" in the spiritual realm, where he conversed with ethereal beings and learned transcendent truths.[22] Pelley soon declared that he was in regular contact with those Ascended Masters. The Masters were also, he added, in contact with Adolf Hitler, who would visit the Bavarian mountains to "get his orders from the Hierarchy of Presiding Dignitaries who meet and counsel with him."[23] (From Pelley's point of view, that was a good thing.) But the Silver Shirts didn't just believe in a Benevolent Conspiracy that beamed ideas to Pelley and the führer. They imagined a malevolent conspiracy they needed to combat, one that included Communists, bankers, the Illuminati, and, of course, the Jews.

A similar movement called Mankind United, founded in San Francisco in 1934 by one Arthur L. Bell, posited an invisible war between a beneficent cabal called the Sponsors and an evil oligarchy known as the World's Hidden Rulers. Bell claimed to have been working secretly for the Sponsors since 1919, when he had supposedly been recruited into one of its covert arms, the International Legion of Vigilantes.

Meanwhile, Christian conspiracists could construe all this literature as essentially true but inverted: The ancient secret brotherhood does exist, the Christians argued, but it's in league with the Devil. Theosophy is denounced in anticonspiracy literature to this day. So is Manly P. Hall, whose work is quoted by writers who think the Order of the Quest is real but despicable. One relatively recent New

Age book, Marilyn Ferguson's best-selling *The Aquarian Conspiracy* (1980), isn't actually about a conspiracy at all; it uses the word as a metaphor for a grab bag of trends in science and society that the author admires. The book was nonetheless interpreted in some quarters as a guide to Satanic subversion.[24] The Christian conspiracy theorist Constance Cumbey quoted copiously from Ferguson, though she pushed back when Ferguson reminded her readers that the Aquarians aren't a genuine conspiracy. "While Marilyn Ferguson and others have protested that the Movement is both leaderless and unstructured," Cumbey warned, "their statements are belied by the abundance of network council organizational charts, matrixes, statements of purpose, and directories—all showing both leadership and structure to an advanced degree."[25] Where Ferguson described a decentralized network of networks, Cumbey imagined a hidden hierarchy. (Cumbey also referred to the Guardian Angels, a collection of grassroots anticrime patrols, as a "para-military organization with ties to the New Age movement."[26] So worrying comes naturally to her.)

It isn't just the New Agers' religious rivals who suspect them of being part of a diabolical conspiracy. The political center is often frightened by "cult" activities, and sects that claim a connection with the Ascended Masters have inspired the same alarm that greeted Mormons and Shakers in the nineteenth century. Both Bell and Pelley were imprisoned for sedition during the first Brown Scare. Around the same time, the government moved against one of the oddest offshoots of the 1930s New Age: the mystical movement called the I AM Activity.

The man behind I AM was Guy Ballard, an Iowa-born mining engineer and self-proclaimed reincarnation of George Washington who borrowed freely from Blavatsky, Lewis, Pelley, and other occultists as he developed a doctrine of his own. Ballard believed, or at least claimed to believe, that Mount Shasta was "one of the most Ancient Foci of the Great White Brotherhood which has been working for man's freedom since his advent upon this planet."[27] In

Unveiled Mysteries, published in 1934, Ballard recounted a visit he had made to Shasta four years earlier. He had been hiking there one day, he claimed, when he encountered Saint Germain at a mountain spring. The immortal count had taken him on a series of astral journeys through space and time: to ancient civilizations, to his own past lives, to a meeting with visitors from Venus, to the Ascended Masters' lair in the heart of the mountain. In those headquarters, Ballard wrote breathlessly, "at the far end of the hall about thirty-five feet from the floor in the wall itself—was a large eye—at least—two feet across. This represented the—'All-Seeing-Eye of the Creator'—forever watching over—His Creation—and from Whom—nothing can be hidden."[28]

A decade before Hall published *The Secret Destiny of America*, Ballard had Saint Germain delivering a similar message about the purpose and future of the New World: "America has a destiny of great import to the other nations of the earth and Those—who have watched over her for centuries—still watch." According to the count, the United States would attain a "form of perfect government," but only "at a later period, when you have cast off certain activities within—that hang like fungi—and sap your strength as a vampire. Beloved ones in America—be not discouraged—when the seeming dark clouds hang low. Everyone of them—shall—show you its golden lining."[29]

It was an attractive pitch, particularly during the Depression. Also attractive were Ballard's promises that followers could acquire limitless wealth, health, beauty, and power. The group attracted tens of thousands of members, and it also attracted a large collection of critics. The loudest of the latter was Gerald Bryan, a former I AMer whose 1940 book *Psychic Dictatorship in America* charged Ballard and his wife with running an authoritarian cult.

Bryan's book made it clear that Ballard was a con artist, and it made a good case that chunks of *Unveiled Mysteries* had been plagiarized from other people's writings. But it also got lost in an effort to argue that Ballard's movement was a fascist Enemy Within. The

House Committee on Un-American Activities had investigated several far-right groups the year before, concluding that they were subversives, racketeers, and "peewee Hitlers."[30] Bryan believed that the Ballards were up to the same game. Pelley of the Silver Shirts, after all, had "started out originally as a psychic or metaphysical leader" before becoming "a political fuehrer with 'storm troopers' or legionnaires in every state." Ballard and his wife "likewise are psychic leaders, but have political ambitions too."[31]

Bryan acknowledged that the Ballards avoided "the Silver Shirts' well-known hatred of the Jew." But they "denounced other 'enemies,'" made a fruitless attempt to attract Pelley's support, and made a more successful bid to bring in disaffected Silver Shirters.[32] One interpretation of this is that Ballard was an opportunist attempting to draw members from a rival organization. Bryan saw it as a sign that Ballard shared Pelley's fascist orientation, and he wondered why the House Committee on Un-American Activities hadn't investigated I AM yet. "No doubt its 'religious' set-up protects it," Bryan concluded. "Racketeers who hide under the cloak of religion are likely to become one of the most dangerous and difficult problems in the future, if not, indeed, at the present time. It is a weak spot in our protective armor against 'Fifth Columns.'"[33]

By the end of the year, the government *was* investigating I AM, not for subversion but for mail fraud. A grand jury held that the sect's leaders "well knew" that their claims to heal the sick and communicate with the divine were bogus and that they therefore were defrauding the followers who sent them money. That verged on having a jury determine whether a religious doctrine was valid—not a comfortably constitutional activity—and the conviction was eventually reversed, though by that time Guy Ballard was dead and his movement had shrunk to a tiny fraction of its former self.[34]

Before we depart the tale of I AM, a word about Ballard's visitors from Venus. This wasn't the first time a guru had reported an encounter with spacemen: Emanuel Swedenborg claimed to have journeyed to several planets way back in 1758,[35] and Blavatsky's Ascended Masters included some Venusian "Lords of the Flame." It wouldn't be the last time either. The years following World War II would see a wave of alleged encounters with extraterrestrials; and though some of the contactees viewed the aliens as a force to be feared, there were others who essentially announced that they had met Ascended Masters from outer space.[36]

Nick Herbert, a physicist with psychedelic inclinations, split the difference the night he got high and started hearing voices in his head. (This was in the sixties, as you may have guessed.) "They claimed to be an ancient group of galactic telepaths traveling through space mind-to-mind rather than in clunky metal ships," he later recalled:

> They were inviting me to join the conspiracy of galactic telepaths. They told me that some of my friends were already members. . . . My initial response was that if this community really existed its goals would differ from human goals as much as human goals differ from the goals of fishes. This group must by necessity be non-human. So by joining it I would in some sense be betraying the human race.
>
> The aliens seemed to understand my misgivings, but assured me that although I qualified for membership, there was no pressure to join. Then they withdrew from my mind and left me alone.
>
> For the next few days I was obsessed with this contact and tried to discover other members of the group. Some of my psychedelic pals in the Stanford psychology department were prime candidates but they all shrewdly denied being galactic telepaths.[37]

As the last line suggests, Herbert had a sense of humor about the experience; he refrained from setting up his own Church of the Mind-Melding Space Brothers. Not every acid-dropping hippie with a cosmic vision would be so reticent.

The idea of the Benevolent Conspiracy always owed a lot to beliefs about angels. The Elizabethan magician John Dee—a man whose name almost invariably comes up when people start listing alleged Rosicrucians—believed that he was in contact with angels and that they had imparted important knowledge to him. There wasn't a huge difference between the spirits he described and the beings that later mystics dubbed Secret Chiefs.[38]

In the middle of the twentieth century, UFOs remade angels in their image: Books on "ancient astronauts" argued that the angels and gods of Earth's mythologies were actually aliens influencing humanity.[39] But the belief in angels *qua* angels didn't go away, and in the 1990s a full-fledged angel fad erupted. These angels were a Benevolent Conspiracy just as much as the Ascended Masters were. In one self-proclaimed psychic's words, they were a "spiritual network in this world."[40]

The angel boom began in 1990 with Sophy Burnham's *A Book of Angels*, a wide-ranging tour through several centuries of angelic lore. It wasn't the first volume about angels to be aimed at a popular audience: The previous decades had seen Gustav Davidson's *A Dictionary of Angels* in 1967, Peter Lamborn Wilson's *Angels* in 1980, and Hope MacDonald's *When Angels Appear* in 1982.[41] But none of those had the cultural impact of Burnham's book, which hopped easily from histories of angels in different spiritual traditions to anecdotes about encounters with the divine, with side excursions into other paranormal topics: ghosts, premonitions, past lives. The book leans heavily on tales of the unexplained, of the kind you might find in a supermarket paperback, but it also includes several stories whose magical content is nothing more than a helpful stranger coming along at just the right moment. "A shiver runs down your spine when you realize it is not our imagination," Burnham wrote. "Something is watching us out there."[42] Those two sentences could have appeared in a terrified paranoid manifesto, but here the watchers are a blessing.

The book began as a private project. Burnham had had several odd and mystical experiences, so she "decided to set them down, just for myself. Not for publication necessarily, but just to understand what's making the world tick."[43] A book began to take shape, and Burnham gave it the working title *Angels and Ghosts I Have Known*. It wasn't until much later—after the first draft of the book was done and after two publishers had expressed an interest in it—that Burnham realized that angels should be at the center of the book. And it was only then that she wrote the literal center of the book, a middle section that pulls back from the personal anecdotes and explores the history of angelology.

Burnham is an engaging stylist and a talented storyteller, and it is no surprise that her book was a commercial success, eventually selling more than a million copies. What might be more surprising is the interfaith approach she adopted, the ease with which a volume studded with Bible quotes could also declare casually that Zoroastrianism "transformed the old Babylonian and Assyrian gods into archangels, whence they crept irrevocably into Judaism and Christianity."[44] Burnham was following in the footsteps of an earlier book: Peter Lamborn Wilson, who is in no sense a Christian, had argued in *Angels* that the angelic archetype appears in almost every religion.[45] She was also drawing on her own hopscotch spiritual path, which included a spell as a Buddhist and a long-standing interest in the faiths of the world. "I have spent a lifetime looking into various religions," she says today, "and realizing that they're all saying the same thing in slightly different words."

Burnham's book also declared forthrightly that its author doesn't believe in Hell: a tolerant, positive outlook for the age of *Oprah* and the self-help shelf. Indeed, the author eventually appeared on *Oprah*, and some stores filed her book in the self-help section. But her books were sometimes filed as Christian literature too, and Burnham doesn't seem displeased about that. When she heard that a priest had told his congregation that everyone should keep two tomes by the bed, the Bible and *A Book of Angels*, she reported the news proudly in a later edition of the text.

As Burnham climbed the best-seller list, vendors took note. A flood of angel tchotchkes cascaded onto the market: angel dolls, angel figurines, angel watches, even angel perfume. And, of course, more angel books. Because they prominently feature the word *angels*, those books attracted a lot of Christian buyers. Some of them were written by conventional Christians, while others strayed even further from orthodoxy than Burnham did. One volume might thank "the helpful research departments at the Christian Broadcasting Network, the Assemblies of God General Council Headquarters, and *Guideposts* magazine."[46] Another might announce that the ranks of angels include "incarnated elementals," which turns out to mean "leprechauns, fairies, brownies, and elves."[47] And both books might sit on the same shelf at Barnes & Noble.

Not surprisingly, the fad annoyed many Christians, some of whom saw Satan's hand at work: the Enemy Outside in an angelic disguise. "As a young man out of college," the religious writer Bill Myers claimed he encountered a medium who said he could transmit messages from angels. The alleged angels

> told me things about myself they couldn't have known except through supernatural means. They knew, for instance, that I was an aspiring writer. In fact, one of the voices assured me that I was going to be a successful author, and that I was going to accomplish great things for God through my writing. Of course, this is what I *wanted* to hear! The "angels" went out of their way to feed my pride and tantalize me with visions of glory. They constantly flattered me and made me feel I was somebody special.
>
> They also seemed to help me achieve this fame by offering to help me write a book proclaiming to be the "deeper mysteries of God's love."
>
> I grew uneasy. I didn't know much about angels then, but I began to suspect that these beings didn't really have my best interest in mind. They were a bit too slick. And instead of encouraging me to grow in humility and love, I sensed them stirring up my pride and desire for success.
>
> Finally, I decided to ask one of these beings a crucial question: "Is Jesus Christ your Lord?"
>
> "Absolutely!" he said. But before I could even breathe a sigh of relief, he added, "In fact, not only is He my Lord. He's also my brother."

> I could feel the hair on the back of my neck rise.
>
> Why? Because I knew Satan and his demons have always been driven by a desire to be considered God's equals.[48]

You thought you were watching *Touched by an Angel*, but that was just a mask: It was *The Exorcist* all along.

Myers's take won't be very persuasive to people who don't share his religious views. But setting theology aside, there is at least one sense in which devils were present at the beginning of the angel boom. Before Peter Lamborn Wilson wrote *Angels*, helping lay the groundwork for the fad, his publisher had invited him to do a book about devils. But Wilson figured devils were boring. It would be more fun, he decided, to write about angels and "make them sexy."[49]

As angel books invaded bookstores, tomes about aliens and Ascended Masters kept coming out alongside them. Other versions of the Benevolent Conspiracy circulated as well. A whole subculture devoted itself to the idea that certain digital time displays, particularly 11:11, might be messages from another plane. I quote a representative article:

> All over the world, people report waking up at night, looking at the alarm clock, and noticing that it is 11:11pm. This happens again the next night, and the next. Soon they begin to see 11:11 everywhere; from computer screens to digital watches to addresses, labels, menus, billboards and advertisements. Is this repetition simply coincidental? At first, it may merely be forgotten as a lone anomaly—an annoyance. But perhaps, these mysterious time prompts are really wake-up calls urging the observer to sit up and pay attention.
>
> *But pay attention to what? And why?*[50]

The proposed answers vary, but several 11:11ers believe that the readouts are signals from a friendly celestial conspiracy. "These 11:11 Wake-Up Calls on your digital clocks, mobile phones, VCR's and microwaves are the 'trademark' prompts of a group of just 1,111 fun-loving Spirit Guardians, or Angels," one website explains; "the 11:11 prompt is their way of using our innate ability for pattern recognition to let us know that they are here."[51] One book declares that an "11:11 Emergency Platoon" is "on loan to our mortal races for the advancement, or upstepping, of spirituality on this Earth."[52]

If *you* start spotting the 11:11s—or, apparently, any memorable time of day, from 2:22 to 12:12—feel free to take the opportunity to talk with the celestial platoon. All you have to do, according to the aforementioned website, is wait for the prompt and then "Acknowledge it out loud. Say—OK guys I hear you, tell me what you want."[53]

There was a time when communion with the Hidden Masters entitled the contactee to a church of his own: If I'm the one in touch with Higher Intelligence, then I get to tell my followers what the Higher Intelligence had to say. And many sects still stick to this model. But these days the typical angel book, like that 11:11 site, is a do-it-yourself manual. The guru, having cavorted with spirits, wants to tell you how *you* can engage the invisible world too. Every Man a Prophet.

Another version of the Benevolent Conspiracy story takes that theme of empowerment a step further. As Jack Sarfatti, one of Nick Herbert's psychedelic physicist friends, described the idea: "Higher intelligence is us in the future. * We will soon master time-travel to the past and will go back in time to the primordial soup and plant our DNA there! * We interfere with our evolution at critical times. * We create ourselves by transcending time."[54] We have met the ancient astronaut, and he is us.

Poke through the lore of the Benevolent Conspiracy and you'll uncover pieces of genuine history amid the pseudohistory and the speculation. The late Frances Yates, an influential historian of the Renaissance and early modern Europe, has made a plausible case that the late sixteenth and early seventeenth centuries did see a Rosicrucian "type of thinker," even if the secret society that supposedly produced the pamphlets wasn't real. Yates's Rosicrucians still believed in older occultist traditions but were also making the first steps toward the scientific revolution; by her account, the prototypical Rosicrucian was John Dee, and "traces of the Rosicrucian outlook could be detected in Francis Bacon and even in Isaac Newton."[55] Put another way, there really was an Invisible College, but it wasn't a secret society guiding humanity behind the scenes. It consisted of innovators operating in the open, influenced by ideas that would eventually be associated with a fictional secret society.

It is also true that several founding fathers—George Washington, Benjamin Franklin, John Hancock, Paul Revere—were Freemasons, though that hardly constitutes a conspiracy in itself. As history, *The Secret Destiny of America* left a lot to be desired. But as myth, it was powerful stuff, capable of inspiring people far removed from Rosicrucianism and Theosophy.

In 1957, a movie star and GE spokesman named Ronald Reagan returned to Illinois to deliver a commencement address at Eureka College, his alma mater. "I have never been able to believe that America is just a reward for those of extra courage and resourcefulness," he told the crowd. "This is a land of destiny, and our forefathers found their way here by some Divine system of selective service gathered here to fulfill a mission to advance man a further step in his climb from the swamps." Then he related Manly Hall's story about the stranger whose speech had inspired the signers of the Declaration of Independence. Reagan misattributed the tale, as Hall did, to Thomas Jefferson.

The story itself can be traced back to 1847, and several versions surfaced between then and Hall's rendition. But the variant that Reagan told features a detail that doesn't seem to have been present before the Theosophists got their hands on the story: that after the Declaration was signed, "When they turned to thank the speaker for his timely words he couldn't be found, and to this day no one knows who he was or how he entered or left the guarded room."[56] Reagan repeated the story in a 1981 article for *Parade*, that time calling it a legend and that time, as the occult historian Mitch Horowitz has noted, using language "very close to Hall's own."[57] It's enough to make you suspect that the president had gotten the yarn, directly or indirectly, from *The Secret Destiny of America*. But even if the similarities are simply a coincidence, Reagan and Hall shared the deeper idea that the country is on a divine mission.

That idea is a lot older than either Reagan or Hall. It is, in fact, one of the oldest American stories. When the Puritans arrived in New England, they believed they were on an errand to build a New Jerusalem. Sometimes they saw America as a way station, a place to hunker down for a spell before returning to England and erecting their utopia there. But at other times the new Israel was to be planted here in the New World, a commonwealth created far from the corruption and idolatry of Europe. That's not so far from the goal Hall ascribed to the Order of the Quest, even if the ideas animating the missions were deeply different.

In 1630, speaking on a boat off the Massachusetts shore, John Winthrop said that the settlers' colony would be a city upon a hill with the eyes of the world upon it. In 1979, announcing his candidacy for the presidency, Reagan quoted Winthrop's words and continued, "A troubled and afflicted mankind looks to us, pleading for us to keep our rendezvous with destiny."[58] An earlier president, Franklin Roosevelt, had declared that his generation had a rendezvous with destiny. Reagan extended the idea to the United States as a whole, and he linked it to the vision laid out at the beginning of the Puritan experiment.

A belief in a benevolent guiding hand can be an antidote to paranoia. "We live now in a culture of extreme fear," Burnham has said. "Look at the absurdity of the security that's been put in since 9/11, where you can't go into any office without having to go through a magnetic screening machine. And someone is going to bomb the Leesburg, Virginia, courthouse? Not likely. The library? Are you out of your mind?" She'd rather think of her angels—of "a spiritual dimension that is on our side, that wants more and better for us than we can imagine."

But beliefs in benevolent and malevolent conspiracies can also go hand in hand. When you think you're pursuing a divine destiny, it's not hard to find yourself watching for all the *other* invisible forces out there: darker, more dangerous powers who don't want your holy mission to succeed. The Puritans saw their city upon a hill besieged by the Devil in the wilderness. And at Eureka in 1957, after Reagan invoked the mystery man who had urged the founders to sign the Declaration, his speech turned to the Red threat. "Some of us came toe to toe with this enemy, this evil force, in our own community in Hollywood," he told the graduates, "and make no mistake about it, this is an evil force. Don't be deceived because you are not hearing the sound of gunfire, because even so you are fighting for your lives."

INTE N ENEMY WITHIN KU KLUX KLAN MIND CONTRO
SSINS 9/11 ANGELS THE MATRIX ENEMY ABOVE OPERA
NCE “BOB” MYSTIC CLAN ENEMY OUTSIDE BACKMASK
E QUEST HIDDEN PERSUADERS FREEMASONRY TRYS
HIEFS JONESTOWN DANITES ILLUMINATI CIA ZOMBIE
ONTROL FEMA COINTELPRO BENEVOLENT CONSPIRAC
E OPERATION CHAOS MEN IN BLACK ELDERS OF ZIO
CKMASKING NIGHT DOCTORS WATERGATE CULTS MAN
RY TRYSTERO SLAVE POWER MKULTRA ENEMY BELO
A ZOMBIES GENEVA CLUB

PART II

ROSICRUCIAN
ENEVOLENT CONSPIRACY DISCORDIAN SOCIETY SATA
ACK ELDERS OF ZION POD PEOPLE HOMINTERN GHOS
RGATE CULTS MANCHURIAN CANDIDATE ORDER OF TH
EMY BELOW VATICAN FLYING SAUCERS SECRET CHIEF
IINTERN ENEMY WITHIN KU KLUX KLAN MIND CONTRO
SSINS 9/11 ANGELS THE MATRIX ENEMY ABOVE OPERA
NCE “BOB” MYSTIC CLAN ENEMY OUTSIDE BACKMASK
UEST HIDDEN PERSUADERS FREEMASONRY TRYSTER
RET CHIEFS

MODERN FEAR

JONESTOWN DAN
WITHIN KU KLUX KLAN MIND CONTROL FEMA COINTEL
ELS THE MATRIX ENEMY ABOVE OPERATION CHAOS ME
CLAN ENEMY OUTSIDE BACKMASKING NIGHT DOCTOR
ADERS FREEMASONRY TRYSTERO SLAVE POWER MKUL
ES ILLUMINATI CIA ZOMBIES GENEVA CLUB ROSICRU
PRO BENEVOLENT CONSPIRACY DISCORDIAN SOCIET
N IN BLACK ELDERS OF ZION POD PEOPLE HOMINTER
ORS WATERGATE CULTS MANCHURIAN CANDIDATE OR
ER MKULTRA ENEMY BELOW VATICAN FLYING SAUCER
ROSICRUCIANS COMINTERN ENEMY WITHIN KU KLU
OCIETY SATAN ILLUMINATI ASSASSINS 9/11 ANGEL
POD PEOPLE HOMINTERN GHOST DANCE “BOB” MYS
NCHURIAN CANDIDATE ORDER OF THE QUEST HIDDE
ATICAN FLYING SAUCERS SECRET CHIEFS JONESTOW
MY WITHIN KU KLUX KLAN MIND CONTROL FEMA COIN
ANGELS THE MATRIX ENEMY ABOVE OPERATION CHAO
TIC CLAN ENEMY OUTSIDE BACKMASKING NIGHT DOC

7

THE WATER'S GATE

America's faith is drowning beneath that cesspool—Watergate.

—*Gil Scott-Heron*[1]

The special agent in charge of the FBI's San Diego office had a plan. An antidraft activist in the area was convinced that the Bureau was watching him—he kept telling people that his phone was tapped, his home bugged, his every move observed. With "a small push in the right direction," the agent believed, the activist would start exhibiting "obvious paranoid tendencies," and that would "completely neutralize him in his several leadership capacities."

So let's make a big show of spying on the man, the investigator suggested. Maybe we could build a spooky-looking mechanism from a bicycle part and an old transistor radio, then drop it off near his front steps one night. "In the event he displayed the contraption to anyone," the officer argued, "its crude construction would ultimately neutralize any allegation that it originated or is being utilized by the FBI." And if the target tried to tell people it was a bugging device, they'd ridicule him.[2]

Headquarters wasn't convinced. The problem wasn't that the plan was unethical, unconstitutional, or absurd. It was that the activist might not be important enough to be "a suitable target for counterintelligence action." The agent was told to investigate the fellow further, then "resubmit your request if his importance to the New Left movement warrants such attention."[3] In other words, the Bureau should spend more time spying on the man before it tried to convince the man he was being spied on.

It was November 1968, and that was just one of hundreds of operations against domestic dissidents that FBI agents were proposing, and frequently carrying out, as a part of COINTELPRO, a program to disrupt and neutralize political movements that the Bureau deemed subversive. When it was launched in 1956, COINTELPRO had been aimed at the remnants of the Communist Party and at the groups the party had allegedly infiltrated. Gradually the program's targets had expanded. COINTELPRO–Communist Party USA was joined by COINTELPRO–Socialist Workers Party, then COINTELPRO–White Hate Groups, then COINTELPRO–Black Nationalist/Hate Groups, then COINTELPRO–New Left.

The White Hate Groups effort was a watershed. The previous COINTELPROs had been designed with the Enemy Outside in mind: The Bureau's target might have nothing to do with Soviet subversion, but the idea that it *might* be linked to Soviet subversion was always in play. But even J. Edgar Hoover, the FBI's famously anti-Communist director, found it difficult to argue that the Reds controlled the Klan. Once the White Hate Groups program began in 1964, the sociologist David Cunningham has noted, many more groups could "be thought of as 'subversive' and therefore suitable targets for counterintelligence programs. No longer did a subversive group have to be controlled by or intimately tied to a hostile foreign power."[4] Because the Bureau was aiming its fire at the radical Right, powerful liberals were happy to sign off on the program, setting a precedent that made it easier later for the Bureau to target the antiwar movement and the Black Panthers.

Under COINTELPRO, FBI agents infiltrated political groups and spread rumors that loyal members were the real infiltrators. They tried to get targets fired from their jobs, and they tried to break up the targets' marriages. They published deliberately inflammatory literature in the names of the organizations they wanted to discredit, and they drove wedges between groups that might otherwise be allied. In Baltimore, the FBI's operatives in the Black Panther Party were instructed to denounce Students for a Democratic Society as "a cowardly, honky group" who wanted to exploit the Panthers by giving them all the violent, dangerous "dirty work."[5] The operation was apparently successful: In August 1969, just five months after the initial instructions went out, the Baltimore FBI reported that the local Panther branch had ordered its members not to associate with SDS members or attend any SDS events.[6]

Sometimes the Bureau's efforts were simply strange. Late in 1968, the FBI's Philadelphia office pondered how it might react to the counterculture's rising interest in the occult. "Some leaders of the New Left, its followers, the Hippies and the Yippies, wear beads and amulets," an agent observed. "New Left youth involved in anti-Vietnam activity have adopted the Greek letter 'Omega' as their symbol. Self-proclaimed yogis have established a following in the New Left movement." Under those "conditions," he argued, it might be effective if "a few select top-echelon leaders of the New Left be subjected to harassment by a series of anonymous messages with a mystical connotation."

As examples of such messages, the agent enclosed two sketches: a beetle, with the caption "Beware! The Siberian Beetle"; and a toad, with the caption "Beware! The Asiatic Toad." The recipient, he explained, would be

> left to make his own interpretation as to the significance of the symbol and the message and as to the identity of the sender.

> The symbol utilized does not have to have any real significance but must be subject to interpretation as having a mystical, sinister meaning.[7]

fbi.gov

If all of COINTELPRO had resembled the Siberian beetle plan, it would be a minor part of history: unconstitutional but clueless and ultimately harmless, the product of the same blundering Bureau that felt the need to file a report on the Monkees. (The Los Angeles field office claimed that a concert by the band had included left-wing "subliminal messages.")[8] But the FBI's activities were often darker and more dangerous. When the Senate investigated COINTEL-PRO, the chief of the Bureau's Racial Intelligence Section claimed that "no one was killed" after the FBI falsely tagged him or her as a snitch. Someone asked if this had been a matter of planning or just sheer luck. "Oh, it just happened that way, I'm sure," the officer replied.[9]

This is where the study of conspiracy theories becomes a hall of mirrors. The feds didn't just infiltrate and disrupt dissident groups; they made sure the groups knew that they were being infiltrated and disrupted, so activists would suspect one another of being police agents. In effect, COINTELPRO functioned as a conspiracy to defeat subversive conspiracies by convincing the alleged subversives that they were being conspired against.

While all that was going on, the CIA was engaged in its own program of domestic political surveillance. With the flair of a villain in a campy James Bond rip-off, the agency called it Operation CHAOS. And in the Nixon White House, an aide named Tom Charles Huston was drawing up plans for yet another countersubversive operation, one that would roll back restrictions Hoover had imposed in 1966 and also expand the powers of the CIA and military intelligence to spy at home. Huston wanted to revive the use of "black bag jobs"—in plain English, the use of break-ins. He wanted to make it easier for the feds to tap phones and read people's mail. He wanted to send more FBI informants to college campuses and devote more CIA resources to watching students abroad. And he wanted the FBI, the CIA, the National Security Agency, and military intelligence to answer to an Interagency Group on Internal Security staffed by the White House.

The Huston Plan was stopped, but not because of anyone's civil libertarian scruples. It was blocked by J. Edgar Hoover, who had no interest in submitting to an interdepartmental committee.

At this point you might be expecting to read the phrase "Or that's the story, anyway." Sorry. Every word I've just written is true. COINTELPRO, CHAOS, and the Huston Plan all existed, and they don't even begin to exhaust the official crimes that were revealed in the 1970s.

The seventies were a golden age of Enemy Above stories. Ordinarily, such narratives may be the most disreputable sort of conspiracy theory, but as press reports and official investigations exposed a long history of misbehavior in the executive branch, it became clear that many Enemy Above tales were true. And as descriptions of those proven plots appeared in the media, it became easier to imagine that still larger and more malevolent conspiracies were lurking.

In other words, the mainstream was absorbing a mind-set that had long been common currency in the counterculture and the New Left. There was nothing like the direct experience of COINTELPRO, CHAOS, and the local equivalents run by Red squads to instill a deep distrust of the government. It was easier to imagine the president ordering a break-in at the Democratic National Committee if you knew that the FBI had repeatedly broken into the offices of organizations devoted to political protest. For that matter, it was easier to think that the government might have murdered Martin Luther King or Malcolm X if you knew that the Chicago cops and FBI had assaulted and killed Fred Hampton and Mark Clark of the Black Panther Party.[10] Documented misbehavior inevitably fueled speculations about undocumented misbehavior.

As the Vietnam War wore on and domestic politics grew more bitter and violent, there was more critical coverage of the federal government in the mainstream media. The first COINTELPRO revelations, for example, came out after the Citizens' Commission to Investigate the FBI broke into the Bureau's office in Media, Pennsylvania, in 1971, making off with more than a thousand documents detailing the agency's attempts to infiltrate and undermine the Left. The anonymous investigators mailed the memos to the media, and *The New York Times*, *The Washington Post*, and other papers then reported their contents. The FBI soon shuttered the program, though it didn't end all the activities that had been carried out in the program's name.

But the fears that were second nature to protesters didn't start to flood into the mainstream until five burglars were arrested at the Watergate Hotel in Washington, D.C., on June 17, 1972. Over the next two years, a chain of evidence emerged that linked their illegal activity to President Richard Nixon, who resigned from office under the weight of the scandal on August 9, 1974. By then there had been a wide range of revelations about the antics of the president's dirty-tricks team, and the exposés continued to come after Nixon left office.

Nixon's men, it was learned, had sabotaged the campaigns of the candidates believed to have the best chance of unseating their boss in 1972. After the authorities started looking into the Watergate burglary, they had done their best to sabotage that investigation too. When the military analyst Daniel Ellsberg leaked the Pentagon Papers, a classified history of the Vietnam War that revealed the government's deceptions about the conflict, Nixon's operatives had burglarized the office of Ellsberg's psychiatrist, looking for information that could be used against him. Nixon staffers had assembled a list of the president's political foes, ranging from the labor leader Leonard Woodcock to the actor Paul Newman. The list's purpose, White House counsel John Dean explained in a confidential memo, was to "use the available federal machinery to screw our political enemies."[11] Within the Internal Revenue Service, a group called the Special Service Staff had been regularly used to harass people for political purposes. When a new IRS chief shut the staff down in 1973, the president had immediately attempted to have him fired.

On top of all that, some of the Watergate conspirators had seriously considered a plan to assassinate the newspaper columnist Jack Anderson.

Suddenly the New Left's warnings seemed much more plausible. (An underground paper in Atlanta greeted the Nixon scandals with the headline WATERGATE: EXCUSE US FOR BRAGGING BUT WE TOLD

YOU SO!)[12] One COINTELPRO memo had declared the need to "enhance the paranoia endemic in these circles."[13] Now "the paranoia" had spread far beyond "these circles." In just a decade, the historian Kathryn Olmsted has pointed out,

> the percentage of people who distrusted the government had risen from 22 to 62 percent. Forty-five percent of Americans polled believed that there were "quite a few" crooks in government, up from 29 percent in 1964. The proportion of those who agreed that the country's leaders had "consistently lied to the American people" rose from 38 percent in 1972 to 68 percent in 1975. . . .
>
> The proportion of Americans who had a "highly favorable" impression of the FBI had fallen from 84 percent in 1965 to 52 percent in 1973. In 1975, that figure dropped again to 37 percent. Although the Gallup organization did not ask Americans about the relatively anonymous CIA before 1973, the agency at that time was held in lower esteem than the FBI: only 23 percent of Americans gave the CIA a highly favorable rating. In 1975, the figure fell to 14 percent. Among college students, the CIA was highly regarded by only 7 percent.[14]

In the 1770s, many Americans had believed that "a deep-laid and desperate plan of imperial despotism has been laid, and partly executed, for the extinction of all civil liberty." As the bicentennial neared, that same suspicion grew again.

Three months after Nixon's resignation, those suspicious voters elected a reform-minded new Congress. Washington now contained more than the usual number of legislators interested in investigating the national security state, and the FBI and CIA faced more congressional scrutiny than either agency had received to date. An investigative committee chaired by Idaho Senator Frank Church soon issued a report on a host of executive-branch abuses, including COINTELPRO, politically motivated IRS audits, CIA assassination plots, an effort to intercept and read Americans' mail, and a particularly creepy program called MKULTRA.

MKULTRA was the CIA's response to the Korean Communists' purported success in brainwashing prisoners of war. Its researchers had investigated "chemical, biological, and radiological materials capable of employment in clandestine operations to control human behavior."[15] Among other things, the Church Committee reported, the operations entailed the "surreptitious administration" of LSD "to unwitting nonvolunteer subjects in normal life settings."[16] More bluntly, the CIA had dosed people with acid without their permission.

A similar committee in the House of Representatives, chaired by the New York Democrat Otis Pike, took a hard look at the intelligence community's budget secrecy and its spotty record in foreseeing foreign crises. In the executive branch, a commission chaired by Vice President Nelson Rockefeller covered some of the same ground the Church Committee did, though not as thoroughly or incisively.

The Left felt affirmed. The center felt shaken. And though much of the Right reacted to the revelations by defending the embattled national security agencies, Republicans also delighted in digging out dirty deeds by earlier administrations and throwing them back in the Democrats' faces. One conservative book of the era, Victor Lasky's *It Didn't Start with Watergate* (1977), made an unpersuasive effort to defend Nixon from the charges against him. But it also included a spirited recital of ugly facts about previous presidents: how Franklin Roosevelt had used the FBI to spy on the critics of his foreign policy; how Harry Truman had owed his career to Tom Pendergast's corrupt, vote-stealing political machine; how John and Robert Kennedy had steamrollered civil liberties in their pursuit of Teamsters leader Jimmy Hoffa; how Lyndon Johnson had used the CIA—including the future Watergate conspirator E. Howard Hunt—to spy on Barry Goldwater's presidential campaign. (Lasky, alas, added some more dubious allegations to the mix as well.)[17]

The result was an argument not so different from a set of positions taken by Noam Chomsky and other radicals of the Left: that political repression had been a bipartisan project, that Richard

Nixon's troubles had begun because he had directed that repression at powerful people instead of outsiders, that with Nixon out of office we would soon be back to business as usual. Chomsky acknowledged the convergence when he commented that Kennedy's and Johnson's illicit FBI operations had been "incomparably more serious than anything charged in the Congressional Articles of Impeachment" against Nixon, and that Nixon's defenders therefore "have a case." Lasky, in turn, quoted Chomsky's words in his book.[18]

But in the mainstream media a simpler story line was taking hold, one in which Watergate was an unfortunate aberration and Nixon's downfall proved that the system worked. A similar sentiment attached itself to revelations about the FBI and the CIA: *Yes, crimes were committed*, the argument went, *but that's just a sign that the CIA had gone rogue and that J. Edgar Hoover was out of control. It's not as though the scandals represented systemic problems.*

Chomsky and Lasky were closer to the truth. Just a decade after the program formally known as COINTELPRO ended, the FBI was using some of the same old tactics against a leftist protest group, the Committee in Solidarity with the People of El Salvador: tapping its phones, intercepting its mail, and (perhaps) burglarizing its offices. Similarly, the Iran-Contra scandal that made headlines in 1986, in which the Reagan administration secretly sold weapons to the Islamic theocracy in Iran and used the proceeds to illegally fund guerrillas in Nicaragua, made it clear that the post-Watergate investigations had not brought a stop to illicit covert operations overseas. In a different context, the anthropologist Nicholas Dirks once described public scandals as "ritual moments in which the sacrifice of the reputation of one or more individuals allows many more to continue their scandalous ways, if perhaps with minimal safeguards and protocols that are meant to ensure that the terrible excesses of the past will not occur again."[19] He was on to something.

Years later we would learn that Deep Throat, the mysterious anonymous source who leaked Watergate tips to the *Washington Post* reporter Bob Woodward, was FBI Deputy Director Mark Felt, whom a jury would later find guilty of conspiring to violate Americans' constitutional rights—one of just two Bureau officials to be convicted for COINTELPRO crimes. Felt's motive in talking to Woodward was not to stop wrongdoing in high places but to become director of the FBI. (He hoped that Nixon, angry to see so many leaks from the Bureau's investigation, would fire FBI chief Patrick Gray and hire Felt for the job instead.)[20] Put that together with Hoover's self-interested motives for blocking the Huston Plan, and it's not hard to see the convulsions of the 1970s as the sparks set off when one set of high-ranking criminals clashes with another.

In establishment circles, though, the Chomsky/Lasky line wasn't welcome. Enemy Above stories were becoming disreputable again, particularly when they indicted more than one political party. Important media figures began to fret that the press had taken their probes too far. The executive branch went on the offensive, charging investigators with hamstringing the nation's defenders, with endangering the lives of American agents abroad, even with McCarthyism.[21] (The key component of McCarthyism was not, apparently, Joseph McCarthy's willingness to ruin people's careers because of their opinions or age-old associations. It was the fact that he was investigating the State Department.)[22] Congress's interest in examining intelligence agencies had largely played itself out by the dawn of Jimmy Carter's presidency, and the chief exception—the House Select Committee on Assassinations, which looked into the deaths of John F. Kennedy and Martin Luther King—would peter out without much effect.

The assassinations committee did raise some eyebrows by concluding, on the basis of acoustic evidence, that a second gunman had fired a shot at President Kennedy in 1963 and that this established "the probability that a conspiracy did exist that day."[23] Later analysis of the same evidence would come to a different conclusion, but even before then the finding didn't do much to change establishment opinion on the Kennedy killing. One syndicated columnist reacted to the report by writing that a second gunman "is not in itself evidence of conspiracy; it is simply evidence that another person, besides Oswald, may have wanted Kennedy dead."[24] The investigatory era was coming to an end.

But the era had left a mark. *The Washington Post* and *The New York Times* were getting warier about what they published, but alternative outlets—*Rolling Stone*, *Mother Jones*, *Inquiry*, a host of urban weeklies, even *Hustler* and *Penthouse*—kept up the skeptical coverage. The door was open for well-grounded investigative journalism. It was open for shakier theories as well.

There was a new wave of assassination books. One of the less plausible efforts, Michael Canfield and A. J. Weberman's *Coup d'État in America: The CIA and the Assassination of John F. Kennedy* (1975), claimed to contain photographic evidence that a group of tramps arrested in Dallas on the day JFK was shot included the future Watergate conspirators E. Howard Hunt and Frank Sturgis. The photos' resemblance to Hunt and Sturgis is, to put it kindly, fleeting. (Weberman, who had already attracted some notoriety as an obsessed fan of Bob Dylan, was a self-proclaimed "garbologist" who believed he could decode Dylan's life and lyrics by rooting through the trash outside the singer's home. So he was experienced at reading meaning into data.)

Then there was "A Skeleton Key to the Gemstone File," an elaborate conspiracy narrative that roped together drug smuggling, the Kennedy assassinations, hypnosis, the Mafia, the fate of Howard Hughes, and more. The document was periodically reprinted in the alternative press; it would later become an Internet mainstay.[25] It both inspired and attracted a lot of paranoia, as the freelance writer (and future FBI operative) Robert Eringer discovered when he called an outlet that had published it:

> The "reporter" who answered my call became almost hysterical at the mere mention of Gemstone. . . . What was I trying to do, get them all murdered? Was I crazy?

"What are you talking about?" I asked.

"They've killed six of us already!" he screamed.

"Who's They?"

"THEM!" he cried. "Don't you understand?!"

"Perhaps you would explain?"

"What? Over the phone? ARE YOU CRAZY??" he wailed. "THEY'RE LISTENING RIGHT NOW!!!"[26]

The anxiety that COINTELPRO had gone out of its way to encourage was now occurring on its own.

Dig deeper and you'd find people like Mae Brussell, a California mom whose friend Paul Krassner once described her as "plump and energetic, wearing a long peasant dress patchworked with philosophical tidbits, knitting sweaters for her children while she breathlessly described the architecture of an invisible government."[27] Brussell's interest in the death of John F. Kennedy had sprawled into an elaborate counterhistory of the postwar United States, one where surviving Nazis were deeply embedded in the national security state; where violent left-wing sects such as the Symbionese Liberation Army were government fronts created to discredit the Left; where America's invisible government had murdered the Kennedys, Malcolm X, Martin Luther King, Jimmy Hoffa, John Lennon, and even the *Chico and the Man* star Freddie Prinze, among others. ("Jimi Hendrix, Mama Cass Elliott, Steve Perron choking from their vomit?" she wrote in 1976. "I doubt it!!")[28] She hosted a weekly program that sometimes had a home on the radio and sometimes existed only in the form of cassettes mailed to subscribers. She inspired a small army of fans, dubbed Brussell Sprouts, who extended her work and offered each other research tips. (You should "talk to people, all the time," Brussell's protégé John Judge advised. "I was explaining Tom Pappas' role in securing Agnew's position in the '68 election, and his connection to heroin from Greece, to a hitchhiker who turned out to be a blood relation.")[29]

One subject that fascinated Brussell was mind control. Drawing on the MKULTRA revelations, she revived the *Manchurian Candidate* scenario of a brainwashed assassin, putting the CIA in the place of the Communists. At the same time, the counterculture had set off a boom in new and unfamiliar religious sects, which in turn had inspired a cult scare comparable to the fears that had seized many mainline Protestants during the Second Great Awakening. Brussell absorbed those anxieties, and then a tragedy in South America allowed her to combine them with her MKULTRA scenario.

In November 1978, a mass murder-suicide left 918 people dead in and near Jonestown, a religious colony in Guyana founded by Reverend Jim Jones of a church called the Peoples Temple. One of the dead was California Congressman Leo Ryan, who had flown to the community on a fact-finding mission after hearing from some of his constituents that family members were being held against their will.

The mainstream press had greeted the new religions of the era with deep suspicion; the mesmerizing prophet and his zombie followers became a media cliché. And the families of the people involved in the massacre were often eager to minimize their relatives' responsibility for what had happened. So it shouldn't be surprising that the *San Francisco Chronicle* would run a story, headlined "'Robot' Behavior of Ryan Murder Suspect," that sounds like something out of a body-snatching movie:

> [R]elatives said Larry [Layton], 32, acted as if he were in a "post-hypnotic trance" as he was drawn further into the Peoples Temple, which he joined in 1968. . . . "The thing I wonder about," said Tom Layton, 36-year-old brother of the suspected gunman, "is if the Peoples Temple ordered Larry to do whatever he's done. I wonder if the Peoples Temple is in any way going to support his defense in court, since he was a loyal servant following orders. . . ."
>
> "He was a robot," said father Laurence Layton, a flat distant timbre in his voice.[30]

Leaping on the story, Brussell offered her take on the Peoples Temple murders. Jonestown had existed, she concluded, so the secret government could "experiment on black people; mind control; electrodes; sexual deprivation; fear; mass suicides." Layton, "a robot in the hands of Jim Jones," had assassinated Ryan to keep the truth from coming out, and the mass slaughter that followed had been a part of the cover-up.[31]

Not every conspiracist shared Brussell's interest in brainwashing. In 1975, the JFK assassination theorist Mark Lane allegedly told her that he'd "never appear with you publicly. People know you're crazy. There's no evidence of mind control in the United States."[32] But Lane had a Jonestown connection of his own: He had been one of the Temple's attorneys, and he had argued shortly before the massacre that "American intelligence organizations" were making "a deliberate effort" to "destroy the Peoples Temple, to destroy Jim Jones, and to destroy Jonestown."[33] Brussell could now quote Lane's words of praise for the Guyana settlement ("It makes me almost weep to see such an incredible experience with such vast potential for the human spirit and soul of this country to be cruelly assaulted by our intelligence agents") as she painted her old rival as a part of the grand machine. "I'm very proud to say that I've hated his guts and tried to expose him for years," she told her audience.[34]

It shouldn't be surprising to see such speculations after COINTELPRO, CHAOS, and other measures fanned the Left's fears of the government. But that wasn't the only factor at work. Every subculture accumulates demons, and by the late 1970s the New Left and the counterculture had plenty of demons to contend with. If it is possible to discuss "the sixties" in reference to events that took place in 1978—and culturally speaking, I think it is—then the deaths at Jonestown, a colony that until its destruction had presented itself to the world as a multiracial socialist utopia, marked the end of the sixties, a moment even more deflating than the Charles Manson murders or the Rolling Stones' lethal concert at Altamont.

The massacre also came within a month of the assassinations of San Francisco's liberal mayor George Moscone and the city's first openly gay city supervisor, Harvey Milk. If there were ever a time when a spirit of doom hung over the California counterculture, this was it.

Brussell's grand conspiracy narrative found a way to link Jonestown to the San Francisco shootings, and it managed to work in the Symbionese Liberation Army, the Manson murders, the Zodiac killer, and the sixties assassinations too. As history, it was a jerry-rigged assemblage of facts, half facts, rumors, and guesses. But as a mythic translation of a jarring historical moment, it had a powerful pull. Brussell transformed a collection of free-floating anxieties into an external enemy with a name. She gave her listeners a way to talk about the meltdown in progress.

You couldn't cite someone like Mae Brussell in mainstream conversations, of course.[35] But you could cite Hollywood. And while she was working, a wave of movies offered a similarly sinister portrait of American elites—so many movies, in fact, that a new phrase eventually entered the critic's vocabulary: the "1970s conspiracy thriller."

The old Motion Picture Production Code, with its restrictions on filmmakers' freedoms, finally collapsed in the late 1960s.[36] A loose group of upstarts took advantage of the more open environment, ushering in the period known as the New Hollywood. The new moviemakers tended to be affiliated with the counterculture, and their films were filled with skeptical takes on established institutions.

Older writers and directors attempted in turn to imitate the young Turks' approach. And with Watergate, the level of skepticism that the public was willing to accept on-screen increased dramatically.

A few films of the sixties, such as Arthur Penn's *Mickey One* (1965) and John Frankenheimer's *Seconds* (1966), had anticipated the atmosphere of dread found in so many of their seventies successors, though both of those examples avoided the later pictures' corporate and governmental villains. Frankenheimer was already a well-established director of conspiracy movies at that point, having made a sharp adaptation of *The Manchurian Candidate* (1962) and the blander but more commercially successful *Seven Days in May* (1964). The latter is a dramatically flat picture that falls periodically into heavy-handed speechifying. But if it isn't a compelling piece of filmmaking, *Seven Days* is still interesting for its politics: It's a Brown Scare story about a right-wing military plot to oust America's elected government. The script was written by Rod "The Monsters Are Due on Maple Street" Serling, and Frankenheimer later reported that President Kennedy had been "most anxious" to see the movie made. JFK had done "everything he could to make our life easy," the director explained, including timing a trip to Hyannis Port so it would be easier for the crew to shoot a scene outside the White House.[37]

There were other precursors to the 1970s conspiracy genre. Filmmakers sometimes got away with disrespectful portraits of intelligence agencies or their stand-ins in movies that were satiric (*The President's Analyst*, 1967) or semisatiric (*The Manchurian Candidate*); or drew heavily on the conventions of the crime movie, where a certain cynicism about the police was often present (*North by Northwest*, 1959; *Mirage*, 1965); or were upmarket adaptations of the new breed of skeptical, world-weary espionage novels (*The Spy Who Came In from the Cold*, 1965). But the modal spy movie of the 1960s featured a Bond clone battling a cartoonish supervillain. The modal spy movie of the 1970s featured an amoral intelligence bureaucracy killing and manipulating sympathetic characters. Even a fairly straightforward entertainment such as Don Siegel's *Telefon* (1977), in which the hero tries to stop a rogue Russian from activating an old network of *Manchurian Candidate*–style assassins scattered around the United States, could give the tale a twist by having that hero work for the KGB rather than the CIA. By the end of the story both the Soviet and the American governments want the protagonist dead, each for similar—and similarly unattractive—reasons. The effect is to make both sides of the Cold War seem like one vast, callous machine.

If Frankenheimer was the preeminent conspiracy director of the sixties, then the king of conspiracy cinema in the seventies was Alan

J. Pakula. After dipping his toes into paranoid waters with *Klute* (1971), a police procedural that avoided overt politics but reveled in showing surveillance and corruption, the director gave us *The Parallax View* (1974). Fredric Jameson called *Parallax* the "greatest of all assassination films";[38] and if you won't go that far it's still hard not to think of it as the *model* assassination film: the first picture that comes to a movie buff's mind when the phrase "1970s conspiracy thriller" is spoken aloud.

Parallax opens with the assassination of a presidential candidate at the top of the Seattle Space Needle. We then learn that witnesses to the killing have been dying under mysterious circumstances. The hero, a reporter, initially refuses to believe that a conspiracy is afoot. But when his former girlfriend joins the ranks of the dead witnesses, he starts probing the story, eventually infiltrating an enigmatic organization called the Parallax Corporation. Parallax turns out to be in the business of producing assassins, and the infiltrator turns out to be in over his head: He thought he was preparing to expose a conspiracy, while in fact the conspiracy was setting him up as the patsy in yet another assassination. At the end of the film, both the reporter and the new target are dead, and a Warren Commission–style group has covered up the truth. "The committee wishes to emphasize that there is no evidence of any wider conspiracy—no evidence whatsoever," its spokesman announces. "It's our hope that this will put an end to the kind of irresponsible speculation conducted by the press in recent months."[39]

The third entry in Pakula's informal trilogy, *All the President's Men* (1976), dramatizes the *Washington Post*'s Watergate investigation. It has moments of tense paranoia, even playing with the idea that Bob Woodward might be killed for his efforts to expose the scandal. But it ends with Nixon expelled from office and the threat to the republic excised, a rather happier ending than we saw in *The Parallax View*. For all its gritty cynicism, *All the President's Men* embraces the story line in which Nixon was an aberration and the system ultimately worked: an Enemy Above story that reaffirms the social order.

But if conspiracy films sometimes ended up expressing comfortably mainstream ideas, the mainstream in turn was inching toward dissent. Look at Sydney Pollack's *Three Days of the Condor* (1975), that rare case where Hollywood sought a mass audience by making a movie more radical than its source material. Like the James Grady novel that inspired it, Pollack's picture pits an isolated CIA analyst against a cabal within the agency and then against the agency itself. But the screenplay—coauthored by Lorenzo Semple, Jr., who also had a hand in writing *Parallax*—takes the scenario further. As Olmsted put it, the film "eliminated the few sympathetic CIA characters who were in Grady's novel. It also changed the central conspiracy from drug smuggling to unauthorized covert action. . . . It was not mere greed that led them to murder but their fanatical, misguided patriotism."[40]

A decade earlier, the filmmakers behind the James Bond movies had been so wary of politics that they had routinely replaced the Bond novels' Soviet villains with an apolitical terror network called SPECTRE. Now a studio considered it commercially savvy to *add* controversial politics to a picture. And the studio's instincts were sound: *Condor* became the seventh most popular film of the year, taking in more than $41 million at the box office.

Executive Action (1973) was scripted by the formerly blacklisted writer Dalton Trumbo from a story coauthored by Mark Lane. It is essentially an assassination procedural: A group of wealthy and powerful men plot the murder of John F. Kennedy, and then their hirelings carry out the killing. The dark center of the movie's worldview comes through when a character explains the secret purpose of the Vietnam War: to bring down the Third World population, so black, brown, and yellow people don't "swarm out of their breeding grounds into Europe and North America." At the same time, the movie has a certain innocence as well. In one scene a reluctant conspirator asks, "There ought to be a better way of settling things like this. Have you researched [Kennedy's] private history?" The historically unlikely reply: "If we could find a way to discredit him, believe me, we would have done it by now."[41]

Such moments of naiveté were absent in *Winter Kills* (1979), a jet-black comedy based on a Richard Condon novel. That one was inspired by the Kennedy killing too, but instead of *Executive Action*'s flat earnestness it offered a wild ride through virtually every conceivable perp in a JFK conspiracy: mobsters, intelligence agencies, anti-Castro Cubans, even Hollywood itself. The mastermind behind the murder turns out to be the president's own father.

Michael Winner's *Scorpio* (1973) opens with the CIA killing an American ally and framing the local opposition for the deed. ("It's not his death that's important," an assassin explains. "It's who appeared to have killed him that counts.")[42] Clint Eastwood's tongue-in-cheek *The Eiger Sanction* (1975) features a murder-happy secret agency run by a vampiric ex-Nazi. Other films followed the example of *Mickey One* and *Seconds*, soaking themselves in paranoia without overtly inserting a secret government into the story. In Francis Ford Coppola's *The Conversation* (1974), Gene Hackman plays a surveillance expert racked with guilt about the possible consequences of one of his assignments. In Arthur Penn's *Night Moves* (1975), Hackman plays a private eye pursuing a mystery that never quite resolves itself. In both pictures he's a lonely loser being manipulated by forces he doesn't understand.

Hackman was a lonely loser in 1977's *The Domino Principle* too, but this time the character has been dropped into a *Parallax View* scenario: He's a convict quietly guided into becoming an assassin for a mysterious, apparently all-powerful cabal. *The Parallax View* ends on a downbeat note, but it still contains the possibility of reform: It shows an America that's been subverted by an identifiable set of villains, one whose virtue could be restored if those criminals were somehow removed. That glimmer of hope is absent here. The film's fatalist worldview is set up in a monologue heard at the beginning of the movie while we watch a disturbing, jaggedly edited montage:

> Do you believe you decided to come to this theater today? That it was your own idea, of your own free will?

> Whether we know it or not, we're all manipulated. It's becoming almost impossible to think or even act for ourselves anymore. We're manipulated. Programmed. Brainwashed. Right from the start. Right from the day we're born. By family, by press, by radio, by television. And more and more we know less and less of who They are.
>
> Who could They be? Is it the boss we work for? Who tells *him* what to do? Is it the government? Whoever's in power, it seems just the same. So who's behind Them?
>
> It's reached the point when They could take an ordinary man and so manipulate him that They could get him to kill the most important man in the world.[43]

Yet this movie wasn't made by a Penn or a Coppola. It was directed by Stanley Kramer, an established filmmaker known for his earnest, preachy message movies promoting liberal reforms. There's no hope of any reform in *The Domino Principle*; the corruption it depicts is all-encompassing and inescapable. Even after Hackman's character kills two of the conspirators at the end of the story, the film's final shot before the credits roll shows the rifle of another assassin, perched above the protagonist and prepared to dispatch him. It's telling that we never explicitly learn the identity of the man Hackman is supposed to murder, though it is strongly suggested that he's the president. Like the gunman ordered to kill him, he's just another interchangeable and disposable cog in the machine.

The movie is unsatisfying in several ways. Hackman is wonderful in his part, and several sequences have an engagingly unsettling quality, but the film has one of those scripts where smart people suddenly do stupid things because the plot requires it, and it includes more than one heavy-handed conversation in which characters articulate themes that didn't really need to be stated aloud. It was not a critical or commercial success: Reviewers wrote it off as a *Parallax View* knockoff, and audiences stayed away. But in its clumsy, derivative manner, *The Domino Principle* demonstrated how pessimistic and paranoid a view of American politics you could get from even the most mainstream popular entertainers.

The suspicious spirit surfaced in other genres too, from science fiction (1977's *Capricorn One*, in which NASA fakes the moon shot) to comedy (1978's *Foul Play*, in which a librarian discovers a plot to assassinate the pope) to detective fiction (1979's *Murder by Decree*, a Canadian import in which Sherlock Holmes uncovers a Masonic conspiracy behind the Jack the Ripper murders). *Westworld* (1973) manages simultaneously to be a conspiracy thriller, a science fiction film, and a western. The 1979 satire *Being There* isn't a "conspiracy movie" in the ordinary sense of the term, but it does casually include a scene in which powerful men select the next president while standing under a Masonic emblem. Another satire, *Network* (1976), ends with group of TV executives organizing the assassination of one of their stars—"the first known instance," the narrator informs us, "of a man who was killed because he had lousy ratings."[44] The seventies also saw a renaissance of the horror film, a genre that deals with the demonic whether or not the story includes a conspiracy. Even Steven Spielberg's *Jaws* (1975), a popcorn movie about a shark, turns on a small-town mayor's attempts to cover up a threat to public safety.[45]

The body-snatchers subgenre had something of comeback, too. An inspired remake of *Invasion of the Body Snatchers* appeared in 1978, with the old anxieties about the anthill society replaced by anxieties about cults and seventies narcissism. And feminists got their own version of the tale with Ira Levin's 1972 novel *The Stepford Wives* and the film it inspired three years later. The villains in Levin's thriller didn't come from outer space. They came from the other side of the bed.

The book opens as Joanna Eberhart and her family move to the apparently idyllic suburb of Stepford, Connecticut, where it soon becomes clear that something is wrong with the town's women. "That's what they *all* were, all the Stepford wives," Eberhart tells herself: "actresses in commercials, pleased with detergents and floor wax, with cleansers, shampoos, and deodorants. Pretty actresses, big in the bosom but small in the talent, playing suburban housewives unconvincingly, too nicey-nice to be real."[46] The women's own husbands, we learn, have conspired to kill off their flesh-and-blood wives and put busty, servile androids in their place. The substitute spouses are uninterested in anything but cleaning their homes, raising their children, and sexually pleasing their men.

There are echoes here not just of *Body Snatchers* but of *Riders of the Purple Sage*. But in Ira Levin's Connecticut, unlike Zane Grey's Utah, there is no escape from the totalitarian enclave. Jane Withersteen gets away from the suffocating Mormon patriarchy. Joanna Eberhart succumbs to the suffocating suburban patriarchy. She too is finally replaced by a robot programmed to enact the 1950s suburban ideal.

Or rather, a satiric spin on that suburban ideal, one that altered the original in an important way. The stereotypical woman in a postwar suburb was a joiner: When she wasn't doing housework or tending to the children, she'd be involved in the PTA, the Cub Scouts, or a charity. But the Stepford wives don't have social lives. The men meet in a lodge called the Men's Association, giving a vaguely Masonic cast to the conspiracy. The women don't meet anywhere. There *used* to be a Women's Club, and it could attract a crowd of fifty to see the feminist icon Betty Friedan give a speech. That ended after the Men's Association imposed the new order. The only organized women's activities in Stepford involve ladies too old to have been replaced.

Friedan's cameo is a tip-off to Levin's intentions. In *The Feminine Mystique*, a best-selling book published in 1963, Friedan warned that "a new breed of women" was coming to the suburbs. "Like the empty plains of Kansas that tempted the restless immigrant," she argued, "the suburbs in their very newness and lack of structured service, offered, at least at first, a limitless challenge to the energy of educated American women." But once those pioneers helped establish the new communities, subsequent settlers "were perfectly willing to accept the suburban community as they found it (their only problem was 'how to fit in'); they were perfectly willing to fill their days with the trivia of housewifery." Men began to fill the most important volunteer jobs, and housework expanded "to fill the time available."[47]

If you bred *Body Snatchers* with *The Feminine Mystique*, Levin's novel would be the result. Except that it appeared in 1972, not 1963, arriving at a time when Friedan's vision of the suburban future had been averted. There was a much more vibrant women's movement in the seventies, and there was much more visible resentment of that movement as well. In effect, Levin took an allegory for Friedan's critique of the postwar suburb and overlaid it with a critique of the antifeminist backlash.

The story struck a chord: The book was a best seller, and the movie did well at the box office.[48] Not everyone enjoyed it, though. Friedan stormed out of a screening, denouncing the film as a "rip-off of the women's movement."[49] Someone had taken her ideas, she fretted, and replaced them with an ersatz Hollywood confection, a superficially similar crowd-pleasing substitute. Call it the invasion of the feminism snatchers.

Television in the 1970s was more vulnerable to regulation and to ad boycotts than the film industry was, and thus it was less prone to airing stories with radical themes. But the change in what it was possible to see on the small screen was even more pronounced than the change in what it was possible to see in a theater.

The national security state wasn't a frequent subject in the sitcoms of the sixties, and when it did appear it was depicted as benign. Consider its cameo on *My Three Sons*, a long-running comedy starring Fred MacMurray as Steve Douglas, an aeronautical engineer raising a trio of kids after his wife's death. In a 1963 episode titled "Top Secret," Douglas is working at home on a classified project. To keep everything secure, the house is put under surveillance.

"It's sure a switch," says one of the watchers, "from public enemies, spies, subversives, saboteurs, kidnappers—to this!"[50] A colleague commiserates: "In all my months of training, they never mentioned tailing a ten-year-old kid." But their boss won't hear it: "We'll handle this job as though the Douglas family was out to blow up New York City. Every word, every move, every meaningful silence—that's our assignment, from Top Level Pentagon." An apparatus built to combat external and internal threats will be used instead on an ordinary American family, for everyone's good.

For the rest of the episode, the feds tap the Douglases' phone, yielding nothing but the installments of a teenager's halting love life. They file dreary reports on the family's movements. ("7 P.M.: Look through window and observe Chip Douglas watch friend Ernie feed white rat.") Steve Douglas himself engages in a little disinformation to mislead the rest of his household about what's going on. At the end, MacMurray's character breaks the fourth wall and addresses the audience directly:

> You know, this security thing was a little tough on my family for a while, but, well, you can see that it was necessary. Of course, now that the project is completed I can tell you what it was all about. You see, what I was really working on was a type of missile—

And then the words TOP SECRET appear over MacMurray's face and his next several sentences are scrambled. The security system that hovered over the Douglases turns out to be in our homes too, intercepting information before it can be heard on our televisions. It is difficult to describe this scene without it sounding like a deeply creepy moment, but the show presents it as perfectly benign. There's even a laugh track.

Just thirteen years later, *Good Times*, a Norman Lear sitcom about a black couple raising three kids in the ghetto, aired an installment called "The Investigation." Like "Top Secret," "The Investigation" is about an ordinary American family falling under federal surveillance, but this episode takes a rather different approach to the subject. One of the children, Michael Evans, attracts the FBI's attention when he writes to the Cuban government. Michael has militant tendencies, but his intentions here are patriotic: The letter was a part of a school project for the bicentennial. "I thought I'd compare the American Revolution with the Cuban Revolution," he says. "They're a dictatorship and we're a democracy—except for a couple wards here in Chicago."[51]

Michael's brother, J.J., blames the correspondence for the fact that he's just lost his job delivering chicken. His mother, Florida, usually the voice of reason, tells him, "I think we're letting our imaginations run away with us." J.J.'s role on the show is to play the fool, and ordinarily the audience would be expected to adopt the mother's point of view. But then J.J.'s father, James, Sr., walks through the door and announces that he's lost *his* job too. A frightened neighbor drops by with a piece of news: The FBI just interrogated her about the Evanses. J.J. starts to worry that the apartment has been bugged, and after he launches a laughable, over-the-top hunt for wiretaps, his parents and sister have a more serious moment, speaking in hushed tones:

> FLORIDA: You think it's possible?
>
> JAMES, SR.: Sure, it's possible. They've done it before.
>
> THELMA: Yeah—to a lot of people.

Then Federal Agent Lloyd knocks on the door. It's an "unofficial visit," he tells them, not looking very happy. The family starts to explain that the Havana letter was nothing but a homework project, but Lloyd cuts them off. "I know," he says. The studio audience reacts with a horrified noise.

"I'm sorry," Lloyd continues, "but we were asked to find out who was receiving Cuban propaganda in the mail. Just routine." The father chews out the agent, who responds with a defensive apology: "We had to ask questions. We never thought your boss would react this way." James is relentless: "Well, how the hell do you expect him to react, man? The FBI comes nosing around asking him questions, he figures there's gonna be trouble, he's got enough already, so goodbye James Evans."

The FBI persuades James's employer to rehire him, but even that happy resolution is undercut. "Well, I got my job back, that's good," the father says. "But how about all them people who ain't so lucky, huh? How about them?" Someone in the audience yells "Right on!" and there's a big burst of applause.

By the end of the show we've learned that the FBI talked only to James's boss, not to J.J.'s—the son lost his job on the merits. But that isn't an exculpation; that's just J.J. providing comic relief while his dad bears the burden of the drama. After the G-man leaves, James puts his arm around his wife and says, "You know something, Florida? I still got the feeling that somewhere, someplace, my name is still in somebody's file." Then he looks directly at the camera, like Fred MacMurray at the end of "Top Secret." This time there's no laugh track.

In 1975, a different TV broadcast was mentioned in a curious *New York Times* article by Clifton Daniel. After listing several CIA operations that had been exposed, Daniel observed that the "agency has even been suspected of assassinations. Last night NBC television showed a 1973 fiction movie, 'Scorpio,' in which six murders are carried out by C.I.A. agents or hired gunmen."[52] Daniel didn't cite any other sources for those suspicions—just a movie that had been on TV. Talk about thin sourcing.

But there's a backstory here. Daniel and other high-ranking *Times* staffers had recently attended a private luncheon with President Gerald Ford. Intent on explaining the need for limits on the intelligence investigations, Ford had declared that the CIA had secrets that it *couldn't* reveal. Stuff that would "ruin the U.S. image around the world."

"Like what?" asked one of the reporters.

"Like assassinations," replied Ford. Realizing what he had let slip, he immediately added, "That's off the record!"[53]

The paper decided to follow Ford's wishes and suppress his gaffe, but some of the people present still wanted to write about what they'd heard. So Daniel used *Scorpio* to allude to a fact that he knew but could not say aloud.

Revelations in the real world had given popular culture a darker, more skeptical tone. Now pop-culture paranoia was expanding Americans' framework for discussing real-world events. Like Mae Brussell's Jonestown fantasy, the conspiracy thrillers weren't just fiction. They were myth.

8

THE LEGEND OF JOHN TODD

. . . no weird story can truly produce terror unless it is devised with all the care & verisimilitude of an actual *hoax*.

—H. P. Lovecraft[1]

On a Sunday night in 1978, a storyteller came to the Open Door Church in Chambersburg, Pennsylvania. Four hundred or five hundred people were there to hear him. It was a respectable turnout, though not an overflowing one; the auditorium had space for more than a thousand people.

Some of the men and women in the room's uncushioned pews may have had a particular interest in the speaker, an intense young visitor from California named John Todd. But mostly this was the standard Sunday crowd, and they probably didn't think they'd hear anything peculiar. Guests were always stopping in to talk about how they'd been saved. The churchgoers might have heard that this fellow had a more unusual background than the others—that before he became a Christian, he'd been a witch. But the man on the stage soon announced that he had been much, much more than that.

"Many things I say are strange to Christians," Todd warned. "Most of you grew up in Christian homes, or even if you were in the world you were not very close to what I was into."[2] But he knew about the wickedness that was out there, and he had come to tell them about it. At that very moment, he said, the witches were meeting in Washington, D.C. "It was in all the front pages of the newspapers down there," he announced. "Christians across the United States say, 'You don't really expect us to believe that witches are that organized.' No, they've just got senators and congressmen and top witches down there all in one convention. They are not that organized, not at all!"

Then he told the story of his life.

According to Todd, he was a scion of the Collins bloodline, the family that had brought witchcraft to America. He had started studying for the witches' priesthood at age thirteen, and when he was fourteen he had been initiated into the outer court of a coven in Columbus, Ohio. ("When the service is over," he added, "I will be glad to talk with any Mason present, and I will compare my initiation to witchcraft, word for word, action for action, with yours. They are identical.") At eighteen he had become a high priest. That had made him exempt from the draft, but he had enlisted anyway because "it was important to get witchcraft started at the different military bases." Then he had a drunken shoot-out with an officer in Germany, right in the middle of downtown Stuttgart. The officer had died, and Todd had expected to spend the rest of his life behind bars.

Instead, one day "my cell door opened. And there stood a senator, a U.S. congressman, a couple of generals, and an honorable discharge." His court-martial records had been destroyed, his file had been classified top secret, and he still had his rank and grade. When Todd got home to Ohio, he was handed an envelope containing $2,000 and a first-class ticket to New York. There he learned that witchcraft wasn't just another religion. It was the religion of a powerful political organization called the Illuminati.

The chiefs of the Illuminati were the Rothschilds, the infamous banking dynasty. Beneath them in the hierarchy was the Council of 13, the Rothschilds' private priesthood; below them was the Council of 33, consisting of the world's most powerful Masons; and below them was the Council of 500, drawn from the wealthiest circles of the ultrarich—Rockefellers, Kennedys, Du Ponts. The Illuminati controlled Standard Oil and Shell Oil, Chase Manhattan and the Bank of America, Sears and Safeway. They controlled the National Council of Churches and the Satanic Brotherhood of America, the Federal Reserve and the American Civil Liberties Union, the Knights of Columbus and the Junior Chamber of Commerce, the John Birch Society and the Communist Party. In the United States, the Illuminati called themselves the Council on Foreign Relations.

Todd was initiated into the Council of 13 and was given a thirteen-state area to run from a base in San Antonio. He was also put in charge of Zodiac Productions, which he told the crowd was the country's biggest booking agency for rock bands. There he learned the secrets of the music industry. (Elton John, for instance, "has never written a song that was not written in witch language.") And he was shown an eight-year plan for the Illuminati to take over the remainder of the world, a scheme scheduled to conclude in December 1980.

"About twelve years ago," Todd explained to the crowd, "Philippe Rothschild ordered one of his mistresses to write an eleven-hundred-page book that would describe to all witches how they would take control of the world through the Illuminati. It was called *Atlas Shrugged*. One of the things in it is happening on the front pages of the newspapers across the United States right now. In fact, it spent a third of the book describing how they would raise the oil prices and later destroy the oil fields and then they would also completely shut down the coal. . . . Their sole purpose is to bankrupt their own companies until they destroy the currency of the entire world and still be so financially strong that they would withstand it."

Meanwhile, Charles Manson ("an old buddy of mine") was assembling an Illuminist army in America's prisons. "They have been promised weapons," Todd exclaimed. "Military weapons!" Congress was preparing a bill to confiscate Americans' guns, leaving us at the mercy of Manson's army. "Manson," Todd warned, "will either be released next year or the following year, they have not decided yet." Then he and his followers would sweep across the country, butchering a million people and giving the government a rationale for imposing martial law.

Soon the Illuminati would cut off all the electricity on the east coast. "*Atlas Shrugged* ended with this: 'When the lights of New York City go out for the last time, we will have the world,'" Todd said. "Now, that meant this: They are going, towards the end, to cut the cities off completely."

At the peak of the chaos, a savior would present himself, a man the Illuminati believed to be the son of Lucifer, "a person so fantastically powered that he could convince people that he was their only salvation." And then their control would be complete.

Todd walked away from all that. In 1972, when he was near the top of the grand conspiracy, he saw the evangelical exploitation movie *The Cross and the Switchblade.* As he left the theater in a daze, someone handed him a tract. It was "Bewitched," a minicomic published by the Christian cartoonist Jack T. Chick. Todd stumbled into the Greengate Club, an old burlesque joint that had turned itself into a Baptist church. There he got saved, and now he was out to tell the world about the conspiracy.

It was risky. There was a price on Todd's head: "They start at ten-thousand-dollar bounties and work up to several hundred thousand." That's one reason why witches are afraid to exit the occult, he explained. Just a few years earlier, an actress in California had tried to leave the craft. The Illuminati had cut her throat and left her hanging by a foot, a tarot-card tableau that told every witch who heard the news that she had died for betraying the faith. The dead woman's name was Sharon Tate.

So Todd and his allies were starting a retreat, a place in the wilderness where witches who came to Christ could live without fear of assassination. "We need fifty thousand dollars," he told the congregation, "and in the month and a half since we have been trying to raise the money my pastor has received twenty five dollars."

The Chambersburg congregation took up a collection for the cause, and Todd walked away with about $1,000.[3]

Dino Pedrone, the pastor at the Open Door Church when Todd came to speak, says there was a fair amount of buzz about Todd in the weeks after his testimony. "We've had many great preachers in our pulpit," he later told *Christianity Today*, "but there was more talk around town after he left than with any other preacher we've had."[4] That doesn't mean the talk was all positive: By Pedrone's recollection, Todd inspired more skepticism than belief. "This guy is giving his testimony, you want to believe what he's saying," he recently remembered. "But I think as time wore on, it just didn't add up."[5]

Still, Todd did attract believers. You don't raise $1,000 from an audience without convincing at least some of the people in the pews that you're telling the truth. And he wasn't convincing them just in Chambersburg; he was speaking at some of the biggest churches on the East Coast, and thousands of his tapes were circulating. "I just remember my dad coming home from a church event at which one or more of Todd's tapes was played and describing in great detail, and with a straight face, Todd's account of an Illuminati/Rothschild hierarchy culminating in Satan," recalled Gary Chartier, a legal scholar at La Sierra University who was raised in an Adventist household in Corona, California. Chartier's father wasn't an ill-educated fool. He had an MD and an MBA, and he passed his CPA exam on the first try: an intelligent professional who found Todd persuasive.[6]

Put yourself in the shoes of a churchgoer in Chambersburg or Corona looking for more information about Todd and his tales.

Maybe you'd pick up one of the comic books that Jack Chick made with Todd's input, or maybe you'd track down some of his tapes.

If you did, you might have heard him saying more about *Atlas Shrugged*. "It was written by a woman named Ayn Rand," he told one audience. "She was already a well-known writer, and her books sell nationwide—mostly people who read her are Communists. . . . They are extremely mad because just this year alone, they sold several million of them—mostly to Christians. And they don't like that. In fact they've tried to stop printing it but people don't want to stop printing it, they're making so much money." The book included about five pages' worth of sex scenes, he cautioned, but "you can tear them out and throw them away. . . . They're stuck in there on purpose to stop Christians from reading the book."[7] The character John Galt was a stand-in for Philippe Rothschild, Todd added, and Galt's retreat in the Colorado mountains was, when decoded by Todd, the Bermuda Triangle.

You might have heard Todd talking about a book that would be harder to acquire: the "Necromonicon," which he called "the original occult bible." Only three copies existed, he said—one in Glasgow, one in London, one in St. Petersburg Cathedral in the USSR—but he had seen it, and he knew it had been a direct inspiration for both the witches' Book of Shadows and the Mormons' Book of Mormon.

You might have heard Todd explain the occult symbols the Illuminati use to mark the companies they control. "They have Sunoco with an arrow through it because that's the sign of casting a spell, the arrow," he explained. "They use 76 because May 1, 1776, is their birth date of the Illuminati. . . . The winged horse in Marathon, Pegasus, is the messenger of the gods. . . . The eightfold path of what a witch must master to be a powerful witch—that's the symbol of Denny's."

You might have heard Todd talking about music. "Rock music didn't come out with Elvis Presley," he preached. "It's thousands of years old. If you take it away, witches can't do witchcraft."[8] When he was in the rock business, "a witch would write the words and we'd dig up an old Druid manuscript containing a melody for the song."[9]

Christian rock wasn't any different: The lyrics might seem better, but it wasn't the lyrics that gave the songs their demonic power. "It's the music. The power's in the music. . . . They don't produce rock music to make money. They don't *need* that money. They own everything anyway! They do it to put demonic influence in your life. The music is a spell."[10] Todd claimed that he had personally delivered a $4 million check to Pastor Chuck Smith of Maranatha Music to infiltrate the churches with "Christian" rock.

Smith espoused charismatic Christianity, an interdenominational movement that stressed the role of the Holy Spirit in believers' lives. And the charismatic churches, Todd preached, were controlled by the Illuminati, though most rank-and-file charismatics didn't realize it. Ralph Wilkerson, the pastor of the Melodyland Christian Center in Anaheim, California, ran "one of the largest independent charismatic Bible schools and universities in the country. And they gave that man so much. Everything that is there, the Illuminati bought and built for him."

You might have heard Todd talking about politics. Every president since Woodrow Wilson had been a member of the Illuminati, he claimed.[11] The conspirators had used dirty tricks to defeat Ronald Reagan's insurgency against Ford in the 1976 primaries, he added: "We have talked with Reagan's son and other people, and they have told us about the violent threats, bribes, death threats, assassinations, and everything that never reached the news media, that went on during the nomination thing for the Republican Party."[12] Having beaten Reagan, Todd explained, Ford had the role of throwing the election to the Antichrist, Jimmy Carter.

You might have heard Todd's survival tips for the coming hard times: how to stockpile food, where to find shelter, what weapons to have on hand. ("The Illuminati has decided if they can't get your guns, they'll make them so bad that they'll blow up in your face. And they've recently bought both Smith & Wesson and Winchester.")[13] You might have run across a publication put together by Reverend Tom Berry, the pastor of a Baptist church in Elkton, Maryland, and the organizer behind Todd's tour through Chambersburg and other eastern cities. It was called "The Christian During Riot and After Revolution," and it was filled with Todd's survivalist advice.

Maybe, after all that, you would have taken Todd's stories to heart and started preparing for the bloodbath to come.

Alternatively, you might have decided he was full of crap.

It certainly wouldn't take much digging to refute his most egregious claims. The Necronomicon, for example—not "Necromonicon," as Todd kept mispronouncing it—was a fictional book invented by H. P. Lovecraft, who referred to it in several stories and encouraged other writers to do the same. ("I think it is rather good fun to have this artificial mythology given an air of verisimilitude by wide citation," he told his fellow pulp writer Robert E. Howard.)[14] Granted, there were Lovecraft cultists who were convinced the book actually existed, and by the time Todd came to Chambersburg more than one volume claiming to be the Necronomicon had been published. But that hardly excuses Todd's claim to have had firsthand contact with the original tome. Clearly he had picked up the idea of the book from a pop-culture source—probably the Lovecraft-inspired 1970 film *The Dunwich Horror*, which Todd described as "one of the strongest movies, truthful, about witchcraft and their beliefs that ever existed."[15]

Similarly, it didn't require a lot of investigation to learn that Sharon Tate's body had not been left in the position Todd described. Or that Ayn Rand was a laissez-faire capitalist, not a Communist—and an atheist, not a witch. (When Rand appeared on Phil Donahue's talk show in 1979, a Toddian in the audience asked, "In your book *Atlas Shrugged*, isn't it true that you gave a blueprint for the world takeover by the Illuminati?" The visibly puzzled Rand replied, "By whom?")[16] You might start to suspect that Todd's claims about the "Collins bloodline" owed less to real history than they did to the TV show *Dark Shadows*. And with time, you'd be able to read journalistic accounts that debunked many of the claims Todd made about his life.

The most important of these were an article by Edward Plowman, printed in the February 2, 1979, edition of *Christianity Today*, and a book by the evangelical writers Darryl Hicks and David Lewis, published later that year. Hicks and Lewis's book, called *The Todd Phenomenon*, identified a pattern that Todd seemed to follow in each place where he settled from 1972 to 1979:

1. Attempt to set up a coffeehouse—teen ministry.
2. Attempt to set up a rehabilitation ministry especially for drugs and the occult.
3. Set up some type of commune, usually thinly disguised as a rehabilitation ministry, or Christian retreat from something or from someone.
4. Have sex with as many seductees (young Christians or otherwise) as possible, all heterosexual according to available reports, but little discrimination as to age.
5. Always target on a select group of "bad guys" in an attempt to alienate "them" from "us."
6. Refuse to submit to any type of authority except when it will expedite one's own purpose.
7. Always manage "murder attempts" and "death threats" on his life, so that the "retreat" idea will be more feasible (and especially more supported by sympathetic followers).
8. Constantly seek promotion using "name dropping," allegations, Biblical knowledge, and amazing ability and command to piece them together with current event information.
9. When the fact/fantasy walls begin caving in . . . seek sympathy from the most ardent followers by using the "What's the use, I might as well go back into the occult, nobody cares anyway, especially Christians" routine.
10. When all else fails—SPLIT![17]

The book included statements from Smith, Wilkerson, and other figures denying the charges that Todd had leveled against them. Like the *Christianity Today* piece, it demonstrated that Todd's tale of a secret court-martial in Germany was extremely unlikely. And like the *Christianity Today* piece, it showed that Todd's religious history was more complicated than he had claimed.

Todd, it turned out, had entered and exited the Christian world several times both before and after his burlesque-house salvation in 1972. After that particular conversion, he had hooked up with a Christian coffeehouse affiliated with the hippieish Jesus Movement. (It was also oriented toward charismatic Christianity, which at that point Todd was not yet denouncing as an arm of the Illuminati.) By the end of 1973, Plowman reported, Pastor Ken Long "began getting reports that Todd was trying to seduce teenage girls at the coffeehouse. (Two later confessed that they had sexual relations with him.) Four girls revealed that Todd wanted them to form a witches' coven and that he told them that he was still in witchcraft. Long later removed Todd from the coffeehouse ministry."[18]

Todd's first taste of fame came when he appeared on *The Gap*, a Christian TV show in Phoenix. There, Plowman wrote, Todd

> claimed that the Illuminati were financing some fundamentalist churches, that he had been the Kennedy family's personal warlock ("John F. Kennedy was not really killed; I just came back from a visit with him on his yacht"), and that he had witnessed the stabbing of a girl by Senator George McGovern in an act of sacrifice.
>
> More than $25,000 was pledged during the telethon and management offered to employ Todd—who was then, reportedly, packing a .38 snub-nosed revolver. He eventually declined. Doug Clark heard of Todd and invited him to appear on his "Amazing Prophecies" show. Overnight Todd became a hit in charismatic circles in southern California, and he and [his then wife] Sharon moved to Santa Ana.
>
> Soon the Todds were hosting dozens of young people at a weekly Bible study in their home. A few young people were converted, said Sharon, but there were distressing things, too. She said that Todd was blending elements of witchcraft with his Christian teaching and seducing some of the girls, several of whom confided in lead-

> ers at Melodyland Christian Center. In an ugly confrontation with Melodyland church leaders around Christmas, 1973, Todd denied the charges and stormed out.[19]

Yes, that's the same Melodyland center that Todd would later denounce as "bought and built" by the Illuminati. It's not hard to imagine what might have motivated that charge.

The next year Todd moved to Dayton, Ohio, where he ran an occult bookstore and conducted classes in witchcraft. Todd's version of the craft turned out to involve a lot of sex rites. When a sixteen-year-old student informed police that Todd had forced her into oral sex, he was sentenced to six months' imprisonment. (He was released after two.) He called on the pagan community for support, and Gavin Frost of the Church and School of Wicca and Isaac Bonewits of the Aquarian Anti-Defamation League soon arrived in Dayton to investigate Todd's claims that he was being persecuted for his beliefs. Frost was so disturbed by what he found that he asked his church to revoke the charter it had granted to Todd's Watchers Church of Wicca. Bonewits warned that "Todd may be using his own peculiar version of the religion of Witchcraft as cover for illegal, immoral and/or infiltrative purposes" and recommended that "as many different Federal, State and Local law enforcement agencies as possible" should investigate him.[20] Frost and Bonewits began to form a conspiracy theory of their own: According to an FBI report, the two pagans told the police that they suspected neo-Nazis had "planted Todd in their midst to disrupt their efforts."[21]

Bonewits also predicted that Todd would soon be firing off "wild accusations" against Frost and himself.[22] Sure enough, Todd soon returned to the Christian circuit with an even more elaborate story to tell, one where the two pagans had offered to make a deal with him if he would stop telling the truth about the Illuminati. He had refused, he said, so they had colluded with the police against him.

By 1978, Todd's lectures had made him more famous than ever before. Then the exposés arrived and his reputation came crashing down. The John Birch Society published a paper condemning Todd. The *Journal Champion*, published by Jerry Falwell's Thomas Road Baptist Church, editorialized that Todd's message was "an unscriptural and deceitful attempt to rob the church of Jesus Christ of its vibrant joy, its aggressive soul-winning, and its trust in God."[23] The Christian Research Institute advised that Todd be "avoided and rejected by the body of Christ until such time as he does repent."[24] Ministers who had hosted Todd at their churches said that they wouldn't have him back. His only significant supporter remaining was Jack Chick.

But if you weren't going to accept Todd's lurid stories, you still might accept one or more of the strains of folklore that Todd drew on as he developed those tales. The people who attacked Todd didn't necessarily reject the concept of a grand conspiracy. Hicks and Lewis's book declares it "very possible that the Illuminati still exists."[25] The *Journal Champion* dismissed the idea that the Illuminati were still out there, but it did raise the possibility that Todd was "an under-cover witch."[26] By the mid-1980s, when Todd was largely forgotten, the idea of a vast Satanic conspiracy survived, taking hold in much of the media and seeping into some police departments.

Think of Todd as a distorted mirror, a surface that could absorb his audiences' fears and shine back a strange, fantastic story about them. Churches that distrusted modernity now had a tale that reinforced their worries about everything from pop culture to the occult to new forms of Christian worship. In a time of economic hardship, the narrative also indicted the oil companies and department stores. The seventies spirit of suspicion toward the government and corporate America affected Christian conservatives as well as secular liberals, and Todd's tales exploited that. With "all these investigations," a minister who had seen Todd speak told the Baltimore *Sun*, "there's very little credibility left in government. And so this guy comes along, and he puts together a package that, at first hearing, makes sense: Eureka, we've found it!"[27] Like Mae Brussell and John Smith Dye, Todd translated anxieties into myth.

It isn't clear to what extent Todd was a con man and to what extent he was a crazy man. His military records included a diagnosis of "emotional instability with pseudologia phantastica" and a comment that he "finds it difficult to tell reality from fantasy."[28] If his talks were compelling enough to convince people he was telling the truth, that might be because he had persuaded himself, some of the time if not all of the time, that the things he preached were true. Either way, his life was a long string of deception and exploitation, and it ultimately led to a prison cell.

But we're not quite ready for that part of the story yet. There are other issues to be explored first, starting with Todd's interest in the Illuminati. How did a half-forgotten bugaboo of the Federalist Party become the starring villain in the John Todd apocalypse show?

The most important figure for the transition is Nesta Webster, an early-twentieth-century British writer who had grown fascinated with secret societies and revolutionary movements. Picking up where John Robison and Augustin Barruel had left off, she argued that the Illuminati and related groups were responsible not merely for the French Revolution of 1789 but for all the revolutions to hit Europe since then. Webster's Illuminati were simultaneously Communist and capitalist, a braid of banks, Bolsheviks, Masons, occultists, Germans, and Jews.

Webster allowed that many Jews "have shown themselves fearless opponents both of Germany and Bolshevism."[29] In other words, her worldview had room for "good" Jews. But she was obsessed with her conspiracy's Jewish qualities, and she was prone to writing such lines as "German Atheism and Jewish antagonism to Christianity have combined to form the great anti-religious force that is making itself felt in the world today."[30] And although she stopped short of pronouncing *The Protocols of the Learned Elders of Zion* authentic, she insisted that the document had "never been refuted."[31]

One person impressed by Webster's arguments was Winston

Churchill. In 1920, he contrasted the Jews he admired with the evil "International Jews" of Webster's books:

> This movement among the Jews is not new. From the days of Spartacus-Weishaupt to those of Karl Marx, and down to Trotsky (Russia), Bela Kun (Hungary), Rosa Luxembourg [*sic*] (Germany), and Emma Goldman (United States), this world-wide conspiracy for the overthrow of civilisation and for the reconstitution of society on the basis of arrested development, of envious malevolence, and impossible equality, has been steadily growing. It played, as a modern writer, Mrs. Webster, has so ably shown, a definitely recognisable part in the tragedy of the French Revolution. It has been the mainspring of every subversive movement during the Nineteenth Century; and now at last this band of extraordinary personalities from the underworld of the great cities of Europe and America have gripped the Russian people by the hair of their heads and have become practically the undisputed masters of that enormous empire.[32]

After Webster, even anti-Illuminists who wanted to avoid anti-Semitism—or at least avoid the appearance of anti-Semitism—sometimes found ways to draw *The Protocols of the Learned Elders of Zion* into their theories. The Canadian conspiracist William Guy Carr drew liberally on the *Protocols* while insisting that the conspiracy had altered the document "in such a way that suspicion was turned away from the directors of the Illuminati"; the "Jews were picked to be the scape-goats."[33] (That didn't keep Carr from using the sort of loaded language you'd expect from an anti-Semite, as with his ruminations on "international Jewry"[34] or his description of the conspiracy as the "Synagogue of Satan.")[35]

Carr wasn't the only Illuminati hunter to follow in Webster's footsteps. I already mentioned that William Dudley Pelley included the Illuminati in the Silver Shirts' demonology. Eli A. Helmick, the inspector general of the U.S. Army from the end of World War I until his retirement in 1927, gave speeches drawing a direct line from Weishaupt to Lenin.[36] Edith Starr Miller, a.k.a. Lady Queenborough—an American transplanted to Europe—declared in her posthumously published 1933 book *Occult Theocrasy* that the Jews were behind the Bavarian Illuminati and that the Illuminati's plans were essentially the same as those of "Judeo-Masonic Russian Soviet Communism."[37] Gertrude Coogan of Chicago, whose populist monetary theories attracted a following during the Depression, wrote in 1935, "All of the theorics and practices advanced by the present-day Socialists are copied directly from the organization known as the Illuminati."[38] That same year the Kansas anti-Semite Gerald Winrod produced "Adam Weishaupt, a Human Devil," a booklet that drew heavily on Webster while arguing that the Illuminati were Jewish. There were less prominent anti-Illuminists too, churning out small-press books and pamphlets with titles such as *Red Shadows* and *Roosevelt and the Illuminati*. Many of the writers drew other secret societies into their theories as well, from the Rosicrucians to the Knights Templar. One student of the literature, the political scientist Michael Barkun, has called the resulting web "a kind of interlocking directorate of conspirators who operate through a network of secret societies."[39]

Some of the writers who followed Webster imagined the Illuminati as an almost all-encompassing force of evil. Carr, for example, believed that the order was behind everything from white-slavery rings to the drug trade to a boating mishap that had killed his dog. Other theorists were relatively restrained. G. Edward Griffin, a writer associated with the John Birch Society, was humble enough to say that we "don't know" whether Adam Weishaupt's secret society was directly linked to the later machinations of Communists and bankers, though he maintained that "we *do* know that it is not impossible, and certainly not absurd."[40]

Not every Bircher adopted Griffin's ambivalence. The group's founder, Robert Welch, was certain that the modern Master Conspiracy could be traced back to the Bavarian Illuminati. The organization was institutionally opposed, however, to the idea that the conspiracy was a Jewish plot.[41] The society's most popular conspiracy book—Gary Allen and Larry Abraham's *None Dare Call It Conspiracy* (1971)—declared that "it is unreasonable and immoral to blame all Jews for the crimes of the Rothschilds as it is to hold all Baptists accountable for the crimes of the Rockefellers."[42] It also included a blurb on the back cover from Barney Finkel, the president of an organization called the Jewish Right, declaring that "people of the Jewish faith have been the number one historical victims of the Communist Conspiracy." Rabbi Marvin S. Antelman went a step beyond that in *To Eliminate the Opiate* (1974), giving the Illuminati a starring role in "a conspiracy . . . to undermine Judaism."[43] (Jew-baiters did join the John Birch Society, but the group made an effort to keep them out. The most prominent anti-Semite in sixties Birch circles, Revilo Oliver, was expelled for his views, at which point he moved to a farther-right group called the Liberty Lobby.)

Anti-Illuminati messages weren't limited to the printed page. Griffin's comments about Weishaupt, for instance, appeared in *The Capitalist Conspiracy*, a filmstrip suitable for showing at a Birch Society meeting or similar venue. And in the late 1960s, an actor, director, screenwriter, and pro-blacklist activist named Myron Coureval Fagan recorded a series of LPs called *The Illuminati and the Council on Foreign Relations*. The records, which drew heavily on Carr's worldview, were produced by a young actor, nightclub entertainer, and music producer and promoter named Anthony J. Hilder, who a few years before had been recording surf rock records but had been drawn into politics by the Goldwater campaign and now was devoted to exposing evil cabals. (Hilder would soon be a target as well as a popularizer of conspiracy theories. He had been handing out literature at the Ambassador Hotel in Los Angeles when Robert Kennedy was assassinated there, and by his account he had stood at one point just a few feet from the shooter, Sirhan Sirhan. Since then, various conspiracists have attempted to implicate Hilder in the assassination.)[44]

Outside the populist Right, you were more likely to hear the

Illuminati invoked as a foolish fear that had foreshadowed anticommunism than as the hidden hand behind communism itself. When the leftist *New Masses* mentioned the secret society in 1940, it did so to mock the "lurid accounts" of the Federalists who had seen the Illuminati as a "dread Comintern"—and, by extension, to mock the opponents of the actual Comintern.[45] The Communist screenwriter John Howard Lawson struck the same note in 1947: "Today the old propaganda machine is again grounding out its lies. The imbecilities of the Illuminati campaign are repeated in our press and on the radio."[46] He meant the Illuminati campaign of the 1790s, not the anti-Illuminati voices of his day.

But within the populist Right, the Illuminati were becoming stock demons. By the time Todd surfaced in Phoenix in 1972, he could draw on any number of sources as he shaped his story. The Council of 13 and Council of 33 came from Carr's books, for example, and one of the comic books Todd made with Jack Chick cited Lady Queenborough. Hicks and Lewis report that Todd listened closely to the Fagan/Hilder records and that Todd's then wife, Sharon, researched the Illuminati at the local library. He also lifted details from *The Satan Seller* by Mike Warnke, a book and author we'll discuss shortly.

Even when Todd wasn't consciously borrowing material from earlier conspiracy theorists, his stories echoed the country's established conspiracy mythos. His vision of Charles Manson's army sacking the United States carries more than a faint trace of the legend of Murrell's rebellion or of Jedidiah Morse's warnings that the Illuminati intended to invade the South with an army of Haitians, inciting slave rebellions as they crossed the countryside. Todd's Illuminati were based outside the country, had infiltrated the government, were preparing a wave of riots, and had undetected agents in almost every institution of ordinary American life. They were simultaneously an Enemy Outside, Above, Below, and Within: a master narrative that could absorb virtually any paranoid story that Todd encountered.

If the 1960s and '70s were a fruitful time for talking to conservative Christians about the Illuminati, they were even more propitious for predicting the collapse of civilization. There was a general cultural fear of an approaching cataclysm, an anxiety circulating in secular as well as religious circles. The environmentalists of the era, for example, were often prone to mistaking ecological problems for imminent planetary doom. (In 1969, *Ramparts* magazine warned on its cover that the oceans could be dead in just a decade.)[47] In Christian America, interest in the end-times was surging. The biggest beneficiary of that interest was Hal Lindsey, the coauthor with Carole Carlsson of the immensely popular *The Late Great Planet Earth* (1970). Lindsey, whose ideas spread rapidly through both the Jesus Movement and the nascent religious Right, interpreted world events through the lens of biblical prophecy and argued that Armageddon was nigh.

This was no John Todd– or Mae Brussell–level phenomenon. The book has sold more than 35 million copies, and no less than Orson Welles hosted a film based on it in 1979. Welles didn't believe the *Late Great Planet Earth* scenario any more than he believed Martians had been invading in 1938: He was doing the project for a paycheck, a way to raise the funds he needed to make his own movies. The author of the film's press kit later claimed that the documentary had been tongue-in-cheek and that his PR materials had been "equally facetious."[48] But Welles's narration in *The Late Great Planet Earth*, unlike his "War of the Worlds," included no announcement that everything was fiction; the movie was made for an audience of potential believers. Meanwhile, Lindsey and Carlsson kept cranking out sequels: *Satan Is Alive and Well on Planet Earth* in 1972, *There's a New World Coming* in 1973, and so on. Nor were they the only figures with their eyes on Armageddon. Even as John Todd was denouncing Chuck Smith as an agent of the Illuminati, for instance, Smith in turn expected the apocalypse to arrive by 1981, just a year after the takeover forecast by Todd.[49]

Even if you weren't anticipating the Antichrist's arrival, you might still be alert to the Devil's influence on the country's culture and the marketplace. The idea that Satanic symbols were concealed in the Denny's and Sunoco logos may not have spread beyond the John Todd audience, but around 1980 a rumor took off that Procter & Gamble had hidden a "666" in its logo, a notion that led to boycotts, vandalism, and, finally, the adoption of a new logo in 1985. The larger culture saw a renewed interest in *Hidden Persuaders*–style subliminal advertising, a fascination fueled by Wilson Bryan Key's best-selling books on the subject. Key was controversial, but his basic argument was endorsed by some of the country's most mainstream institutions.[50] (I first encountered Key's ideas in a public elementary school in the early eighties, when my class was assigned to look for concealed come-ons in magazine ads.) The Procter & Gamble crusade was surely influenced by these ideas.

Key believed that messages were hidden not just in ads but in rock records. He endorsed the idea that the Beatles' "Hey Jude" was a song about drugs, a notion previously advanced by Gary Allen of the John Birch Society; and he declared that Simon and Garfunkel's "Bridge over Troubled Water" was "a drug user's guide to withdrawal into a syringe-injected hallucinatory drug experience—most probably heroin."[51] Such songs were part of a general program of "cultural conditioning for addiction," he explained.[52]

But the most popular rumor about subliminal messages in music sounded more like Todd than Key. When played backward, the story went, many of the most popular rock records revealed references to Satan. This tale wasn't limited to the conservative church crowd. In 1982, the Minnesota DJ Chris Edmonds attracted attention by playing "backmasked" clips on the radio and telling his listeners what hidden phrases they were allegedly hearing.

Some pop acts *had* inserted backward Easter eggs into records, though they tended to be nonsensical or comic rather than Satanic. The Electric Light Orchestra's "Fire on High," for example, parodied the panic with the backward message "The music is reversible, but time is not. Turn back, turn back, turn back, turn back." More often, the supposed messages were the product of suggestible minds finding patterns in noise. If you listen to Led Zeppelin's "Stairway to Heaven" backward without being told what to expect, you'll probably hear nothing but strange sounds. If you listen after being informed that there's a Satanic message in there, on the other hand, you might pick up the phrase "sweet Satan." And if you're watching the allegedly encoded words projected on a lecturer's screen while the reversed music plays, you might hear not just "sweet Satan" but a spooky word salad: "So here's to my sweet Satan. The one whose little path would make me sad, whose power is Satan. He will give those with him 666. There was a little tool shed where he made us suffer. Sad Satan."[53]

A decade earlier, rock fans had searched for evidence that Paul McCartney was dead. ("Turn me on, dead man," a backmasked Beatle purportedly said in "Revolution 9.") Now they were searching for Lucifer's fingerprints. The fact that the bands almost always denied that they'd put the messages there didn't matter. Even if they were telling the truth, the argument went, Satan could have inserted the incantations himself.

If you wanted to hear more about Satan's maneuvers, purported defectors were willing to tell tales from the belly of the beast. The most famous of them wasn't Todd. It was Mike Warnke, a star of the Jesus Movement's coffeehouse circuit. Warnke made his first splash in 1972, when he showed up at a San Diego Christian convention with the Witchmobile, a mobile exhibition of alleged Satanic paraphernalia. In public appearances and in a 1973 book called *The Satan Seller*, Warnke claimed to have emerged from a world of drugs, violence, and ritual sexual abuse, serving as high priest of a three-city, 1,500-member Luciferian organization that was an arm of, yes, the Illuminati. Jon Trott and Mike Hertenstein of the Christian magazine *Cornerstone*, who exposed Warnke as a fraud in 1992, have suggested that Warnke picked up the idea of the Illuminati from the Baptist pastor Tim LaHaye, who would later become famous as the coauthor of the *Left Behind* series. "I brought up the term Illuminati first," LaHaye told them. "I had been reading a book on the subject called *Pawns in the Game* [by William Guy Carr], and I tried testing him to see if he really knew anything about it. He didn't seem to have ever heard the word before."[54]

Warnke was much more successful than Todd, both in the size of his audience and in the length of time he was able to extend the deception. Hicks and Lewis's book on Todd includes a brief foreword by Warnke, who wrote that his rival "could possibly turn into another Jim Jones" and reminded readers "to be careful of those who take the name of the Lord in vain."[55] You don't say. As we'll see, Warnke eventually penetrated the mainstream, appearing as a cult expert on several secular TV shows in the 1980s.[56]

In one of the more perceptive passages of "The Paranoid Style in American Politics," Hofstadter highlighted the role of the alleged defector in spreading conspiracy tales. A "special significance," he wrote, "attaches to the figure of the renegade from the enemy cause. The anti-Masonic movement seemed at times to be the creation of ex-Masons; it certainly attached the highest significance and gave the most unqualified credulity to their revelations. Anti-Catholicism used the runaway nun and the apostate priest, anti-Mormonism the ex-wife from the harem of polygamy; the avant-garde anti-Communist movements of our time use the ex-Communist."[57] Warnke and Todd carried on that tradition. One man who was especially interested in defectors' stories was Jack Chick. In addition to endorsing Todd's testimony, Chick became the preeminent platform for Alberto Rivera, a purported ex-Jesuit who blamed the Catholic order for everything from Jonestown to the Holocaust to the creation of Islam. Later Chick would promote the claims of Rebecca Brown, a former physician who claimed to have been a high priestess in a Satanic cult. It eventually emerged that Brown had lost her license to practice medicine, in part because she had been in the habit of diagnosing patients as demonically possessed and attempting to treat them with exorcisms.

Chick was also interested in Satan's penetration of popular culture: His comics denounced rock ("heavy metal has turned millions into rock-a-holics. . . . They've become zombies"),[58] the game Dungeons & Dragons ("***THE INTENSE OCCULT TRAINING THROUGH D&D PREPARED DEBBIE TO ACCEPT THE INVITATION TO ENTER A WITCHES' COVEN***"),[59] the sitcom *Bewitched* ("*that* show paved the way for all our occult and vampire programming viewed by ***MILLIONS*** today!").[60] And though his tracts weren't exactly mainstream material, the ideas he expounded weren't always confined to the country's margins.

Take Pat Pulling, a mother who blamed Dungeons & Dragons for the 1982 suicide of her sixteen-year-old son. D&D, she decided, "uses demonology, witchcraft, voodoo, murder, rape, blasphemy, suicide, assassination, insanity, sex perversion, homosexuality, prostitution, satanic type rituals, gambling, barbarism, cannibalism, sadism, desecration, demon summoning, necromantics, divination and other teachings. There have been a number of deaths nationwide where games like Dungeons and Dragons were either the decisive factor in adolescent suicide and murder, or played a major factor in the violent behaviour of such tragedies."[61] She sued the game's publisher, petitioned the government to regulate or ban D&D-related products, appeared on many popular TV shows, and distributed pamphlets to police departments around the country. (One of her suggested questions for cops interviewing gamers: "Has he read the Necronomicon or is he familiar with it?")[62] She also endorsed Jack Chick's anti-D&D tract "Dark Dungeons."

One person who found Pulling persuasive was Tipper Gore, the wife of Senator Al Gore. Mrs. Gore had launched a crusade against indecent rock lyrics in 1985, and it didn't take long before the targets of her campaign incorporated more than just music. In her 1987 book *Raising PG Kids in an X-Rated Society*, the spouse of the future vice president pitched herself as a moderate liberal who was adept with sociological evidence and concerned about feminist issues. Yet she included an entire chapter on the dangers of the occult, and one of the alleged occult dangers she discussed was D&D. "According to Mrs. Pat Pulling, founder of the organization Bothered About Dungeons and Dragons," Gore wrote, "the game has been linked to nearly fifty teenage suicides and homicides."[63]

As Todd reached the peak of his fame in 1978, his public statements grew more apocalyptic. On Friday the 13th of October, at a restaurant near Elkton, Maryland, he held what he said would be his final workshop. "I received a telephone call from John Todd that this would be his last meeting," Tom Berry explained in an invitation to the session. "He was told by a former CIA agent that [word has] come down through the CIA to 'not stop until John Todd is dead.' Consequently, John has canceled all the bookings scheduled beyond October 13 and plans to go underground at that time."[64] By January, Todd was telling Darryl Hicks that the "riots have already started. You can't stop it once it's started, and it's already started. In just a few days, John Todd will have vanished."[65] That same month, Todd's wife Sheila sent his followers a communiqué from a ten-acre farm near Florence, Montana. "We get letters continually asking for us to defend ourselves against the many rumors going around," she wrote. "Brothers and Sisters, we just cannot constantly defend ourselves. All we can say in defense is that if you will wait and watch things will come to pass as John has said they will."[66]

Todd's reputation was battered by the exposés and the failed predictions, but he still had some believers. When the *Journal Champion* attacked Todd, it received many letters criticizing its story.[67] And when Todd gave a talk at a Holiday Inn near Chicago in 1979, the crowd wasn't happy when a reporter from *Cornerstone* asked him some tough questions. While Todd grew more belligerent in his responses, finally screaming at his interrogator, one man in the audience yelled, "Use the whip!" As the reporter and four colleagues left the room, they heard people murmuring that they were "demons of rebellion."[68]

As late as 1982, Todd was spotted speaking to a half-empty

room at a Holiday Inn in Iowa. He wore a gun, and he kept glancing over his shoulder as he spoke. He had been brought in by a couple named Randy and Vicki Weaver, who had heard his tapes and been intrigued. But Vicki found herself turned off by Todd and by some of the people he attracted. "Watch out for him," she told a friend, pointing to a man in the room. "He's a neo-Nazi."[69]

Meanwhile, Todd's warnings had been taken to heart by the Zarephath-Horeb Community Church, a Christian community in the Ozarks that would eventually evolve into a paramilitary group called the Covenant, the Sword, and the Arm of the Lord, or CSA. (The initials deliberately echoed another CSA, the Confederate States of America.) The group's "propaganda minister," Kerry Noble, heard his first Todd tape in 1978 and immediately shared it with his church's elders. "With that first John Todd tape I was given, our group embraced everything Todd preached," Noble later recalled. "He seemed to confirm all that we felt was wrong in this country, as well as what we believed would happen in the future." Under Todd's influence, the church began to arm itself: "[F]rom August 1978 to December 1979, we spent $52,000 on weapons, ammunition, and military equipment, and we began to train militarily." They also "built our homes with defense in mind, strategically placing them against an attack from the outside. Many of the houses had bunkers built underneath. Those that didn't usually had a foxhole bunker built nearby."[70]

The church soon mixed Todd's teachings with the ideas of other conspiracy theorists, many of them affiliated with Christian Identity, a racist movement that believed Anglo-Saxons rather than Jews are the real descendants of the ancient Israelites. The results could be seen in Noble's brief book *Witchcraft and the Illuminati*. The chief difference between Todd's tapes and Noble's book was that Noble was antiblack, anti-Semitic, and obsessed with homosexuality. Todd denied that there was an international Jewish conspiracy, but Noble's book cited *The Protocols of the Learned Elders of Zion*, described Jews as "the most highly organized race of people on the face of the earth," warned that they "control nearly every major organization in existence," and called the Talmud "one of the most vile, anti-Christian, satanic books ever written." The book also declared that "rebellious BLACKS" are among "the enemies of God" and accused many famous figures—including Mike Warnke—of being gay.[71]

The group's fears grew increasingly apocalyptic. "It will get so bad that parents will eat their children," church leader James Ellison predicted. "Death in the major cities will cause rampant diseases and plagues. Maggot-infested bodies will lie everywhere. Earthquakes, tidal waves, volcanoes, and other natural disasters will grow to gigantic proportions. Witches and satanic Jews will offer people up as sacrifices to their gods, openly and proudly; blacks will rape and kill white women and will torture and kill white men; homosexuals will sodomize whoever they can. Our new government will be a part of the one-world Zionist Communist government. All but the elect will have the mark of the Beast."[72]

The CSA began to hatch plans for terrorist attacks, and Noble nearly bombed a gay church in Kansas City, discovering only at the last moment that he could not bring himself to do it. On April 19, 1985, the group found itself under siege by the Bureau of Alcohol, Tobacco, and Firearms. The four-day standoff ended after Noble, increasingly disillusioned with the church, helped negotiate a surrender.

You can take that as a lesson about the dark places where ideas like Todd's can lead. But before you draw too neat a conclusion from the story, you should think about what happened to another two people who encountered John Todd and his worldview.

Increasingly attracted to far-right politics, Randy and Vicki Weaver moved from Iowa to the mountains of the Pacific Northwest, where they planned to live as self-sufficiently as possible. Then the Bureau of Alcohol, Tobacco, and Firearms entrapped Randy on a minor weapons violation and offered him a deal: The charge would be dismissed if he became an informant in the local white separatist movement. Instead Weaver moved his family to a cabin in the wilderness and failed to appear for his trial. It is possible that he deliberately decided to skip it, but he probably wouldn't have shown up either way—he had been sent the wrong date.

When federal agents arrived on the scene, they shot the family dog. The Weavers' son, Sam, not realizing what was going on, fired a shot in response and then fled, at which point an agent shot him in the back. Kevin Harris, a visiting friend, fired at the attacking cops, killing a U.S. marshal. The FBI's snipers went on to wound both Randy and Harris, and one of the agents killed Vicki, firing a bullet into her head while she held her ten-month-old daughter.

The ensuing standoff lasted eleven days. After Weaver surrendered, he and Harris were found not guilty of murder. A subsequent internal report concluded that the FBI had violated the Weavers' constitutional rights, though the man who killed Vicki Weaver never went to jail.

If the story of the CSA shows how a marginal group's paranoia about the government can drive it to violence,[73] the tale of the Weavers shows how the government's paranoia about marginal groups can drive *it* to violence. The FBI looked at a family with fringe views and perceived a potential CSA, and as a result a woman, a boy, a dog, and one of the government's own agents were killed.

The problem of Ruby Ridge was repeated a year later, when the ATF raided the Mount Carmel Center, home of the Branch Davidian sect, near Waco, Texas. The feds believed that the church was stockpiling weapons (and claimed, in a request for military support, that its members might have been manufacturing meth as well). It was an ill-conceived operation from the beginning: There was little evidence that the group's weapons were illegal, there was no evidence at all of the drug lab, and in any event there were several less confrontational ways to arrest the sect's leader. The situation went south when the Davidians shot at the raiders, killing four agents and starting a fifty-day standoff that ended with an FBI raid, a fire, and nearly all the Davidians dead.

While the feds confronted the Davidians, the media spread stories, some exaggerated and others simply false, of sexual depravity, weird rituals, and a plot against the outside world—the same sorts of fables that the medieval authorities told about Jews and heretics. The Davidians' paranoia was no match for the paranoia of their enemies.

By that time the fear of Satanists had spread far beyond the evangelical world, mixing with three secular scares to create a new face for the Enemy Within.

The first of those scares was the country's sudden obsession with missing children, an interest reflected in the new practice of printing lost kids' faces on milk cartons. The fear began with some high-profile kidnappings and murders—the Atlanta child killings of 1979 to 1981, the 1979 disappearance of six-year-old Etan Patz, the 1981 abduction and decapitation of six-year-old Adam Walsh—and it was amplified by misleading statistics that often appeared in the media. An estimate of the number of missing children, for example, might include runaways, teens who returned home within twenty-four hours, and kids taken by parents in custodial disputes. The number of children abducted by strangers was much smaller. But the missing-children cases discussed in the news—and in the movies, and on TV shows, and in novels about child-grabbing conspiracies—highlighted the more rare and horrifying cases.[74]

The panic may have reached its most ridiculous moment on April 15, 1986, when police raided the home of the punk rock performer Jello Biafra, searching for evidence to support the obscenity charges that would soon hit Biafra's band. One of his roommates had been collecting and posting pictures from milk cartons, and the decor alarmed an officer. "What are all those pictures of missing milk carton kids doing on your kitchen wall?" the cop asked the singer. *"Do you know where they are?"*[75]

The second scare was a surge in charges of child molestation. Aware that such crimes had frequently been swept under the rug in the past, many advocates were loath to disbelieve any allegations that came their way, even if they contained obvious fantasies and even if they did not emerge until after the kids had undergone lengthy sessions with sketchy therapists. While that impulse was found in parts of the feminist movement, another source of the fear had a more antifeminist cast. For many people, day care centers represented women's willingness to abandon their children. With that mind-set, they found it easy to believe that terrible abuses were taking place behind day care center doors.

The most infamous episode involved the McMartin Preschool in Manhattan Beach, California, a case study in how interrogators can manipulate small children. Kids were badgered when they said they hadn't been victimized, and they were praised when they said what the interviewer wanted to hear. The more the children said, the more positive reinforcement they got, and the questioners didn't seem to mind when the tales grew outlandish. One child, Debbie Nathan and Michael Snedeker report in their book on the case, began by saying she had no secrets to share, then eventually declared that she had been raped. After more days of questioning, she said "she was forced to drink [a teacher's] urine and to consume his feces covered with chocolate sauce." With time the girl "was talking about animals being slaughtered at the school and about how she was taken to a 'mansion' to be molested," about adults "forcing her to take drugs, about fellating animals, about trips to a church and 'devil land,' and about being made to touch dead people."[76]

The members of the press were initially credulous about the claims. Tom Jarriel, previously ABC's chief White House correspondent, described McMartin as "a sexual house of horrors" in a 1984 report for the show *20/20*.[77] Even when the case against the alleged molesters started to fall apart, similar witch hunts erupted in other locations without much public objection. Indeed, when prominent figures did urge caution or challenge unlikely evidence, they often found themselves accused of participating in the crimes themselves.

If you joined or led the attacks, on the other hand, you weren't likely to pay a penalty. One politician who oversaw two overreaching child-abuse prosecutions was a Miami prosecutor named Janet

Reno. In 1993, having made a name for herself, Reno went on to become the country's attorney general; one of her first acts in that office was to approve the FBI raid that brought the federal standoff with the Branch Davidians to a fiery end. She had given the order, she explained, because she had been told that "babies were being beaten" within the compound.[78]

From mid-September 1986 to mid-February 1987, one sociologist reported, "Popular magazines published an average of one story about child abuse, child molestation, or missing children each week."[79] Add a third secular scare—the anticult agitation that had been bubbling since the 1970s—and the culture was receptive to the idea that a network of Satanic sects was engaged in the ritual abuse and slaughter of innocent children.

To see how much of the Todd/Warnke worldview the mainstream had absorbed, consider the special report that *20/20* devoted to the subject in 1985. The show's anchor, Hugh Downs, declares at the start that "police have been skeptical when investigating these acts, just as we are in reporting them. But there is no question that something is going on out there."[80] Then Tom Jarriel starts describing that *something*. A drug-related killing in which the murderer appeared to have Satanic leanings. Reports of animal mutilations around the country, which "often" were "clearly used in some kind of bizarre ritual" but have "no official explanation." An Alabama investigation of "what appears to have been a ritual" with "various Satanic paraphernalia, including pictures of the devil." And then there's the "Satanic graffiti" that's "turning up on public buildings and abandoned buildings, where police suspect secret meetings are being held." The camera zeroes in on several specimens of the graffiti, including an eye in a pyramid, which Jarriel describes as "the evil eye."

From there we go to a potted explanation of who Satan is, a long clip from the movie *Rosemary's Baby* (in which "modern Satanism was shockingly dramatized"), and an interview with Mike Warnke, uncritically identified as "a former Satanist," who displays some suitably spooky-looking Devil-worship paraphernalia. We are told that a teenager hanged himself after writing on his body "666," "Satan lives," and "I'm coming home, master." Then we wade deeper into conspiracy territory, with statements from two police officers, Sandi Gallant of San Francisco and Dale Griffis of Tiffin, Ohio. "We have kids being killed," Griffis intones gravely. "We have people missing in America. We have our own MIAs right here." Not content to invoke the ghost of Vietnam, he adds, "We have cattle being killed. We have all types of perversion going on."

A trip to a shopping mall reveals "how easy it is for children, or adults for that matter, to get their hands on Satanic material." The video store, we see, stocks a lot of horror movies. (Cut to Warnke. "If the devil has PR, then it is cinema," he says.) The mall bookstore sells Anton LaVey's *The Satanic Bible* and other occultist texts. And the music store is filled with heavy metal albums, plus records that have what "some believe" are backward Satanic references. (Cut to Chris Edmonds, who demonstrates the "sweet Satan" allegedly hidden in "Stairway to Heaven.")

We hear about a grisly murder committed by a teenager who was interested in *The Satanic Bible*. An assistant attorney general in Maine condemns the book as "dangerous." We get a brief sketch of the Church of Satan, and the narrator notes that police have never found a link between the religion and Satanic crimes. "However," Jarriel adds as we see some old documentary footage of a Church of Satan service, "some incidents described to us by witnesses from around the country are strikingly similar to these ritualistic scenes."

Finally the show tackles the topic of underground Satanic cults. These, we're told, *are* linked to crimes . . . maybe. "Nationwide, police are hearing strikingly similar horror stories," Jarriel tells us. He acknowledges that "not one has ever been proved," and then he plunges into the unproved cases, as alleged participants and their relatives describe the murders that the cults supposedly force children to commit. Two boys reenact the reported ritual with a knife and a doll. Jarriel gives us a "checklist" of "Satanic practices to look for," from sexual abuse to cannibalism to cremation. Cremation could explain why we never actually find the bodies of the sacrifice victims, Jarriel informs us: They've been burned. But "so far police have failed to make the connection."

At the end of the report, Barbara Walters pronounces the story "terrifying." It *is* rather terrifying that Hugh Downs believed the *20/20* team had "been skeptical," given that the reporters apparently failed to interview a single skeptical voice. If you look past the program's fearmongering tone to see what the show actually demonstrated, you get this:

- Certain segments of pop culture like to play around with Satanic imagery.
- Disturbed people who commit crimes sometimes like to spout Satanic mumbo jumbo.
- There are many unsolved animal mutilations around the country, and some people think Satanists may have something to do with it.
- There is a group called the Church of Satan, which no one has ever credibly connected to a ritual crime.
- Some children claim to have been forced to participate in murderous Satanic rituals.

The program did not distinguish between pop-culture material that presents itself as pro-Satan, such as LaVey's bible, and material that denounces the Devil, such as *The Exorcist*.[81] The program did not explore whether it was Satanism that drew those criminals toward homicide or, as seems more likely, someone who already has homicidal tendencies might also to be attracted to the idea of worshipping evil. The program did not mention that scientists had been investigating animal mutilations since the 1970s and consistently concluded that the great majority of the beasts had died of natural causes. The only item on the list that seems to support the conspiracy narrative is the last one, in which kids become cult murderers, and it has the disadvantage of relying on claims that almost certainly were not true. The bodies of the alleged victims were never discovered, and we've seen in the McMartin case how children can be guided to level outlandish charges. Indeed, the McMartin case itself eventually degenerated into conspiracy theories about a secret Satanic cult.

As early as 1974, John Todd had been promoting the idea that Satanists were kidnapping young people for ritual sacrifices.[82] Now a widely respected news program on a major television network was broadcasting the legend to an audience far larger than the crowd at the Open Door Church. Many more programs followed: Over the next four years, Oprah Winfrey, Larry King, and Sally Jessy Raphael all did shows on the Satanic menace. (Warnke was a repeat guest.) Geraldo Rivera devoted at least three broadcasts to the topic. "Satanic cults!" he announced in one of them. "Every hour, every day, their ranks are growing. Estimates are there are over one million Satanists in this country. The majority of them are linked in a highly organized, very secret network. . . . The odds are this is happening in your town."[83] Charles Manson, Rivera averred in another show, was "reportedly linked to the Devil-worship underground."[84]

Some cops were getting in on the act, too. In 1989, an FBI agent complained in *Police Chief* magazine about "a flood of law enforcement seminars and conferences" about occult crimes, where police would hear talks about heavy metal, Dungeons & Dragons, and "satanic groups involved in organized conspiracies, such as taking over day care centers, infiltrating police departments, and trafficking in human sacrifice victims." Sometimes, he added, the presenters would even invoke the "'Big Conspiracy' theory, which implies that satanists are responsible for such things as Adolf Hitler, World War II, abortion, pornography, Watergate, and Irangate, and have infiltrated the Department of Justice, the Pentagon, and the White House."[85]

One new fashion in Big Conspiracy circles was "The W.I.C.C.A. Letters," purportedly the minutes of a meeting of a "Witches International Coven Council Association" in Mexico in 1981. According to the *Protocols*-like document, "decoded" and circulated by a member of the San Diego County Sheriff's Department, the witches' plans included "infiltrating boys'/girls' clubs and big sister/brother programs," "infiltrating schools, having prayers removed, having teachers teach about drugs, sex, freedoms," "instigating and promoting rebellion against parents and all authority," and changing the country's laws to facilitate "removing children from [the] home environment and placing them in our foster homes."[86] In one of Geraldo Rivera's broadcasts, a California cop invoked the letters' claims as though they were demonstrably true.

John Todd continued his sexually aggressive ways. In 1984, living in Louisville, Kentucky, he molested a niece, a crime that led to five years' probation. In 1987, living in Columbia, South Carolina, he started inviting female college students to work for a publishing company that he claimed to be launching. One applicant was invited to "role-play" different situations with Todd, an activity that ended with him forcing her to perform fellatio. Another woman thought she was applying for a job that paid $50,000 a year. When she met with Todd, he demanded sex, saying, "What do you think the $50,000 is for?"[87] He then pulled a knife, forced her to take three pills, and raped her. Before she left, he warned her that a network of men was protecting him. "If you try to hurt me I could have you killed," he said.[88]

With that, Todd was arrested and charged with criminal sexual assault. Two teenagers who had been taking karate lessons from Todd came forward to say he had molested them too; their accusation led to two additional charges of committing lewd acts on children. He attempted suicide twice while awaiting trial, and in January 1988, after he was convicted on the rape charge, he tried to kill himself again. Then he started filing lawsuits against the authorities. In the first suit, he demanded that the government return property it had seized as evidence, including a pair of women's pink panties.

In 1991, Todd released a tape from prison, claiming that he had been railroaded by Senator Strom Thurmond. (The senator, Todd explained, was upset that Todd had exposed him as "the highest ranking Mason in the world.")[89] Three years later, when a Christian visiting from Britain interviewed him, Todd declared that he was a witch again. "Raised up in Wicca, you *never* lie," he declared. "Christians break their word. All I ever saw for 18 years was Christians breaking their word. . . . I waited five years for Christians to help. I went back to Wicca." Not that he was pro-Illuminati now. "Wiccans see the Illuminati as Jews and Christians," he said.[90]

By 2005, Todd had adopted the name Kris Sarayn Kollyns and sued the South Carolina Department of Mental Health for failing to provide "medical and psychological treatment" for gender identity disorder.[91] A 2006 suit accused several state employees of insulting the inmate's Wiccan beliefs and confiscating the women's undergarments that the prisoner liked to wear. The judge sided with the state, declaring that the "plaintiff could pose a serious security threat by changing and being half-clothed in his homemade women's underwear while in plain view of other residents in the program."[92] Finally, in November 2007, the prisoner formerly known as John Todd died.

Todd had traveled a long way since that evening in Chambersburg, from Christian survivalist to cross-dressing witch. But by this time Todd the human being and Todd the legend had been completely divorced. There were rumors that Todd was still alive, that Todd had been killed way back in 1979, that Todd had been released from prison in 1994 and assassinated the same day; there were rumors that the imprisoned rapist was an imposter, and there were rumors that Todd had been framed. When a viewer on YouTube mentioned Todd's criminal record, another viewer replied:

> Never heard about setting up???Of course they just maded upp stories like rape etc. and Illuminati is really well known for doing that.Look at Eminen for example,after he braked up with the high ups he got arrested and look at DXM..Even worse!!!
>
> So wake upp ffs!!![93]

9

OPERATION MINDFUCK

We should be grateful that we live in a culture so insulated from true horror it can afford to play with fear as entertainment.

—*Grant Morrison*[1]

In 1969, *The East Village Other* was the trippiest paper in New York: a kaleidoscopic combination of absurdist headlines and psychedelic graphics that made *The Village Voice* look as stuffy as *The New York Times*. The actual articles could be pretty freaky too: outré stuff about LSD and UFOs, sex and revolution. And conspiracies.

In the spring and summer of '69, *EVO* published an interview with an alleged defector from the Minutemen, a man who claimed the group was in league with America's intelligence agencies and that a violent right-wing revolution would be attempted "before 1972."[2] It ran an occult advice column that touched on Rosicrucianism and Theosophy. It printed a two-part interview with Mark Lane. And in the June 4 issue, it included this diagram:[3]

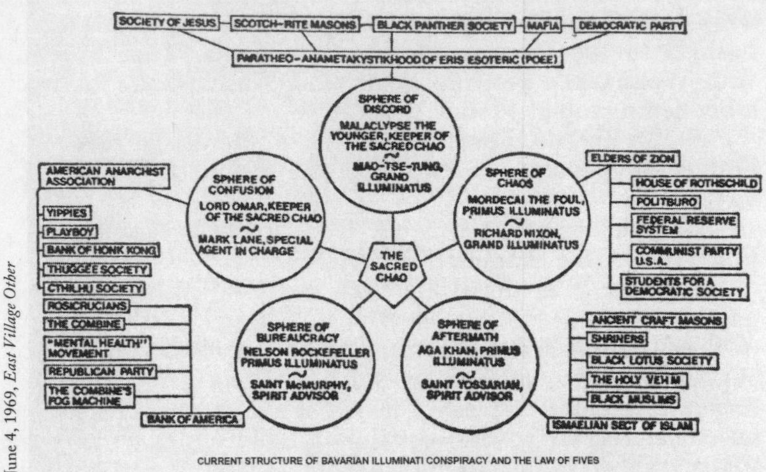

CURRENT STRUCTURE OF BAVARIAN ILLUMINATI CONSPIRACY AND THE LAW OF FIVES

June 4, 1969, *East Village Other*

The chart appeared with no editorial explanation, but savvy readers surely inferred that the graphic was satiric. "The Combine" was a reference to Ken Kesey's novel *One Flew over the Cuckoo's Nest*, "Saint Yossarian" to Joseph Heller's *Catch-22*, the "Cthulhu Society" to the tales of H. P. Lovecraft. As we've seen, some people have trouble separating Lovecraft's fiction from reality, but the Kesey and Heller fan bases had never displayed such a problem. Even if you didn't recognize the literary allusions, you probably knew how absurd it was to claim that anarchists ran the Bank of Hong Kong or that Chairman Mao controlled the Jesuits, the Democrats, and the Mafia. "Mark Lane, Special Agent in Charge" was a nice touch too. The chart was a joke. Obviously. Right?

Then again, conspiracy buffs are certainly capable of asserting bizarre connections and mixing pieces of pop culture into their theories, as John Todd would soon be demonstrating in churches across the country. Instead of taking this as satire, you might decide it was the work of a sincere kook. You might even take a hit from your roommate's bong and decide to believe the thing. *The East Village Other* was a hippie paper. Its readers were willing to entertain all sorts of unusual ideas. If you bought the Minutemen story, why not take another step into Conspiracyville and buy this one too?

As it happened, the chart really was a joke, the brainchild of a band of pranksters called the Discordians. The Discordians, particularly a quietly influential writer named Robert Anton Wilson, were pioneers of the ironic style of American conspiracism, a sensibility that treats alleged cabals not as intrigues to be exposed or as lies to be debunked but as a mutant mythos to be mined for metaphors, laughs, and social insights. "A certain class of reader values bizarre and paranoid theories precisely because they are bizarre and paranoid," the novelist Thomas M. Disch once observed. Disch didn't approve, but he understood. "They must see themselves not as liars, or even romancers, but as poets," he wrote.[4]

From Swift to Orwell, dystopian writers have exaggerated social trends they dislike, forging those artful distortions into satires. Conspiracy folklore does the same thing for the same reason, except that most of those dystopians believe in the worlds they've invented. But the ironists don't necessarily believe them. In the ironic style, the most interesting thing about a conspiracy theory isn't that it might or might not be true; it's that it constructs a story out of the everyday truths we only hazily perceive. As the cultural critic Mark Dery said of a certain sort of Lovecraft fan, the ironists like to "have their critical distance and eat it, too, believing as if rather than believing in."[5]

As the ironic style was emerging, so too was a second sensibility. In the past, people adopted the conspiracy theories peculiar to their own ideologies or social circumstances. If you were worried about Communist subversion, you did not naturally progress to fearing the Pentagon. But in the heat of the 1960s and '70s, something new was appearing: a focus on conspiracy *in itself*, an appetite for "conspiracy research" that transcended the standard Left/Right barriers. With time this interest would become a full-fledged subculture. That subculture wouldn't be a mass phenomenon until the 1990s, but it was around as early as the 1970s, when it became possible to read publications with such names as *Conspiracies Unlimited* and *Conspiracy Digest*.

In 1995, Michael Kelly would call this outlook *fusion paranoia*. It was a frame of mind, he wrote, that "draws from, and plays to, the left and the right" but "rejects that bipolar model for a more primal polarity: Us versus Them."[6] It would have horrified the man to think it, but in a way the hidden father of fusionism was Richard Hofstadter. Once the idea came into common currency that a "paranoid style" linked the country's conspiracy theorists, it was just a matter of time before some of those theorists would embrace the insult and explore the ideas other paranoids were proposing. In denouncing conspiracy thinking, Hofstadter helped to remake it.

The fusionists, unlike the ironists, are dead serious. Or at least they're serious when they aren't also being ironists: It is fairly easy to switch from one mode to the other, and some writers managed to straddle the boundary between the two. With the "conspiracy" category in place, an earnest interest in conspiracies could turn ironic, or vice versa.

The ironists love to construct elaborate paranoid visions, some so baroque that they make that *EVO* diagram look like a simple pie chart. Sometimes these creations are just jokes, and sometimes they're something more: Like a spiritual seeker who plunges into different religious rituals without embracing any faith as the literal truth, the ironist can appreciate conspiracy theories as a makeshift mythology. Occasionally that mythology will be so transfixing that he will lose his sense of irony and start to believe it.

The ironic style emerged in the 1960s, but its roots stretch back far earlier. Three influences were especially important in shaping the ironists' outlook: the Forteans, the political pranksters, and a church dedicated to the worship of chaos.

We'll start with the Forteans. Charles Fort, born in Albany in 1874, was a writer obsessed with anomalies. He spent years in the New York and London libraries, assiduously gathering reports that seemed to confound established theories: tales of poltergeists, of monsters, of blood and worms and fish and frogs falling from the sky. He was full of dark and playful hypotheses to explain those accounts. Most famously, he proposed that we are the property of an extraterrestrial force that guides the world through some "cult or order" of human beings who "function like bellwethers to the rest of us." As for why the aliens find us useful, Fort wrote:

> Pigs, geese, and cattle.
>
> First find out that they are owned.
>
> Then find out the whyness of it.[7]

You shouldn't assume that Fort literally believed that thesis. He liked to try on ideas for the hell of it, and he wasn't afraid to be deliberately outlandish. "I conceive of nothing," he explained, "in religion, science, or philosophy, that is more than the proper thing to wear, for a while."[8] The point of his books wasn't to advance any particular oddball theory. It was to show the gaps in the mainstream theories, the ways inconvenient irregularities are shunted aside so our belief systems can stay intact. On the surface, Fort may sound like a mad poet reading the *Weekly World News*. But lurking below the lyrical strangeness of his books, you'll find an impish philosopher of science.

After Fort died in 1932, an eccentric platoon of writers kept the Fortean tradition alive. One of them was John Keel, a reporter who chased tales of flying saucers and paranormal creatures. Keel's writing was by turns funny and frightening, as if someone had crossed a slapstick comedy with the horror stories of H. P. Lovecraft; it suggested a world plagued by conspiracies that would never make sense to human minds because the forces behind them were not human themselves. There has always been a strain in the ufological literature that feels like the theater of the absurd: the Wisconsin man who claimed that an alien had given him pancakes, or the woman in Italy who insisted that spacemen had stolen her flowerpot. Most saucer buffs preferred to brush past such surrealist stories, but Keel thrived on them.

Keel played with Fort's idea that the human race is the property of some unseen power, suggesting in one book that Earth was, to quote his title, a *Disneyland of the Gods*. If "you give it just a little thought," Keel noted, "you will realize that billions of people have understood and believed this very thing for thousands of years. This belief is the foundation of all our great religions."[9] His best-known book is probably 1975's *The Mothman Prophecies*, a compulsively readable piece of Fortean New Journalism in which the author investigated the odd phenomena reportedly besetting the town of Point Pleasant, West Virginia, in 1966 and '67: strange yarns about cattle mutilations, Men in Black, a gigantic winged creature called the Mothman, and more.

At times Keel sounds as though he's describing a Bizarro World COINTELPRO: visits from inhuman agents, strange phone calls, a mysterious imposter claiming to be Keel's secretary. While Black Panthers and SDS activists were having their telephones tapped, the people of Point Pleasant, by Keel's account, were experiencing incidents like this:

> Every night when she returned home from work at 5 o'clock her phone would ring and a man's voice would speak to her in a rapid-fire language she could not understand. "It sounds something like Spanish . . . yet I don't think it is Spanish," she complained. She protested to the phone company, but they insisted they could find nothing wrong with her line. . . .
>
> When you unscrew modern telephone earpieces you will often find a small piece of cotton which serves as a cushion for the magnet and diaphragm. You shouldn't find anything else. But when I opened this woman's handset I was startled to find a tiny sliver of wood. She said no one, not even the repairmen, had ever opened up her phone before. The wooden object looked like a piece of matchstick, sharpened at one end and lightly coated with a substance that looked like graphite. Later I showed it to telephone engineers and they said they'd never seen anything like it before. I put it in a plastic box and stored

it away. Years later while visiting a magic store in New York (sleight of hand is one of my hobbies), I glanced at a display of practical jokes and discovered a cellophane package filled with similar sticks. Cigarette loads! Somehow an explosive cigarette load had gotten into that Point Pleasant telephone! Who put it there, when, how, and why must remain mysteries.

Soon after my investigation, the woman's phone calls ceased. Maybe I exorcised the phone by removing the stick.[10]

That was typical of Keel, who sometimes seemed serious but at other times might be suspected of pulling his readers' legs.[11] At other moments, you might suspect that someone was pulling *his* leg. Gray Barker, a writer who published supposedly true stories about UFOs while privately calling saucers "a bucket of shit,"[12] was doing his own snooping in Point Pleasant while Keel was there. Barker, who had more or less launched the legend of the Men in Black in his 1956 book *They Knew Too Much About Flying Saucers*, had a propensity for hoaxes, and he apparently decided to start prank-calling his competitor. Keel's book mentions that "a few of the ego-tripping characters in ufology" were prone to "placing prank calls,"[13] but the author seems oblivious to the fact that Barker was one of them:

At 1 A.M. on the morning of Friday, July 14, 1967, I received a call from a man who identified himself as Gray Barker from West Virginia. The voice sounded exactly like Gray's softly accented mellifluous own, but he addressed me as if I were a total stranger and carefully called me "Mr. Keel." At first I wondered if maybe he hadn't been out celebrating. The quiet, familiar drawl told me that he knew I wrote for newspapers and he had just heard about a case which he thought I should look into. It was, he said, similar to the Deren*stein* case. Gray and I had visited Woodrow Derenberger together so I knew this was not the kind of mistake he would make.

Around that time I had received a number of reports from people in the New York area who had been receiving nuisance calls from a woman who identified herself as "Mrs. Gray Barker." I knew that Gray was not married but when I mentioned these calls to this "Gray Barker" he paused for a moment and then said, "No, Mrs. Barker hasn't been calling anybody up there." He returned to his recital of an absurdly insignificant UFO sighting near West Mifflin, Pennsylvania. It was not the kind of incident that would have inspired a long-distance call. Later I did try to check it out and found all the information he gave me was false.

We talked for about ten minutes and throughout that period "Gray" sounded like a man under duress . . . as though someone was holding a gun to his head. I tricked him several times with different meaningless references and by the time I hung up I was definitely convinced that this man was not the real Gray Barker.

An hour later my phone rang again and a young man said, "Gray *Baker* has been trying to reach you . . . he asked us to give you this number and to please call him." He recited a number that was identical to my own except for the last digit.

There were more calls from strangers that night, and more pointless messages from Gray *Baker*.

The next day I called Gray long distance and he denied having placed the call, naturally.[14]

He would, wouldn't he?

In private Keel suspected that at least some of the stuff Barker was feeding him wasn't true. In one letter to the prankster, he wrote: "Let's stop all this happy horseshit."[15] James Moseley, another ufologist with a history of hoaxing, later recalled that his pal Barker "was delighted that Keel was reporting all sorts of 'persecutions' and paranoia."[16] At one point Barker wrote a letter to Moseley and sent it to Keel instead, as though he had accidentally addressed the envelope inaccurately; it was filled with mysterious comments seemingly designed to make Keel paranoid.[17]

University Books, 1956

"The diehard fanatics who dominated sauceriana during the early years were a humorless lot," Keel wrote in *Mothman*, "and Gray's mischievous wit baffled and enraged them. At times it baffled me, too."[18]

Barker's playful deceptions bring to mind the second wellspring of the ironic style: the pranksters—most notably, a prankster named Paul Krassner, who launched a magazine in 1958 called *The Realist*.

The Realist's great innovation was to refuse to label which articles were truthful and which were jokes, and sometimes to add just enough truth to a piece of fiction that readers would be left completely befuddled as to what, if anything, they should believe.[19] With time Krassner would make that a matter of policy: "*The Realist* never labels an article as either satire or journalism," he wrote in 1991, "in order not to deprive you the pleasure of discerning for yourself whether it's actually true or metaphorically true."[20] But the practice didn't begin as a deliberate attempt to confound people. Krassner had simply assumed that everyone would be able to tell the satiric from the sincere. When it turned out that many readers found that difficult, he didn't look for ways to clear up the confusion; he looked for ways to have fun with it.

The result was one of the most infamous hoaxes of the 1960s. "The Parts That Were Left Out of the Kennedy Book," published in 1967, posed as a series of outtakes from William Manchester's popular account of the JFK assassination, *The Death of a President*. Krassner's piece began with a true story: When LBJ had been competing with Kennedy for the 1960 presidential nomination, he had called his rival's father a Nazi sympathizer. The article went on to describe the president's infidelities, which were well known in journalistic circles but had not yet been reported, and then it grew steadily less reliable, concluding with a scene of Lyndon Baines sticking his Johnson in the president's throat wound. It is a testament to Krassner's literary skill—or the average reader's gullibility, or LBJ's unpopularity—that many people were fooled. When Krassner met Daniel Ellsberg, the famous leaker confessed that he had believed the Johnson story. "Maybe it was just because I *wanted* to believe it so badly," he said.[21]

The hoax was not, at its heart, about a conspiracy, but the penultimate paragraph had a paranoid touch. In the margins of the Manchester manuscript, *Realist* readers were informed, this handwritten note appeared: "Is this simply necrophilia or was LBJ trying to change entry wound into exit wound by enlarging?"[22]

As Krassner strove to top his Kennedy piece, and as his personal interest in conspiracy theories grew, secret plots moved to the center of his hoaxes. He began to conceive of himself as an "investigative satirist," detailing plots that didn't exist in order to expose the deeper social truths that did.

After Robert Kennedy's death, the magazine announced that it would reveal "the rise of Sirhan Sirhan in the Scientology hierarchy."[23] The article hadn't actually been written yet, but the title alone was enough to prompt the Church of Scientology to file a lawsuit against the magazine. That only encouraged Krassner to dig deeper, searching for facts that would give his tale the texture of authenticity. Soon he was assembling an elaborate story about Scientology, assassination, and intelligence agencies, with Charles Manson replacing Sirhan Sirhan at the center of the saga.

You can see the ironic style coming into focus here. When Mae Brussell blamed an anticountercultural conspiracy for the Manson murders, she created fiction with mythic resonance but she thought she was exposing hard truths. Krassner skipped the hard truths except insofar as they helped him achieve that mythic resonance. Or at least that was his plan until he encountered Brussell along the way—but we'll save that part of the story for later.

Krassner wasn't the only investigative satirist in *The Realist*'s stable. Writing under the pseudonym "Reginald Dunsany," a lawyer named James Curry produced a piece claiming that Jim Garrison, the controversial New Orleans D.A. who was helming his own investigation of President Kennedy's assassination, had uncovered "a secret international terrorist ring more deadly than the Ochrana, GPU and Gestapo combined—the Homintern."[24] Several pages of allegations about an international homosexual conspiracy followed. Nearly four decades later, in his otherwise excellent study *The Lavender Scare*, David K. Johnson would mistake Curry's satire for an earnest piece of paranoid gay-baiting.[25]

Outside *The Realist*'s efforts, the most notorious conspiracy hoax cum spoof of the 1960s was the *Report from Iron Mountain on the Possibility and Desirability of Peace*. The book, published in 1967, presented itself as a leaked classified report produced by the Special Study Group, a conclave tasked with considering what Washington should do if a "general condition of peace" should break out.[26] War is a social stabilizer, the purported panel concluded. It allows planners to judiciously burn off excess economic inventory, it channels "antisocial elements" into "an acceptable role," it establishes "the basic authority of a modern state over its people," and it helps "preserve whatever quality and degree of poverty a society requires as an incentive."[27] The whole thing was written in a scathing parody of the prose found in a report from the RAND Corporation or some similar think tank. The book's comic peak comes when the Special Study Group ponders other ways to fulfill war's nonmilitary functions, including the creation of "fictitious alternate enemies."[28]

The jape was inspired by a newspaper headline: "Peace Scare Drives Market Down." When the liberal journalist Victor Navasky saw that, he said to himself, "Peace? Peace is supposed to drive the market *up*."[29] Then he and some friends conceived the satire, which was classified as nonfiction when it entered the best-seller lists. The book's primary author, Leonard Lewin, confessed to the hoax in 1972, but that didn't stop people from believing the *Report* was real. The members of the Liberty Lobby printed their own edition—since they thought it was a government document, they assumed it was in the public domain—and they didn't stop selling it until Lewin sued them.[30] In 1990, the Associated Press distributed a story about the history of Iron Mountain, the spot in New York state where the Special Study Group was supposed to have met. The article casually cited the book's claims as a part of the place's past. "After two years of meetings, the commission decided that permanent peace was a bad idea," the reporter recounted, then quoted Lewin's introduction to the book and moved on to the next stage of the location's history.[31]

People still tout the *Report* as a genuine window into the mind of the Enemy Above. Some of them don't seem to be aware of Lewin's confession; others know about it but just don't believe it. "The government claimed it was a HOAX," wrote Stewart Best, the director of the DIY documentary *Iron Mountain: Blue Print for Tyranny*. "The Eastern Establishment claimed it was a HOAX. Eventually the writer of the forward [*sic*], a Mr. Leonard Lewin, claimed it was a hoax, a political satire, written to generate interest in the problems of war and peace, disarmament, etc. The only problem with all of this is the simple fact that IT WAS PUBLISHED AS NON-FICTION, and it was claimed at the time of the release that it was AUTHENTIC by both Lewen [*sic*] and the Editor-in-Chief of Dial Press."[32]

You might get the impression that Best does not comprehend how a hoax works.

The third source of the ironic style was Discordianism, a spoof religion founded in the late 1950s by a couple of Californians named Greg Hill and Kerry Thornley.[33] If you believe the mock faith's mock bible, the *Principia Discordia*—and just to be clear, it is unwise to take anything in the *Principia Discordia* at face value—the church was born with a blinding epiphany in a bowling alley. "This particular evening," the *Principia* relates, "the main subject of discussion was discord." Hill and Thornley

> were complaining to each other of the personal confusion they felt in their respective lives. "Solve the problem of discord," said one, "and all other problems will vanish." "Indeed," said the other, "chaos and strife are the roots of all confusion." . . .
>
> *Suddenly the place became devoid of light. Then an utter silence enveloped them, and a great stillness was felt. Then came a blinding flash of intense light, as though their very psyches had gone nova. Then vision returned.*
>
> The two were dazed and neither moved nor spoke for several minutes. They looked around and saw that the bowlers were frozen like statues in a variety of comic positions, and that a bowling ball was steadfastly anchored to the floor only inches from the pins that it had been sent to scatter. The two looked at each other, totally unable to account for the phenomenon. The condition was one of suspension, and one noticed that the clock had stopped.
>
> *There walked into the room a chimpanzee, shaggy and grey about the muzzle, yet upright to his full five feet, and poised with natural majesty. He carried a scroll and walked to the young men.*
>
> *"Gentlemen," he said, "why does Pickering's Moon go about in reverse orbit? Gentlemen, there are nipples on your chests; do you give milk? And what, pray tell, Gentlemen, is to be done about Heisenberg's Law?" He*

> *paused. "SOMEBODY HAD TO PUT ALL OF THIS CONFUSION HERE!"*[34]

That was followed by a vision of Eris, the Greek goddess of chaos, who became the duo's object of worship.

Should that story seem hard to believe, here is an alternative account. Hill and Thornley were high school pals in East Whittier, California, where they shared an affection for crackpots, a distaste for religion, and a fondness for pranks. (Once they created what Thornley's biographer Adam Gorightly described as a "seemingly mundane radio program" interrupted periodically by reports that "Soviet planes were invading the U.S. and dropping bombs."[35] They loaded this latter-day "War of the Worlds" into a concealed reel-to-reel tape player, set up an ordinary radio that appeared to be the source of the broadcast, and let it play during drama class, scaring the hell out of their classmates.) Discordianism was a drunken prank of a theology, a couple of smart-asses cracking jokes. It probably wouldn't have outlasted their teen years if Hill and Thornley hadn't found themselves corresponding in the early sixties, reviving their old high school gag in their letters.

By that time Thornley had spent some time in the marines, where he had befriended a private named Lee Harvey Oswald. When Oswald defected to the Soviet Union, Thornley wrote a novel, *The Idle Warriors*, that attempted to make sense of his old friend's decision. He finished it in 1962—surely the only book to have been written about Oswald *before* the death of John F. Kennedy. Thornley had trouble finding a publisher for the manuscript, which didn't see print until 1991.[36] But in the wake of Kennedy's death, in 1965, he did produce a paperback, called *Oswald*, that attempted to analyze the assassin's mind. It included no conspiratorial speculations. At that point, Thornley believed that Oswald had been a lone gunman.

That same year he contributed some pages to another book, though in this case I am using the word "book" loosely. *The Principia Discordia, or How the West Was Lost* was a collection of antireligious, antistatist, and generally antiauthoritarian humor assembled by Hill; only five copies were printed. It included an early attempt at a Discordian mission statement. "Why are the secrets of the atom used to promote chaos among men? Why are the most generous motives of men played upon to produce slavery? Why do otherwise sane people attend church on Sunday?" asked a passage contributed by Thornley. "The purpose of The Discordian Society is to provide false, comforting answers to questions of this sort; to give mystical reasons for the disorder around us; to promote unworkable principles of discord—in short, to provide the world with a workshop for the insane, thus keeping them out of mischief as Presidents, Ambassadors, Priests, Ministers, and other Dictators."[37]

As this and other texts circulated among the church's growing circle, Hill and Thornley and their collaborators kept adding to the new faith's mythos. Discordians, they decided, were discouraged from praying, prohibited from eating hot dog buns, and encouraged to break the prohibition on eating hot dog buns. And every Discordian was a pope. Or at least all the male Discordians were. The women were called momes.

Much of this appeared in the radically revised 1969 edition of the *Principia*, now subtitled *How I Found Goddess and What I Did to Her When I Found Her*, which had a print run of much more than five and would be reprinted several times in the ensuing decades. It was silly stuff, but some serious ideas could be spotted floating behind the jokes. Order, the Discordians argued, is in the eye of the beholder. "The real reality is there," the *Principia* explained, "but everything you KNOW about 'it' is in your mind and yours to do with as you like. Conceptualization is art, and YOU ARE THE ARTIST."[38]

It was natural that the Discordians would become fascinated by conspiracy theories, the fringier the better. What better example could there be of a mind organizing signals into an intricate imaginary order than a crank's mad attempts to explain the irrational world? As one Discordian pope put it, "Nesta Webster had all sorts of spooks in her head (I always imagine her looking under the bed for Illuminati agents at night), but she was so modest that she didn't recognize herself as the artist creating all that. She imagined it was going on outside her."[39]

The pope in question was Robert Anton Wilson, a novelist, journalist, and essayist who wrote frequently about conspiracy theories. All three streams flowed into his work: He was a Fortean, a Discordian, and a regular contributor to *The Realist*. You could see those influences in the literary method he called *guerrilla ontology*. Since ontology is the study of being, he explained, "the guerilla approach is to so mix the elements of each book that the reader must decide on each page 'How much of this is real and how much is a put-on?'" That, he said, was the "basic technique of all my books," be they nominally fiction or nominally nonfiction.[40] It was a perfect fit for the ironic style.

Wilson's writing was marked both by skepticism and by a playful willingness to suspend his skepticism. He believed conspiracies were "standard mammalian politics,"[41] but he also recognized, as in his comments about Webster, that conspiracy theories often revealed more about the theorist than they did about the actual objects of the theorizing. He was also extremely antiauthoritarian in his politics, and this attitude made him both more willing to believe that powerful people were engaged in criminal plots and less willing to believe that the conspirators were capable of carrying out those plots competently. In 1975, he and Robert Shea would publish *Illuminatus!*, a three-volume novel that both embodied the ironic style and played a large role in bringing the Illuminati into contemporary popular culture.

Robert Edward Wilson—he traded the Edward for an Anton after he started writing professionally—was born in Brooklyn in 1932. Wilson's father lost his job not long after the boy was born, and the family had to move to a coal-heated bungalow on an unpaved road in Gerrison Beach, an Irish Catholic enclave on Long Island. In that place and time, Wilson later recalled, the angry unemployed "were divided into two hostile camps. The first group said The Depression resulted from the machinations of the Wicked Jews, but the other group said it resulted from the selfish scheming of the Wicked Republicans. My father was in the second group. Despite their ideological differences, both groups of heretics voted for Roosevelt religiously." Well, *almost* all of them voted for Roosevelt religiously: There were a few odd ducks such as Wilson's uncle Mick, an acolyte of the anti-Semitic radio priest Charles Coughlin. Mick Wilson thought the president "was actually a rich Jew, who had changed his name from Rosenfelt," his nephew later recalled.[42] When Wilson's dad joined the CIO, his uncle took to singing, "Hi-ho, hi-ho / I joined the CIO / I paid my dues to a bunch of Jews / Hi-ho, hi-ho, hi-ho."[43]

Wilson's dad and uncle did agree on one thing: Neither one wanted the United States to enter World War II. Mick still suffered from the poison gas he had encountered as a soldier in the previous big war, and neither he nor his brother wanted Americans to be sent off to battle again.

Wilson contracted polio as a child, and his doctors told his parents that he would be paralyzed for life. He overcame that, thanks to the Sister Kenny method, a controversial treatment developed by an Australian nurse who is now regarded as a pioneer of physical therapy. As a result, he wrote, "the major event of my early childhood consisted of being cured of a major crippling illness which left most of its victims permanently confined to wheelchairs, *by a method which all recognized Experts regarded as unscientific and useless*. This instilled me with certain doubts about Experts."[44] The objects of his doubt soon grew to encompass the Catholicism that dominated his neighborhood. When he went to Brooklyn Technical High School and encountered the liberals who taught civics there, he found he had doubts about some of their ideas, too—particularly their support for Franklin Roosevelt's war. He started reading antiwar historians, despite the disapproval of his teachers.

He also, at age seventeen, became a Trotskyist, finding that the Trots "agreed with me about how capitalist wars get started, but they weren't anti-semitic nuts like Uncle Mick."[45] That phase didn't last long. Though he was the only member of his party cell who actually came from a working-class background, the others kept accusing him of having "bourgeois tendencies." Fed up, he left the organization and adopted the ideas of Ayn Rand instead. He quickly discarded those dogmas, too.[46]

Wilson was working his way through a variety of ideologies, incorporating individual ideas that he liked but growing steadily more suspicious of large-scale belief systems in general. (In later years, he would frequently point out that "belief system" can be abbreviated as "b.s.") He found that he had absorbed Uncle Mick's distrust of banks and governments even as he recoiled from his uncle's bigotry and ideological certainty.[47] He knew he didn't like the form of capitalism that prevailed in the United States in the middle of the century, and he knew he didn't like the form of socialism that had taken hold in the eastern bloc either. He started investigating alternative systems, looking for ideas that "transcend the hackneyed debate between monopoly Capitalism and totalitarian Socialism."[48] His favorite was the individualist anarchism promoted by Benjamin Tucker and other nineteenth-century libertarians.

He was also intrigued by the theories of Wilhelm Reich, a radical psychiatrist who had fallen prey to the paranoia of the postwar era. Reich had already, in Wilson's admiring words, been "expelled from the International Psychoanalytical Society for being too Marxist, from the Communist Party for being too Freudian, and from the Socialist Party for being too anarchistic."[49] After arriving in the United States in 1939, Reich attracted sensationalist press coverage by preaching sexual liberation and touting the allegedly curative properties of "orgone," a cosmic energy that the psychiatrist believed he had discovered. Before long there was a Food and Drug Administration investigation and then an injunction ordering the destruction not just of Reich's orgone accumulators—the devices that had attracted the FDA's attention—but of all of Reich's books that invoked orgone energy or "allied material." When Reich did not cooperate, he was charged with contempt and sentenced to two years in prison, where he died.

Historians often attribute the psychiatrist's legal difficulties to the witch-hunting atmosphere engendered by McCarthyism. It is possible that they are partly right; it's not hard to imagine intersections between the Red scare and the Reich scare. But as with Fredric Wertham's anticomics crusade, the driving forces behind the war on Reich hailed from the left. Wertham himself denounced the psychiatrist in *The New Republic* in 1946, describing one of Reich's books as "exactly what the fascists preach."[50] The next year in the same magazine, the prominent consumerist Mildred Edie Brady pointed to Reich and his "cult of no little influence" to remind psychiatrists of "the responsibility of their profession to discipline itself if it is not to be disciplined by the state."[51] Her article inspired the FDA's investigation.

Brady had been on the receiving end of an inquisition in 1941, having lost her job at the Office of Price Administration when Representative Martin Dies charged the agency with harboring Communist sympathizers.[52] Now one of her articles set into motion the process that culminated with Reich imprisoned at the Lewisburg Federal Penitentiary and his books dumped into an incinerator. Disciplined by the state, indeed.[53]

It was the incineration that caught Wilson's attention. He recoiled at the thought that the U.S. government was burning books, and he decided to seek out Reich's forbidden writings and judge the ideas for himself. He came away from the experience enchanted by the writer. Reich's politics mixed easily with Wilson's interest in antiauthoritarian ideas; Reich's ideas about orgone meshed with Wilson's growing interest in Buddhism, Taoism, and other sorts of mysticism; and Reich's calls for sexual liberation offered a link between the two, a way Wilson could connect political and psychological repression.

By that time Wilson had married the playwright Arlen Riley, adopted her two children, and sired two more. He worked at a series of straight jobs to support his family while writing after hours for *The Realist* and other alternative outlets. Sometimes he landed jobs that allowed him to write for a living, though the nature of that writing varied considerably from one employer to another. In Passaic, New Jersey, he churned out ad copy for the Popular Club Plan. In Lane's End, Ohio, he lived on a homestead and edited a decentralist journal that had been called *Balanced Living*. (He changed the name to *Way Out*, amped up the magazine's anarchist and Reichian content, started publishing poetry by Allen Ginsberg and Norman Mailer, and alienated a lot of readers.) Back in New York, he was a staffer at *Fact*, where he profiled both *Mad* and *The National Inquirer*.

And for three months he worked for a company he called "the country's leading schlock factory," editing three pulp magazines and writing an ESP column for a tabloid paper. "I read the predictions that had appeared over the past several months," he later recounted, "and began grinding out my own predictions, out of the blue. It was surprisingly easy. Among other things, I predicted that Lyndon Johnson would be assassinated, that anti-American riots would occur in another Latin American nation, that the $15,000,000 pornography collection on the closed shelves of a large public library would be robbed by a mob led by a defrocked priest 'well known in occult circles,' that flying saucers would be in the news again, that shocking discoveries would be made at Stonehenge throwing new light on ancient Egypt and revealing how man came to be on earth (ESP bugs, I reasoned, are generally also the types who believe that man was deposited here by flying saucers and that Egypt is full of occult mysteries), that peanut butter would be found to contain radioactive isotopes, and that a Hollywood star would be involved in a sex-and-LSD orgy." Soon he was getting fan letters. "Many of them congratulated me on the number of my predictions that came true, although actually *none* of them ever came true."[54]

His big break came in 1966, after *Playboy* spotted a scathing attack on Hugh Hefner that Wilson had written for *The Realist* a few years before and was impressed enough to offer him a job. (Or at least that was how Wilson described the hiring process to Paul Krassner.) Wilson moved to Chicago, where the magazine put him in charge of the Playboy Forum, a letters column that dealt frequently with individual rights and abuses of power. After he published a discussion of spying by the U.S. Post Office, the editors of the libertarian newsletter *Innovator* sent him an issue featuring a story about private alternatives to the post office.[55] Not long afterward, *Innovator* received and printed a letter about private police and arbitration agencies, signed by one "Simon Moon."[56] Moon was really Wilson, and *Innovator*'s editors included Kerry Thornley. The two began a correspondence, and Thornley introduced his new friend to Discordianism, which Wilson immediately embraced.

Meanwhile, Wilson's encounters with paranoid politics were coming closer to home. He was going to antiwar rallies, contributing to underground newspapers, having Black Panthers over to visit, and otherwise behaving in ways that might attract unwelcome official attention. There was a fair amount of pot and psychedelic drugs in the apartment too, amping up the fear of the police. "I learned you don't say anything that somebody who's tapping the phone is gonna wanna know," his daughter Christina later remembered. "You don't answer the door because it could be the FBI."[57]

But if Wilson was wary about the long arms and ears of the law, he also saw the absurdity of living your life in constant fear. "I think it's probably what inspired my novels," he told an interviewer years later. "I learned to live with that without getting paranoid."[58] The Discordian spirit of play and the sixties spirit of paranoia intermingled as Wilson, Thornley, and their allies began Operation Mindfuck, a free-form art project that was part political protest, part parade of pranks. In a weird way, it resembled the more bizarre COINTELPRO operations: something you might do if you learned about the FBI's Siberian beetle plot and attempted to emulate the surrealist sensibility that must have come intuitively to the federal agent who conceived it.

Wilson laid out the basic instructions for Operation Mindfuck in a memo sent to several friends (including Krassner). Participants were "to circulate all rumors contributed by other members," and they were "to attribute all national calamities, assassinations or conspiracies to the other member-groups." The one great risk, he cautioned, was that "the Establishment might be paranoid enough to believe some wild legend started by one of us and thereupon round up all of us for killing Abraham Lincoln."[59]

So they sent a letter on Bavarian Illuminati stationery to the Christian Anti-Communist Crusade, just to confirm that "we've taken over the Rock Music business. But you're still so naïve. We took over the business in the 1800s. Beethoven was our first convert."[60] Robert Welch of the John Birch Society got a letter informing him that Gary Allen was an Illuminati agent. When a New Orleans jury refused to convict one of the men Jim Garrison blamed for the JFK killing, Garrison's booster Art Kunkin of the leftist *Los Angeles Free Press* received a missive from the "Order of the Phoenix Angel" revealing that the jurors were all members of the Illuminati. The telltale sign, the letter explained, was that none of them had a left nipple.

The Discordians planted stories about the secret society in various leftist, libertarian, and hippie publications, introducing the Illuminati to the counterculture. "We accused everybody of being in the Illuminati," Wilson recalled. "Nixon, Johnson, William Buckley, Jr., ourselves, Martian invaders, all the conspiracy buffs, *everybody*." But they

> did not regard this as a hoax or prank in the ordinary sense. We still considered it guerrilla ontology.
>
> My personal attitude was that if the New Left wanted to live in the particular tunnel-reality of the hard-core paranoid, they had an absolute right to that neurological choice. I saw Discordianism as the Cosmic Giggle Factor, introducing so many alternative paranoias that everybody could pick a favorite, if they were inclined that way. I also hoped that some less gullible souls, overwhelmed by this embarrassment of riches, might see through the whole paranoia game and decide to mutate to a wider, funnier, more hopeful reality-map.[61]

They inserted that chart into *The East Village Other.* They placed odd ads in *Innovator.* They practically took over the Chicago paper *rogerSPARK*, which once had been a fairly staid New Left outlet affiliated with the 49th Ward Citizens for Independent Political Action.[62] The Discordians filled it with anarchist politics and surrealist satire: Someone scanning the classifieds might see an ad declaring, "PARANOIDS UNITE; you have nothing to fear but each other! Send for the informative booklet 'How to Start Your Own Conspiracy'. Free from the Office of the District Attorney, New Orleans."[63] In the summer of 1969, the paper accused Chicago's mayor of being an arm of the octopus, running the front-page headline DALEY LINKED WITH ILLUMINATI.[64]

In the April 1969 edition of the Playboy Advisor column, right after an inquiry about blue balls, this missive appeared:

> I recently heard an old man of right-wing views—a friend of my grandparents'—assert that the current wave of assassinations in America is the work of a secret society called the Illuminati. He said that the Illuminati have existed throughout history, own the international banking cartels, have all been 32nd-degree Masons and were known to Ian Fleming, who portrayed them as SPECTRE in his James Bond books—for which the Illuminati did away with Mr. Fleming. At first, this all seemed like a paranoid delusion to me. Then I read in *The New Yorker* that Allan Chapman, one of Jim Garrison's investigators in the New Orleans probe of the John Kennedy assassination, believes that the Illuminati really exist. The next step in my galloping descent into credulity occurred when I mentioned this subject to a friend who is majoring in Middle Eastern affairs. He told me the Illuminati were actually of Arabic origin and that their founder was the legendary "old man of the mountains," who used marijuana to work up a murderous frenzy and who fought against both the Crusaders and the orthodox Moslems, adding that their present ruler is the Aga Khan; but, he said, it is now merely a harmless religious order known as Ismailianism.

> I then began to wonder seriously about all this. I mentioned it to a friend from Berkeley. He immediately told me that there is a group on campus that calls itself the Illuminati and boasts that it secretly controls international finance and the mass media. Now (if *Playboy* isn't part of the Illuminati conspiracy), can you tell me: Are the Illuminati part of the Masons? Is Aga Khan their leader? Do they really own all the banks and TV stations? And who have they killed lately?[65]

The letter was signed "R.S., Kansas City, Missouri," but it had actually been cooked up by Wilson and Thornley. Wilson's reply, written in the light and neutral tone expected of the Playboy Advisor, cleared up most of the historical confusions contained in the letter (though it added the unsupported claim that Weishaupt's Illuminati were "based loosely" on the Old Man of the Mountain's order). The Berkeley Illuminati, Wilson added, were "a put-on by local anarchists."

It wasn't always easy to tell where Operation Mindfuck ended and sincere paranoia began. "The Discordian revelations seem to have pressed a magick button," Wilson later wrote. "New exposés of the Illuminati began to appear everywhere, in journals ranging from the extreme Right to the ultra-Left. Some of this was definitely not coming from us Discordians." Not that it was always clear who "us Discordians" were either. Though some of the Berkeley Illuminati were acquainted with Thornley, they had independently invented the joke of posing as an ancient conspiracy.[66] At one point, Wilson recalled, the *Los Angeles Free Press* printed "a taped interview with a black phone-caller who claimed to represent the 'Black Mass,' an Afro-Discordian conspiracy we had never heard of. He took credit, on behalf of the Black Mass and the Discordians, for all the bombings elsewhere attributed to the Weather Underground."[67]

Wilson and Thornley met only once in that period, when Wilson spent the night at Thornley's place in Tampa in 1968. They smoked some pot and started ruminating about their project. "What if there really is an Illuminati?" Wilson asked. "Maybe they'll find out about us and be pissed."

"I doubt if there is," Thornley replied. "And if there by some chance is, they would probably be very happy to have wildass fools like us covering up for them by spreading bizarre theories."[68]

In 1969, Wilson and another *Playboy* editor, Robert Shea, began to work on what would become the most influential element of Operation Mindfuck. Inspired by the nutty letters the magazine often received, Shea and Wilson decided to write a novel "perched midway between satire and melodrama, and also delicately balancing between 'proving' the case for multiple conspiracies and undermining the 'proof.'"[69] The result was *Illuminatus!* It was basically finished in 1971 but it wouldn't be published for another four years, with significant cuts and with the book sliced into three volumes.[70] (A one-volume edition finally appeared in 1984.)

Illuminatus! is the *ur*-text of the ironic style—the book that, as the comics writer Alan Moore later put it, "changed paranoia from an illness into an illuminating game."[71] It is often described as a story in which all the world's conspiracy theories turn out to be true, but it would be more accurate to say that it treats every interpretation of the world, conspiracist or not, as equally plausible and equally ridiculous.

The novel layers one conspiracy atop another atop another, creating a mosaic that refuses to be reduced to a single straightforward narrative. Various characters suggest early on that the Illuminati are the master conspiracy pulling the strings of the world's elites, and we meet a loose alliance of anarchist organizations fighting against them: the Legion of Dynamic Discord, the Erisian Liberation Front, the Justified Ancients of Mummu, even a band of talking gorillas. But each new revelation undermines the information the reader thinks he knows. It's the sort of story where several conspiracies independently show up in Dallas on the same day to kill John F. Kennedy, and even the assassins aren't entirely sure which one fired the decisive bullet. By the end we learn that the allegedly all-powerful Illuminati are as baffled by the world as everyone else.

All the primal myths are invoked in *Illuminatus!*—the Enemy Above and the Enemy Below, the Enemy Outside and the Enemy

Within, even the Benevolent Conspiracy. I wouldn't dare attempt to summarize the novel's labyrinthine plot. I'll just say it's as good a guide as you'll find to the apocalyptic fever dreams of the 1960s and '70s: an acute critique of paranoia that is all the more powerful for being so deeply paranoid itself.

The conspiracy-hunting community wasn't sure what to make of *Illuminatus!* In the Michigan-based newsletter *Conspiracy Digest*, editor Peter McAlpine introduced an interview with Wilson by commenting that many of his readers believed "that Wilson, himself, was an Illuminati agent attempting to lampoon and discredit conspiracy theories." Others, on the other hand, "felt sure he was doing his best to slip the truth past Establishment censors by disguising the truth as a titillating parody." And some readers, aware of Wilson's "occult-Gnostic-psychedelic connections," thought *Illuminatus!* "was a reliable guide to the inner doctrines of the hidden world of the secret societies alleged to control the conspiracy."

The conversation that followed was cordial but contentious. The most telling exchange might be this one:

> McALPINE: Nesta Webster in her *Secret Societies and Subversive Movements* claims that the inner doctrine of the Illuminati was (is?) antiauthoritarian anarchism: the destruction of Church and State. On the other hand, *Illuminatus!* and some of the Illuminati secret records (see Robison's *Proofs of a Conspiracy*) suggest that Weishaupt's real goal was (or is?) a new and absolute state tyranny (now achieved?). Was anarchism a cover for the Illuminati's real goal? Or was the Illuminati's anarchism sponsored by the International Bankers only until the ancient order of kings and queens was destroyed, making way for the bankster dictatorship?
>
> WILSON: Beats the hell out of me. The only safe conclusion about Dr. Weishaupt and his buddies is that their attempt to main-

> tain secrecy has worked marvelously well: no two investigators of the Illuminati have come to the same conclusion about the real purpose of the Order. My *Cosmic Trigger: Final Secret of the Illuminati* asserts that the real inner secret was that they had contact with Higher Intelligence in the system of the double star Sirius. I don't think that's any more preposterous than any other theories about the Illuminati, and I'll bet a lot of my readers believe it. The evidence is so good that I'd believe it myself if I didn't know what a great artist I am and how easy it is for me to produce baroque and beautiful models to fit any weird facts you give me to work with.[72]

Wilson warned McAlpine, "One reality-tunnel is as limiting as another. We are all blind men investigating the elephant. You have to jump quickly from reality map to reality map, time after time, to begin to 'see the Elephant,' in the Sufi phrase, and realize how complex and funny this whole terrestrial drama is."

McAlpine didn't share Wilson's sense of the absurd, but he did agree about the importance of exploring multiple perspectives. McAlpine had his own worldview—"only philosophies based on self-interest as the highest individual value make any sense to me," he once wrote[73]—but he went out of his way to weigh the claims being made in other parts of the political spectrum. In one issue he interviewed Mae Brussell. In another he interrogated Lyndon LaRouche, a veteran of the New Left who had started drifting toward the radical Right. (LaRouche was known for his elaborate conspiracy theories, which frequently featured Henry Kissinger and the queen of England; for the internal authoritarianism of his political organization, which was frequently called a cult; and for a series of assaults he dubbed Operation Mop-Up, in which LaRouche's followers attacked the members of other leftist groups with bats, chains, and other weapons.[74] *Conspiracy Digest* cited LaRouche's theories fairly frequently, and it just as frequently added editorial caveats.) The debut *Digest* featured a four-page review-essay on anti-

Semitic conspiracy literature, with an introduction explaining that McAlpine "refuse[d] to ignore any source" no matter how much he might disagree with the source's opinions.[75] In a sign that even McAlpine was willing to flirt with the ironic style, he at one point mentioned a book called *We Never Went to the Moon*. "We don't take this one seriously," he explained, "but collectors of conspiracy apocrypha may want it anyway."[76]

McAlpine's readers might have enjoyed *Cover-Up Lowdown*, a cartoon syndicated to underground and college newspapers for about half a year in 1976—sort of a *Ripley's Believe It or Not!* for conspiracy buffs. But the comic's entertaining approach could hardly be more different from the *Digest*'s dry earnestness. Written and drawn by Jay Kinney and Paul Mavrides, each *Cover-Up Lowdown* consisted of a single panel built around an allegation about the Enemy Above, with the source of the claim identified in a footnote. One cartoon, for example, reported that "**JFK**'s preserved **brain** and related **slides**, important for fixing the true flight path of the fatal shot, were discovered **missing** from the **Nat'l. Archives** in '72. There's still no clue as to who took them or where they are."[77] The report was sourced to Robert Sam Anson's 1975 book *They've Killed the President*, and it was illustrated by a picture of a brain and several slides walking out of the archives, looking like a mother duck and her ducklings.

Other installments of the comic covered wiretapping, environmental contamination, the CIA's alliance with the Mafia, the attempted assassination of George Wallace, and the deaths of Robert Kennedy, Martin Luther King, the nuclear whistle-blower Karen Silkwood, and the Native American activist Anna Mae Aquash. Despite the funny drawings, the cartoonists were sincere about what they were doing. "That was at a time when investigative journalism was probably at its peak," Kinney later recalled, "when all of the revelations had been coming out about Watergate, about the intelligence agencies' misdeeds. So there was a lot of material out there that we could draw upon. I think our notion was: Okay, let's try to get this out to people who may not be reading the daily newspaper or

serious journalistic investigations, but we'll distill it down to factoids and crack a joke about it. But getting the info out was the main goal."[78]

When Rip-Off Press collected the cartoons in a comic book, Kinney and Mavrides added several stories in the ironic style. In the first one Bud Tuttle, a right-wing broadcaster devoted to exposing the "machinations of Zionist one-worlders and would-be cattle mutilators in Washington," spends a dollar, which then passes through the hands of a series of malevolent cabals, from a cult led by Baba Black Sheep to the Soma Broadcasting System, a media combine controlled by Cthulhu, Inc.[79] There is also an absurdist eight-page story about the "Solar Czars of Cornutopia," a quiz headlined "You Killed Kennedy! And Here's the Proof . . . ," a comic about cattle mutilations that ends with some cows devouring a dead relative, and an elaborate conspiracy chart designed to be cut out and twisted into a Möbius strip. In the last feature, the Vatican, the Communists, the Theosophists' Great White Brotherhood, and other forces sit atop a diagram that incorporates everyone from Scientology founder L. Ron Hubbard to Big Brother, who is shown to be in direct command of both George Orwell and Janis Joplin.

"We were partly reacting to a certain kind of conspiracy mongering that presumed that everything under the sun connected up into one big conspiracy, which we found to be somewhat absurd and overblown," Kinney would later explain. "The sort of ironic intention was to take that to such an extreme that it collapsed under its own weight." In short, the comic book was both ironist and fusionist, mixing gags with serious allegations and trusting readers to tell the difference.

In 1982, the Tulsa-born, Austin-based game designer Steve Jackson created an Illuminati card game. He was inspired by *Illuminatus!* but he didn't want to do a direct adaptation of such a convoluted story: "[E]ven if you could figure out who was on whose side, which I didn't think I could, how could you make a game out of it?" Instead he created his own scenario, using Wilson and Shea's books "as spiritual guides, but not as actual source material."[80] In the game that resulted, several contending conspiracies—the Bavarian Illuminati, the Discordian Society, the Servants of Cthulhu, and others—battle and bargain for control of a host of smaller cabals, from the Mafia, the CIA, and the International Communist Conspiracy to the Trekkies, the Dentists, and, naturally, the Conspiracy Theorists.

It was both a fun pastime and an effective satire. In Jackson's words, "The cards take a sardonic attitude toward absolutely everything," because "in the world of the game, nobody is innocent. Every organization is a puppet or a manipulator, and most are both."[81] Shea liked what Jackson had done and wrote an introduction to the first expansion set. Wilson was less enthusiastic, complaining to his agent that the game infringed on his intellectual property rights.[82] His agent disagreed, and no legal battle ensued. In practice, the game probably helped rather than hurt Wilson's bank account, since it served as an advertisement for *Illuminatus!*

It also served as a catalyst for still more creativity, as fans produced their own versions of the game and its sequels. "I have seen people recast everything from their offices to their cities in terms of Illuminati," Jackson has said. The games would also inspire some sincerely held conspiracy theories, of which we'll have more to say in chapter 12.

But the biggest development of the 1980s, on the ironist front at least, was the Church of the SubGenius. This group resembled the Discordian Society, except that whereas the Discordians borrowed their goddess from classical mythology, the SubGenii assembled their mythos from more modern sources, from UFO cults to sales manuals. It was centered on the worship of a pipe-smoking messiah named J. R. "Bob" Dobbs. The Church of the SubGenius has two histories: the real one and a fictional saga spread by its devotees. Jay Kinney, who had been appointed the church's minister of propaganda, wrote up the imaginary version in a mock exposé published in *Whole Earth Review* and *Weirdo*. "Church old-timers like Rev. Ivan Stang of Dallas date their involvement in the cult back to the late '50s," he wrote, identifying Dobbs as a former aluminum siding salesman and "bit-actor in C-movies" who founded the SubGenius Foundation after he began to believe he was receiving messages from aliens and/or from "Jehovah-1 the Space God." Dobbs's teachings initially reflected his Birchite political ideas, Kinney continued, but after an "extended love affair with LSD in the late 1960s and early 1970s" his movement "evolved into a Church." Eventually, the church began to allow individual SubGenii to add their own gods and demons to the pantheon, transforming the "monotheistic neo-UFO cult" into "a polytheistic grab-bag."

The church might seem to be "a harmless eccentric sect sprung from the same sun-baked environment that Jack Ruby and Lyndon Johnson both called home," Kinney concluded, but it "has long since outgrown its humble roots and is stalking bigger game. Consider it all a joke at your own risk."[83] At least one academic who read the account failed to recognize it as a put-on, gravely reporting that "Kinney fears that the Church's absolute cynicism is tantamount to fascism" and adding, "Sharing that fear, we note that Bob's world is a white phallocracy."[84]

In fact, J. R. "Bob" Dobbs never existed. The church was dreamed up in the late 1970s by a couple of Texas wiseacres named Doug Smith and Steve Wilcox, or, as they referred to themselves in their SubGenius lives, Ivan Stang and Philo Drummond.

Stang grew up in the Dallas/Fort Worth area, watching monster movies and producing his own amateur films and science fiction fanzines. As an adult he became a freelance movie editor and director, working on industrial films, documentaries, fund-raising films for nonprofits, and music videos. When Drummond moved to Dallas from Austin, Stang recalled, the two men bonded over their shared love of "what you might call kook pamphlets or extremist literature"[85]—Jack Chick comics, Bircher tracts, Scientology questionnaires. They also noticed a face that kept recurring in the ads in old magazines: "This square-looking guy smoking a pipe, and he would always be grinning." That man's face inspired the face of "Bob," and the tracts they were reading and sci-fi movies they were watching inspired the church's mythology.

From around 1976 to 1979, the idea for the church gestated. "We have to have an enemy, you know," Drummond had told Stang as they were inventing the faith. "Let's just call it The Conspiracy." This wouldn't be just any old cabal. "It's not just the people who shot JFK or the crashed flying saucer in Area 51 or Roswell," Stang later explained. "It's everybody. Every normal person is out to get every abnormal person. Just instinctively. They don't even think about it. You know, harking back to when you're a nerd getting bullied in school all the way up to when you're an outsider in the office in a way that might as well be high school." ("And for that matter," he added, "the whole stupid thing even continues in the little society of active SubGeniuses.")[86]

The group's first pamphlet was printed on January 2, 1980. The cover announced: "REPENT! Quit Your JOB! ¡SLACK OFF! The World Ends Tomorrow and YOU MAY DIE!" (Then, in smaller type: "Well, no, probably not . . . but whatever you do, just keep reading!")[87] It was followed by more SubGenius pamphlets, by SubGenius films, by a SubGenius magazine called *The Stark Fist of Removal*. You can get a taste of the church's style of humor, and a hint of the perspective lurking behind the humor, in this passage from 1983's *The Book of the SubGenius*:

> They aren't *readying* us for takeover, THAT'S already HAPPENED. **ONE WORLD GOVERNMENT IS HERE.** It just isn't *obvious* yet. But any day now the media will have people not only prepared for the realization, but *welcoming* it. One World Government is "hip." . . .
>
> Sounds like kook-talk, huh? That's because they're always one jump *ahead* of you. THEY ENGINEERED THE SPREAD OF CRAZY CONSPIRACY THEORIES, because even though many of the theories are *true*, they *still sound crazy*: the Rockefeller Conspiracy, the C.F.R., The Round Table, the Bilderbergers, the JFK "cleanup," ALL OF IT.
>
> The C.F.R. and the Trilateral Commission: oh, they're bad guys, alright, but compared to the REAL controllers they're just the *clerks* at the *front desk*. They're just the sales force of a far larger "company." Sure, they have more control than any sane American ever dreamed possible, but they themselves are more controlled than THEY ever dreamed possible. According to "Bob," some of the *top men* there *actually still believe* they're preserving a *two*-party system in America. . . .
>
> For that matter, you'd be CRAZY not to suspect that the Church of the SubGenius is one of Their *cleverest ruses*. . . . We're not, and

> we don't care who believes it, but that IS how tricky They REALLY ARE.[88]

The older ironists liked the new church. Robert Anton Wilson joined. Paul Mavrides got involved early on and participated heavily in the ensuing decades. Kerry Thornley contributed a sidebar to *The Book of the SubGenius*, and he later declared the "Bob" cult a "sister faith or brother religion" to Discordianism—"or at least our Marine-Corps buddy theology."[89] John Keel came to a SubGenius party, where by Stang's account the old ufologist got drunk and confessed that his books regularly fudged the facts: "I'm from a carnival background. You think that stuff's real?"

By the mid-1980s, SubGenius influence was creeping into the larger culture. The face of "Bob" appeared in the credits of the kids' show *Pee-Wee's Playhouse*. Steve Jackson and the church put together *INWO: SubGenius*, a "Bob"-based version of one of Jackson's Illuminati games. David Byrne, the lead singer of the arty pop band Talking Heads, became a SubGenius. So did the members of another rock group, Devo. (In the SubGenius video *Arise!*, Devo singer Mark Mothersbaugh described The Conspiracy as "the human condition. It's things falling apart. It's fat ladies in double-knit jumpsuits beating their kids in Kroger's. . . . It's Christ without a penis.")[90] Richard Linklater's 1991 film *Slacker*, which presented an Austin filled with conspiracy theorists and other artists and cranks, drew directly on SubGenius lore.

As *Slacker* entered theaters, another movie dived even deeper into the ironic style. *Tribulation 99: Alien Anomalies Under America* was written and directed by a card-carrying SubGenius named Craig Baldwin.[91] *Tribulation* was constructed largely from found footage, combining B movies, newscasts, and other sources to illustrate a secret history of the Western Hemisphere. It was a seminal independent film, a significant step in the evolution from earlier found-footage filmmakers to the mash-up artists inhabiting YouTube today. But as fascinating as Baldwin's rapid montage of fragments from our shared cultural past can be—he has compared the effect of watching his movies to gazing at "shards of a mirror"[92]—the most impressive thing about *Tribulation 99* is the carefully nested narrative that allows Baldwin to sketch out a conspiracy theory as bizarre and comic as anything in *Illuminatus!* or *The Book of the SubGenius* while threading through it a serious critique of U.S. foreign policy.

The surface story of *Tribulation 99* involves extraterrestrials colonizing the inner earth and brave heroes in Washington struggling to protect the planet from the aliens' machinations. The feverish narration, which draws heavily on crank literature that Baldwin found via Stang's 1988 book *High Weirdness by Mail*, sketches out a fantastic scenario that seems to justify terrible crimes in high places—but since the story is too ridiculous to take seriously, the effect is to expose rather than excuse the abuses of power. We are informed, for example, that when the CIA overthrew the Guatemalan president Jacobo Árbenz, it was really displacing "the aliens' well-placed humanoid double."[93] Árbenz's land reforms are presented as a masquerade: "He claims the idle land is to be distributed among 100,000 peasant families, but actual[ly] plans for more sacrificial pyramids to satisfy the mutants' blood lust." Another leader overthrown by the CIA, Chilean president Salvador Allende, is described as a "cybernetic replicant" trying to "alter the earth's polar axis." The "Watergate martyrs" were "plumbing a possible alien pipeline in Democratic Party headquarters when tripped up by the trivial technicalities of local burglary law."

Throughout the film, titles appear on the screen. Some of them echo the story line with screaming tabloid headlines. Others, printed in another typeface, offer a nonironic description of the underlying facts. While the narrator gives us one explanation for Washington's shift from backing the Panamanian dictator Manuel Noriega to overthrowing him—"Our good friend Noriega is suddenly replaced by a grotesque, voodoo-spouting freak!"—the words on-screen offer a real-world explanation: "Noriega refuses to participate in anti-Sandinista arms-cache hoax."

Completing the Möbius strip, these critiques contain conspiracy theories of their own. The narrator endorses an especially absurd lone-gunman theory of JFK's death: "His assassination *must* have been by an android like Oswald, since no lone human being could possibly hit a distant moving target two times within 1.8 second." Meanwhile, the on-screen title informs us that "Ex-CIA chief Allen Dulles serves on the Warren Commission, supports single-assassin theory." In effect, Baldwin was using images of the Enemy Within, Enemy Outside, and Enemy Below to point an accusing finger at the Enemy Above.

Not everyone was able to distinguish a sincere conspiracy theory from a satiric effort. We've already seen how Krassner's hoaxes and the *Report from Iron Mountain* were mistaken for evidence of actual cabals. The same thing happened to Robert Anton Wilson, whose novels have been cited in all sorts of conspiracy theories, often by the fundamentalist Christians who were the targets of much of his satire.[94] "A lot of them have found that selective passages from my books, out of context, are very useful to them," he told one interviewer. "I don't mind that at all," he added. "I regard that as a marvelous joke."[95]

Even the Church of the SubGenius attracted some bona fide believers. "That has actually been the biggest regret for me," Stang said in 2012. "We were just trying to be like the [psychedelic comedy group] Firesign Theatre and underground comics, our heroes. And what we ended up with is this flypaper for kooks, to a certain degree. Or maybe just people who are ignorant and gullible. Or maybe they're just getting into this stuff for the first time. And they should be damned glad it was us and not Heaven's Gate or Jonestown. . . . I've been told by quite a few people that the Invisible College or something like that was channeling this stuff through me. And I go, 'No, they're not. My buddies and I just get high and we come up with this crap.'"[96] In church circles the believers are dubbed "Bobbies" and mocked, often mercilessly. "A whole lot of SubGeniuses are people who got burned in their childhood by some religion," Stang notes. "Maybe Orthodox Judaism, or fundamentalist Christianity of some kind, or Catholic school. They've got a bone to pick, and they're angry."

That isn't true of Stang, who was raised by secular humanists. "My interest in religion is very, very much like my interest in monster movies," he said. "When you're a kid you read the Greek and Norse religions and they're full of cyclopses and dragons and monsters and they're really cool. And for that matter, even the Book of Revelation has some pretty good monsters in it, my favorite being the Whore of Babylon. . . . I've never lost my love for monsters. As long as somebody else's religion or political party has something like a monster in it, I'm still interested.

"To us, 'Bob' is the ultimate monster," he added. "Because he's the epitome of a mind-control guru. He's like the guy who can make you sit in the sweat lodge until you burn, literally dying. And then die. And then act like it was your fault."

It wasn't just outsiders who sometimes mistook the ironists' efforts for evidence of real conspiracies. The ironists themselves sometimes fell down a rabbit hole and started taking their creations seriously. That happened to Krassner, who eventually returned from his trip around the bend, and to Thornley, who didn't.

Krassner's descent began when he started researching his Scientology story. "I began to work on 'The Rise of Sirhan Sirhan in the Scientology Hierarchy,'" he reminisced later. "But then, in the course of my research, a strange thing happened. I learned of the *actual* involvement of Charles Manson with Scientology." Sure enough, Manson had dipped his toes into Hubbard's church before deciding to go into the guru business himself. "Suddenly I had no reason to use Sirhan as my protagonist. Reality will transcend allegory every time."[97] At that point Krassner got a call from Mae Brussell, who had read about the Scientologists' lawsuit against *The Realist* and wanted to tell him that the church hadn't actually killed any Kennedys. "Oh, I knew that," he replied, "but the article was just gonna be a satire, and they took it seriously. I'm working on something else now instead. Let me ask, do you know anything about the Manson case?"

"Of course," she said. "The so-called Manson murders were actually orchestrated by military intelligence in order to destroy the counterculture movement. It's no different from the Special Forces in Vietnam, disguised as Vietcong, killing and slaughtering to make the Vietcong look bad."[98]

Krassner started getting drawn into Brussell's worldview. When he finally met three of the Manson killers, the women asked him who really ran the country. Pulling a pyramid-shaped seashell from his pocket, he launched into a rap about secret societies, organized crime, military intelligence, and the corporate world. Serious conspiracy stories began to rub shoulders with *The Realist*'s investigative satires, including a 1972 piece by Brussell on the Watergate affair.

Krassner began to think that people were following him. Once, on a bus, he became convinced the man sitting in front of him was in the CIA. To let the guy know that he was on to his game, Krassner pulled out a ballpoint pen and started clicking it like a telegraph, saying "Paul Krassner calling Abbie Hoffman" over and over. (Krassner later told Hoffman, a prominent Yippie, about the incident. "Oh, yeah," Hoffman replied. "I got your call, only it was collect, so I couldn't accept it.")[99]

"I had wanted to explore the Charles Manson case," Krassner later wrote, "but ultimately I had to face the reality of my *own* peculiar darkness. Originally, I had wanted to expose the dangers of Scientology, but instead I *joined* a cult of conspiracy. . . . I thought that what I published was so important that I *wanted* to be persecuted, in order to validate the work. In the process, I had become *attached* to conspiracy."[100]

Krassner's return from paranoia didn't end his interest in conspiracy theories. It just grounded it. "I was able to examine more closely in terms of what could be a conspiracy and what could be misinterpreted," he explained. "The way conspiracy people work, they start with a premise automatically—'This is an assassination, not a suicide'—and then they go back and back through the facts and make them fit that conclusion that they already have." Instead he tried to foster a spirit of "conscious innocence," of approaching a mystery with "as little predisposition as possible."[101]

In the meantime, he kept cracking conspiracy-themed jokes. When HBO hired Krassner to help write a comedy special in 1980, only one of his gags made it to the air: a Secret Service man ordering a drink he calls a Lee Harvey Wallbanger. The censors cut the next line, when the bartender asks, "Yes, sir, will that be one shot or two?"[102]

Thornley, for his part, managed to get drawn into the JFK assassination circus. Jim Garrison tried to get him involved in his investigation of the Kennedy killing, and after Thornley rebuffed the D.A., Garrison started suggesting that Thornley himself had been a part of the plot. Garrison put out a press release claiming that the Discordian had been "closely associated with Lee Oswald," not just in the marines but "at a number of locations in New Orleans" in September 1963.[103]

Thornley gave a deposition before a New Orleans grand jury at the beginning of 1968, and the experience convinced him that Garrison's team wasn't interested in justice. Among other things, the team members seemed intent on pigeonholing him as a Birch-style conservative. "I explained several times to them that I am neither a traditionalist nor a nationalist nor a racist—that I oppose the John Birch Society and what passes today as political Conservatism," Thornley wrote shortly afterward. "I went on to say that I am a 'rightwinger' in so far as I favor individualism, but my rightism is more anarchistic than authoritarian. They looked at me blankly, not seeming to hear."[104]

As Garrison's allegations spread through the underground press, Thornley put out his side of the story in every venue available to him. (The subscribers to *Ocean Living*, a low-circulation zine that Thornley helped edit, were surely surprised when the material they were used to—a typical article informed readers that plankton "can be gathered in nets and used as a nourishing foodstuff"[105]—was now mixed with statements by the assassination theorists David S. Lifton and Sylvia Meagher criticizing Garrison for his pursuit of Thornley.) Garrison was soon spreading the story that Thornley, who bore some physical resemblance to his marine friend, had served as a "double" for the accused assassin, posing as Oswald in the time before the president's murder so as to create a false trail of Oswald's activities.

As he fended off Garrison's attacks, Thornley reconsidered his assumption that Oswald had acted alone in Dallas. In 1973, he read a feature in the Yippie tabloid *Yipster Times* that would later be expanded into Canfield and Weberman's book *Coup d'État in America*. Thornley wasn't just convinced: He began to suspect that he really *had* been involved in the assassination without his knowledge, a hypnotized zombie held in reserve in case something went wrong with the Oswald plan. He started typing up his speculations, boosted by new "memories" of things that he believed had happened to him years before, and he circulated the manuscripts among his contacts. After that, he perceived various odd events as the secret government's reactions to those memorandums.

Some of the incidents would scare anyone: At one point armed bandits in ski masks had raided a party he was attending, stealing Thornley's identification along with everyone else's money. But Thornley was also capable of accusing his girlfriend of working for the conspiracy. He wrote to Greg Hill, "I am literally surrounded by the Intelligence Community, but after the first three attempts to murder me things seem to have cooled down and most of the spies now appear to be on my side."[106] At one point he became convinced that a coworker at the Sunshine Floral Company was really Robert Anton Wilson, "living incognito with [Timothy] Leary in Atlanta for reasons I obviously could not fathom."[107] He wondered whether the collapse of the New Left was caused by "foreign intelligence agencies . . . dosing organizers with a substance causing heart disease, thereafter maintaining control over them by means of a microwave device capable of instantly halting a Pacemaker."[108] By the 1990s, he believed that he was "the product of a Vril Society breeding/environmental manipulation experiment."[109]

In the midst of this, the real Wilson cut off his correspondence with Thornley. It was hard, he told Gorightly years later, "to communicate with somebody when he thinks you're a diabolical mind-control agent and you're convinced that he's a little bit paranoid."[110] Thornley continued to write, sometimes with wit and self-awareness, sometimes not. He spent the last few years of his life working at menial jobs in Atlanta and selling trinkets and essays on the street. It was a chaotic conclusion to a chaotic life—a darkly poetic fate, I suppose, for a man who worshipped Eris. "You know," Thornley told Hill in one of his more lucid moments, "if I had realized all of this was going to come *true*, I would have chosen Venus."[111]

10

THE GHOST OF RAMBO

On Wednesday we'll sing patriotic songs and pretend I said none of the above.

—*Good Guys Wear Black*[1]

In the 1980s, the United States rediscovered its faith in its leaders. Or at least that's the standard gloss on the era, and there's certainly some truth to it. If the iconic political footage of the seventies featured Richard Nixon resigning, the eighties brought the nation's TV screens a Ronald Reagan ad declaring it morning in America.

But the same cynicism about the government that powered a great deal of the seventies Left also helped elect Reagan, and that attitude didn't disappear when the candidate became president. Reagan refused to attack Nixon for Watergate, and he called the investigation that felled the thirty-seventh president a "lynching" and a "witch hunt."[2] But as the liberal pundit Thomas Frank would later grumble, the Nixon scandals also "poisoned public attitudes toward government and stirred up the wave that swept Ronald Reagan into office six years later—and made antigovernment cynicism the default American political sentiment."[3] Reagan co-opted that cynicism, but he didn't kill it. The skeptical seventies spirit didn't disappear so much as it mutated into new forms and hid in plain sight.

One of the forms it took was the shirtless Sylvester Stallone firing a machine gun. When Stallone's Rambo movies came to theaters, many critics hailed or damned them as a sign that the sixties were dead and a new patriotic moment had arrived. Far fewer recognized that they were watching a brawny, bloody descendant of *The Parallax View*.

There are three things people tend to forget about the Rambo series. One is the original book. Before there were any Rambo movies, there was *First Blood*, a 1972 novel by a young literary scholar named David Morrell.[4] It's about a Green Beret called Rambo—the name was inspired partly by Rambo apples and partly by the French poet Arthur Rimbaud—who has come home from Vietnam and is tramping across the United States. It's also about a sheriff named Will Teasle, who doesn't want the long-haired, unshaven kid bringing trouble to his corner of Kentucky. Their conflict eventually engulfs an entire town, with countless people dying meaningless deaths. The book is told alternately from both characters' point of view, switching back and forth until their identities essentially merge. In the end they both die.

It isn't immortal literature, but it's an intelligent thriller. It was respected enough to be assigned occasionally as classroom reading, though "by the mid-eighties," Morrell later wrote, "the controversy generated by the films had caused teachers to shy away from the book."[5] Morrell's Rambo is more loquacious than Stallone's. He is also more of a cold-blooded killer, picking off policemen who pose no real threat and enjoying the thrill of battle. He's one of the first manifestations of what would become a media stereotype: the deeply damaged Vietnam veteran who has trouble adjusting to the home front and finally snaps. In real life, Americans who survived that war have been more likely to be married, college-educated, and gainfully employed than other members of their generation.[6] But in popular culture and the press, they were often portrayed as time bombs waiting to explode.

You can't blame Morrell for that. His Rambo is a well-rounded character with his own motives for what he does, not a cookie-cutter copy of a movie cliché. Morrell meant his story as a metaphor for the culture war breaking out at home while another war raged in Southeast Asia. "The final confrontation between Rambo and Teasle," he wrote, "would show that in this microcosmic version of the Vietnam War and American attitudes about it, escalating force results in disaster. Nobody wins."[7]

When *First Blood* became a movie in 1982, both the story and the metaphor changed. Rambo became more sympathetic: He kills only once in the film, a slaying that is both accidental and an act of self-defense. Teasle, in turn, grows less appealing. Brian Dennehy's textured performance keeps him from being entirely one-dimensional, but he's still a redneck sheriff pointlessly persecuting a war hero. His officers mistreat the man in jail, and the film compares their abuses directly to the torture the soldier received as a prisoner of war. It's clear that Rambo is a little crazy—by the end of the movie, he's more than a little crazy—but it's also clear that viewers are supposed to root for him. "*My* intent was to transpose the Vietnam war to America," Morrell complained. "In contrast, the *film's* intent was to make the audience cheer for the underdog."[8]

But there was more to the movie than that. That's the second thing people forget about the Rambo films: The first one is explicitly antiwar and surprisingly radical. Director Ted Kotcheff's earlier credits include *North Dallas Forty*, a jaundiced take on professional football, and *Fun with Dick and Jane*, a crime comedy that mocks middle-class materialism and the corporate world. *First Blood* continues in that antiestablishment vein.

The film opens with Rambo learning that one of his war buddies has died of exposure to Agent Orange. He wanders into a small town, and almost immediately the sheriff starts to harass the soldier: "Wearing that flag on that jacket, and looking the way you do, you're asking for trouble around here," Teasle tells him. The reference to the flag may seem to signify intolerance toward veterans, but the second clause adds the implication that Teasle doesn't like Rambo because of his appearance—that is, because he looks like a hippie drifter. When the sheriff's men finally find out that Rambo is a Green Beret who served in Indochina, one of them exclaims, "Jesus! That freak?"[9]

This identification of Rambo with the counterculture is a residue of Morrell's novel, which was partly inspired by a news report. "In a southwestern American town," Morrell recalled, "a group of hitchhiking hippies had been picked up by the local police, stripped, hosed, and shaved—not just their beards but their hair. The hippies had then been given back their clothes and driven to a desert road, where they were abandoned to walk to the next town, thirty miles away. . . . I wondered what Rambo's reaction would be if, after risking his life in the service of his country, he were subjected to the insults that those hippies had received."[10]

The most jarring thing about the movie's politics comes later. Everyone remembers Rambo's much-quoted soliloquy at the end of the film, the one where he complains about "maggots at the airport, protesting me, spitting on me, calling me a baby killer." What isn't quoted as often is a conversation between Teasle and Colonel Sam Trautman, the Special Forces officer who trained Rambo. Trautman describes his student's immense skills as a fighter, and he suggests that the police should defuse the situation by letting Rambo escape, waiting a few days, then putting out a nationwide all-points bulletin and picking him up later. Teasle refuses.

> TRAUTMAN: You want a war you can't win?
> TEASLE: Are you telling me that two hundred men against your boy is a no-win situation for us?
> TRAUTMAN: You send that many, don't forget one thing.

TEASLE: What?

TRAUTMAN: Plenty of body bags.

A small but committed guerrilla force humiliating a larger power that doesn't comprehend the fight it's in—the comparison to Vietnam is obvious. It's also a little discomforting, because it puts Rambo in the role of the Vietcong. Morrell was wrong: The movie *does* transpose the Vietnam War to the United States. It just does it in a radically different way from the novel, and with radically different implications. It asks the audience to cheer for a guerrilla hero.

That was surprisingly common in the superficially right-wing cult movies of the eighties. Consider John Milius's *Red Dawn* (1984), in which a small group of Colorado high school jocks battle a Soviet occupation. The film outraged liberal critics, but farther to the left it had some supporters. In a witty and perceptive piece for *The Nation*, the socialist writer Andrew Kopkind called it "the most convincing story about popular resistance to imperial oppression since the inimitable *Battle of Algiers*," adding that he'd "take the Wolverines from Colorado over a small circle of friends from Harvard Square in any revolutionary situation I can imagine."[11] The sole sympathetic character among the occupying forces is a Cuban colonel with a background in guerrilla warfare. At one point he tells a Russian officer, voice dripping with disgust, that he used to be an insurgent but now is "just like you—a policeman."[12] Increasingly sympathetic to the Coloradan rebels, at a key moment the Cuban allows two of them to escape.

First Blood drew from several other genres as well: the redneck movie, the revenge movie, the war film, the western. One sequence, in which the sheriff's men track the fugitive soldier through the woods only to discover that he's hunting them rather than the other way around, feels like a slasher flick, with Rambo in the Jason/Freddy/Michael Myers role. The difference—and it's a substantial one—is that unlike the villains of *Friday the 13th* and *Halloween*, Rambo has the audience's sympathy. In that, he's more like the monster in Universal's old Frankenstein series. *Frankenstein* was, in fact, one of the inspirations for the script: According to Susan Faludi, who interviewed several people involved in the Rambo sequence for her 1999 book *Stiffed*, Stallone "envisioned the drama 'like the Frankenstein monster and the creator,' a creator who 'understood what he made' and 'felt guilty' for it."[13] (Stallone's role in creating the Hollywood Rambo should not be underestimated. He cowrote all four films and directed at least one, perhaps two of them—George P. Cosmatos, credited as the director of *First Blood Part II*, was reportedly a figurehead.)[14]

First Blood ends with a confrontation between Rambo, the sympathetic monster, and Colonel Trautman, his creator. As originally shot, it concluded with Stallone's character committing suicide, but the test audiences hated to see their hero die. So the filmmakers changed the ending. The veteran was sent to prison instead, preparing the way for a series of sequels.

Like the monster emerging from the pit beneath the burning mill at the beginning of *Bride of Frankenstein*, 1985's *Rambo: First Blood Part II* starts with the title character being freed from a prison that Trautman calls a "hellhole." Dangling the possibility of a pardon, Trautman asks if Rambo is willing to go on a covert reconnaissance mission to find MIAs in Communist Vietnam. Rambo accepts with just one question: "Do we get to win this time?"[15]

So begins the movie everyone remembers; or, rather, the movie everyone thinks he remembers. If Stallone's speech about the mistreated vet serves as a screen memory that conceals the more radical implications of the first Rambo picture, the hype and hysteria around the follow-up film have done something similar for *First Blood Part II*. Yes, it's an ultraviolent story about a supersoldier refighting the Vietnam War. Yes, it implies that we could have won Vietnam the first time around if our hands hadn't been tied by liberals back home. Yes, Ronald Reagan co-opted it, joking at the end of a hostage crisis, "After seeing *Rambo* last night, I know what to do the next time this happens."[16] The word *Rambo* entered the language, in phrases such as *Rambo foreign policy*. Some veterans picketed the picture. One vet—Gustav Hasford, the author of the book that became the movie *Full Metal Jacket*—called it "*Triumph of the Will* for American Nazis."[17]

All of which makes it easy to forget that the film is as cynical about the government as any 1970s conspiracy thriller. Indeed, the POW/MIA rescue genre, of which *Rambo* was merely the most popular example, evolved directly from those post-Watergate pictures.

The transition film was Ted Post's *Good Guys Wear Black* (1978), a conspiracy movie that contained the seeds of the POW/MIA cycle to come. The story begins with an ill-fated effort to free some prisoners of war. The rest of the picture is a poor man's *Parallax View*, with Chuck Norris and Anne Archer tracking down the plotters who sabotaged the mission. It's no salve for Vietnam hawks: Early in the film, while teaching a class, Norris's character calls Vietnam "a war that never should have begun, in a country we never should have entered," adding that "the reasons for the war were beyond any rules of logic." (At that point a bell rings, signaling the end of the class. Norris cracks a joke: "On Wednesday we'll sing patriotic songs and pretend I said none of the above.") But there are elements of another old narrative here, along with that familiar seventies story of the Enemy Above. As part of the Paris peace agreement, we learn, the North Vietnamese negotiator secretly demanded "a sacrifice" in which U.S. soldiers are killed. The line recalls the story colonial soldiers whispered about Governor Edmund Andros, that he had "brought them theither to be a sacrifice to their heathen Adversaries." Ghosts of the Indian wars haunt the picture, and sometimes the symbolism is overt. Stateside, our heroes are trailed by a pair of Vietnamese assassins, one a man, one a woman; when the woman shoots a former CIA agent, she does it at the Squaw Valley ski resort.

In other words, the movie has merged the Enemy Above and the Enemy Outside.[18] When he finally confronts the chief conspirator, a few hours before the villain is scheduled to be sworn in as secretary of state, Norris mentions one of the Vietnamese assassins: "At first I assumed he worked for *them*, whoever *they* were—but of course, *they* are *you*, and *you* are all *one*."

It's a bleak film that ends with Norris killing the would-be secretary of state. A friend in the CIA is complicit in the death and helps smooth things over; when the story is done, it's hard to say whether you've seen a justification for revolutionary violence or just for another lawless covert operation. But the movie's general opinion of the nation's establishment is clear. When Norris and the grand conspirator have their first extended dialogue, the politician invokes a wilderness metaphor familiar from many tales of the Enemy Outside, then transfers it someplace new. "I understand, Major Booker, that you were quite a jungle fighter," he tells Norris. "Well, this is my kind of jungle."[19]

In *First Blood Part II*, as in *Good Guys Wear Black*, we learn that Rambo was never supposed to find any prisoners; he rescues them only by ditching the authorities' plan and setting off on his own. (Morrell's novelization of the film is even more skeptical about the government, with a scene in which Rambo chuckles darkly as he informs the disbelieving POWs that Ronald Reagan has become president. He "couldn't bring himself to tell them that Vietnam was about to change its name to Nicaragua.")[20] Stallone doesn't follow in Norris's footsteps and have his character assassinate an American official. But Rambo does return to the computerized command center in the movie's climax, and there he pumps pounds of ammo into its alienating array of machinery. It's a violent, cathartic revision of an old sixties slogan. *I am a soldier. Do not fold, bend, spindle, or mutilate me.*

Like the previous picture in the series, *First Blood Part II* owed a lot to the western.[21] But while the first film resembles those existential stories about a stranger entering a corrupt frontier town, *Part II* is about a cowboy who rides deep into the wilderness to save white captives from savage Indians. Complicating the racial dynamics, Rambo is now identified as a half-breed, part civilized and part wild: We learn that he's half Native American himself (his other half—paging Gustav Hasford!—is German), and he has a brief affair with a Vietnamese woman. But you can still trace the core plot to the Indian captivity narratives that first flourished in seventeenth-century New England and have manifested themselves in the American imagination countless times since.

The movie may have had a more recent antecedent as well. In the late 1970s, a self-promoting soldier named Bo Gritz staged several unsuccessful efforts to rescue American POWs from Indochina. It is often claimed that Gritz's exploits helped inspire *First Blood Part II.* Whether or not that's true, the movie certainly had an impact on Gritz, who started to bill himself as the "real-life Rambo" after the film became a hit.

With that in mind, you can imagine two men walking away from the movie: Hollywood Rambo and Real-Life Rambo. Hollywood Rambo embodies the popular gloss on the eighties; he's either a simpleminded jingoistic killer or a warrior-hero we can have faith in, depending on whether or not you like the Reagan years. Real-Life Rambo is a very different figure, a bridge from the Watergate seventies to the militia nineties.

Hollywood Rambo appeared in another picture, 1988's *Rambo III*, in which he fights alongside the mujahideen in Afghanistan. It's another bringing-Vietnam-home film, but this time Stallone is bringing it home to the Soviets. (In this one Colonel Trautman—the same man who warned Sheriff Teasle about those body bags—informs the Russians, "This war is your Vietnam, man. You can't win!")[22] Hollywood Rambo got his own TV cartoon, *Rambo and the Forces of Freedom*, in which he works for a military peacekeeping unit and battles a global conspiracy called S.A.V.A.G.E. This is the Rambo of "Rambo foreign policy," the Rambo of popular memory; it is invoked by both the fans and the foes of Reagan's bombing raid over Libya and Oliver North's illicit efforts to aid the Nicaraguan Contras.

And Real-Life Rambo? In the late 1980s, Gritz continued to build on that suspicious post-Watergate mood, accusing the intelligence community of connections to the drug trade and speaking to audiences of both the radical Left and the radical Right. In 1992, he ran for president, drawing support from the precursors to the militia movement. His core constituency was a bunch of angry patriots, many of them veterans, who said they loved their country but feared their government. Later in the nineties, their rallying cry would be the confrontation between the Branch Davidians and federal police at Waco, a conflict that was retold in two very different ways. For the authorities and most of the media, it was another version of the captivity narrative, with the ATF and FBI unsuccessfully attempting to rescue children from a sexually depraved death cult. In the alternative story, the police were the villains and the confrontation was a massacre, part My Lai and part Wounded Knee. Like the Mormons of the nineteenth century, elements of the populist Right rewrote the American story with themselves in the role of the Indians.[23]

There are people—real people, not archetypes—who stopped playing one Rambo role and took up the other. Tom Posey was the head of Civilian Material Assistance, a paramilitary group that trained and armed the Nicaraguan Contras in the 1980s. Both the CIA and the National Security Council were aware of Posey's activities and encouraged them. But with the end of the Cold War, Posey's anger shifted from the government in Managua to the government in Washington, and he started hatching plans for a revolution at home. He was thinking along these lines as early as 1990, but after the deaths at Waco his rage intensified.[24]

Meanwhile, the 1997 documentary *Waco: The Rules of Engagement* includes footage of cops in camouflage gathered outside the Branch Davidians' compound before the feds' final assault. A Klansman turns up in the middle of the standoff to offer his services in stopping the group's leader. "Give him an ultimatum, give him a deadline," he suggests. One officer declares himself "honed to kill." A buddy compares him to Rambo.[25]

Which of the two Rambos prevailed? When the Cold War ended, Stallone's movies lost their hold on the culture and decayed into eighties kitsch, while distrust of the government intensified and crossed what used to look like sharp ideological lines. When the wounds of 9/11 were fresh, the outrage of the heartland populists turned outward again; it was a moment made for Hollywood Rambo. After a while, the failures of the Iraq occupation drove many of them back to an antigovernment stance; the spirit of Real-Life Rambo was dominant again. And with the Obama era . . .

Sorry, we're getting ahead of ourselves; we aren't quite ready to cover the Obama years yet. But as long as we've taken a detour to the twenty-first century, let's pause to consider the fourth Rambo movie, released in early 2008. The critics mostly disliked it, deploying such phrases as "enough jingoistic imperialism to make Kipling puff up his chest with pride"[26] and "the *Schindler's List* of B-list butchery."[27] (If you're going to be compared to a movie about Nazis, I guess *Schindler's List* beats *Triumph of the Will*.) David Morrell was more impressed, calling it "the first time that the tone of my novel *First Blood* has been used in any of the movies."[28]

For the most part I'll have to join in the jeers. This is basically a paint-by-numbers action picture that has almost as little to say as its taciturn protagonist. But the film does show a brief glimmer of something thoughtful beneath the monosyllabic grunts and the CGI gore.

The fourth film in the Frankenstein series was called *The Ghost of Frankenstein*. The fourth film in the Rambo franchise is ghostly as well: After an absence of two decades, both the series and its protagonist feel a little undead. An early version of the script pitted Stallone's alter ego against a right-wing American paramilitary group—sort of a *Rambo vs. Rambo* scenario. But the finished product takes us back to Southeast Asia instead. When we return to Stallone's character, he is a numb man hunting snakes for a living in Thailand. Vietnam is deep in his past, and the country's more recent wounds don't seem to have touched him—the word *Iraq* appears nowhere in the movie, and neither does *Al Qaeda*, *Islam*, *9/11*, or *bin Laden*. The writer/director/star told *Ain't It Cool News* that he had taken this approach because "the idea of Rambo dealing with Al-Qaeda, etc. would be an insult to our American forces that are actually dying trying to rid the world of this cancer. To have at the end of a 90 minute movie the character of Rambo seizing Osama bin Laden in a choke hold then dragging him into the Oval Office then tossing him in the President's lap declaring 'The world is now safe, Chief' would be a bit insulting."[29] I don't doubt Stallone's sincerity, though World War II–era GIs didn't seem to mind the fact that Superman, Captain America, and the rest were fighting alongside them in the comic books.[30]

Instead we get a one-man humanitarian intervention in Burma, where brutal soldiers have seized a group of missionaries tending to Christian villagers. Rambo sets out to rescue them, arriving just in time to save a young woman—the closest we have to a female lead—from a rape.

In other words, Stallone has returned to the classic Indian captivity narrative. Remember Richard Slotkin's summary of the archetypal captivity story:

> a single individual, usually a woman, stands passively under the strokes of evil, awaiting rescue by the grace of God. . . . In the Indian's devilish clutches, the captive had to meet and reject the temptation of Indian marriage and/or the Indian's "cannibal" Eucharist. To partake of the Indian's love or his equivalent of bread and wine was to debase, to un-English the very soul.[31]

There are films that intelligently explore the racial and sexual anxieties that underlie this tale. The most famous is John Ford's 1956 film *The Searchers*, in which the captive woman does not want to leave the Indian community; her would-be rescuer, a complex antihero played by John Wayne, would rather kill her than watch her become an Indian.[32] The 2008 *Rambo*, by contrast, merely adopts those old anxieties as its own. The woman prisoner is almost comically pure, kind, white, and blonde, while every Asian character except one—a thoroughly Westernized mercenary who was obviously raised in the United States—is either a victim or a savage. When the original Indian captivity narratives enjoyed their peak of popularity, Slotkin writes, "It almost seems as if the only experience of intimacy with the Indians that New England readers would accept was the experience of the captive (and possibly that of the missionary)."[33] *Rambo* gives us both, and little more. It doesn't seem to have anything to say about the country's scars in Vietnam or the Middle East. Or rather, it doesn't until the final scene, when Stallone does something unexpected.

The Searchers concludes with John Wayne's character turning his back on home and hearth and walking into the western landscape, unable to join the civilized world. Stallone's movie inverts that: Rambo returns to civilization, hiking down an Arizona road toward the house where he grew up. As the old soldier strides down a driveway to his family homestead, the film finally seems to say something that resonates in an era of occupation and empire.

Come back from that violent foreign wilderness, it tells us. *Come home.*

11

THE DEMONIC CAFETERIA

The Cold War was supposed to end in a nuclear inferno that killed everyone. It wasn't supposed to just have the air go out of it. And a deferred eschaton has unusual power. Culturally, we spent decades expecting that we were all going to die. The reprieve didn't suddenly make everybody less pessimistic. It just turned that pessimism inward.

—*Philip Sandifer*[1]

It is June 1994, and Anthony J. Hilder is selling tapes at a convocation called The New World Order. Hilder, whom we last spotted passing out right-wing literature the night Robert Kennedy was shot, is now the host of two talk shows, *Radio Free America* and *Radio Free World*, that continue in the vein of the anti-Illuminati records he produced in the 1960s. Above him, two overhead projectors beam the covers of books about Masonic conspiracies onto the walls of the smoke-filled room.

It might sound like a gathering of the xenophobic Right. In fact it was a multiracial rap/rock concert in downtown Los Angeles, featuring Fishbone, Ice Cube, Ice T, and Body Count, among other performers. The event was organized not by a white man decked out in camouflage but by a black DJ called Afrika Islam, and the smoke thickening the air was not burning tobacco but burning marijuana.

In the 1990s, as the world's cultures and subcultures traded and blended more easily than ever before, so did its schools of fear. Militiamen, hippies, black nationalists, ufologists: one group's legends flowed freely into another's. Figures on the right found ways to work flying saucers into their litany of official crimes and cover-ups. Activists opposed to drug-war abuses extended their outrage to Waco. Alienated African Americans discovered the conspiracy theories and curious legal doctrines of the sovereign citizens, a subculture that also overlapped with the world of white separatists.[2]

The 1990s were boom years for Enemy Above theories, even more than the 1970s had been. But while paranoia had reached the public eye through the front door in the seventies, enshrined by congressional committees and investigations in the country's leading newspapers, two decades later it was a side-door affair, a phenomenon not of broadcasting but of narrowcasting. Its greatest engine was the Internet, which did not merely enable theories from outside the mainstream to reach a much larger audience; it gave those theories new opportunities to mix. The conspiracy subculture that had been developing since the Nixon era was now in full bloom. It was in the 1990s that Michael Kelly coined the phrase *fusion paranoia*, and it was in the 1990s that Michael Barkun identified a phenomenon that he came to call *improvisational millennialism*. Once it had been typical for a conspiratorial or apocalyptic vision to stick to a single tradition, Barkun wrote, but the eclectic new breed could "draw simultaneously on Eastern and Western religion, New Age ideas and esotericism, and radical politics, without any sense that the resulting mélange contains incompatible elements."[3]

For decades, religious leaders had been complaining about "cafeteria spirituality," a mentality in which people customized their beliefs, jettisoning doctrines that didn't appeal to them and mixing in elements from other faiths. With the 1990s, cafeteria demonology came of age.

Meanwhile, the transition from one Rambo to the other took place. The Cold War came to an end, removing a potent Enemy Outside from the country's psychic landscape and allowing many Americans to shift their fears toward the Enemy Above. The confrontations at Ruby Ridge and Waco hastened the process, as suspicions that had once been directed at Communists abroad and their alleged agents at home were redirected at federal police agencies. The Enemy Outside didn't disappear, but it became more diffuse: a ghostly, shape-shifting presence, more a generalized dread about globalization than a fear of a specific foreign power.

In the militia world, the most popular conspiracy theories held that Waco was a trial run for future assaults on independent Americans; that concentration camps were being built within the country's borders; that foreign troops were being imported to impose the new authoritarian order; and that the destruction of local self-government by federal forces would be conjoined with the destruction of national self-government by global forces. When President George H. W. Bush described the post–Cold War world with the phrase "new world order," a phrase that many conspiracy theorists had long associated with a plot to impose a one-world government, suspicious populists saw it as a sign that individual liberty and U.S. independence faced an imminent threat. If conspiracy theories reflect the anxieties and experiences of the people who believe them, these theories were what you'd expect from Americans concerned about a loss of freedom and sovereignty.

Those rising fears of the Enemy Above were met by a growing concern about the Enemy Within and the Enemy Below, as the centrist establishment adopted its own conspiracy theories about militias and other radical groups. Those worries went into overdrive in 1995, when Timothy McVeigh, a Desert Storm vet enraged by Waco, bombed the Alfred P. Murrah Federal Building in Oklahoma

City, killing 168 people, including more than a dozen kids in a day care center.

In the popular imagination, the militia movement was a paranoid pack of racists plotting McVeigh-style attacks. The historian Robert Churchill has called this "the narrative of 1995," a story line in which "the militias and the Patriot movement took on the guise of a perfect, racist 'other,' and the threat they posed was best articulated by Morris Dees' apocalyptic vision of a 'gathering storm.'"[4]

That vision was promoted by a collection of groups dedicated to tracking the radical Right, notably the Anti-Defamation League and Dees's Southern Poverty Law Center. Their narrative dominated the media. "In news coverage, popular novels, episodes of *Law and Order*, and movies such as *Arlington Road*," Churchill wrote, "the public became well acquainted with the archetypal militiaman, usually portrayed as warped by racial hatred, obsessed with bizarre conspiracy theories, and hungry for violent retribution."[5] In *Searching for a Demon*, a 2002 study of how the media portrayed the militias, the sociologist Steven Chermak summed up their image: They were "irrational terrorists—a dangerous, growing outsider threat that needed eradicating."[6]

The figures who promoted that image often traced the militia movement to a weekend meeting in 1992, when Peter J. Peters, an anti-Semitic preacher associated with the Christian Identity movement, organized a gathering of the far-right tribes in Estes Park, Colorado. About 160 people reportedly attended, including one, John Trochmann, who later played a significant role in the militia milieu. (Trochmann denies that he was there.) By that account, the militias were a direct sequel to the violent racist underground of the 1980s, represented by such groups as the Aryan Nations and the Order, a terrorist gang that robbed banks, counterfeited money, and murdered a Jewish talk-show host. For writers such as the Seattle-based journalist David Neiwert, the militias were "specifically geared toward mainstreaming some of the basic tenets of [the racist Right's] worldview."[7] If the militias didn't seem to express the same set of concerns as those predecessors, that was merely a mask.

Churchill offered a more persuasive origin story. He agrees that the militias overlapped with the older, broader populist Right—the sorts of people who gathered around Bo Gritz's presidential campaign—but he also distinguishes the militias from those precursors. The movement began to congeal not in 1992 but in the early months of 1994, as activists reacted to the lethal federal raid on the Branch Davidians. Rather than tracing the phenomenon back to groups such as the Order, Churchill used a series of case studies to explore the long American tradition of armed resistance to intrusive government.

The militias of the 1990s, he argued, were reacting primarily to the rise of paramilitary police tactics. Their causes célèbres—the standoffs in Waco and Ruby Ridge—were only the most visible examples of what could go wrong when policemen regarded themselves as soldiers rather than peace officers. The militias formed and grew, Churchill wrote, as their members "came to the conclusion that the federalization and militarization of law enforcement had created a paramilitary culture of violence."[8] He backed up his interpretation with many quotes from militia figures, including denunciations of the beating of Rodney King in Los Angeles and the rape of Abner Louima, a Haitian man whom New York police sodomized with a broomstick in 1997. Churchill also cited militia publications that covered botched paramilitary police raids. Ohio's *E Pluribus Unum* once listed fifteen raids gone wrong, including three that had left civilians dead, under the headline "Just Who Are the Terrorists?"[9]

Meanwhile, neither McVeigh nor his accomplice Terry Nichols turned out to be a member of a militia. After the Oklahoma City attack, a Michigan Militia spokesman said that his group's closest contact with the bombers had come when James Nichols, Terry's brother, showed up to speak during the open-forum portion of a meeting. As the spokesman told it, Nichols attempted to distribute some literature, urged those present to cut up their driver's licenses, and was eventually asked to leave. (There are conflicting accounts as to whether McVeigh attended a Michigan Militia meeting, but even the witness who believes he was there states that he attended as a guest, not a member. And although some media outlets reported that McVeigh once served as a bodyguard to Michigan Militia leader Mark Koernke, that turned out to be a case of mistaken identity: The man in question was named *McKay*.)[10]

In the years between Oklahoma City and 9/11, some would-be terrorists on the fringes of the militia milieu were nabbed for planning attacks. (By the most generous definition of *militia*, there were about a dozen plots.)[11] Such events bolstered the narrative of 1995, but the details of the schemes reveal a much more complicated picture. Several of the plans originated with the government's own infiltrators. Many of the "militias" involved were tiny operations run by hotheads who'd been expelled from more established militia groups. In at least three cases—a plan to assault a series of government and media targets in Michigan; a plot to bomb gay bars, abortion clinics, and antimilitia groups in Oklahoma; and a strange scheme to prevent a Chinese invasion by attacking Fort Hood, Texas—the conspirators were arrested after militia members themselves got wind of the plans and alerted the police.

Even the identification of the militias with the far Right isn't entirely stable. The Left/Right crossovers that we saw bubbling beneath the paramilitary movies of the 1980s went even further in the following decade, as the fusion paranoia that Michael Kelly described found a receptive audience in much of the militia world. "We don't want to hear about left and right, conservative and liberal, all these bullshit labels," Militia of Montana activist Bob Fletcher told Kelly. "Let's get back to the idea of good guys and bad guys, righteous governments—the honest, fair, proper, American government that all of us have been fooled into believing was being maintained."[12]

The fusionist style had continued to develop in the previous decade, with different figures putting their own stamps on the sensibility.

When a new journal called *Critique* debuted in 1980, mixing articles about conspiracies and social control with essays on mysticism and the paranormal, it became clear just how eclectic the conspiracy subculture could be.

Critique was created by Bob Banner, a young man who first stumbled into the conspiracy world at Santa Rosa Junior College in the mid-1970s. He was in his early twenties, and his life felt aimless: "I was drinking a quart of beer, fucking as many women as I could possibly find, and I was in a spiritual crisis, a psychological crisis."[13] Then he took a course in comparative religion from an instructor named Norman Livergood. When Banner found out that Livergood had a small center of his own—"it was like a secret society, it was like a mystery school"—he asked if he could join. They told him he had to get a haircut, shave his beard, buy a suit, and a find a full-time job. He did all of the above, and Livergood let him into the group: about a dozen people sharing a house and studying esoteric ideas.

According to Banner, Livergood's eclectic interests ranged from the mysticism of G. I. Gurdjieff to the political theories of Lyndon LaRouche, and he had a shelf full of publications from the Institute for Historical Review, an organization infamous for arguing that the Holocaust never happened. Banner adds that Livergood was intrigued by UFOs and by Wilhelm Reich's ideas about sex. At one point, Banner told me, there was talk of "using our sexual attractiveness to other people to possibly bring them into the group." Here Banner paused. "It sounds like I was in a cult. And yes, to a certain degree I was. We were a cult trying to figure out what the fuck we were."[14]

Livergood eventually kicked Banner out, but he left a mark on his former student. The first issue of Banner's magazine included an editorial that seemed simultaneously to reflect Livergood's social critique and to turn it against Livergood himself:

> During the 60s there were created "movements" which infiltrated American culture and politics. We were living in an emotionally strife

> era where racism, sexism, ageism, imperialism, corporatism, psychiatrism, patriotism and nuclear familyism were being attacked ruthlessly and irresponsibly. Movements were created overnight to destroy any new "disease" located in our cultural psyches. People who had the slightest degree of leadership capability amassed alien, atomized individuals to commit their time, rage, money and energy for purposes which these self-appointed leaders assumed to be meaningful.
>
> We didn't question the possibility that we were being duped. Our new beliefs were considered to be our own. We held onto them like cherished artifacts discovered in a cave of lost treasure. We wore them like clothes to distinguish us from our "enemies": that multitude who did not believe the way we did. We didn't see that we were becoming as attached to ideas and belief systems as those people we categorically lumped together on the *other* side. We didn't see it because we didn't want to. It was too easy and comfortable to align ourselves with ideas that were in opposition to the "established reality."

Critique, he hoped, would evoke "the spirit to think, reflect, create and act toward gaining a deeper understanding of the often invisible manipulating influences and of who, in fact, we are and who we are becoming."[15]

When Banner describes this period of his life today, he makes his younger self sound simultaneously skeptical and naive. On one hand, he was willing to interrogate not just the normal assumptions of American society but the assumptions of the most popular alternative social visions as well. At the same time, he was the sort of person willing to follow one of those trails into the arms of a group he came to consider a cult. Make that *two* groups that he came to consider cults: At the dawn of the nineties, feeling aimless again after a decade of publishing *Critique*, Banner joined Xanthyros, an intentional community in Vancouver led by a guru named Robert Augustus Masters. *Critique* was revamped as a New Age magazine called *Sacred Fire*, and Masters took it over, with Banner serving as little more than a typesetter until he left the community.

That mixture of skepticism and naiveté characterized *Critique* as well. "What I really found refreshing about *Critique*," Jay Kinney recalled in 2012, "was that he was in some ways like a newborn with no taboos, would publish anything that challenged consensus reality. He even published Holocaust revisionist material, in what I would call a rather naïve fashion, but he was sincerely engaged with the notion of, 'Well, what if what we know about that isn't true?'" Some of the weirder material was included for novelty value or comic relief: Banner wasn't being serious when, in the midst of a roundup of plausible or at least thinkable conspiracy news items, he threw in someone's theory that "Carter looks like a zombified robot" because he "was killed in July of 78 and replaced with a 'double.'"[16]

Banner discovered a drawback to that approach when he manned a *Critique* table at an event near his home. "This guy shows up," Banner told me, "and he's so excited that he sees *Critique*. He loves my magazine. And he's got mental problems." The man rattled off references to drugs and aliens, to conspiracy theories and alternate realities; he sat on the ground leafing through back issues as he sang the publication's praises. "And it's the first time that I'm actually scared," Banner recalled. "What the fuck am I doing if I'm attracting psychopaths or psychotic people or people who maybe really believe this shit I'm putting out? I'm doing it as an intellectual exercise to continually play with ideas and hold these ambiguities in my head. . . . Someone's actually paying attention, and I need to be cautious."

Banner was very different from Peter McAlpine, and *Critique* was very different from *Conspiracy Digest*. But the two men read and appreciated each other's work, and they were recognizably a part of the same subculture, a world the libertarian activist Samuel Edward Konkin III, writing in 1987, dubbed "Conspiracy Fandom."[17] By the time *Critique* was supplanted by *Sacred Fire*, new conspiracy fanzines were arriving to take its place, each with its own tone and flavor. *Steamshovel Press* launched in 1988. *The Excluded Middle* and *Paranoia* both followed in 1992. *Flatland* and the book catalog from which it emerged were a bit older, but they moved into the conspiracy culture only gradually. They came out of the Left, beginning as an adjunct to an anarchist printing collective in the mid-1980s. *Flatland* was still selling books on anarchism in the subsequent decade, but by then it also had a large stock of material on assassinations, mind control, UFOs, Wilhelm Reich, "suppressed science," and the sovereign citizens movement. It even sold Bob Fletcher's militia videos. The editor, Jim Martin, placed his operation firmly in fusionist territory when he called himself "an anarchist for Perot."[18]

Where there's fandom, conventions frequently follow. In 1991 and 1992, you could attend PhenomiCon in Atlanta, a place where earnest UFO buffs such as William Cooper, the author of *Behold a Pale Horse*, could rub shoulders with ironists such as Robert Anton Wilson and the SubGenius crowd. A contingent from the Georgia Skeptics came the first year, eager to debate people with strange beliefs. One of the skeptics got more than he bargained for, according to the group's newsletter, when he went to "a discussion on 'Atomic Radio,' billed as 'the communications technology suppressed by the government since the late '40s.'"[19] As the skeptic argued that the alleged technology violated the laws of physics, agents invaded the presentation and appeared to kill everyone present. The skeptic, it turned out, had wandered into a live-action role-playing game. No one at the session actually believed in "Atomic Radio" at all.[20]

Fandoms tend to take root on the Internet, too. A discussion group called alt.conspiracy had already appeared on Usenet at the tail end of the eighties. As of 1993, you could subscribe to an e-mail newsletter called *Conspiracy for the Day*, run by Brian Redman of Champaign, Illinois. (The title parodied the "Thought for the Day" messages available from various online sources.) One of Redman's e-mails might contain part of a *Science News* report about crop circles; another might feature an excerpt from a book about CIA brainwashing experiments; another might reprint an Abbie Hoffman critique of the drug war. It's hard to generalize about how the newsletter's recipients perceived what they were reading. I had friends who subscribed to it under the impression that it was at least partly tongue-in-cheek and who made a habit of forwarding the items that they found especially funny or strange. But though Redman didn't accept every idea he printed—he wanted, he later said, to "leave it open so people could just decide for themselves"[21]—his interest in conspiracies was sincere.

Redman hadn't paid much attention to world affairs until he hit his forties, when Waco got him interested in alternative news sources. After he had been putting out his daily e-mail for a while—he soon renamed it *Conspiracy Nation*—he got in touch with Sherman Skolnick, a Chicago-based conspiracy chaser who had been active since the sixties. In the days before mass access to the Internet, Skolnick had shared his ideas through a series of recorded messages that you could access by calling a phone number; now he became Redman's mentor. Skolnick's career had begun with a fairly well grounded argument that a couple of judges were corrupt, then had gradually descended into increasingly bizarre claims.[22] Eventually they became too bizarre for Redman, who went his own way after Skolnick started declaring, to give just one example, that sinister forces had deliberately steered Hurricane Katrina into New Orleans.

Skolnick came out of the radical Left but contributed to whatever publications would have him, including the Liberty Lobby's paper *The Spotlight*. Redman had started as a Democrat, but in the nineties his outlook became more libertarian. The sources used in *Conspiracy for the Day* and *Conspiracy Nation* spanned the spectrum from liberal muckrakers to followers of Lyndon LaRouche. That sort of range was not unusual in the 1990s conspiracy scene.

In that environment, it shouldn't be surprising to see Anthony Hilder, who once had belonged to a group that sold "Support Your Local Police" bumper stickers, selling tapes at an event featuring Ice T and Body Count, musicians infamous for a song called "Cop Killer."

Hilder and the concert's organizers hailed from very different political traditions, but they shared some of the same conspiracy theories.

That shouldn't be surprising, since they shared some of the same fears. Both were wary of the government's growing police powers. Both resented the abuses of civil liberties that have come with the war on drugs, and both accused government officials of being involved with the drug trade themselves. The firebombing of MOVE in Philadelphia and the beating of Rodney King in Los Angeles aroused the same resentment among blacks that the Ruby Ridge standoff prompted among many whites. In much of the mass media, Americans angry about the Waco fires were classified with Klansmen. But nearly half the Branch Davidians killed at Mount Carmel were minorities—twenty-eight blacks, six Hispanics, and five Asians.[23] "As things get worse," Bob Fletcher concluded, "blacks and whites will be thrown into the same trash pail."[24]

Two organizations played prominent roles at that black/white intersection: the Nation of Islam and the Universal Zulu Nation. The Nation of Islam dates back to the 1930s, but Zulu Nation was born in the early days of hip-hop. Afrika Bambaataa has been a DJ and community organizer in New York since the 1970s; along with Grandmaster Flash, Kool Herc, and others, he was one of the founding fathers of rap. He created Zulu Nation as an alternative to gangs, inviting young people to the Zulus' world of rapping, break dancing, and graffiti instead. By the 1990s, the group included musicians, filmmakers, and others around the world, from France to Japan to Africa. One of the "primary functions of getting in," according to Afrika Islam, was sharing theories about the New World Order.[25]

In 1994, Islam's friend Hilder appeared on *The Front Page*, a popular talk show on the black-oriented Los Angeles radio station KJLH. There Hilder mixed the conspiracy theories popular in the patriot movement with appeals aimed at a black community ruptured by unemployment and crime. One listener who tuned in that day was Rasul Al-Ikhlas, the host of *The Story of Soul*, a local public-access television program. Al-Ikhlas invited Hilder onto his show, and at his guest's suggestion he had Fletcher come along as well.

Eager to reach still more of the black community, Hilder eventually tried his skills as a rapper, reciting apocalyptic verses over an electronic beat:

Masonic mind manipulation
Inciting riots, it's crisis creation
Biochip implantation
Vaccinate your kid for U.N. identification[26]

If you were hoping that Hilder's tolerance would extend past the region of race and into sexual orientation, I'll have to disappoint you: He also rhymes "Albert Pike" with "Janet Reno, dyke."

News of the newcomers traveled via the Universal Zulu Nation network. (Hilder's black girlfriend had the amusing experience of visiting a village in Belize only to be recognized by a native who had heard a tape of her speaking on the radio.) Islam introduced Hilder to Michael Moor, a reporter for the Nation of Islam's newspaper *The Final Call*, and shortly afterward Moor appeared on Hilder's radio show. There they argued that the powers that be are driving the United States toward a race war and that men and women of all ethnicities should work together to defuse the battle before it starts—the same story line that the John Birch Society preached in the 1960s, but now pitched to an audience that was more black than white. Other Muslims, such as Cedric X Welch of *The Final Call*, began to show an interest in the militia/patriot worldview.

Many readers, learning that elements of the Black Muslim and militia communities wanted to cooperate, will assume that the common ground was bigotry. Both groups, after all, have been plagued by accusations of anti-Semitism. There is indeed a lot of anti-Jewish sentiment in the Black Muslim community—Hilder had an unpleasant confrontation with the infamous Khalid Abdul Muhammad, whom he subsequently described as a "crazy" who wants to kill all whites, especially the Jewish ones—but it does not seem to have played a major role in the black-white crossover. "The blacks that are anti-Semitic won't have anything to do with me," Hilder noted at the time, "because they're also antiwhite."[27] That said, Cedric X Welch does have a history of anti-Semitic statements, and Hilder did share a microphone once with Steve Cokely, a black militant prone to citing *The Protocols of the Learned Elders of Zion* and casually using the word "Jewboy." The pairing didn't work out: After the program, Cokely and his companions snubbed Hilder because of his race. (Hilder himself, though a Christian, is a former member of the Jewish Defense League.)

Even ignoring the problems posed by people like Cokely, this was an unstable alliance. Covering the story for a magazine article in 1995, I called Moor for an interview. I learned that he had cooled to the idea of black-white cooperation—and to other sorts of black-white interaction, too. "I don't talk to the white media no more," he told me gruffly. "Every time we talk to whitey, something happens." The militias "seem sincere," he continued, "but you have to wonder what their hidden agenda is, who's pulling their strings." There's always the chance that "behind closed doors, we're all still niggers to them. I'm not necessarily talking about Anthony [Hilder], but sometimes I don't even know where he's coming from." After all, "They're getting too much pub' from the white media. . . . After they overthrow the overlords, maybe they'll start lording it over people of color."[28]

But even when blacks had no use for the militiamen, they could be drawn to the conspiracy stories that some of those militiamen believed. Marc Lamont Hill, a professor of African-American studies at Columbia, has noted an effect the "cultural nationalist tradition within hip-hop and within black culture" had in the 1990s and afterward. "People were going to black book stores like Hakims in West Philly or Robbins downtown," he told the *Philadelphia Weekly*, "and buying books like *Behold a Pale Horse*," William Cooper's UFO tract, which was also influential in the militia movement. "They were talking about the Illuminati and the Rothschilds and Bilderbergs," Hill added.[29] Professor Griff of the hip-hop group Public Enemy took to quoting Cooper. One MC/producer made "William Cooper" his stage name.

Tony Brown, the black host of the PBS show *Tony Brown's Journal*, thought the patriot movement was a bunch of "armed-and-dangerous militias of disgruntled White supremacists."[30] But he also believed, like Anthony Hilder and Gary Allen, that the ruling class was trying to foment a race war. The militias, Brown wrote, were "America's 'Manchurian candidates,'" and although they "may not have been hypnotically programmed, they are nevertheless being psychologically prepared to kill Blacks, Browns, Yellows, Reds, Jews, and non-WASP White immigrants when the appropriate cue is given."[31] And who was going to give that cue? An "evil cabal of elitists and money lords that pulls the strings: the Illuminati Ruling Class Conspiracy."[32]

One African-American militiaman—James Johnson of Columbus, Ohio—received a fair amount of public attention, if only because his prominent position in the movement made him hard to ignore. But he was treated as an aberration or, worse yet, a token. (One writer compared him to "the rare black nationalist who appears at a Klan meeting to endorse 'separation of the races.'")[33] The press frequently treated the militia movement as a simple continuation of the 1980s racist underground. Yet the leaders of the older groups weren't so quick to recognize the new crew as their children. "They are not for the preservation of the white race," Aryan Nations chief Richard Butler complained to *New York Post* reporter Jonathan Karl. "They're actually traitors to the white race; they seek to integrate with blacks, Jews, and others."[34]

That's not to say that members of the racist Right didn't join militias, make an effort to recruit from the militias, or try to capitalize on the militias' prominence. Some of them appended the word *militia* to their groups' names in the 1990s, giving us organizations such as the tiny Oklahoma Constitutional Militia, led by an anti-Semite who'd been kicked out of the mainline militia movement. But even as bigots sometimes appeared in militia circles, so did blacks, Hispanics, and Jews. Churchill divided the movement into two distinct though sometimes overlapping tendencies: the constitutionalists and the millenarians. The former organized in public, emphasized gun rights and other civil liberties, and saw themselves as a deterrent to repression and abuse. The latter organized sometimes in secret cells, emphasized elaborate conspiracy theories, and saw themselves as survivors in the face of a coming apocalypse. The millenarians were more likely to tolerate racists, while groups in the constitutionalist wing sometimes went out of their way to pick political fights with white supremacists.

To understand just how oversimplified the story of militia racism was, look back to a nearly forgotten scandal that erupted the same year as the Oklahoma City bombing. For a decade and a half, it was discovered, federal, state, and local law enforcement officials had been attending an event in Tennessee called the Good O' Boy Roundup. A Department of Justice investigation found "ample evidence of shocking racist, licentious, and puerile behavior" at the gathering, including a sign saying "No Niggers" and a self-appointed group that stopped drivers to announce that they were "checking cars for niggers."[35]

What does this have to do with the militia movement? It was the Alabama-based Gadsden Militia that learned about the event, infiltrated it, and exposed it to the press, eventually triggering the official investigation. Faced with racist cops, those militiamen didn't see allies in the belly of the beast; they saw another government abuse to be exposed.

Militia critics nonetheless insisted that the movement was bigoted at its core. A representative text is the 1996 book *A Force upon the Plain*, written by the attorney Kenneth Stern. Stern essentially argued that when militia members weren't racist themselves, they were duped by racists. When militia conspiracy theorists fretted over an international cabal led by Freemasons, the Illuminati, or the Trilateral Commission, Stern suggested, they were *really* imagining a cabal led by Jews. Such theories, he wrote, were "rooted in the *Protocols of the Elders of Zion*" because the worldviews were structurally similar. "The militia movement today believes in the conspiracy theory of the *Protocols*," Stern concluded, "even if some call it something else and never mention Jews."[36]

The argument resembled Woody Allen's syllogism "Socrates is a man. All men are mortal. Therefore, all men are Socrates." And Stern's history was as bad as his logic. The *Protocols* did not emerge until the late nineteenth century and was not widely popularized until 1903. As we've seen, anti-Masonic theories were common throughout the eighteenth and nineteenth centuries, and the English-speaking world's first anti-Illuminati panic broke out in 1797.

An even odder argument held that the militias were a gateway drug. Stern attributed that idea to Ken Toole of the Montana Human Rights Network, who compared the movement to a funnel. People enter it for many reasons, he acknowledged. But as they're sucked in, they begin to embrace conspiracy theories and revolutionary rhetoric. At the far end of the funnel are the hard-core bigots. Stern conceded that not all of the militiamen are at the funnel's eye. But by virtue of being a part of the movement, he believed, they were heading there.

This theory would make sense only if white supremacy were the logical conclusion of opposing globalism, federal power, and paramilitary policing. But you'd expect the most extreme members of such a movement to embrace a radical *decentralism*, not racism. Perhaps anticipating this objection, Stern argued that decentralist rhetoric is itself racist.

"The ideas of 'states' rights' and 'county supremacy' that fuel so much of the militia movement are covers for bigotry," he asserted. "The former has always been used to shield local governments from criticism over discriminatory practices."[37] (Yes, he wrote "always." When state officials object to federal raids on medical marijuana clubs, Stern presumably believes that they have a veiled racist agenda.) What's more, "When a political movement rejects the idea of common American values and says, 'Let me do it my own way,' it usually means it wants to do things that are objectionable, and yearns to do them undisturbed and unnoticed." Stern did note that ordinary arguments "about federal intrusiveness, silly regulations, mounds of red tape" need not be efforts "to remake America into a weak whole comprising fifty herculean states that can do as they wish."[38] But by using the phrase "it usually means," he suggests that only a minority of decentralist arguments are innocuous. Combine this with Ken Toole's funnel theory, and the implication is that any critic of centralized power, from a governor protesting unfunded mandates to an eco-conscious locavore, is potentially a part of the problem.

When you blur the boundaries of a scapegoated group, there's a useful side benefit: You can discredit mainstream as well as radical political opponents. There was a turning point in the mid-nineties standoff between President Bill Clinton, a Democrat, and House Speaker Newt Gingrich, a Republican—a moment when the White House was able to start setting the terms of the debate and the GOP went on the defensive. In most accounts, the shift came when the Republicans' willingness to "shut down" the federal government backfired during the budget battle at the end of 1995. But the April bombing in Oklahoma City and the militia panic that followed were at least as important in shifting the grounds of the argument. They allowed Clinton's supporters to play up the "extreme" antigovernment rhetoric coming from Gingrich's supporters in the talk-radio Right and to link that to the "extremism" of McVeigh and the militias.

The White House was well aware of what was going on. Eight days after the bombing, Clinton's adviser Dick Morris presented the president with a proposal to take advantage of the blast. As Morris explained the thinking in his memoir, Republican leaders were "not themselves extremists," so directly accusing them of radical sympathies would probably have backfired. But the president could "advocate executive and legislative measures to counter right-wing hate groups and limit their access to weapons of destruction," Morris felt. "Reluctant to alienate part of their political base, the Republican leaders were certain to rise in opposition," thus creating a link to the extremists themselves. The memo called that strategy the "ricochet" approach.[39]

If that sounds like the Red Scare and Brown Scare tactics of the past, it's because it was consciously influenced by them. Morris's memo explicitly cited McCarthyism as a precursor, noting that Republicans in 1952 had been able to use the "communism issue against Democrats" by pointing to the party's "flirtation with extremists"—i.e., liberal defenses of Communist civil liberties. The document also described how the public's fear of groups such as the John Birch Society and the Minutemen had been used against Goldwater in 1964 and how the fear of black rioters and student demonstrators had been used against Democrats in 1968. Clinton could do the same thing, Morris advised, if he would stress the "weird lifestyles, paranoia, and aberrant behavior" of right-wing groups; create a "President's List" of dangerous organizations that must disclose their members and donors; and call for "preventative surveillance" of such extremists.[40]

Some of that scenario, though not all of it, would play out over the next year and a half. Clinton proposed an antiterror bill that included serious limits on civil liberties, and Republican leaders weathered a lot of criticism when they excised the most restrictive parts of the law. Even so, Morris felt that Clinton didn't "emphasize the menace of right-wing extremism" to the extent that he had suggested.[41]

The president certainly didn't go as far as Hollywood did. In the intensely paranoid film *Arlington Road*, an Enemy Within thriller from 1999, a suburban professor learns that his next-door neighbors are planning an attack on a federal building. The movie feels as though it had been only barely updated from the Red Scare films of the fifties, though its ending owes more to *The Parallax View*: The protagonist not only fails to prevent the attack but also becomes the patsy who's blamed for it, and the real perps move on to commit their next outrage. In the world of *Arlington Road*, the normal-seeming family next door might be terrorists, the man accused of terrorism might be an antiterrorist hero, and the seemingly sedate districts where middle-class Americans live might be breeding destruction.

The militias received a different treatment on *The X-Files*, the science fiction series often identified as the most paranoid TV show of the 1990s. Actually, they received two different treatments. In "Unrequited" (1997), the show's heroes—the maverick FBI agent Fox Mulder, who is quick to believe tales of extraterrestrials and conspiracies; and his partner Dana Scully, who is more skeptical—encounter a Bo Gritz–esque veteran who leads a paramilitary group called the Right Hand. He is initially presented as a potential villain, but by the end of the episode his claims about a POW/MIA cover-up have turned out to be true. "The Pine Bluff Variant" (1998) is closer to the narrative of 1995: A militia called the New Spartans is plotting to use biological weapons against Americans, and Mulder has to infiltrate the group to stop it. But the episode isn't a simple Brown Scare story. We learn that the feds infiltrated and manipulated the militia long before Mulder arrived on the scene. The group's bioweapons did not come, as we were initially told, from Russia; they came from a secret U.S. arsenal. And the New Spartans intended to spread the pathogen by spraying it onto a bank's supply of money, thus transforming one of the United States' central institutions—cash—into a tool of terror.

There are also signs that Mulder shares the militia's concerns, even if he despises their methods. That's how he landed in a position where he was able to join the group in the first place. "He spoke at a UFO conference in Boston," an official explains, "where he apparently broadcast his feelings about the government and their conspiracies against the American people." A militiaman saw him as a potential ally and reached out for his help.[42]

If any popular anxiety was afoot, be it conspiracist or more broadly paranoid, it was likely to turn up on *The X-Files*. (Sometimes the franchise managed to catch a fear *before* it entered the larger culture. Six months before 9/11, the debut episode of a short-lived spin-off, *The Lone Gunmen*, featured a plot to crash a jet into the World Trade Center.) The series found villains in the military, in corporate America, and in the skies. Its heroes encountered hackers and vampires, psychics and disgruntled postal workers, surveillance cameras and the country's most pervasive species of shadow government: a neighborhood association and its Covenants, Conditions, and Restrictions. Many episodes reflected a generalized dread about globalization and porous borders, reflecting the Enemy Outside's newly diffuse status. "The central image of threat during the Cold War was a nuclear explosion—destruction that starts at a clear central point and spreads outward," the critic Paul Cantor has observed. "The central image of threat in *The X-Files* is infection—a plague that may begin at any point on the globe and spread to any other."[43]

The program's episodic, monster-of-the-week structure allowed all those threats to coexist in the same framework without weaving them into one vast explanatory narrative. At the same time, the show attempted to build such a narrative anyway. That proved to be its undoing. The grand conspiracy that had once stayed in the background—more an enticing set of hints than anything else—began to intrude more and more, and good storytelling gradually gave way to a plot that seemed less interesting with each new revelation. When the series went off the air in 2002, it set the first half of the final episode in a courtroom (a secret military tribunal, naturally). The trial allows the chief characters to summarize the vast conspiracy they uncovered. After this goes on for a while, the judge asks angrily, "Is this leading anywhere?"[44] What longtime *X-Files* viewer never exclaimed the same thing?

A better episode—I'd call it the show's best episode—is "Jose Chung's *From Outer Space*," an installment scripted by Darin Morgan and first broadcast in 1996. In a series whose hero focused so emphatically on exposing the Truth, Morgan's story casts doubt on the very notion of a single Truth—or, at least, of a Truth that can be captured in a master narrative. It is framed around the efforts of a writer named Jose Chung—imagine John Keel with a touch of Richard Condon[45]—to investigate an alleged alien abduction in Washington state. The result is a *Rashomon*-style collection of mutually inconsistent accounts of the same event, which appears by turns as an extraterrestrial contact, a CIA operation, and even a journey to the inner earth. There is an "alien autopsy" video, inspired by a hoax that had been broadcast on network television the year before, and there is the part left out of the autopsy video, in which the alien turns out to be a man in a rubber suit. Mulder meets the Men in Black, and he discovers that they are, or at least appear to be, the quiz-show host Alex Trebek and the pro wrestler Jesse Ventura.[46] Another character decides that Mulder and Scully themselves are Men in Black. There is an air force officer who creates false flying saucer sightings as disinformation and who then doesn't know what to believe when he seems to witness an alien contact himself. Everyone, even Mulder, is an unreliable narrator, and at the conclusion we still aren't sure what happened on the night of the apparent abduction. Instead the episode ends with Chung invoking "those who care not about extraterrestrials, searching for meaning in other human beings. Rare or lucky are those who find it. For although we may not be alone in the universe, in our own separate ways on this planet, we are all alone."[47]

It made sense that *The X-Files* would have room for an episode such as this one. If the program was going to explore almost every American phobia, from the fears held by militias to the fears held *about* militias, then it ought to have some space for the ironic style.

The ironic style was, in fact, more visible than ever before. By the 1990s, even mainstream news stories about conspiracy theorists sometimes adopted a lightly ironic tone, allowing readers to try on some odd worldviews while maintaining their distance.[48] And where mainline papers merely dipped their toes, alternative outlets such as *The Nose* and *Mondo 2000* plunged in merrily.

Mondo, a glossy mag for the cyberpunk subculture, ran a series of bizarre letters to the editor from one "Xandor Korzybski" alleging one strange plot after another. A typical effort opened by invoking "the bloodsucking aliens' Master plan to take over the world from their plush caverns in the U.S. deserts and make us into spaceship-building slaves by 1994, in cahoots with U.S. and Soviet government officials who will escape to Mars just before the world ends in 1999."[49] From there the letter just got weirder. Korzybski's rants were so popular that the magazine eventually gave him a column.

Was he kidding, or was he a kook? Opinions differed. Did you take him seriously, or did you just dig the craziness? That was up to you. Ken Goffman, who coedited the magazine under the pseudonym R. U. Sirius, thinks that Korzybski "at once believes this and knows it's absurd, or perhaps alternatively, depending on the mood."[50] But that's just an informed guess. "I don't think we ever discussed if he took it seriously or not, but that was the way at *Mondo* then," he recalls today.[51]

Goffman sums up the editorial attitude with a quote often attributed to the founder of a medieval Muslim secret society, the Order of Assassins: "Nothing is true, everything is permitted." It was a perfect line for the 1990s, that pause in history after the Cold War ended and before the War on Terror began. Then a very different Muslim conspiracy brought down two towers in New York, and a different sort of plot spotting seized the day: less fun, more urgent, and more dangerous.

12

EVERYTHING IS A CLUE

I think he was trying to tell me something, like it had some sort of a meaning.

—George Costanza[1]

October 7, 2001: less than a month after 9/11. Police in Maryland decide that two trucks on Interstate 270 might be carrying explosives. The alert cops block traffic for an hour, searching the vehicles for tools of terror. The cargo turns out to be stage equipment headed to a memorial service for the firefighters killed in the attack.

A forgivable mistake, given the circumstances? Perhaps.

In Tyler, Texas, a few days earlier, federal agents, city police, and bomb experts from far-flung cities had descended on a family's mailbox to grapple with a gadget jerry-rigged from wires, batteries, and green duct tape. The streets were blocked; the neighbors were evacuated. The device turned out to be an eight-year-old's homemade flashlight, built as a school project and left in the mailbox for safekeeping.

Still forgivable? Maybe—though on reflection, it doesn't seem likely that the killers who organized the attacks on the World Trade Center and the Pentagon would select a neighborhood in east Texas as their next target. But why, after learning that the bomb was actually a flashlight, did the authorities still feel the need to confiscate it?

When George W. Bush was president, the group most frequently invoked as a symbol of political paranoia was the 9/11 truth movement, nicknamed the *truthers*, who believed that a cabal within the U.S. government had either organized the 9/11 attacks or deliberately refrained from preventing them.[2] But the truthers were ultimately a side attraction. The most prevalent form of paranoia after 9/11 was the mind-set that allowed officials to mistake a harmless school project for a jihad. Americans were on edge, waiting for the next deadly attack. And in a change from the Cold War, when we at least knew the form such an attack would take, all sorts of activities or objects could be construed as a threat.

It was the same species of fear that had flared during earlier hunts for spies and saboteurs. But now the consequences of failing to spot the conspirators seemed much more catastrophic. Anything might be a weapon; anything might be a clue.

We've seen how the loosely structured Al Qaeda was misperceived as a tightly centralized organization, and we have compared this to the ways earlier Americans mistook scattered Indian raids for a tightly controlled conspiracy. But there was another antecedent to Al Qaeda's image: the global networks of mayhem found in the James Bond movies and their imitators. To show how the image of the Bond villain was conflated with the reality of the jihadist, Michael Barkun points to the

> speculation about Osama bin Laden's Tora Bora cave complex in the final days of the U.S. attack on the Taliban and al-Qaeda in Afghanistan. The myth of bin Laden's subterranean fortress began with a story in the London *Independent* newspaper on November 27, 2001, which described a mountain honeycombed with tunnels, behind iron

> doors, with "its own ventilation system and its own power, created by a hydro-electric generator," capable of housing 2,000 people "like a hotel." This story was quickly picked up and embellished by American media. The result was that on November 29th the *Times* (London) published a cut-away drawing titled "Bin Laden's Mountain Fortress," showing thermal sensing equipment and tunnels wide enough for a car to drive through. . . . When "Meet the Press" was broadcast on December 2nd, Tim Russert showed the drawing to Defense Secretary Donald Rumsfeld, who suggested there might be many such sophisticated redoubts, and not only in Afghanistan.[3]

When American forces arrived at Osama's actual lair, they found something somewhat simpler. They found some caves.

"There's a tendency for people to say, 'First the World Trade Center, then the Pentagon, now something near me,'" the sociologist Joel Best remarked after the attacks.[4] Sure enough, after September 11 and the smaller anthrax attacks that followed, the country was dotted with terrorism scares.[5] Baltimore-Washington International Airport shut down an entire concourse when someone mistook some powdered coffee creamer for anthrax spores. In Nevada, a man called in the police after receiving a suspiciously lumpy package that, when opened, turned out to contain a pair of lace panties and a love letter. An airline bound for Los Angeles was diverted to Shreveport, Louisiana, when a man handed a stewardess a note she described as "bizarre" but not actually threatening. ("It didn't make a lot of sense," she later said, "but at the same time it was alarming.")[6] Another flight was diverted on its way to New Jersey when some passengers aroused suspicion by speaking a foreign language in the back of the plane. A thorough investigation revealed that the men were two Jews praying.

It was an understandably cautious time, and some of those incidents seem ridiculous only in retrospect. Others were simply preposterous. Even the most sympathetic observer will have a hard time defending the airport guards in Philadelphia who nabbed Neil Godfrey before the twenty-two-year-old could board his flight to Phoenix. According to Gwen Shaffer's report in the *Philadelphia City Paper*, a National Guardsman's suspicions had been aroused because Godfrey was reading a novel—Edward Abbey's *Hayduke Lives!*—whose cover illustration included some dynamite.[7] United Airlines refused to let Godfrey board his plane, then barred him again when he tried to take a second flight.

As 9/11 receded into the past, incidents like those happened less often. But they didn't disappear. In January 2007, guerrilla marketers erected illuminated signs in locations around ten cities, each displaying one of the Mooninite characters from the *Aqua Teen Hunger Force* TV cartoon. In nine of those cities, the campaign went off without incident, but in Boston the cops construed the signs as bombs and essentially locked down the town. On learning that the installations were not explosives, officials started calling them a "hoax," as though the advertisers had expected people to mistake the Mooninites for weapons. "It had a very sinister appearance," Massachusetts attorney general Martha Coakley said of one of the signs. "It had a battery behind it, and wires."[8]

When people enter an apocalyptic frame of mind, the historian Richard Landes has observed, "everything quickens, enlightens, coheres. They become semiotically aroused—everything has meaning, patterns."[9] In the months following 9/11, that mentality was almost inescapable. Consider some of the flotsam on the Internet after the attacks. One frequently forwarded e-mail gave readers instructions on how to fold a $20 bill, revealing an image that seemed to predict the planes hitting the towers:

Another message asked readers to open Microsoft Word, enter the initials NYC, and then switch the font to Wingdings. The results:

Some people might take that as a curious coincidence; some might declare it evidence that Microsoft was somehow involved in the plot.[10] But every interpretation, from the most levelheaded to the most cracked, demanded that the reader pause to interpret the material in the first place. The world was filled with unexpected connections and irregular details. With clues.

After the attacks, the government expanded its apparatus for collecting its own clues and interpreting them. Congress created a federal Department of Homeland Security. The USA PATRIOT Act, rushed through in October 2001, permitted secret searches and warrantless Internet surveillance, gave police access to accused terrorists' phone records (again without a warrant), and required retailers to report suspicious customer transactions to the Treasury; it also provided other extensions of state power.[11]

Muslim-baiting hucksters from a variety of backgrounds gave presentations to law enforcement agencies on how to identify Islamic terror plots. At their worst, they resembled the alleged experts on Satanism who peddled paranoid misinformation to the police in the 1980s. ("When you have a Muslim that wears a headband, regardless of color or insignia, basically what that is telling you is 'I am willing to be a martyr,'" Sam Kharoba, the founder of the Counter Terrorism Operations Center, told a crowd of cops at one course.)[12] Across the country, law enforcement agencies established institutions called fusion centers: intelligence-sharing shops run on the state and local levels but heavily funded by the Department of Homeland Security. Some fusion centers and Homeland Security contractors extended the rhetoric of counterterror in disturbing ways. The Missouri Information Analysis Center devoted a dossier to the remnants of the militia movement, plus a host of other dissidents it roped in with the militiamen. The fact sheet, which was distributed to police throughout the state, declared that "it is not uncommon for militia members to display Constitution Party, Campaign for Liberty, or Libertarian material. These members are usually supporters of former Presidential Candidate: Ron Paul, Chuck Baldwin, and Bob Barr."

The document also warned that the Gadsden flag, a familiar historical banner bearing the slogan "Don't Tread on Me" below a coiled rattlesnake, "is the most common symbol displayed by militia members and organizations."[13] Watch out, highway patrolman: That history buff with the flag on his bumper just might be a terrorist!

The Virginia Fusion Center's "terrorism threat assessment" covered not just real terrorists but such groups as the Garbage Liberation Front, an ecological organization whose activities, the report explained, "include dumpster diving, squatting and train hopping."[14] A Texas center warned that "Middle Eastern Terrorist groups and their supporting organizations" were "gaining support for Islamic goals in the United States and providing an environment for terrorist organizations to flourish." Among its examples: public schools that allowed Muslim students to take prayer breaks, a Treasury Department conference on financial services in the Islamic world, and certain "marketing schemes" in "hip hop fashion boutiques."[15] The Institute of Terrorism Research and Response, a terror-tracking company hired by the Pennsylvania Office of Homeland Security, sent out alerts that subversives were plotting to hold a candlelight vigil, organize a gay and lesbian festival, and screen the antifracking film *Gasland*. One of its memos revealed that

> anti-government groups, convinced that the US government is intent on incarcerating them in FEMA prison camps, injecting them with micro-electronics while giving them the flu vaccine, and planning to seize their firearms will be out in full force in support of the "Fed is Dead" protests being held the weekend of 21–22 November 2009.

> TAM-C [the Targeted Actionable Monitoring Center, a division of the company] analysts hasten to add that not all of the protestors marching against the Federal Reserve System are conspiracy theorists. But enough of the protesters possess these types of theories that cause the TAM-C to alert law enforcement personnel that some of the marchers have a different view of reality than most people.[16]

You're forgiven if you expected people tasked with preventing terrorism to concern themselves with whether a political group includes anyone *who is violent*, not whether it includes anyone with "a different view of reality."

In 2012, Senate investigators offered a devastating judgment on the fusion centers' output. After reviewing thirteen months' worth of the centers' reports, the investigators concluded that the documents were "oftentimes shoddy, rarely timely, sometimes endangering citizens' civil liberties and Privacy Act protections, occasionally taken from already-published public sources, and more often than not unrelated to terrorism." Nearly a third of the reports were not circulated after they were written, sometimes because they contained no useful information and sometimes, the Senate study said, because they "overstepped legal boundaries" in disturbing ways: "Reporting on First Amendment–protected activities lacking a nexus to violence or criminality; reporting on or improperly characterizing political, religious or ideological speech that is not explicitly violent or criminal; and attributing to an entire group the violent or criminal acts of one or a limited number of the group's members." Homeland Security usually refused to publish these problematic reports, but the department also retained them for an "apparently indefinite" period.[17]

Meanwhile, mission creep was setting in. By the time the Senate conducted its investigation, many centers had adopted an "all-crime, all-hazards" philosophy that shifted their focus away from stopping terrorism and onto a broader spectrum of threats.

In itself, this was arguably a wiser use of public resources. Terrorism is rare, after all, and the practical effects of a terrorist attack can be functionally identical to the practical effects of a natural or technological disaster. Unfortunately, when fusion centers looked past terrorism, they were less concerned with such collective hazards than with drug and immigration offenses.

In the words of the disaster researcher Kathleen Tierney, all-hazards planning—a staple of traditional emergency management—asks institutions to "focus generically on tasks that must be performed regardless of event type, and then plan for specific contingencies, guided by risk-based assessments of what could happen." The DHS was rhetorically committed to the all-hazards idea, but in practice it was oriented toward more specific threats; and since the department had absorbed the Federal Emergency Management Agency, those threats took priority in places with worries far larger than terrorist conspiracies. Under Homeland Security Presidential Directive 8, Tierney wrote, communities that once had assessed their own risks and vulnerabilities were "required to develop plans and programs for dealing with fifteen different scenarios, thirteen of which involve terrorism, [weapons of mass destruction], and epidemics." Worse still, "as we saw so vividly in Hurricane Katrina, the government's stance is that the public in disaster-ravaged communities mainly represents a problem to be managed—by force, if necessary—and a danger to uniformed responders."[18]

The sociologists who study disasters are wary about using the word *panic*. In real-world disasters, as we noted in chapter 3, genuine panic is rare and spontaneous social cooperation is the norm. But in 2008, the Rutgers sociologists Lee Clarke and Caron Chess suggested that events like Katrina can spark something they called an *elite panic*. When the hurricane hit New Orleans, there were rumors that dozens of dead bodies were stacked in the convention center where refugees had taken shelter, that men were firing weapons at the helicopters coming to rescue them, that roving bands of rapists were assaulting people willy-nilly, that survivors of the storm had turned to cannibalism.[19] "Misinformed about conditions on the ground and overly fearful of the loss of property," Clarke and Chess wrote, "officials turned resources away from rescue in New Orleans. Elites responding after Katrina were disconnected from non-elites and obviously fearful of them. Further, their actions and inactions created greater danger for others."[20]

Panic may or may not be the appropriate word here. But *paranoia* is a term that fits. The effects of the elites' fears were far greater than the effects of, say, the grassroots rumors that the authorities had deliberately blown up New Orleans' levees to drive out black residents, even if the latter idea was more likely to be invoked in discussions of public paranoia during the disaster.

The first decade of the twenty-first century saw three particularly notable eruptions of elite paranoia. The first came with the reactions to the 9/11 attacks. The second was the response to Katrina, when powerful people's fears both fed and were reinforced by the centralization and militarization of disaster relief. And the third began when Barack Obama became president, as commentators treated a group of unconnected crimes as a grand, malevolent movement. As is often the case with paranoid perspectives, this connect-the-dots fantasy said more about the tellers' anxieties than it did about any order actually emerging in the world.

This third scare had been bubbling since the final months of the 2008 election, but it exploded after a summertime shoot-out at the United States Holocaust Memorial Museum in Washington, D.C.

On June 10, 2009, an elderly man entered the Holocaust museum, raised a rifle, and opened fire, killing a security guard named Stephen Tyrone Johns. Two other guards shot back, wounding the gunman before he could kill anyone else.

The killer was soon identified as James Wenneker von Brunn, an eighty-eight-year-old neo-Nazi. Von Brunn acted alone, but there was no shortage of voices eager to spread the blame for his crime. Pundits quickly linked the murder, in a free-associative way, to the assassination ten days earlier of the Kansas abortionist George Tiller. This, we were told, was a "pattern" of "rising right-wing violence."

More imaginative pundits tried to tie the two slayings to a smattering of other crimes, from an April shoot-out in Pittsburgh that had killed three cops to a double murder at a Knoxville Unitarian church the year before. The longest such list, assembled by the blogger Sara Robinson, included a variety of incidents linked only by the fact that the criminals all hailed from one corner or another of the paranoid Right. One of the episodes involved a mentally disturbed anti-Semite who had stalked a former classmate for two years before killing her in May. "This is how terrorism begins," Robinson warned.[21]

Crime wave thus established, the analysts moved on to denounce the unindicted instigators. Those weren't just killers, the narrative went; they were killers inflamed by demagogues. Bonnie Erbe of *U.S. News & World Report* pinned the museum guard's death on "promoters of hate," adding: "If yesterday's Holocaust Museum slaying of security guard and national hero Stephen Tyrone Johns is not a clarion call for banning hate speech, I don't know what is."[22] In *The New York Times*, the columnist Paul Krugman warned that "right-wing extremism is being systematically fed by the conservative media and political establishment."[23] His *Times* colleague Bob Herbert wrote that he "can't help feeling" that the crimes "were just the beginning and that worse is to come"—thanks in part to "the over-the-top rhetoric of the National Rifle Association."[24] Another *Times*man, Frank Rich, announced that "homicide-saturated vituperation is endemic among mini-Limbaughs." After the museum murder, Rich wrote, Glenn Beck "rushed onto Fox News to describe the Obama-hating killer as a 'lone gunman nutjob.' Yet in the same show Beck also said von Brunn was a symptom that 'the pot in America is boiling,' as if Beck himself were not the boiling pot cheering the kettle on."[25]

When critics blamed prolife partisans for the death of George Tiller, there at least was a coherent connection between the pundits' antiabortion rhetoric and the assassin's target. Say what you will about Glenn Beck and Rush Limbaugh, but neither is known for railing against the Holocaust Museum. If Beck, to borrow Rich's mixed metaphor, was cheering on a kettle, it wasn't the kettle that produced James von Brunn.

The attempt to draw those connections was a form of paranoia, just as much as the jittery responses to powdered coffee creamer and a kid's homemade flashlight were. Like those earlier excitements, it found a home at the Department of Homeland Security. In 2009, DHS analyst Daryl Johnson produced a report on the threat of "rightwing extremism." He seemed to cast a wide net. "Rightwing extremism in the United States," he wrote, "can be broadly divided into those groups, movements, and adherents that are primarily hate-oriented (based on hatred of particular religious, racial or ethnic groups), and those that are mainly antigovernment, rejecting federal authority in favor of state or local authority, or rejecting government authority entirely. It may include groups and individuals that are dedicated to a single issue, such as opposition to abortion or immigration."[26]

The charitable reading of this passage is that it's a sloppily phrased attempt to list the ideas that drive various right-wing extremists, not a declaration that *anyone* opposed to abortion or prone to "rejecting federal authority" is a threat.[27] But even under that interpretation, the report is inexcusably vague. It focuses on extremism itself, not on violence, and there's no reason to believe that its definition of "extremist" is limited to people with violent inclinations. (A DHS report on *left-wing* extremism cites such nonviolent groups as Crimethinc and the Ruckus Society.)[28] In the words of Michael German, an FBI agent turned policy counsel for the American Civil Liberties Union, the bulletin focuses "on ideas rather than crime." One practical effect, he noted, is that the paper "cites an increase in 'rhetoric' yet doesn't even mention reports that there was a dirty bomb found in an alleged white supremacist's house in Maine last December. Learning what to look for in that situation might actually be useful to a cop. Threat reports that focus on ideology instead of criminal activity are threatening to civil liberties and a wholly ineffective use of federal security resources."[29]

Like the liberals who voted to recharter the House Committee on Un-American Activities in 1938 only to find the same tool used against the Left a decade later, conservatives who supported the spying apparatus erected during the War on Terror found that it could be deployed in more ways than they'd anticipated. Republican leaders protested Daryl Johnson's report loudly, and the consequences were quick: The DHS adopted a civil liberties and privacy review process, and it reduced its staff devoted to the domestic Right. Johnson, who soon left the agency, later claimed that his team was "left floundering day-to-day without any meaningful work to do"[30] as higher-ups retreated in the face of criticism.

It was a substantial victory for civil libertarians, but it's important not to overstate how far it went. The review process didn't end the production of inappropriate fusion center reports, though it did largely prevent them from being published. Johnson may have left the federal Homeland Security bureaucracy, but he stayed in the homeland security business, running a consulting company called DT Analytics that contracts with police departments, fusion centers, and other institutions. And in the press, the new Brown Scare continued to flourish, as incidents were uncritically presented as evidence that political rhetoric was inciting political violence.

In September 2009, when a Kentucky census worker named Bill Sparkman was found bound and lifeless with the word FED on his chest, the *Huffington Post*'s Allison Kilkenny called the death "the kind of violent event that emerges from a culture of paranoia and unsubstantiated attacks."[31] Under the headline "Send the Body to Glenn Beck," *True/Slant*'s Rick Ungar wondered whether "the time has come for the FCC to consider exactly what constitutes screaming fire over the publicly owned airwaves."[32] Two months later, police concluded that the death had been a suicide. Sparkman, they reported, had staged it to look like a murder for insurance reasons.

When a software engineer named Joe Stack flew a plane into an Austin IRS office in early 2010, pundits reached for the same narrative. Stack's personal manifesto did not, in fact, fit into any conventional political category; it revealed a mix of left-wing resentments, right-wing resentments, and painfully specific resentments from Stack's own life. Yet the prominent blogger Josh Marshall, highlighting the pilot's reference to "Mr. Big Brother IRS man," greeted the document with the headline "Ideas Have Consequences," as though no American would resent the tax man if it weren't for the GOP's antitax rhetoric.[33]

Several statistics circulated through the press that seemed to suggest a crisis. On closer examination, they revealed something less:

• On August 28, 2009, CNN's Rick Sanchez reported that a source close to the Secret Service "confirmed to me today that threats on the life of the president of the United States have now risen by as much as 400 percent since his inauguration," going "far beyond anything the Secret Service has seen with any other president."[34] In the ensuing weeks, the number was widely repeated in other press outlets. It was also widely challenged, and Sanchez eventually backed down from his report.

The statistic had come from Ronald Kessler's book *In the President's Secret Service*, published a few weeks before the Sanchez broadcast.[35] In early 2010, I asked Malcolm Wiley, a Secret Service spokesman, about the claim. He wouldn't give out the correct figures, but he denied that Kessler's number was correct. According to Wiley, there was a period while Obama was still a candidate when he had received more threats than the sitting president. "But since he became president, that has leveled off," he continued. "The number of threats he has received has been consistent with the number received by Bush, Clinton, Reagan, and others."[36] Secret Service director Mark Sullivan offered a similar assessment to the House Homeland Security Committee in late 2009, testifying that "threats are not up."[37]

• After Joe Stack flew his plane into an IRS building, the press reported that threats against employees of the Internal Revenue Service had increased 21.5 percent from fiscal year 2008 to fiscal year 2009. In that case, the claim was accurate: As a Treasury official told *The Wall Street Journal* in early 2010, there had been a "steady, upward trend" in such threats.[38] But the trend had started in 2006, when a Republican was in the White House and the loudest angry rhetoric about internal revenue involved tax cuts, not tax hikes.

In the absence of more detailed data, it isn't obvious what factors fueled the increase. But when someone decides to assault an IRS employee, one government official told me, it's "usually a personal event that's a catalyst."[39]

• Here's Paul Krugman in early 2011: "Last spring Politico.com reported on a surge in threats against members of Congress, which were already up by 300 percent. A number of the people making those threats had a history of mental illness—but something about the current state of America has been causing far more disturbed people than before to act out their illness by threatening, or actually engaging in, political violence." Krugman declared that "toxic rhetoric" was the force compelling them to act out.[40]

Politico did indeed report the 300 percent increase, though Krugman's statement that threats were "already" rising implies that the number had continued to climb until his column appeared. In fact, the spike took place during the debate over Obama's health care law, and there is no reason to assume that the level stayed that high after the bill was passed. *Politico*'s sources did not reveal how that figure compares with the data for the debates over other hotly contested legislation, leaving readers unsure whether that was an unusually large spike in death threats or if it was typical of what happens when a substantial segment of the population is strongly opposed to a bill that is likely to pass. The Capitol Police, alas, are as tight-lipped about such statistics as the Secret Service, and the agency refuses to release the comparable figures. The best we can do is search through past press accounts, which reveal, for example, that at least three representatives received death threats because of their votes for the

North American Free Trade Agreement. But the information available that way is spotty at best.

• The Southern Poverty Law Center releases new reports each year listing different kinds of "extremist" groups. In 2010, for example, the SPLC's Mark Potok announced that an "astonishing 363 new Patriot groups appeared in 2009, with the totals going from 149 groups (including 42 militias) to 512 (127 of them militias)—a 244% jump." If you worry about political violence, he warned, that growth "is cause for grave concern."[41]

There are good reasons to believe that the Patriot milieu grew substantially in 2009, though the SPLC's numbers aren't as conclusive as they might initially seem. (If a group splinters into two or more pieces, that probably indicates that it's getting weaker, but the faction fight will show up as growth if all you're counting is the number of organizations on the ground.) The biggest problem with the SPLC list is that it lumps together a very varied set of organizations, blurring the boundary between people who might have sympathy for aggressive violence and people who would want no part of it. "Generally," the center explains, the groups on its Patriot roster "define themselves as opposed to the 'New World Order,' engage in groundless conspiracy theorizing, or advocate or adhere to extreme antigovernment doctrines."[42] That covers a lot of ground. Using such a list to track the threat of right-wing terrorism is like tracking the threat of jihadist terrorism by counting the country's mosques.

The SPLC acknowledges that not all the groups on its list "advocate or engage in violence or other criminal activities."[43] But its spokespeople regularly suggest that there's a slippery slope at work. Potok, for example, told the *Las Vegas Review-Journal* that he wouldn't accuse any member of the Oath Keepers, a group whose chapters take up fifty-three spots on the 2010 watch list, "of being Timothy McVeigh." But the Oath Keepers are spreading paranoia, he continued, and "these kinds of conspiracy theories are what drive a small number of people to criminal violence."[44] The article didn't mention the possibility that the Oath Keepers could pull people interested in those ideas *away* from criminal violence. The whole point of the Oath Keepers, after all, is to persuade the government's agents to refuse to obey orders the group considers unconstitutional. That is a central tactic not of terrorism but of nonviolent civil resistance.

To see how misleading the SPLC number can be, consider the Hutaree, a Michigan-based sect raided in 2010 and accused of plotting a mass assassination of police officers. The defendants were ultimately acquitted of most charges, but let us assume, for the sake of argument, that they really were a violent threat.

In Robert Churchill's typology of the militia movement, the Hutaree are extreme millenarians. There was no love lost between them and the area's dominant militia, the constitutionalist Southeast Michigan Volunteer Militia, which greeted the arrests by denouncing the Hutaree as a religious cult. One member of the SMVM, Mike Lackomar, even told *The Detroit News* that the Hutaree had called his militia to ask for assistance during the raids and had been rebuffed. "They are not part of our militia community," he said.[45]

Skeptical readers may object that this is exactly what you'd expect an organization to do if its erstwhile allies are facing federal charges. (David Neiwert greeted Lackomar's claim by declaring that the militiaman was "throwing the Hutaree folks under the bus.")[46] But we have independent confirmation of the tensions between Lackomar's group and the Hutaree. Amy Cooter, a doctoral candidate in sociology at the University of Michigan, had been doing fieldwork in the state's militia movement for about two years when the arrests happened. She had first heard of the Hutaree long before the arrests, when members of Lackomar's organization had told her a "story about some crazy people who came to train with them once"; the visitors had handled themselves unsafely and were "told not to come back." Cooter also noted that the SMVM, a secular group that included a convert to Islam, distrusted the "strong anti-Muslim sentiment" it detected in the Hutaree. Lackomar's militia did "keep the lines of communication open" with the group, "but that was to keep an eye on them as much as anything else."[47]

What did "keep an eye on them" mean? Both Lackomar and another militiaman, Lee Miracle, told *The Detroit News* that they had warned the FBI about the Hutaree more than a year before the arrests. Miracle said he urged the agency to check out the sect's website, telling his contact, "See if they creep you out the way they creep me out."[48]

The Hutaree and the Southeast Michigan Volunteer Militia both appeared on the SPLC's list. In other words, the roster did not merely mix people who were potential terrorists with people who were not; it mixed people who were potential terrorists with people willing to call the cops on potential terrorists. That is the sort of distinction you miss when you treat the size of the list as a proxy for the likelihood of insurrectionary violence.

• By early 2013, the fear of right-wing violence was no longer as intense as it had been three years earlier. But it received another burst of attention when the press discovered a paper by Arie Perliger, the director of terrorism studies at West Point's Combating Terrorism Center. Perliger's study stated that the number of violent right-wing incidents reported each year—everything from vandalism to mass murder—had risen more than 400 percent since the early 1990s.

Perliger's data did indeed show such an increase, though he also included an important caveat. The "quality of, and accessibility to, data on hate crimes and far right violence has improved during the last two decades," he noted, so "we need to take this into consideration when interpreting findings relating to fluctuations in levels of violence."[49] In other words, it's not clear to what extent the apparent growth from 1990 to 2011 reveals a real increase in activity and to what extent it just means our measurements are becoming more accurate.

But if it's unwise to use Perliger's numbers to compare the present with twenty years ago, you needn't be as cautious if you narrow your focus to a briefer period of time. And if you do that, you see something remarkable:

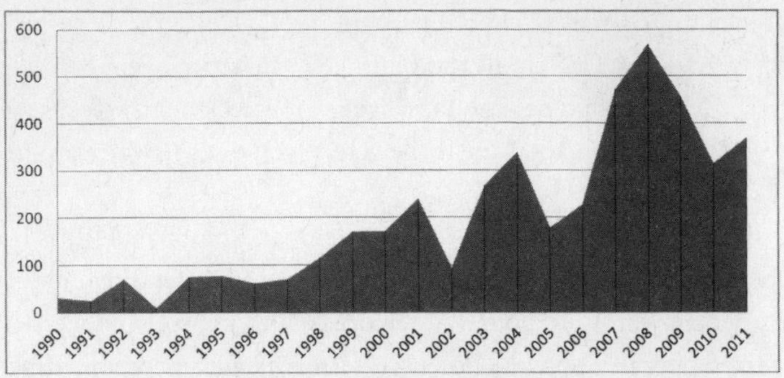

In 2009 and 2010—the period when the "rising right-wing violence" narrative was ubiquitous in the media—the number of violent right-wing incidents was actually declining. Let me repeat that: As pundits were issuing frantic warnings about the great beast stirring in the fever swamps, the number of attacks was going down.

Instead, the bulk of the increase took place under Bush, not Obama, with a peak during the 2007–2008 election season. Perliger argued that this is part of a broader pattern in which "presidential election years and the preceding year are characterized by an increase of far-right violence," and he suggested that the increase in 2011 might represent the same cycle repeating itself.[50]

What happens if you take out the white supremacists, the anti-abortion killers, and so on, and just stick to the people Perliger called the "anti-federalist movement"—militias, sovereign citizens, and others opposed to the concentration of power in Washington? Then his data did show a brief spike in 2010. Usually, he reported, there are about one to four violent incidents involving antifederalists each year. In 2010, the number jumped to thirteen. The next year, it dropped back down to two. Contrast those figures with the Southern Poverty Law Center's warnings that the number of patriot groups has been growing since 2008, and you'll see another reason not to treat the SPLC's count as a proxy for the threat of political violence.

The backdrop to all this fear of the right was the rise of the Tea Party movement, a surge in conservative and libertarian activism against new federal interventions in the economy. Some Tea Partiers were prone to conspiracy theories of their own, from the claim that Obama's health care bill would establish "death panels" to the familiar charge that FEMA was preparing internment camps. Discussions of the movement frequently highlighted such theories, often arguing that they proved the Right had "gone crazy" since the Democrats had retaken the White House.

On the face of it, that was an odd argument to make. When George W. Bush was in office, there was no shortage of conspiracy theories on the right; it's just that they tended to be aimed at foreigners, Muslims, and the left-wing opposition rather than the White House. On the paramilitary right, the social space once occupied by the government-fearing militia movement was filled in Bushtime by the illegal immigrant–fearing Minuteman movement, which organized patrols of the U.S.-Mexico border. (This is not the same group as the anti-Communist Minutemen of the 1960s.) As the Tea Party movement rose, the faction-prone Minutemen continued to fracture and the militias began to grow again.[51] Broadly speaking, the grassroots Right of 2009 was more libertarian than the grassroots Right of five years earlier, so its conspiracy theories were more likely to involve the Enemy Above. But it is far from clear that the Right was more prone to conspiracy theories in general. It merely pointed many of those theories in a different direction.

That said, the most notable right-wing conspiracy theory of the period was not particularly libertarian. I refer to the idea that Barack Obama and his allies are covering up the true circumstances of the president's birth. The exact details of the story vary from theorist to theorist, but the usual payoff is that Obama was born in Kenya, not Hawaii, and therefore is ineligible for the presidency.

By mid-2009 the birthers, as they became known, threatened to replace the truthers as the media's favorite emblem of political paranoia.[52] The radio and TV hosts Lou Dobbs and Glenn Beck gave their thesis a sympathetic hearing, and in July, ten House Republicans cosponsored a birther-backed bill that would require prospective presidential candidates to release their birth certificates before running. The obsession didn't diminish until the president released his original long-form birth certificate in April 2011, and even then the story still circulated among some die-hard clue hunters.

At least three significant motives ran through the birther milieu, each inflaming different (though sometimes overlapping) groups.

Wishing for a magic bullet. This is the most obvious motivation: the search for a bolt of lightning that would end Obama's career without the pain of political persuasion. Birtherism was born not in the GOP but during the 2008 Democratic primaries, when Hillary Clinton's supporters started wishing for a miracle that would remove her chief rival for the nomination. After Clinton left the race, the theory continued to attract new believers, but suddenly they hailed from the right, because that's where Obama's new foes were to be found. First came the political need, then came the belief. If you went to a birther convention in 2009, one pair of sentences you would almost certainly not hear was "I strongly support Obama's ideas about economic stimulus and health care reform. It's just too bad he's ineligible to be president."

Fear of foreign influence. For many birthers, Obama's origins were bound up with a general suspicion of the foreign. It's no surprise that the highest-profile media figure to give their arguments a friendly venue was Lou Dobbs, at the time a fiercely protectionist and anti-immigrant voice. Discussing Obama's birth certificate on his radio show, Dobbs declared that he was "starting to think we have a, we have a document issue. You suppose he's un— No, I won't even use the word *undocumented*. It wouldn't be right."[53]

He was making a pun. I assume that Dobbs didn't actually believe that Obama is an illegal alien. But jokes have meanings, and

Dobbs—perhaps intuitively, perhaps by design—was bringing an implicit link into the open: the connection between the fear of foreign settlers and the fear of a foreign president.

Where Dobbs will only joke and wink, others spoke in earnest. Later that month, on the cable show *Hardball*, the old Watergate hand G. Gordon Liddy was asked what Obama would be if he had been born abroad and never naturalized. "An illegal alien," Liddy replied.[54]

While the obvious anxiety here involves the influx of immigrants from Mexico, that wasn't the only factor at work. It isn't a big leap from the fear of foreign Muslims to the fear that a powerful figure is covertly foreign and/or Muslim. (In addition to the birther theories, Obama has been plagued by rumors that he secretly subscribes to Islam.) And there was already plenty in Obama's biography to fan nativist anxieties about the Enemy Outside. He spent a chunk of his childhood in Indonesia. His father came from Kenya. When young Obama did live in the United States, he was in Hawaii, the one American state that isn't actually a part of the Americas. If you don't conceive of the United States as a multicultural nation, the president's life is reason enough to consider the man metaphorically foreign. And if there's one thing conspiracy theories are good at, it's transmuting the metaphorical into the real.

Excessive reverence. In a perverse way, birtherism is the flip side of Obama's fervent fan base: It's a way to keep your respect for the Oval Office intact while hating the man who occupies it. In his 2008 book *The Cult of the Presidency*, Gene Healy noted that although trust in our presidents has declined since Watergate, "the inflated expectations people have for the office—what they want from a president—remain as high as ever. . . . From popular culture to the academy to the voting booth, we curse the king, all the while pining for Camelot."[55]

What happens when someone who reveres the presidency despises the president? In the past you might, say, denounce Bill Clinton as a "stain" on the institution, thus mentally separating office from officeholder. But if you can challenge the president's legitimacy entirely, that's all the more satisfying. The throne is still the throne; it's just that the man sitting in it is a pretender.

I can't claim credit for that metaphor. Surf through the birther hangouts online, and you'll see a lot of semiroyalist rhetoric on display. One writer declared that "when Barack Obama officially entered the office of President, he became, in essence, a 'pretender to the throne.'"[56] Another called him "our present Pretender to the Presidency."[57] Another suggested that the man might be a "usurper."[58] Yet another, mixing monarchist and nativist rhetoric, jumped from describing Obama as "the quasi-Muslim, marginal American in the White House" to calling him—yes—"almost certainly a Pretender to the Throne."[59]

Birtherism wasn't just paranoid in itself. It fed the paranoid narrative about "rising right-wing violence," as when Heidi Beirich of the Southern Poverty Law Center told NPR that birther-style theories might presage another Oklahoma City bombing.[60]

To hear some people tell it, just about *anything* might presage another Oklahoma City bombing. On January 8, 2011, a young man named Jared Lee Loughner attempted to assassinate Representative Gabrielle Giffords of Arizona in a parking lot near Tucson. She survived, but he killed six others in the process. The airwaves and Internet were quickly clogged with claims that Loughner had been incited by talk radio, by violent political imagery, by right-wing conspiracy theories, even by a map the former vice presidential candidate Sarah Palin had released during the 2010 elections, in which the congressional districts that she was targeting (including Giffords's) were illustrated with crosshairs icons. Right after the shooting, Markos Moulitsas of *The Daily Kos* tweeted: "Mission accomplished, Sarah Palin."[61] Michael Daly of the New York *Daily News* wrote that "now that Palin may have the blood of more than some poor caribou on her hands, I wonder if she will continue putting people in cross hairs and calling on folks to RELOAD!"[62] An article in *The Guardian* strained very hard to find traces of the Tea Party movement in Loughner's YouTube videos, at one point noting that "The US constitution, the bible of the Tea Parties, features heavily."[63]

The narrative fell apart when Loughner's actual worldview began to emerge. Instead of revealing a passion for Tea Party politics or an interest in Sarah Palin's PAC, the texts and videos the killer posted on the Internet advocated an "infinite source of currency,"[64] warned that the government is using grammar to control people's minds, and expressed what one journalist described delicately as "indecipherable theories about the calendar date."[65] Here is a typical Loughner passage:

> If I define sleepwalking then sleepwalking is the act or state of walking, eating, or performing other motor acts while asleep, of which one is unaware upon awakening.
>
> I define sleepwalking.
>
> Thus, sleepwalking is the act or state of walking, eating, or performing other motor acts while asleep, of which one is unaware upon awakening.
>
> I'm a sleepwalker—who turns off the alarm clock.[66]

Even then, there was some confusion about just what forms of crankery were influencing Loughner. Mark Potok, for example, wrote a day after the shootings that it was "pretty clear that Loughner is taking ideas from Patriot conspiracy theorist David Wynn Miller of Milwaukee," a claim that has yet to yield any substantive supporting evidence.[67]

Loughner's friend Zach Osler provided a more useful clue when he told ABC that the killer wasn't interested in mainstream political debates and that he was a fan instead of Peter Joseph's 2007 documentary *Zeitgeist*. Joseph's movie is one-third arguments that religion is a fraud, one-third trutherism, and one-third conspiracy theories about bankers. Its online study guide cites a rainbow coalition of sources—libertarians, leftists, Birchers, even a cameo by

Lyndon LaRouche—and the results do not easily fit the label *left* or *right*. In 2009, Joseph founded a full-blown Zeitgeist Movement, with a platform heavy on futurism, sustainability, and utopian economics. There's no sign that Loughner's love of the *Zeitgeist* movie extended into a love of the Zeitgeist Movement. That isn't likely, given that Joseph now calls not for a new currency but for the abolition of money altogether. Whatever Loughner got out of the video is obviously just one element of his worldview.

Loughner was also interested, for example, in lucid dreaming, in reality-bending movies such as Richard Linklater's *Waking Life* (2001) and Richard Kelly's *Donnie Darko* (2001), and in the science fiction novels of Philip K. Dick, a writer whose paranoid plots often hinge on the idea that reality itself is a fraud. Another friend of Loughner, Bryce Tierney, told *Mother Jones* that the shooter was "fascinated" with the idea that "the world is really nothing—illusion."[68]

Interviewed by MSNBC on the day of the shooting, Potok gamely tried to link lucid dreaming to the radical Right, noting that the conspiracy theorist David Icke is interested in the subject. A much more plausible hypothesis—but still just a hypothesis—is that Loughner's interest in alternate realities was at the core of his worldview and that he was attracted to those elements of fringe politics that seemed to reinforce his suspicion that the waking world is a lie.

Not that this in itself would be enough to drive a man to murder. Many, many people have been playing with those ideas recently, and most of them do not try to kill anyone.

In the late 1990s and early 2000s, a wave of cult movies drew on the most extreme form of the Enemy Within story—the narrative where life is a masquerade and what we experience as reality is a false and perhaps malevolent illusion. The idea wasn't new, but suddenly it was everywhere: in *The Truman Show* (1998), *Dark City* (1998), *The Matrix* (1999), the Canadian *eXistenZ* (1999), *The Thirteenth Floor* (1999), the TV series *Harsh Realm* (1999–2000), *Vanilla Sky* (2001), and other motion pictures.[69] The broader idea of prowling about in a virtual world, possibly located in someone else's head, turned up in still more pictures, from *What Dreams May Come* (1998) to *Being John Malkovich* (1999) to *The Cell* (2000) to one of Loughner's favorites, *Waking Life*.

You can credit part of this glut to imitation. But too many of the projects were created simultaneously and independently for that to explain everything. For whatever reasons, audiences at the turn of the twenty-first century were receptive to paranoid thrillers about inauthentic realities. Call it the Demiurge cycle, after the Gnostic notion that our world is governed by a mad ersatz God.

The most influential of the Demiurge films was *The Matrix*, an extremely popular picture written and directed by Andy and Larry (later Lana) Wachowski. It told the story of Neo, a computer programmer played by Keanu Reeves who learns that our world is just a simulation, something to occupy our minds while we live in tiny pods and malevolent machines harvest our bioelectrical energy. *The Matrix* and its two sequels could pass as a capsule history of baby-boom rock. The first film is a three-chord riff of a movie: a simple, familiar idea—"What if reality is a great big fake?"—amplified and transformed into an irresistible hook. *The Matrix Reloaded* (2003) is a 1970s prog-rock concept album: sprawling, pretentious, and ultimately incoherent, but brimming with ideas and virtuoso displays. And *The Matrix: Revolutions* (2003) is an over-the-hill pop star recycling someone else's material: the sort of music you'd hear on a Michelob commercial, circa 1987.

The Demiurge genre didn't die when the *Matrix* trilogy ended—*Inception*, the most notable recent specimen, was a critical and commercial success in 2010—but *Revolutions* did signal that the boom was coming to a close. Unlike its two predecessors, *Revolutions* barely bothers to engage the idea that set the *Matrix* series in motion. No longer trapped in a false world devised by an evil intelligence, the heroes are now trapped in an anthology of war movie clichés; no longer skeptical and alienated, they proclaim the tritest sort of faith. When critics comment on the Demiurge cycle, they often cite Philip

K. Dick as its patron saint. There is no trace of Dick in *The Matrix: Revolutions*.[70]

If the king of the world builders was J. R. R. Tolkien—the man who devoted so much of his life to creating the Middle-Earth of *The Lord of the Rings*, complete with an elaborate philology of his imaginary languages—then Dick was the fellow who confessed, in an essay called "How to Build a Universe That Doesn't Fall Apart Two Days Later," that he liked "to build universes that *do* fall apart. I like to see them come unglued, and I like to see how the characters in the novels cope with this problem."[71] In a Dick story, true as well as false realities threaten to crumble away, and false as well as true realities are waiting to be discovered.[72]

Only a few entries in the Demiurge cycle, notably *eXistenZ* and *Being John Malkovich*, take things that far. As a result, most of them never acknowledge a curious social fact that lurked in the background while they flickered on our Cineplex screens. In a Demiurge movie, either the protagonist or the whole world is trapped in an alternate universe of someone else's making. Yet the films became popular as more and more people were willingly immersing themselves in ever more elaborate alternate universes, many of which they had helped to build.

The paradox at the heart of the *Matrix* movies is that a story about people struggling to free themselves from an imaginary world should evolve into an imaginary world that millions of people are eager to enter. You can become a *Matrix* character by playing a best-selling video game; you can explore the *Matrix* universe by playing a collaborative online puzzle game; you can build unauthorized add-ons to that universe by devising your own *Matrix* parody or fan fiction. People might not like to be forced or tricked into a false world. Evidently, though, they'll jump at the opportunity to enter and exit one at will.

That brings us back to the hunt for clues. The Web, multiplayer computer games, and fan communities are not merely places where people adopt or construct their own fake realities; they are places where those realities bump against one another in unpredictable ways, leaving trails to entice or confuse the devoted clue hunter.

Look at what happened when music lovers across England mourned the death of Jamie Kane, the scandal-tinged veteran of the boy band Boy*d Upp whose solo career was, to quote Wikipedia, "mildly successful."[73] He was killed in a helicopter crash en route to a video shoot in 2005; the BBC's *Top of the Pops* website reported that Kane's aircraft "experienced some technical difficulties on the flight, and crashed into the sea some miles from its destination."[74] Some suspected foul play.

Nearly everything in the previous paragraph is untrue. There never was a boy band called Boy*d Upp, there never was a pop star named Jamie Kane, he never faced a scandal, he never died, and no one ever mourned him. The BBC did report his death, though, and an outline of his alleged career did surface briefly in Wikipedia. And when people realized that those fictions were appearing in venues theoretically devoted to fact, the whiff of foul play did waft through the air.

Jamie Kane was a character in an alternate reality game, or ARG. The first major ARG was *The Beast*, an elaborate puzzle created to promote Steven Spielberg's 2001 film *A.I.* It was widely regarded as far superior to the movie it advertised, and it wound up setting the template for the ARG genre.[75] In the words of the game's designer, Jane McGonigal, *The Beast* "co-opted real environments." Among other things, that meant thousands of Web pages planted throughout the Internet, clues dropped unannounced into newspaper and TV ads, real-world phone calls and faxes to players, packages in the mail, even carefully placed bathroom graffiti. Some ARGs have dealt directly with conspiracies: *Plot 49* was inspired by Thomas Pynchon's paranoid novel *The Crying of Lot 49*, and *The Secret World*'s story includes the Illuminati, the Knights Templar, and other staples of secret-society literature. But even when a game's story wasn't especially paranoid, it required the sort of attention to potential connections that comes naturally to the conspiracy theorist. "*The Beast* recognized no game boundaries," McGonigal wrote; "the players were always playing, so long as they were connected to one of their main everyday networks." It had a devilishly paranoid slogan: "This Is Not a Game."[76]

By asking players to live simultaneously in the real world and the game world, ARGs required the sort of double vision encouraged by the ironic style. (Operation Mindfuck was, in its way, a precursor to ARGs, even if it offered no puzzle to solve.) In the case of *The Beast*, the lines became so blurry that when terrorists took down the World Trade Center, a forum dedicated to solving the game's puzzles began to buzz with plans to "solve" 9/11 as well. A characteristic post argued that "this sort of thing is sorta our MO. Picking things apart and figuring them out."[77] Eventually, the founders of the group felt obliged to intervene, pointing out the difference between "clues hidden that were gauged for us" and clues left in the wake of the attacks.[78]

At least the would-be terror sleuths knew that 9/11 wasn't really a game. In the case of Jamie Kane, the ARG's puppet masters dropped pieces of their puzzle into places that were supposedly off-limits to play. If you Googled "Jamie Kane," you could land not just at a fake fan site with girl-friendly publicity stills or a fake official site with samples of Kane's music but at the aforementioned *Top of the Pops* report of his death; Kane also appeared in a Radio 1 directory that otherwise excluded deliberate fictions. When the blog *Boing Boing* revealed that people had placed entries for Kane and Boy*d Upp in Wikipedia, the news produced such an uproar that the BBC was forced to deny that it had been responsible for the posts; it blamed them on two fans acting independently, one of whom "happens to work for the BBC" but had posted his disinformation "without the knowledge of anyone in the Jamie Kane Team or BBC Marketing."[79] That might be true and it might be false, and it might be a deeper sort of deceit. There is, after all, a subspecies of marketer who believes that all buzz is good buzz. As one observer wrote at the time, "Did the Beeb just turn BoingBoing into part of the game?"[80]

In the middle of the twentieth century, several psychologists and psychiatrists, notably Eric Berne and the pre-psychedelic Timothy Leary, pioneered the theory of transactional analysis, which treats social roles as gameplay and social behavior as a series of games. Leary held on to the metaphor after he started experimenting with drugs: When Robert Anton Wilson interviewed him for *The Realist* in 1964, Leary referred casually to Harvard's "verbal game," his guests' "visiting game," and his countrymen's "nationality game"; describing his first trip on magic mushrooms, he declared: "The space game came to an end, then the time game came to an end, and then the Timothy Leary game came to an end."[81] In 2005, the Jamie Kane game, aimed at telling a story and attracting public attention, clashed with the Wikipedia game, aimed at presenting truth rather than fiction.

It also exposed the viral marketing game, a form of advertising that declares This Is Not an Ad as defiantly as an ARG announces This Is Not a Game. As the furor gained momentum, an anonymous reader wrote to *Boing Boing*: "I can't say who I am, but I do work at a company that uses Wikipedia as a key part of online marketing strategies. That includes planting of viral information in entries, modification of entries to point to new promotional sites or 'leaks' embedded in entries to test diffusion of information."[82] If you think you see a similarity between the way a game's puppet masters scatter clues, a viral marketer scatters buzz, and an intelligence agency scatters disinformation, you're not alone.

When *Beast* players tried to solve the real-life murder of three thousand people with the same techniques they had used to decipher a high-tech narrative, it wasn't the only time someone confused a recreation with the much more byzantine complex of games that constitute human society. I'm not just thinking of the fellow from the Georgia Skeptics who unwittingly wandered into a live-action role-playing game at PhenomiCon. Stephen Dollins, a John Todd–like figure who claims to be a former priest of Satan, has given talks about *Illuminati: New World Order*, one of Steve Jackson's Illuminati games. Dollins highlights a card captioned "Terrorist Nuke," which features an illustration of an explosion at the World Trade Center; it resembles an image of the Twin Towers in the short period after the buildings were struck and before they collapsed. Another card depicts an explosion at the Pentagon. Those pictures, Dollins decided, were clues linking the Illuminati to the attacks.

"Remember," he claimed to one audience, "in the 1990s, the word 'Illuminati' was not even a household name. Nobody knew what anybody was talking about, except just for a chosen few. You had people out there, evangelists like John Todd, some of the other ones that were out there, showing about the seal, the Great Seal on the back of the dollar bill, and telling you that this was the seal of the Illuminati and telling you what it stood for. And he also came out and told what some of their plans were for future events. And people thought at that time that he and all those other people were crazy. Now they look back at him and say, 'Gee, we should have listened.' . . . We've seen a lot of things that they said take place exactly as they said they were going to. They're right on schedule."[83]

Dollins isn't the only one to see precognition rather than satire in Jackson's cards. "Since 9/11 there has been a thread, mostly online, of people who find similarities between the card titles and images and real-world events. Or at least events in *their* real world," Jackson told me in an e-mail. "Typically, these people post Web pages showing some of the cards and their interpretations, much as if they were trying to interpret a Tarot deck, and ask 'How did he *know*?' Sometimes they post YouTube videos in which they zoom in and out of card images and play portentous music." In addition to 9/11, theorists have claimed that the cards have predicted everything from a Japanese earthquake to the 2012 massacre at a Colorado screening of *The Dark Knight Rises*.[84]

The Internet gave Illuminati buffs an unprecedented ability to exchange ideas, even more than in the era that produced alt.conspiracy and *Conspiracy for the Day*. With "the rise of broadband Internet," the pop critic Jonah Weiner wrote in 2011, "Illuminati conspiracies have enjoyed the same steroidal super-boost as pornography and cat photography."[85] Anytime an entertainer died, Internet forums lit up with speculations that the secret society from Bavaria was to blame. ("Donna Summer, latest illuminati sacrifice victim?")[86] Thanks to platforms such as YouTube, it is now relatively easy to rip and post clips from movies and TV and highlight the Masonic symbolism allegedly concealed within them. And people have found that symbolism *everywhere*, from music videos to superhero movies: a massive clue hunt across the entire pop-culture landscape.

You can attribute part of this increased interest to some relatively high-profile conspiracy theorists who made a habit of invoking the Illuminati, such as the radio host Alex Jones. You can attribute part of it to the long shadow of the *Illuminatus!* trilogy, whose direct and indirect influence touched a lot of the pop landscape. And you can attribute a great deal of it to the hip-hop community, which hasn't forgotten the New World Order lore that Afrika Islam was spreading in the 1990s. Illuminati allusions have appeared in the lyrics of rappers ranging from Dr. Dre ("Ain't tryin' to stick around for Illuminati," he announced in 1996)[87] to Common ("Eye on a dollar like Illuminati," he rapped in 2012).[88] Prodigy's 2008 track "Illuminati" featured this chorus: "Illuminati want my mind, soul, and my body/ Secret society tryin' to keep their eye on me/But I'ma stay incogni'/ In places they can't find me/Make my moves strategically."[89]

By the time Prodigy accused Jay-Z of being a member of the Illuminati, Adam Weishaupt's organization had become the stuff of celebrity gossip; tattoos, hand gestures, and video imagery all became fodder for fans determined to figure out which performers were initiates of the order. You can get the flavor of the fears from an exchange the rapper 50 Cent had on a Philadelphia radio station in 2009.

> TARSHA JONES: Have you ever been approached by the secret society that, when a rapper—and I'm talking about musicians, black artists—reach a certain level, this secret society still wants to infiltrate and control the minds of our youth, and so they incorporate you into the secret society, and so secretly you put out messages, but you don't go against their grain? It's like you're dressed like us, but you speak for them.
>
> 50 CENT: I haven't been approached by anybody like that.[90]

Jay-Z reacted to the rumors by rapping the line "I said I was amazin', not that I'm a Mason."[91]

Hip-hop records weren't the only pop artifacts alluding to the secret society. A 1999 episode of *Buffy the Vampire Slayer* set the show's heroine against an order of the undead called "El Eliminati." The *New Avengers: Illuminati* comic books borrowed the name "Illuminati" for a secretive supergroup that included such iconic costumed heroes as Iron Man and Doctor Strange.[92] In movie theaters, the Illuminati were the villains of the 2001 film *Lara Croft: Tomb Raider* and the suspected villains of the 2009 film *Angels & Demons*. The latter was based on a novel published nine years earlier by Dan Brown, who followed up his Illuminati thriller with what might be the single most widely read English-language conspiracy novel of the twenty-first century thus far, *The Da Vinci Code*.

The Da Vinci Code's plot, which owed a heavy debt to the conspiracy tracts *Holy Blood, Holy Grail* and *The Templar Revelation*, hinges on the notions that Jesus was married to Mary Magdalene, that they spawned a holy bloodline, and that the Vatican has engaged in a long, bloody cover-up to hide the truth.[93] (Curiously, the plot also hinges on the idea that the truth has already been exposed. Rather than uncovering an unknown secret history, the protagonists learn it in dribs and drabs from a well-informed character who claims that the "royal bloodline of Jesus Christ has been chronicled in exhaustive detail by scores of historians.")[94] The novel was released at a propitious time: 2003, right on the heels of the biggest uproar to hit the Vatican in decades. The book's fan base included many Catholics who had been disillusioned to learn that their church had been hushing up priestly pederasty and who were now primed to believe in all sorts of Vatican cover-ups.

Yes, *believe*. It is common for thriller writers to drop hints that parts of their story might be real, allowing readers to enjoy not just the pleasures of vicarious sex and gunplay but the frisson of suspecting they're getting a glimpse of a hidden truth. When Brown placed a note at the beginning of his novel claiming that various elements of his story really exist, he was probably doing this standard scene setting. Inadvertently, he landed in the perfect position to launch a cult. Since it doesn't claim to be the literal, infallible truth, *The Da Vinci Code* isn't easily damaged by the sort of skeptical inquiry that digs out contradictions or obvious inaccuracies in holy texts. Like H. P. Lovecraft and Robert Anton Wilson before him, Brown wrote a yarn that will attract believers no matter how many times its author assures them that the tale isn't true.

The characters in *The Da Vinci Code* are constantly deciphering puzzles. In that spirit, the publisher sponsored a somewhat ARGish contest to promote the novel, announcing that several codes were concealed on the book's jacket. They turned out to include a phrase from Freemasonry and the coordinates of a sculpture just outside the CIA's headquarters in Langley, Virginia.[95] Even on the cover of a best-selling potboiler, anything might turn out to be a clue.[96]

In June 2008, some Web surfers came across a curious site called Notes to Mary. It featured several threatening letters from one high school student to another, and it was, they quickly concluded, an alternate reality game. Word spread through the Internet hubs where ARG fans congregate, and the players set to work deciphering the puzzle. The site's owner "began interacting with players," an observer recalled at the Web forum MetaFilter, "sending them strange messages and several series of numbers that appeared to be some sort of code."[97]

After a while, a log-in link appeared at the Notes to Mary site. The players worked hard to figure out the password, and finally they seemed to solve the puzzle. They eagerly logged in, and there they found the object of their quest.

It was a video of the eighties pop star Rick Astley singing "Never Gonna Give You Up." In 2008, this was the Internet equivalent of a joy buzzer.

There had never been a game. The man behind the site "just thought it would be funny to put up some creepy notes and see what sort of attention they got," the MetaFilter writer explained. When people decided it was an ARG, "he decided to play along. The numerical 'codes' he sent out? Random numbers and dates plucked out of the air."

He provided the noise; the players perceived the pattern. They imagined a labyrinth as elaborate as bin Laden's legendary fortress in Tora Bora. They found an empty cave.

EPILOGUE

THE MONSTER AT THE END OF THIS BOOK

We find human faces in the moon, armies in the clouds; and by a natural propensity, if not corrected by experience and reflection, ascribe malice and good will to everything that hurts or pleases us.

—*David Hume*[1]

As soon as Mark Phillips heard that the World Trade Center was on fire, he ran to the roof of his Brooklyn home. He didn't know what had set the building ablaze. He just knew, as a journalist, that he needed to photograph what was happening. He took his first picture right after the second plane crashed, and within half an hour the Associated Press was distributing his images to the world.

It wasn't till later that week that he learned what people were seeing in that first photo. "Mark," his agent told him on the phone, "you have a face in your picture."

Phillips took another look, and there it was. "The image I saw was distinct," he later recalled. "Eyes, nose, mouth, horns. It was an image from a nightmare, leering at us, triumphant in its evil as it hung onto Tower 2 of the World Trade Center."[2] There, in the contours of the smoke, he found the face of Satan.

Search online and you'll see still more 9/11 pictures where people perceive the shapes of demons. Some of the photos are fakes, but not all. And if some of them require you to squint pretty intently to see the spirits allegedly encoded within them, there are others, like the photo Phillips took, where the face isn't hard to see.

There's no shortage of theories about what the faces mean. "An act of hatred and violence is a thrill ride for a demon," one website suggests. "Demons knew what was going to happen in New York and they gathered there to jump in at the point of the impact, like a human jumping onto a moving train to have a thrill."[3] The Christian conspiracist Texe Marrs identifies the imagery with the Enemy Outside: "Just as the Arab terrorists led by the Devil left their own trail of evidence, wanting the world to know their names of infamy, so, too, does the Devil, as proven in this photograph, cackle out loud and boast, *'I did it—and I'm proud of what I did!'*"[4] Another writer, on the other hand, sees the Enemy Above at work: "Don't these photos of Satan at the world [*sic*] Trade Center catastrophe tell us that the current seat of Satan's power is the World Trade Center? Don't these photos depict Satan being awakened from his hiding place in the World Trade Center? For it is the international bankers who operate from Fed, the CFR and the World Trade Center who create first, second and third world debt."[5]

Some even see the face as a signal from a Benevolent Conspiracy, or at least from a benevolent power. One website calls the image "a much needed edict from Allah—a final ruling from the highest authority possible which decrees once and for all that the use of terrorism is never permitted in Islam."[6]

Then there's the explanation I prefer. The faces are the result of *apophenia*, the process of projecting patterns onto data. More specifically, they are *pareidolia*, in which those patterns are perceived as meaningful shapes or sounds. It is pareidolia that allows us to see a man in the moon, to hear a Satanic incantation when "Stairway to Heaven" is played backward, or to conjure the image of your subconscious choice while taking a Rorschach test. Indeed, pareidolia makes the whole world a Rorschach test. The Web is filled with delightful pareidolia-themed photo sets, where unexpected forms appear in mountains, pasta, fire, clocks, clouds.

The apparitions in the pictures range from an octopus to an angel, but we are especially prone to seeing faces. That sink's knobs and spigot look like two eyes and a nose. That house's windows and door look like two eyes and a mouth. That cloud of smoke billowing from an unimaginably evil attack looks like the author of evil himself.

Spotting such images is an act of creativity, though it's a kind of creativity that is often invisible to the creator. It's easy to believe the face is really *there* in the photo rather than in the interaction between the photo and the observer. Remember what Robert Anton Wilson said about Nesta Webster: "She was so modest that she didn't recognize herself as the artist creating all that."

Many people do understand that they're the artists in the situation. Some even transform their experiences of pareidolia into artworks that others can enjoy. The Spanish surrealist Salvador Dalí called this the *critical-paranoiac method*. At a lecture in Connecticut in 1934, he illustrated the idea with a slide: a postcard photo of tribesmen in front of a hut. He then showed the same image on its side, and pareidolia did its work: With some priming from the painter, the audience could see an image of a human head.

Salvador Dalí, unknown, c. 1931

More examples followed, including a vulture that Freud had perceived in Leonardo da Vinci's *The Virgin and Child with St. Anne*.[7] "These more or less accidental ideas Mr. Dali is concentrating upon in his own work," *The Hartford Courant* reported the next day, "but instead of allowing them to be accidental, he is trying to cultivate them."[8]

In a conspiracy context, the ironic approach entails a similar sort of cultivation. A group of scholars learned this in 2010, when they played a game they called *The Paranoid Style*. The historian Rob MacDougall, who organized the exercise, reported afterward that he started it with "a little briefing on pareidolia and apophenia." Then, after asking each player to pick a well-known historical figure, he

> told them we were looking for evidence of the secret conspiracy of vampires that has pulled the strings behind the world for hundreds of years. So we went through what we knew about each of our historical figures and found "evidence" of each one's role for or against the Great Vampire Conspiracy. . . . If anything, they were *too* willing to indulge me: we very quickly spun out a goofy little chronicle of the vampire-vs-electricizer war behind the world, but we probably didn't work at it long enough to get to the real kick of autohistoric apophenia, when the evidence starts to line up all too well with the fantasy you have just concocted, and you skate right up to the edge of believing. It's a powerful and uncanny feeling, and if it serves as good inoculation against pseudohistorical thinking, it also colors your relationship with "real" history ever after.[9]

Tim Powers, whose novels often attribute historical events to supernatural conspiracies, encounters something similar when he researches his books. You reach a point, he has said, where you need to start "resisting paranoia" because "your research genuinely does seem to support whatever goofy theory you've come up with."[10] As Paul Krassner put it after his Manson satire seemed to come to life around him, "Had I accidentally stumbled into a real conspiracy when I thought I was merely making one up?"[11]

Human beings have a knack not just for finding patterns in chaos but for constructing stories to make sense of events, especially events that scare us. I can hardly condemn that habit. I just devoted an entire book, after all, to the patterns I think I've glimpsed in American history.[12] But when building a narrative you can fall into a trap, one where a combination of confirmation bias and serendipity blinds you to the ways your enticing story might fail to describe the world.

A conspiracy story is especially enticing because it imagines an intelligence behind the pattern. It doesn't just see a shape in the smoke; it sees a *face* in the smoke. It draws on one of the most basic human characteristics, something the science writer Michael Shermer calls *agenticity*—a "tendency to infuse patterns with meaning, intention, and agency."[13] Sometimes the story a conspiracy theorist tells is correct. At other times he mistakes a chicken joint for a sterilization scheme, an unusual sect for a body-snatching cult, a Mooninite for a terror plot.

The conspiracy theorist will always be with us, because he will always be us. We will never stop finding patterns. We will never stop spinning stories. We will always be capable of jumping to conclusions, particularly when we're dealing with other nations, factions, subcultures, or layers of the social hierarchy. And conspiracies, unlike many of the monsters that haunt our folklore, actually exist, so we won't always be wrong to fear them. As long as our species survives, so will paranoia.

Yet we can limit the damage that paranoia does. We can try to empathize with people who seem alien. We can be aware of the cultural myths that shape our fears. And we can be open to evidence that might undermine the patterns we think we see in the world. We should be skeptical, yes, of people who might be conspiring against us. But we should also be skeptical—deeply, deeply skeptical—of our fearful, fallible selves.

AFTERWORD TO THE PAPERBACK EDITION

"Leaking is tantamount to aiding the enemies of the United States."

—*Insider Threat Program*[1]

As the hardcover edition of this book was going to press, a young NSA contractor named Edward Snowden leaked an enormous cache of data exposing the agency's domestic surveillance, among other illicit and/or embarrassing activities. As revelation after revelation emerged from the Snowden documents, the story became the biggest scandal to hit the national security state in years.

The NSA's spying was a bona fide government conspiracy, but that's not the only way the saga seemed to echo the book I'd just written. When the government's defenders attempted to push back against the NSA's critics, many of them also adopted the language of conspiracy, spinning speculative scenarios in which Snowden worked for the Russians or another foreign power. And an ongoing Enemy Within crackdown, begun in response to an earlier series of leaks, intensified after the Snowden story hit the headlines.

According to the McClatchy newspapers, the government had been operating something called the Insider Threat Program since October 2011. The initiative, which stretches across multiple departments, encourages federal employees and contractors to keep an eye on allegedly suspicious indicators in their co-workers' lives, from financial trouble to divorce. A brochure produced by the Defense Security Service, tellingly subtitled "Combating the ENEMY within your organization," sums up the spirit of the program: "It is better to have reported overzealously than never to have reported at all."[2]

The word "espionage" appears ten times in that pamphlet, while "leak" isn't used even once. But that doesn't mean leakers aren't being targeted. The effort blurs the boundary between spies and whistleblowers: an agent of a foreign power is considered an "insider threat," and so is someone releasing information to the media. The program has been adopted in agencies that have little or nothing to do with national security, including the Social Security Administration, the National Oceanic and Atmospheric Administration, the Department of Education, and the Peace Corps. A tutorial for Agriculture Department employees includes a long list of "examples of behaviors that may indicate an individual has vulnerabilities that are of security concern," ranging from sleeping at his desk to expressing "bizarre thoughts, perceptions, or expectations."[3] The list was imported, word for word, from a Defense Department document.

Whether or not this exercise in profiling can identify potential leakers, it isn't likely to stop leaks. As the security specialist Bruce Schneier wrote in 2010, after the WikiLeaks website started to publish thousands of classified State Department cables, "The government is learning what the music and movie industries were forced to learn years ago: it's easy to copy and distribute digital files."[4] Nearly five million federal employees or contractors have access to at least some of that secret information.

That creates a double bind: The more the government trusts someone with sensitive data, the more it has reason to fear that person. Trust breeds mistrust. It's the sort of situation that could make a person paranoid.

Did anyone ever imagine a government so scared of its own shadow? I can think of at least two people who did. One is Robert Anton Wilson, whose essay "The Snafu Principle" suggested that any secret police agency must be monitored by another arm of the government, lest it be infiltrated by its enemies. But then, he wrote, "a sinister infinite regress enters the game. Any elite second order police must be, also, subject to infiltration. . . . So it, too, must be monitored, by a secret-police-of-the-third-order," and so on. "In practice, of course, this cannot regress to mathematical infinity, but only to the point where every citizen is spying on every other citizen or until the funding runs out."[5]

The other prescient figure is WikiLeaks founder Julian Assange. "The more secretive or unjust an organization is, the more leaks induce fear and paranoia in its leadership and planning coterie," he wrote in 2006.[6] That fear will engender more secrecy, he continued, which in turn will make it harder for the institution to act. In the words of Aaron Bady, who wrote a lucid analysis of the man's thinking in 2010, Assange expected leaks to prompt an authoritarian organization to "turn against *itself* in self-defense, clamping down on its own information flows in ways that will then impede its own cognitive function." The fear of the Enemy Within would undermine the Enemy Above; WikiLeaks would make its target "so paranoid *of itself* that it can no longer conspire."[7] The Insider Threat Program suggests that Assange was on to something.

So does another development. After the WikiLeaks cables came out, the Department of Defense put out word that its personnel and contractors should avoid the WikiLeaks site: "There has been rumor that the information is no longer classified since it resides in the public domain. This is NOT true."[8] In the military, visiting an outlet that merely discussed the revelations could prompt your computer to warn you that "YOU HAVE SELECTED A SITE THAT MAY POTENTIALLY CONTAIN CLASSIFIED DOCUMENTS." The message would then go on to explain that "once a user identifies the information as classified or potentially classified, the individual should immediately cease viewing the item and close their web browser."[9] For a while, employees of the Air Force couldn't use their work computers to read the *New York Times*, the *Guardian*, *Le Monde*, *Der Spiegel*, or twenty-one other publications that had published a portion of the WikiLeaks cables. No longer able to prevent information from reaching the public, the government instead attempted to prevent the info from reaching itself.

If some of those *verboten* reports made their way to a federal employee anyway, an exorcism might be called for. After the Snowden leaks, the *Monterey Herald* reported that "if an employee accidentally downloaded classified information," the authorities might respond with "the wipe or destruction of the computer's hard drive."[10] And that's how a war on leaks can degenerate into a government deliberately destroying its own property.

The authorities eventually charged Snowden with espionage. You're forgiven if that feels a little disorienting. Legal definitions aside, people generally conceive of spies as someone's *agents*, extracting information for a firm or a foreign country. But the prosecutors, unlike some of the anti-Snowden conspiracy theorists, were not accusing the leaker of working for Moscow. As far as they were concerned, Snowden was a spy even if he was "spying" for the public.

Even so, Snowden's critics frequently fell into something like the myth of the superchief, treating the networks around the whistleblower as though they were more centralized and statelike than they were. Stuart Stevens, formerly the chief strategist for Mitt Romney's presidential campaign, took this to absurd lengths in an article for *The Daily Beast*:

> Snowden's U.S. passport has been rescinded and now he is, in effect, fleeing the U.S. authorities on a WikiLeaks passport. The organization is acting like a digital state with enemies and allies. Fine. Let's treat it accordingly and address the threat WikiLeaks presents not

> as a simple criminal act by random individuals but as the organized effort of a virtual state. As such, we should employ the full set of tools—ranging from diplomacy and world opinion to espionage and military force—we use when dealing with any other state. . . .
>
> WikiLeaks has made clear its interest in taking on the United States. Let's do now what we failed to with al Qaeda in the decade before 9/11: take it at its word, respect its capabilities and stated intent, and respond with our own not-so-modest capabilities to defend the United States.[11]

There is a history of treating groups like WikiLeaks and its allies like a *metaphorical* world power. In 2003, James F. Moore wrote a widely cited essay titled "The Second Superpower Rears Its Beautiful Head," arguing that the "collective power of texting, blogging, instant messaging, and email across millions of actors cannot be overestimated. Like a mind constituted of millions of internetworked neurons, the social movement is capable of astonishingly rapid and sometimes subtle community consciousness and action." This "new superpower," he argued, was "a new form of 'emergent democracy'" in which action comes "not from the top, but from the bottom"; as an example, he offered the coalescing opposition to the war in Iraq.[12] Stevens seemed to be taking this idea literally.[13]

He wasn't the only person making that sort of error. Two days before Stevens' article appeared, Turkish Prime Minister Recep Tayyip Erdogan looked out at two more expressions of the second superpower—the protests shaking his country and a similar people-power movement exploding in Brazil—and thought he saw a vast conspiracy. "The same game is being played in Brazil," he announced at a rally. "There are the same symbols, the same posters. Twitter, Facebook is the same, so are international media. They are controlled from the same centre. They are doing their best to achieve in Brazil what they could not achieve in Turkey. It is the same game, the same trap, the same goal."[14]

Now, it's certainly true that civil resistance movements around the world have been keeping an eye on each other, imitating tactics that seem successful, and sometimes even interacting directly. But the protests in Turkey and Brazil had different roots, appeared in different contexts, and, far from being centrally controlled, were notably resistant to control. They were, in the Brazilian sociologist Giuseppe Cocco's phrase, "self-convening marches that nobody manages to represent, not even the organizations that found themselves in the epicenter of the first call."[15] But people in authority can have a hard time comprehending such loose, decentralized action. Hence the persistence of elite paranoia, not just in the U.S. but around the globe.

That leads me to one last point. Some readers have misconstrued this book's thesis, mistaking my focus on the United States for a belief that conspiracy theories are a particularly American phenomenon. I thought I made it clear on page 18 that I don't believe that, but evidently it bears repeating.

So let me stress this: *I don't have any reason to think that Americans are unusually prone to political paranoia.* Conspiracy stories flourish all over the world, from Iran to Indonesia and from Mozambique to Mexico.[16] In just the last couple of years, Europe has undergone one of its periodic panics about international child-stealing Gypsy conspiracies and the Nigerian press has accused a TV host of being a high-ranking member of the Illuminati.[17] I strongly suspect that the conspiracy theories believed in other nations could be divided in the same five-fold way that I have divided the theories believed in the United States, though the archetypal examples will surely vary from place to place. The Enemy Outside you might imagine in a frontier society, for example, will likely be different from the Enemy Outside you'll imagine if you're bordered by world powers.

Americans aren't distinguished by the fact that we're suspicious. We're just suspicious in distinctive ways. Every country's conspiracy stories reflect that country's culture, and that's as true of the United States as anyplace else. There is an American style of paranoid politics.

And that style permeates the political spectrum. It's comforting to imagine that irrational, sometimes violent fear appears only on the far left or the far right. Comforting, but false. From the Indian scares of the seventeenth century to the Leak Scare of today, the American elite has found its own ways to cringe in fear. You thought you were watching the sober center, but that was just a mask: They were prone to paranoid fevers all along.

ACKNOWLEDGMENTS

It took a vast conspiracy to write this book. As I worked on it and on the earlier articles that fed into it, many people were generous with their thoughts and their time. I'd like to thank everyone who answered my questions, whether that involved replying to a couple of e-mails or sitting down for a multihour conversation: Rasul Al-Ikhlas, Craig Baldwin, Bob Banner, Joel Best, Sophy Burnham, Gary Chartier, Amy Cooter, Robert Eringer, Rita Fellers, Leslie Fish, Bob Fletcher, Erich Goode, Anthony Hilder, Afrika Islam, Steve Jackson, Philip Jenkins, Jay Kinney, Paul Krassner, Michael Moor (not Moore!), Christina Pearson, Dino Pedrone, Arie Perliger, Sharon Presley, E. L. Quarantelli, Brian Redman, Lewis Shiner, R. U. Sirius, Ivan Stang, Jeannette Sutton, Mike Vanderboegh, Malcolm Wiley, and Peter Lamborn Wilson.

Many other people passed along leads, helped dig up documents, offered useful advice, or otherwise lent a hand. Thank you to Bryan Alexander, Ceredwyn Alexander, Antero Alli, Sandy Asirvatham,

Radley Balko, Greg Beato, Chris Bray, Tim Cavanaugh, Robert Churchill, Dan Clore, Dave Cushing, Soren Dayton, Eric Dixon, Jared Farmer, Thomas Fleming, Charles Paul Freund, the late Mary Frohman, David J. Halperin, Henry Hardy, Gene Healy, Mollie Hemingway, Robert Higgs, Mike Holmes, Jeffrey Rogers Hummel, Tom Jackson, Ben James, Lene Johansen, Bill Kauffman, Steve Kaye, Bruce Kodish, Psyche Lamplighter, Martin Levinson, Jim Lippard, Monica Lopossay, Rob MacDougall, Dave Mandl, Paul Mavrides, Daniel McCarthy, Don Meinshausen, Victor Morton, Michael C. Moynihan, Mark Murrell, Debbie Nathan, Ted Pappas, Jeffrey Pasley, Rick Perlstein, Mark Phillips, Virginia Postrel, Will Potter, Des Preston, Stacia Proefrock, Eric Rabkin, Dave Rahbari, Karen Rockney, Gabriel Rossman, Thaddeus Russell, Joel Schlosberg, George H. Smith, Randy Smith, Sam Smith, Thomas Ruys Smith, Seth Soffer, Clare Spark, Lester Spence, Lucy Steigerwald, Clark Stooksbury, Luis Vasquez, Timothy Virkkala, Dave Weigel, Cosmo Wenman, Shawn Wilbur, the late Robert Anton Wilson, and Oberon Zell. Thanks in particular to everyone who gave me feedback on all or part of the manuscript: George Baca, Amy Cooter, Brian Doherty, Jeet Heer, Jay Kinney, Rona Kobell, Ed Krayewski, Charles Pearson, and Amy Sturgis.

It would have been a lot harder to write this book without the assistance of the Baltimore County Public Library's interlibrary loan department: Jennifer Baugher, Deb Brothers, Helen Hughes, Timberly Johnson, and Joan Lattanzi. I also spent valuable time at the Labadie Collection at the University of Michigan's Hatcher Graduate Library, where Julie Herreda, Kate Hutchens, and the rest of the staff were extremely helpful. So were the employees of the Library of Congress in Washington, D.C. And a warm thank-you to Mars De Ritis and Jim Dwyer for their hospitality while I was in Michigan doing archival research at Labadie.

Matt Welch, my editor at *Reason*, didn't just let me work out some of my thoughts in his publication's pages; he let me take time off work to write the book, and he let me draw on the magazine's resources in countless ways. My thanks to him and to everyone else at *Reason* who assisted in one way or another, including Mike Alissi, Ronald Bailey, Barbara Burch, Brian Doherty, Jim Epstein, Matthew Feeney, Nick Gillespie, Ed Krayewski, Katherine Mangu-Ward, Chris Mitchell, Ray Ng, David Nott, Mike Riggs, Damon Root, Scott Shackford, Peter Suderman, Jacob Sullum, Mary Toledo, J. D. Tuccille, and, not least, the interns who transcribed several of my interviews: Julie Ershadi, Melanie Kruvelis, John K. Ross, Nick Sibilla, and Calvin Thompson.

My agent, David Kuhn, and his staff were instrumental not just in getting a publisher interested in my book proposal but in shaping the proposal itself. Billy Kingsland in particular was full of good ideas, and the book is much better for his and David's work. My editor at HarperCollins, Barry Harbaugh, has been an inexhaustible source both of enthusiasm for the project and of suggestions that have improved it. Thanks also to Lynn Anderson for her copyediting, to Nancy Wolff for creating the index, to Michael Correy for designing the book's interior, and to Jarrod Taylor for designing the cover.

Finally, I'd like to thank my family for all their patience and love: my parents, David and Marjorie Walker; my brother, Andrew Walker; my wife, Rona Kobell; and our children, Maya and Lila Walker. I owe more to them than to anyone else. Except, of course, the Order of the Illumin— Ah, but I am not supposed to speak of that.

NOTES

Chapter 1: The Paranoid Style Is *American Politics*

1. William Isaac Thomas and Dorothy Swaine Thomas, *The Child in America: Behavior Problems and Programs* (Knopf, 1928), 572.
2. "Case of Richard Lawrence," *Niles' Register*, February 14, 1835.
3. Quoted in Edwin A. Miles, "Andrew Jackson and Senator George Poindexter," *The Journal of Southern History* 24, no. 1 (February 1958).
4. See Richard C. Rohrs, "Partisan Politics and the Attempted Assassination of Andrew Jackson," *Journal of the Early Republic* 1, no. 2 (Summer 1981).
5. John Smith Dye, *The Adder's Den; or the Secrets of the Great Conspiracy to Overthrow Liberty in America* (privately published, 1864), 29.
6. Ibid., 94.
7. On the medical mistreatment of William Henry Harrison, see Will

Englund, "Remember the Flu of '41," *The National Journal*, October 10, 2009.

8. Naturally, Dye's revised book blamed Lincoln's murder on the same culprits. Dye's son, Sergeant Joseph M. Dye, wound up testifying as a witness in the trial that followed the Lincoln assassination, claiming to have seen Booth and his confederates conferring outside Ford's Theatre.
9. "New Books," *The New York Times*, October 8, 1864; "Poisoning Presidents," *Chicago Tribune*, June 28, 1866.
10. Favorable reviews from the *Philadelphia Daily Telegraph*, the *Philadelphia Evening Bulletin*, the *Philadelphia Daily Press*, the *Harrisburg Daily Telegraph*, the Trenton *Daily State Gazette*, *The New York Daily Tribune*, the *Easton Express*, and *The New York Evening Express* are reprinted in John Smith Dye, *Life and Public Services of Gen. U.S. Grant: The Nation's Choice for President in 1868*, 10th ed. (Samuel Loag, 1868), 93–96.
11. David Wylie, letter to Abraham Lincoln, January 25, 1861, in *The Lincoln Mailbag: America Writes to the President, 1861–1865*, ed. Harold Holzer (Southern Illinois University Press, 1998), 4.
12. A Maine Country Girl, letter to Abraham Lincoln, 1860, memory.loc.gov/mss/mal/maltext/rtf_orig/mal012f.rtf.
13. See George Duffield, *The Nation's Wail* (Advertiser and Tribune Print, 1865), 10–11; William Goodwin, *A Discourse on the Assassination of Abraham Lincoln, President of the United States, April 14, 1865* (David B. Moseley, 1865), 9. Beecher's article is quoted in John Smith Dye, *History of the Plots and Crimes of the Great Conspiracy to Overthrow Liberty in America* (privately published, 1866), 305.
14. Quoted in David O. Stewart, *Impeached: The Trial of President Andrew Johnson and the Fight for Lincoln's Legacy* (Simon & Schuster, 2009), 101.
15. "By the Bullet and the Bowl," *New-York Tribune*, May 16, 1868.
16. Russel B. Nye, "The Slave Power Conspiracy: 1830–1860," *Science & Society* 10, no. 3 (Summer 1946).
17. Abraham Lincoln, "Draft of a Speech" (1858), in *Lincoln: Speeches and*

Writings, 1832–1858, ed. Don E. Fahrenbacher (Library of America, 1989), 488.

18. There is, for example, this elaborate metaphor for the policies that allowed slavery to extend westward:

> We cannot absolutely *know* that all these exact adaptations are the result of preconcert. But when we see a lot of framed timbers, different portions of which we know have been gotten out at different times and places, and by different workmen—Stephen, Franklin, Roger, and James, for instance—and when we see these timbers joined together, and see they exactly make the frame of a house or a mill, all the tenons and mortices exactly fitting, and all the lengths and proportions of the different pieces exactly adapted to their respective places, and not a piece too many or too few—not omitting even scaffolding—or, if a single piece be lacking, we see the place in the frame exactly fitted and prepared yet to bring such piece in—in *such* a case we find it impossible not to *believe* that Stephen and Franklin and Roger and James all understood one another from the beginning and all worked upon a common plan or draft drawn up before the first blow was struck.

Abraham Lincoln, "'House Divided' Speech" (1858), ibid., 431.

19. Henry Wilson, *The Death of Slavery Is the Life of the Nation: Speech of Hon. Henry Wilson (of Massachusetts,) in the Senate, March 28, 1864. On the Proposed Amendment to the Constitution Prohibiting Slavery Within the United States* (H. Polkinhorn, 1864), 8.
20. The article originated as a lecture delivered at Oxford in November 1963, just a day before the assassination of John F. Kennedy; it was then published in the November 1964 *Harper's*. A revised version appeared in Richard Hofstadter, *The Paranoid Style in American Politics and Other Essays* (Harvard University Press, 1965). Unless otherwise noted, my quotes are drawn from the 1965 version of the essay.
21. Hofstadter, *The Paranoid Style in American Politics*, 5, 7.
22. That is, the *Harper's* version.
23. Thomas Hargrove, "Third of Americans Suspect 9-11 Government Conspiracy," Scripps Howard News Service, August 1, 2006.

24. "John F. Kennedy's Assassination Leaves a Legacy of Suspicion," ABC News press release, November 16, 2003.
25. Frank Newport, "What If Government Really Listened to the People?" Gallup Poll, October 15, 1997. As this book went to press, Public Policy Polling released a survey asking Americans about a wide variety of conspiracy theories. The results showed a smaller but still substantial portion of the public—51 percent—believing that a conspiracy larger than Lee Harvey Oswald was responsible for the Kennedy assassination, with 24 percent unsure. Just 11 percent believed that the U.S. government knowingly allowed the 9/11 attacks to happen, with 11 percent unsure. These changes from the earlier polls could be a product of a greater distance from the events being discussed. (The anger that led people to blame 9/11 on Washington, for instance, may have cooled somewhat since George W. Bush left office.) It is also possible that the different numbers reflect different methodologies. People may, for example, be less inclined to embrace JFK and 9/11 theories when they are proposed alongside such obvious kook-bait questions as "Do you believe Paul McCartney actually died in a car crash in 1966 and was secretly replaced by a look-alike so that the Beatles could continue, or not?" and "Do you believe that shape-shifting reptilian people control our world by taking on human form and gaining power to manipulate our societies, or not?" For the full results, see Public Policy Polling, "Democrats and Republicans Differ on Conspiracy Theory Beliefs," April 2, 2013, publicpolicypolling.com/pdf/2011/PPP_Release_National_ConspiracyTheories_040213.pdf.
26. Monica Crowley, *Nixon in Winter: His Final Revelations About Diplomacy, Watergate, and Life Out of the Arena* (Random House, 1998), 309.
27. Webb Hubbell, *Friends in High Places: Our Journey from Little Rock to Washington, D.C.* (William Morrow, 1997), 282. Hubbell insisted that Clinton "was dead serious."
28. Stanley Cohen, *Folk Devils and Moral Panics*, 3rd ed. (Psychology Press, 2002), 1.
29. Erich Goode, e-mail to the author, November 9, 2001.
30. Cohen, *Folk Devils and Moral Panics*, 47.

31. Clifford Griffith Roe, *The Girl Who Disappeared* (World's Purity Federation, 1914), 200.
32. For a comparison between the Bureau's role in stoking fears of vice rings during the white-slavery panic and its role in stoking fears of Communist conspiracies after the First World War, see Regin Schmidt, *Red Scare: FBI and the Origins of Anticommunism in the United States* (Museum Tusculanum Press, 2000), 83–86.
33. Hofstadter, *The Paranoid Style in American Politics*, 9.
34. Quoted in Norman Pollack, *The Populist Response to Industrial America: Midwestern Populist Thought* (Harvard University Press, 1962), 129.
35. "What Does It Mean?" *Winfield Daily Courier*, October 4, 1888.
36. "Clinched!" *Winfield Daily Courier*, October 18, 1888.
37. Hofstadter, *The Paranoid Style in American Politics*, 32–33. Hofstadter here is elaborating on an argument in an earlier essay: David Brion Davis, "Some Themes of Counter-Subversion: An Analysis of Anti-Masonic, Anti-Catholic, and Anti-Mormon Literature," *Mississippi Valley Historical Review*, September 1960.
38. Walter Reuther, Victor Reuther, and Joseph Rauh, "The Radical Right in America Today," December 19, 1961.
39. Rick Perlstein, *Before the Storm: Barry Goldwater and the Unmaking of the American Consensus* (Hill and Wang, 2001), 157.
40. Ibid., 149.
41. David Frum, "What Is Going On at Fox News?" March 16, 2009, web.archive.org/web/20100317185437/http://www.frumforum.com/what-is-going-on-at-fox-news.
42. David Graeber, *Fragments of an Anarchist Anthropology* (Prickly Paradigms Press, 2004), 25–26.
43. Ibid., 27.
44. Sam Smith, "America's Extremist Center," *The Progressive Review*, July 1995.
45. As I was writing my manuscript, another book that treats conspiracy theories as a modern mythology appeared. I enjoyed it, though its approach was ultimately rather different from mine. See Robert Guffney, *Cryptoscatology: Conspiracy Theory as Art Form* (TrineDay, 2012).

46. The term comes from the Czech Communist Jan Kozak, who used it to describe how his party came to power. For an influential example of the idea being used in a Birchite context, see Gary Allen with Larry Abraham, *None Dare Call It Conspiracy* (Concord Press, 1972), 113–27.
47. "Brief lesson for paranoiacs: setting your open-ended conspiracy metaphors loose upon the world, they become (like anything) eligible for manifold repurposing. Free your mind and an ass may follow." Jonathan Lethem, *They Live* (Soft Skull Press, 2010), 43.
48. Hofstadter, *The Paranoid Style in American Politics*, 3–4.
49. *Fact*, September–October 1964.
50. Hadley Cantril, *The Invasion from Mars: A Study in the Psychology of Panic* (Transaction Publishers, 2005 [1940]), 3, 47.
51. Michael J. Socolow, "The Hyped Panic over 'War of the Worlds,'" *The Chronicle of Higher Education*, October 24, 2008. Socolow also described Cantril's methodological problems in detail, showing why the numbers in *The Invasion from Mars* are doubtful.
52. W. Joseph Campbell, *Getting It Wrong: Ten of the Greatest Misreported Stories in American Journalism* (University of California Press, 2010), 36.
53. Walter Lippmann, "The Modern Malady" (1938), in *The Essential Lippmann: A Political Philosophy for Liberal Democracy*, ed. Clinton Rossiter and James Lare (Harvard University Press, 1963), 174–75.
54. Socolow, "The Hyped Panic over 'War of the Worlds.'"

Chapter 2: The Devil in the Wilderness

1. Michael Paul Rogin, *Ronald Reagan: The Movie, and Other Episodes in Political Demonology* (University of California Press, 1987), 50.
2. Joseph Mede, letter to William Twisse, March 23, 1635, quoted in *Collections of the Massachusetts Historical Society*, 2nd ser., vol. 6 (Massachusetts Historical Society, 1815), 680–81.
3. Cotton Mather, *Magnalia Christi Americana; or, The Ecclesiastical History of New-England; From Its First Planting, in the Year 1620, unto the Year of Our Lord 1698*, vol. 1 (Silas Andrus and Son, 1853 [1702]), 41.

4. Cotton Mather, *The Wonders of the Invisible World: Being an Account of the Tryals of Several Witches Lately Executed in New-England* (John Russell Smith, 1862 [1693]), 63.
5. William Hubbard, *A Narrative of the Indian Wars in New England* (William Fessenden, 1814 [1677]), 323.
6. Cotton Mather, *Magnalia Christi Americana*, vol. 2 (Silas Andrus and Son, 1853 [1702]), 623.
7. Richard Slotkin, *Regeneration Through Violence: The Mythology of the American Frontier, 1600–1860* (University of Oklahoma Press, 1973), 94.
8. Mather, *Magnalia Christi Americana*, vol. 2, 42.
9. Increase Mather, *Relation of the Troubles Which Have Happened in New England by Reason of the Indians There* (Kessinger Publishing, 2003 [1677]), 74.
10. James David Drake, *King Philip's War: Civil War in New England, 1675–1676* (University of Massachusetts Press, 1999), 70.
11. For a discussion of the questions left open about the physical evidence, see Yasuhide Kawashima, *Igniting King Philip's War: The John Sassamon Murder Trial* (University Press of Kansas, 2001), 88–100.
12. The Mohegan leader named Uncas used this tactic repeatedly to get military assistance from the colony of Connecticut. See Drake, *King Philip's War*, 64–65.
13. Samuel Gorton, letter to John Winthrop, Jr., September 11, 1675, in *Collections of the Massachusetts Historical Society*, 4th ser., vol. 7 (Massachusetts Historical Society, 1865), 628. Lest I give the impression that *every* settler held such beliefs, I should point out that Gorton himself rejected them firmly, writing: "[F]or my own part I feare no such thing" and "People are apt in these dayes to give credit to every flying and false report."
14. Samuel Gardner Drake, *The Present State of New-England with Respect to the Indian War* (Dorman Newman, 1833 [1675]), 30.
15. *Extracts from the Itineraries and Other Miscellanies of Ezra Stiles, D.D., LL.D., 1755–1794, with a Selection from His Correspondence*, ed. Franklin Bowditch Dexter (Yale University Press, 1916), 232.

16. Pedro de Feria, quoted in Fernando Cervantes, *The Devil in the New World: The Impact of Diabolism in New Spain* (Yale University Press, 1997), 35. For a detailed account of this episode, see Kevin Gosner, "Caciques and Conversion: Juan Atonal and the Struggle for Legitimacy in Post-Conquest Chiapas," *The Americas* 49, no. 2 (October 1992).
17. William Hubbard, *A General History of New England from the Discovery to MDCLXXX* (Massachusetts Historical Society, 1815 [1682]), 26.
18. William S. Simmons, "Cultural Bias in the New England Puritans' Perception of Indians," *The William and Mary Quarterly*, 3rd ser., 38, no. 1 (January 1981).
19. See Alfred A. Cave, "Indian Shamans and English Witches in Seventeenth-Century New England," *Essex Institute Historical Collections*, 128 (1992).
20. Drake, *King Philip's War*, 70.
21. Jeffrey L. Pasley, "Native Americans," in *Conspiracy Theories in American History: An Encyclopedia*, vol. 2, ed. Peter Knight (ABC-CLIO, 2003), 523–24. Pasley borrowed the word *superchief* from Russell Bourne, *The Red King's Rebellion: Racial Politics in New England, 1675–1678* (Oxford University Press, 1992), 202. But the identification of the broader pattern was Pasley's, not Bourne's.
22. See Alden T. Vaughan, *New England Frontier: Puritans and Indians, 1620–1675*, 3rd ed. (University of Oklahoma Press, 1995), 157–60.
23. Daniel Wetherell, letter to John Winthrop, Jr., June 30, 1675, in *Collections of the Massachusetts Historical Society*, 3rd ser., vol. 10 (Massachusetts Historical Society, 1849), 119.
24. Daniel Gookin, *An Historical Account of the Doings and Sufferings of the Christian Indians in New England in the Years 1675, 1676, 1677* (Kessinger Publishing, 2003 [1677]), 494.
25. Harvard Charter of 1650, library.harvard.edu/university-archives/using-the-collections/online-resources/charter-of-1650.
26. Increase Mather, *An Earnest Exhortation to the Inhabitants of New-England, To hearken to the voice of God in his late and present Dispensa-*

tions As ever they desire to escape another Judgement, seven times greater than any thing which as yet hath been (John Foster, 1676), 12.

27. Ibid., 6.
28. Slotkin, *Regeneration Through Violence*, 68.
29. People who think the space where cultures mix is "wholly foreign," the political scientist Anne Norton has written, "exhibit the same symptoms: fear of conspiracy and a sense of omnipresent danger." Anne Norton, *Reflections on Political Identity* (Johns Hopkins University Press, 1988), 55. Riffing on Norton, James David Drake noted that the Puritans most eager to exclude Indians from the New England community were the ones who held "the most paranoid fears of attacks from all Indians, regardless of the relationship of those Indians to other English colonists." Drake, *King Philip's War*, 78.
30. William Hand Browne, ed., *Archives of Maryland: Proceedings of the Council of Maryland, 1687/8–1693* (Maryland Historical Society, 1890), 77.
31. It wasn't the first time Coode had played a role in spreading such rumors. After some Indian raids in 1681, he had helped circulate the story that the natives were attacking the Protestants on behalf of the Catholics. When Coode and company took power in 1689, they stood by those earlier stories, maintaining that the "incursion . . . of the said Northern Indians in the year 1681" had been "conducted into the heart of this Province by French Jesuits." Ibid., 106.
32. Quoted in Mary Beth Norton, *In the Devil's Snare: The Salem Witchcraft Crisis of 1692* (Alfred A. Knopf, 2002), 97. Andros, in turn, blamed his political troubles on a conspiracy of Boston merchants.
33. Increase Mather, *Early History of New England; Being a Relation of Hostile Passages Between the Indians and European Voyagers and First Settlers: And a Full Narrative of Hostilities, to the Close of the War with the Pequots, in the Year 1637; Also a Detailed Account of the Origin of the War with King Philip* (J. Munsell, 1864 [1677]), 217.
34. "An Act Against Jesuits and Popish Priests in New York," passed July 31, 1700.
35. John Perceval, summarizing a letter from Georgia's founder, James

Oglethorpe, in *Manuscripts of the Earl of Egmont: Diary of the First Earl of Egmont (Viscount Percival)*, vol. 2 (His Majesty's Stationery Office, 1923), 246.

36. Quoted in Peter Silver, *Our Savage Neighbors: How Indian War Transformed Early America* (W. W. Norton, 2009), 98.
37. Maria Monk, *Awful Disclosures, or, The Hidden Secrets of a Nun's Life in a Convent Exposed* (privately published, 1836).
38. Though the Enemy Outside is more likely to turn up in prowar rhetoric, some elements of the story are standbys in antiwar arguments too. The image of the outside world as a hostile wilderness best avoided has an obvious appeal to opponents of military intervention. Though there's a long tradition of imperialists denouncing the devils outside our borders, there is also John Quincy Adams's oft-quoted admonition not to go abroad "in search of monsters to destroy." And if there have been conspiracy theories, some accurate and some fanciful, about foreign plots to attack Americans, there have also been conspiracy theories, some accurate and some fanciful, in which foreign powers try to draw Americans into their conflicts abroad.
39. Richard M. Dorson, *American Folklore*, 2nd ed. (University of Chicago Press, 1977), 18.
40. Rex Alan Smith, *Moon at Popping Trees: The Tragedy at Wounded Knee and the End of the Indian Wars* (University of Nebraska Press, 1981 [1975]), 98. Smith discusses the limits to Sitting Bull's real-world authority on pp. 98–100.
41. Elbridge Streeter Brooks, *The Master of the Strong Hearts: A Story of Custer's Last Rally* (E. P. Dutton and Co., 1898), 50–52.
42. This might have been inspired by the Mormon endowment robe, which weapons allegedly could not penetrate.
43. James McLaughlin, quoted in *Sixtieth Annual Report of the Commissioner of Indian Affairs to the Secretary of the Interior* (Government Printing Office, 1891), 125.
44. Quoted in Smith, *Moon at Popping Trees*, 111.
45. Quoted ibid., 112.
46. Quoted ibid., 139.

47. L. Frank Baum, *Our Landlady*, ed. Nancy Tystad Koupal (Bison Books, 1999), 144.
48. Brooks, *The Master of the Strong Hearts*, 305.
49. Quoted in David M. Kennedy, *Over Here: The First World War and American Society*, 2nd ed. (Oxford University Press, 2004), 68.
50. Frederick Luebke, *Bonds of Loyalty: German-Americans and World War I* (Northern Illinois University Press, 1974), 255–56.
51. Committee on Public Information, "Spies and Lies" (1917), reprinted in James R. Mock and Cedric Larson, *Words That Won the War: How the Creel Committee on Public Information Mobilized American Opinion Toward Winning the World War* (Princeton University Press, 1939), 64.
52. "Stamping Out Treason," *The Washington Post*, April 12, 1918.
53. Mock and Larson, *Words That Won the War*, 15–16.
54. David Ignatius, "The bin Laden Plot to Kill President Obama," *The Washington Post*, March 12, 2012.
55. George Michael, *Lone Wolf Terror and the Rise of Leaderless Resistance* (Vanderbilt University Press, 2012), 127.
56. For an extended argument along these lines, see Jason Burke, *Al-Qaeda: Casting a Shadow of Terror* (I. B. Tauris, 2004).

Chapter 3: The Devil Next Door

1. *Invasion of the Body Snatchers*, directed by Don Siegel, screenplay by Daniel Mainwaring, from a novel by Jack Finney, Allied Artists, 1956.
2. Nathaniel Hawthorne, "Young Goodman Brown" (1835), in *Selected Short Stories of Nathaniel Hawthorne*, ed. Alfred Kazin (Ballantine Books, 1966), 102.
3. Ibid., 108–9.
4. Ibid., 110.
5. For an extended reading of the story along these lines, see David Levin, "Shadows of Doubt: Specter Evidence in Hawthorne's 'Young Goodman Brown,'" *American Literature* 34, no. 3 (November 1962).
6. John Putnam Demos, *Entertaining Satan: Witchcraft and the Culture of*

Early New England (Oxford University Press, 1982), 11. The individual cases are listed on pp. 401–9. Demos's count included six women accused of witchcraft in and near Stamford, Connecticut, in 1692, the same year the Salem witch hunt began. For a detailed discussion of that episode, which followed a rather different course from the Salem trials, see Richard Godbeer, *Escaping Salem: The Other Witch Hunt of 1692* (Oxford University Press, 2005).

7. I'm relying here on the tally in Mary Beth Norton, *In the Devil's Snare: The Salem Witchcraft Crisis of 1692* (Alfred A. Knopf, 2002), 3–4.
8. Salem Village is now Danvers, Massachusetts. Salem Town became the modern Salem.
9. Hugh Trevor-Roper, *The Crisis of the Seventeenth Century: Religion, the Reformation, and Social Change* (Liberty Fund, 2001 [1967]), 145. This body count, I should note, is not as well documented as the numbers we have for New England.
10. John Hale, "A Modest Inquiry into the Nature of Witchcraft" (1702), in *Narratives of the Witchcraft Cases, 1648–1706*, ed. George Lincoln Burr (C. Scribner's Sons, 1914), 413.
11. A few scholars have suggested that Tituba was of African descent, an idea that has also appeared in some literary accounts of the trials. Though I don't find their arguments convincing, that hardly matters. The important issue for our purposes is what the Puritans believed, not whether they were right to believe it. And the contemporary record, to the extent that it engaged the issue at all, described Tituba as an Indian.
12. Hawthorne, "Young Goodman Brown," 101.
13. Ann Putnam, Jr., quoted in *The Salem Witchcraft Papers: Verbatim Transcripts of the Legal Documents of the Salem Witchcraft Outbreak of 1692*, vol. 1, ed. Paul Boyer and Stephen Nissenbaum (Da Capo Press, 1977), 164.
14. Cotton Mather, *Magnalia Christi Americana; or, The Ecclesiastical History of New-England; From Its First Planting, in the Year 1620, unto the Year of Our Lord 1698*, vol. 2 (Silas Andrus and Son, 1853 [1702]), 620.

15. Cotton Mather, "A Brand Pluck'd Out of the Burning" (1693), in Burr, *Narratives of the Witchcraft Cases, 1648–1706*, 282–83.
16. Thomas Newton, quoted in Paul Boyer and Stephen Nissenbaum, *Salem Possessed: The Social Origins of Witchcraft* (Harvard University Press, 1974), 32.
17. Chadwick Hansen, *Witchcraft at Salem* (George Braziller, 1969). I think Hansen greatly overstated his case, but it was unquestionably true that some colonists attempted to harness magic for their own ends. In one illuminating pre-Salem deposition, a woman's healing powers—that is, her skills as a white witch—were offered as evidence that she might be a "destroying witch" as well. Quoted in Samuel G. Drake, *Annals of Witchcraft in New England, and Elsewhere in the United States, from Their First Settlement* (W. E. Woodward, 1869), 281.
18. Richard Weisman, *Witchcraft, Magic, and Religion in 17th-Century Massachusetts* (University of Massachusetts Press, 1984), 121.
19. Quoted in Boyer and Nissenbaum, eds., *Salem Witchcraft Papers*, vol. 1, 66.
20. Quoted in Eve LaPlante, *Salem Witch Judge: The Life and Repentance of Samuel Sewall* (HarperCollins, 2008), 2.
21. Deodat Lawson, quoted in Charles Upham, *Salem Witchcraft; with An Account of Salem Village, and A History of Opinions on Witchcraft and Kindred Subjects*, vol. 2 (Wiggin and Lunt, 1867), 525–26.
22. Amos Taylor, *A Narrative of the Strange Principles, Conduct and Character of the People Known by the Name of Shakers: Whose Errors Have Spread in Several Parts of North-America, but Are Beginning to Diminish, and Ought to Be Guarded Against* (Isaiah Thomas, 1782), 3.
23. Valentine Rathburn, quoted in Elizabeth A. De Wolfe, "'A Very Deep Design at the Bottom': The Shaker Threat, 1780–1860," in *Fear Itself: Enemies Real and Imagined in American Culture*, ed. Nancy Lusignan Schultz (Purdue University Press, 1999), 107.
24. A Protestant [Calvin Colton], *Protestant Jesuitism* (Harper & Brothers, 1836), 13–14.
25. Ibid., 35.

26. Ibid., 30.
27. Ibid., 16.
28. Ibid., 107.
29. Ibid., 111.
30. Ibid., 132.
31. Robert S. Levine, *Conspiracy and Romance: Studies in Brockden Brown, Cooper, Hawthorne, and Melville* (Cambridge University Press, 1989), 128. Levine also suggested that "Young Goodman Brown" was partly inspired by the Anti-Masonic movement and its "attack on aristocratic plotters," noting that the story features "a typically Antimasonic image of the community's religious, judicial, and political leaders leagued in secretive fraternity." I'll have more to say about the movement against Masonry in chapter 5. Here I'll just note that though it's certainly possible that Anti-Masonic imagery influenced elements of Hawthorne's tale, the alleged conspiracy in "Young Goodman Brown" extends beyond the respectable classes; the witches' camp meeting also includes "men of dissolute lives and women of spotted fame, wretches given over to all mean and filthy vice, and suspected even of horrid crimes." The Anti-Masons of the 1820s and '30s feared the Enemy Above. Goodman Brown's fears were not limited to any single social class.
32. Calvin Colton, *Thoughts on the Religious State of the Country; with Reasons for Preferring Episcopy* (Harper & Brothers, 1836), 177–78.
33. La Roy Sunderland, *Pathetism; with Practical Instructions* (P. P. Good, 1843), 210.
34. Pleasant Hill Ministry, quoted in Stephen J. Stein, *The Shaker Experience in America: A History of the United Society of Believers* (Yale University Press, 1994), 98.
35. The Book of Mormon, 3 Nephi 3:9, Helaman 6:26–29.
36. For a discussion of the Gadianton robbers in Mormon folklore, see W. Paul Revere, "'As Ugly as Evil,' and 'As Wicked as Hell': Gadianton Robbers and the Legend Process Among the Mormons," in *Between Pulpit and Pew: The Supernatural World in Mormon History and Folklore*, ed. W. Paul Revere and Michael Scott Van Wagenen (Utah State University Press, 2011), 40–65.

37. David Brion Davis, "Some Themes of Counter-Subversion: An Analysis of Anti-Masonic, Anti-Catholic, and Anti-Mormon Literature," *Mississippi Valley Historical Review*, September 1960.
38. *Female Life Among the Mormons; A Narrative of Many Years' Personal Experience* (J. C. Derby, 1855), 47. The title page attributes the book to "The Wife of a Mormon Elder, Recently from Utah," but the narrator identifies herself as Maria Ward in the text. Some scholars have suggested that Ward was a pseudonym for Cornelia Ferris, whose (non-Mormon) husband worked for Utah's territorial government. Whether or not that's true, the book is clearly fiction.
39. John C. Bennett, *The History of the Saints; or, An Exposé of Joe Smith and Mormonism* (Leland & Whiting, 1842), 223.
40. Davis, "Some Themes of Counter-Subversion."
41. Harrington O'Reilly [and John Young Nelson], *Fifty Years on the Trail: A True Story of Western Life* (Chatto & Windus, 1889), 180.
42. Mark Twain, *Roughing It* (American Publishing Company, 1873), 106.
43. The most telling attack on the Mormons' economic enterprises came from New England, not Idaho. Writing in the 1880s, Samuel Porter Putnam complained that the "Mormons are money-getters, like the Jews." Quoted in Dyer D. Lum, "Mormon Co-Operation," *Liberty*, July 3, 1886.
44. Recall that Wovoka studied both the Mormons and the Shakers before he revived the Ghost Dance. Outsiders observed the two sects' influence on him, and conspiratorial speculation predictably followed. Catherine Weldon, an Indian rights advocate who didn't approve of the Ghost Dance, claimed that "the Mormons are at the bottom of it all & misuse the credulity of the Indians for their own purposes." Quoted in Rex Alan Smith, *Moon at Popping Trees* (University of Nebraska Press, 1981), 110.
45. Zane Grey, *Riders of the Purple Sage* (Grosset & Dunlap, 1912), 310.
46. Ibid., 26.
47. Ibid., 160–62.
48. Ibid., 172.
49. Ibid., 174.

50. Don Siegel, *A Siegel Film: An Autobiography* (Faber and Faber, 1993), 178.
51. *It Came from Outer Space*, directed by Jack Arnold, screenplay by Harry Essex, from a story by Ray Bradbury, Universal Studios, 1953. Sources differ as to how much of a role Ray Bradbury played in writing the movie. The film was produced by William Alland, who earlier had acted in Orson Welles's "The War of the Worlds."
52. Harl Vincent, "Parasite," *Amazing Stories*, July 1935.
53. Campbell's novella was the basis of Howard Hawks's 1951 film *The Thing from Another World*, which removed the body-snatching element of the plot but maintained the atmosphere of paranoia. The theme of imposture was restored in the second movie to be based on the story, John Carpenter's *The Thing* (1982). For a clever reimagining of the scenario from the alien's point of view, see Peter Watts, "The Things," January 2010, clarkesworldmagazine.com/watts_01_10.
54. *The Puppet Masters*, in keeping with its Enemy Outside leanings, does end with the hero preparing to battle the invaders at their home base on Titan. In Britain, meanwhile, the sequel to *Quatermass II*—the six-part serial *Quatermass and the Pit* (1958–59)—features a mind-controlling Satanic alien that has been lying dormant beneath the earth.
55. *Hearings Before the Subcommittee to Investigate Juvenile Delinquency of the Committee on the Judiciary, United States Senate, Eighty-Third Congress, Second Session, Pursuant to S. 190* (United States Government Printing Office, 1954), 93.
56. Vance Packard, *The Hidden Persuaders* (Ig Publishing, 2007 [1957]), 32. Packard was a former staffer at *Collier's*, the same magazine that serialized Jack Finney's *The Body Snatchers*.
57. Ibid., 33.
58. Ibid., 219–20.
59. That worldview was widespread not just among the critics of advertising but also among the admen themselves, many of whom "contemplated the rise of the modern mass man with fear and contempt," according to the historian Roland Marchand. Advertisers were aware

that this fear and this contempt were also becoming prevalent in the larger society, and they found ways to exploit both. As early as the 1930s, as pitchmen recognized "a rising public fear of submergence in mass conformity," ads "frequently appealed to this concern by advertising products on the strength of their capacity to lift the individual out of the crowd." Roland Marchand, *Advertising the American Dream: Making Way for Modernity, 1920–1940* (University of California Press, 1985), 268–69.

60. *The Whip Hand*, directed by William Cameron Menzies, screenplay by George Bricker and Frank L. Moss, from a story by Roy Hamilton, RKO, 1951. Menzies's next credit would be the aforementioned *Invaders from Mars*.
61. Thomas Doherty, *Cold War, Cool Medium: Television, McCarthyism, and American Culture* (Columbia University Press, 2003), 146–47. Philbrick was played by Richard Carlson, who was also the lead in *It Came from Outer Space*.
62. Ibid., 146.
63. On the 1950s fear of brainwashing and its influence on Condon's book, see Louis Menand, "Brainwashed," *The New Yorker*, September 15, 2003. As Menand pointed out, American observers exaggerated the brainwashers' power: "the former prisoners who had come home praising the good life to be had in North Korea soon reverted to American views."
64. Richard Condon, *The Manchurian Candidate* (Four Walls Eight Windows, 2004 [1959]), 32. This edition of Condon's book reprints Menand's essay as an introduction.
65. Ibid., 41.
66. Richard H. Rovere, *Senator Joe McCarthy* (University of California Press, 1996 [1959]), 51.
67. Kerouac's views on McCarthy are discussed, with different degrees of sympathy, in Dennis McNally, *Desolate Angel: Jack Kerouac, The Beat Generation, and America* (Da Capo Press, 2003 [1979]), 185–86; Bill Kauffman, *America First! Its History, Culture, and Politics* (Prometheus Books, 1995), 172; and Barry Miles, *Jack Kerouac: King of the Beats*

(Virgin Books, 2010 [1998]), 239. To see Burroughs praising Pegler, read William S. Burroughs, letter to Allen Ginsberg, December 24, 1949, in *The Letters of William S. Burroughs, 1945–1959*, ed. Oliver Harris (Penguin Books, 1993), 57.

68. See Leo Ribuffo, *The Old Christian Right: The Protestant Far Right from the Great Depression to the Cold War* (Temple University Press, 1983). The term *Brown Scare* is also sometimes used to describe fears of Mexican subversion. The historian Ricardo Romo attached the phrase to an anti-Chicano crusade of the 1910s that "developed peculiar dimensions on the West Coast," including fear of "a revolution which would claim the entire American Southwest for Mexico." Ricardo Romo, *East Los Angeles: History of a Barrio* (University of Texas Press, 1983), 90.
69. Erich Fromm, *Escape from Freedom* (Avon Books, 1969 [1941]), 266–67.
70. "The Monsters Are Due on Maple Street," *The Twilight Zone*, CBS, March 4, 1960.
71. Even as the fear of the herd mind was riding high in the 1950s and early '60s, social scientists were doing research that undercut the idea that mass panic was a common response to disaster. Much of their work was funded by the Pentagon, which was worried about how the public would act in a nuclear war and was surprised by the conclusions that E. L. Quarantelli, Charles Fritz, and other sociologists reached.
72. Erich Neumann, *Depth Psychology and a New Ethic*, trans. Eugene Rolfe (G. P. Putnam's Sons, 1969), 52. (First published in German in 1949.)
73. Gore Vidal, *The City and the Pillar*, 2nd ed. (New American Library, 1965), 158. Vidal was not the first writer to compare homosexuality to freemasonry: Richard Burton and Marcel Proust, among others, had used the same metaphor.
74. R. G. Waldeck, "Homosexual International," *Human Events*, April 16, 1952.
75. *Congressional Record*, May 1, 1952.
76. Quoted in David K. Johnson, *The Lavender Scare: The Cold War Per-*

secution of Gays and Lesbians in the Federal Government (University of Chicago Press, 2004), 112.

77. Ibid., 76. The Lavender Scare rebounded on some of the McCarthyists as well, eventually grazing against Joseph McCarthy himself. See Andrea Friedman, "The Smearing of Joe McCarthy: The Lavender Scare, Gossip, and Cold War Politics," *American Quarterly* 57, no. 4 (December 2005).
78. Johnson, *The Lavender Scare*, 183–84.
79. Quoted ibid., 187.
80. Ibid., 188.
81. Harry R. Jackson, Jr., quoted in Van Smith, "Holy War," *City Paper* (Baltimore), October 3, 2012.
82. Quoted ibid.

Chapter 4: The Beast Below

1. Bertram Wyatt-Brown, *Southern Honor: Ethics and Behavior in the Old South*, 2nd ed. (Oxford University Press, 2007), 413.
2. The North River is now known as the Hudson River.
3. Quoted in Daniel Horsmanden, *A Journal of the Proceedings in the Detection of the Conspiracy Formed by Some White People, in Conjunction with Negro and Other Slaves, for Burning the City of New-York in America and Murdering the Inhabitants* (John Clarke, 1747), 100. The first printing of Horsmanden's book appeared in 1744.
4. Quoted ibid., 26.
5. Quoted ibid., 14. In the text, "goddamn" is rendered as "---damn."
6. Quoted ibid., 16.
7. For a detailed accounting of the accused and their fates, see Jill Lepore, *New York Burning: Liberty, Slavery, and Conspiracy in Eighteenth-Century Manhattan* (Alfred A. Knopf, 2005), 248–59.
8. "Great Newes from the Barbadoes" (1676), in *Versions of Blackness: 'Oroonoko,' Race, and Slavery*, ed. Derek Hughes (Cambridge University Press, 2007), 341. Jill Lepore has argued that the Barbados conspiracy charges were an early example of what the English thought

"a slave plot looked like," with elements of the story reappearing in subsequent crackdowns through the years. "In Barbados in 1676," she wrote, "slave rebels sent signals using trumpets made of elephant tusks; in Antigua in 1736, dancing plotters swished an elephant tail. The New York confessions seem so formulaic that, if pachyderm tusks and tails were plausibly to be had on the banks of the Hudson, they might have made an appearance in John Hughson's tavern," if not in fact then at least in the accusers' imagination. Lepore, *New York Burning*, 10–11.

9. Nathaniel Saltonstall, "A Continuation of the State of New-England" (1676), in *Narratives of the Indian Wars, 1675–1699*, ed. Charles H. Lincoln (Charles Scribner's Sons, 1913), 73.
10. Horsmanden, *A Journal of the Proceedings in the Detection of the Conspiracy*, 18.
11. Ibid., 20.
12. Ibid., 300.
13. Ibid., 340.
14. For an early example of a skeptical take, see the 1810 edition of Horsmanden's own book, released just thirty-two years after the author's death. Horsmanden had written his account to defend the prosecutions, but a new preface declared that the conspiracy's "extent could never have been so great as the terror of those times depicted."
15. See, for example, Peter Linebaugh and Marcus Rediker's lively *The Many-Headed Hydra: Sailors, Slaves, Commoners, and the Hidden History of the Revolutionary Atlantic* (Beacon Press, 2000), 174–210.
16. Horsmanden, *A Journal of the Proceedings in the Detection of the Conspiracy*, vii.
17. Ibid., 378.
18. Quoted in Suzanne Lebsock, *The Free Women of Petersburg: Status and Culture in a Southern Town, 1784–1860* (W. W. Norton, 1984), 91.
19. See William Johnson, "Melancholy Effect of Popular Excitement" (1822), in *Denmark Vesey: The Slave Conspiracy of 1822*, ed. Robert S. Starobin (Prentice-Hall, 1970), 68–70.

20. Peter Charles Hoffer, *Cry Liberty: The Great Stono River Slave Rebellion of 1739* (Oxford University Press, 2010).
21. George Baca, *Conjuring Crisis: Racism and Civil Rights in a Southern Military City* (Rutgers University Press, 2010), 48.
22. Quoted in T. C. Parramore, "Conspiracy and Revivalism in 1802: A Direful Symbiosis," *Negro History Bulletin* 43, no. 2, April–June 1980. For more on the suppression of independent black churches, see Peter P. Hinks, *To Awaken My Afflicted Brethren: David Walker and the Problem of Antebellum Slave Resistance* (Pennsylvania State University Press, 1997), 60–62.
23. Herself [Harriet Jacobs], *Incidents in the Life of a Slave Girl* (privately published, 1861), 98.
24. Ibid., 99.
25. Ibid., 102.
26. Baca, *Conjuring Crisis*, 48. According to Jacobs, some whites protected slaves from the mob by putting them in jail for the duration of the riot.
27. Peter Charles Hoffer, *The Great New York Conspiracy of 1741: Slavery, Crime, and Colonial Law* (University Press of Kansas, 2003), 23–25.
28. Quoted in "Monthly Record of Current Events," *Harper's New Monthly Magazine*, January 1860.
29. Mark Twain, *Huck Finn and Tom Sawyer Among the Indians and Other Unfinished Stories* (University of California Press, 2011), 142–43.
30. Mark Twain, *Life on the Mississippi* (Penguin, 1984 [1883]), 211. The Murrell gang is invoked in *Tom Sawyer's Conspiracy* too, though there it's called "Burrell's Gang."
31. Joseph S. Williams, *Old Times in West Tennessee: Reminiscences—Semi-Historic—of Pioneer Life and the Early Emigrant Settlers in the Big Hatchie Country* (W. G. Cheeney, 1873), 200–1.
32. Augustus Q. Walton, *A History of the Detection, Conviction, Life and Designs of John A. Murel, the Great Western Land Pirate* (George White, 1835), 26–27.
33. Quoted in Edwin A. Miles, "The Mississippi Slave Insurrection Scare of 1835," *The Journal of Negro History* 42, no. 1 (January 1957).

34. At about the same time, an Anti-Gambling Committee in Vicksburg, Mississippi, expelled the town's gamblers from the city limits. The men who refused to go were hanged without a trial. It is unclear to what extent that outbreak of lynch law was connected to the Murrell lynchings, but the two events were linked afterward in public memory, and subsequent accounts sometimes treated the Mississippi gamblers as part of the conspiracy. In one historian's words, "the terms 'Murrell,' 'gambler,' and 'abolitionist' became essentially interchangeable." Thomas Ruys Smith, "Independence Day, 1835: The John A. Murrell Conspiracy and the Lynching of the Vicksburg Gamblers in Literature," *Mississippi Quarterly* 59, no. 1–2 (Winter–Spring 2006).
35. Compare: "The central idea of slavery, from the masters' point of view, was the absolute submission of the slave to the master. Theoretically, the slave represented no more than an extension of the master's will." Eugene Genovese, "Class, Culture, and Historical Process," *Dialectical Anthropology* 1, no. 1 (November 1975).
36. Annalee Newitz, "A History of Zombies in America," November 18, 2010, io9.com/5692719/a-history-of-zombies-in-america.
37. Zombies became extremely popular in the early twenty-first century. Some stories played with the notion of sympathizing with the zombies, an approach that dates back at least as far as Romero's 1985 film *Day of the Dead* but became increasingly common in this period. Other storytellers stuck with the idea of the undead as feral subhumans who deserve to be dispatched. Some survivalists refer to postapocalyptic looters as "Mutant Zombie Bikers." The term is tongue-in-cheek; the fear isn't.
38. "Outrages by Tramps," *The World*, October 4, 1879.
39. *The World*, October 24, 1879.
40. Quoted in "The Vagrant Class," *The New York Times*, September 7, 1877.
41. Horatio Seymour, "Crime and Tramps," *Harper's New Monthly Magazine*, December 1878.
42. *Galveston Daily News*, August 25, 1877.
43. Earlier in the century, one legal weapon the government had used

against unions had been to prosecute them as criminal conspiracies. You didn't have to be a slave to have something to fear from the broad application of conspiracy law.

44. Kevin Kenny, *Making Sense of the Molly Maguires* (Oxford University Press, 1998), 7. Kenny credited Benjamin Bannan, the nativist editor of *The Miners' Journal*, with introducing the term to the anthracite region, using it as what Kenny calls "a shorthand term for the various aspects of 'the Irish character' he found most objectionable and threatening."
45. Quoted in Allan Pinkerton, *The Molly Maguires and the Detectives*, 2nd ed. (G. W. Dillingham, 1905), 521.
46. As capitalists worried about labor conspiracies, union activists sometimes fretted about conspiracies bubbling among the immigrants who competed with them for jobs. Denis Kearney, the Irish-American leader of the Workingmen's Party, saw the "debauched, offal-eating, devil-worshipping, leprous Chinese" as the pawns of a capitalist plot to undercut white wages and undermine the republic. Quoted in "John Chinaman in America," *All the Year Round*, December 10, 1881.
47. "The Communists of New York—Their Secret Meetings and Movements," *New York Herald*, January 18, 1874.
48. Gary Alan Fine and Patricia A. Turner, *Whispers on the Color Line: Rumor and Race in America* (University of California Press, 2001), 48.
49. "Race Riots," *The New York Times*, July 28, 1919. The editorial's gallery of villains also includes Germany and the Industrial Workers of the World.
50. Quoted in Howard W. Odum, *Race and Rumors of Race: The American South in the Early Forties* (Johns Hopkins University Press, 1997 [1943]), 133, 135. Odum also collected rumors in which the secret power behind a black conspiracy was First Lady Eleanor Roosevelt, who supposedly lent her name to subversive "Eleanor Clubs." The clubs' purported motto: "A white woman in every kitchen by 1943." Ibid., 73–80.
51. Governor's Commission on the Los Angeles Riots, *Violence in the*

City—An End or a Beginning? December 2, 1965, usc.edu/libraries/archives/cityinstress/mccone.

52. Gary Allen, "The Plan to Burn Los Angeles," *American Opinion*, May 1967. All subsequent Allen quotes in this chapter come from this article.
53. There is more than a faint parallel between Allen's fear of what white retaliation might bring and the antebellum planters' fear of a black insurrection setting off white lawlessness. Allen, like the planters, preferred that the suppression of the Enemy Below be channeled through the state. On a related note: In the 1960s, the John Birch Society believed that the international conspiracy was manipulating not just the civil rights movement but the various Klan and neo-Nazi groups as well, with the aim of using both sides to incite a race war. In later years, Bircher accounts of the civil rights era would assign their most heroic role to the FBI infiltrators who targeted the Klan.
54. John Schmidhauser, quoted in Rick Perlstein, *Nixonland: The Rise of a President and the Fracturing of America* (Scribner's, 2008), 142.
55. Terry Ann Knopf, *Rumors, Race, and Riots* (Transaction Books, 1975), 131.
56. *Subversive Influences in Riots, Looting, and Burning, Part 1: Hearings Before the Committee on Un-American Activities, House of Representatives, Ninetieth Congress, First Session, October 25, 26, 31, and November 28, 1967* (U.S. Government Printing Office, 1968), 835.
57. Quoted in Gerald Horne, *Fire This Time: The Watts Uprising and the 1960s* (University Press of Virginia, 1995), 267.
58. Quoted in "Hard-Core Leftists Exploit L.A. Negroes, Says Graham," *The Spartanburg Herald*, August 18, 1965.
59. Quoted in "Outside Agitators Took Part in Riots, Says Frisco Mayor," *St. Joseph News-Press*, October 1, 1966.
60. Quoted in Perlstein, *Nixonland*, 199. On Johnson's push for the FBI to find a Communist conspiracy behind the riots, see Kenneth O'Reilly, *"Racial Matters": The FBI's Secret File on Black America, 1960–1972* (Free Press, 1989), 229ff.

Chapter 5: Puppeteers

1. Quoted in Bernard Bailyn, *The Ideological Origins of the American Revolution* (Harvard University Press, 1967), 94.
2. Oliver Noble, *Some Strictures upon the Sacred Story Recorded in the Book of Esther, Shewing the Power and Oppression of STATE MINISTERS Tending to the Ruin and Destruction of GOD's People:—And the Remarkable Interpositions of Divine Providence, in Favour of the Oppressed* (E. Lunt and H. W. Tinges, 1775), 6.
3. Edmund Burke, *Thoughts on the Cause of the Present Discontents* (J. Dodsley, 1770), 15–16.
4. Noble, *Some Strictures upon the Sacred Story*, 26.
5. John Adams, letter to Henry Niles, February 18, 1818, in *The Works of John Adams*, vol. 10, ed. Charles Francis Adams (Little, Brown and Company, 1856), 288.
6. Quoted in Bailyn, *The Ideological Origins of the American Revolution*, 101.
7. Quoted ibid., 119–20.
8. George Washington, letter to Bryan Fairfax, August 24, 1774, gwpapers.virginia.edu/documents/revolution/letters/bfairfax3.html.
9. Quoted in Bailyn, *The Ideological Origins of the American Revolution*, 119.
10. First Continental Congress, "Address to the People of Great Britain," September 5, 1774.
11. It's the Declaration of Independence. Do I really need to footnote the Declaration of Independence?
12. Alexander Hamilton, letter to George Washington, February 7, 1783, in *Hamilton: Writings*, ed. Joanne B. Freeman (Library of America, 2001), 122.
13. Cassius [Ædanus Burke], *Considerations on the Society or Order of Cincinnati; Lately Instituted by the Major-Generals, Brigadiers, and Other Officers of the American Army* (A. Timothy, 1783), 8, 28–29.
14. Abraham Yates, quoted in Bill Kauffman, *Forgotten Founder, Drunken Prophet: The Life of Luther Martin* (ISI Books, 2008), 27.

15. Luther Martin, "The Genuine Information, Delivered to the Legislature of the State of Maryland, Relative to the Proceedings of the General Convention, Held at Philadelphia, in 1787" (1787), oll.libertyfund.org/?option=com_staticxt&staticfile=show.php%3Ftitle=1787&chapter=96564&layout=html&Itemid=27.
16. Quoted in Kauffman, *Forgotten Founder, Drunken Prophet*, 75.
17. Quoted in Donald Henderson Stewart, *The Opposition Press of the Federalist Period* (State University of New York Press, 1969), 490.
18. Quoted in Louise Burnham Dunbar, "A Study of 'Monarchical' Tendencies in the United States from 1776 to 1801," *University of Illinois Studies in the Social Sciences* 10, no. 1 (March 1922).
19. Quoted ibid.
20. Bailyn, *The Ideological Origins of the American Revolution*, 56.
21. George H. Smith, "'That Audacious Document': Notes on the Declaration of Independence," November 8, 2011, libertarianism.org/publications/essays/excursions/audacious-document-notes-declaration-independence.
22. J. L. De Lolme, *The Constitution of England, or An Account of the English Government* (privately published, 1777), 203. Americans who used the phrase included Richard Henry Lee, who quoted it in a 1787 letter to George Mason; and Samuel Bryan, who invoked it around the same time in an Anti-Federalist essay.
23. Gordon S. Wood, "Conspiracy and the Paranoid Style: Causality and Deceit in the Eighteenth Century," *The William and Mary Quarterly*, 3rd ser., 39, no. 3 (July 1982).
24. Quoted in Carl Bridenbaugh, *Mitre and Sceptre: Transatlantic Faiths, Ideas, Personalities, and Politics, 1689–1775* (Oxford University Press, 1962), 215–16.
25. Those reasons are laid out in William M. Hogue, "The Religious Conspiracy Theory of the American Revolution: Anglican Motive," *Church History* 45, no. 3 (September 1976).
26. Thomas Jefferson, letter to George Washington, April 16, 1784, in *The Portable Thomas Jefferson*, ed. Merrill D. Peterson (Penguin Books, 1975), 368.

27. Quoted in Markus Hünemörder, *The Society of the Cincinnati: Conspiracy and Distrust in Early America* (Berghahn Books, 2006), 46.
28. In case you were wondering: The city in Ohio was named for the Society of the Cincinnati, not the other way around. The group took its name from the Roman dictator Lucius Quinctius Cincinnatus.
29. The most extreme advocates of Tory-style hierarchy and privilege—the group that would become the Essex faction of the Massachusetts Federalist Party, derided by Jeffersonians and moderate Federalists alike as a conspiratorial "Essex Junto"—were dissatisfied with the Constitution from the other political direction, arguing that the document was too democratic. Nonetheless, they supported ratification, believing it the best politically realistic option. See David H. Fischer, "The Myth of the Essex Junto," *The William and Mary Quarterly*, 3rd ser., 21, no. 2 (April 1964).
30. This is not the same argument as Charles Beard's economic interpretation of the Constitution, which attempted to reduce the framers' motives to narrow financial self-interest and which has been pretty much refuted.
31. R. Lamb, *An Original and Authentic Journal of Occurrences During the Late American War, from Its Commencement to the Year 1783* (Wilkinson & Courtney, 1809), 8.
32. Bailyn, *The Ideological Origins of the American Revolution*, 151.
33. Quoted in Marshall Smelser, "The Jacobin Phrenzy: Federalism and the Menace of Liberty, Equality, and Fraternity," *The Review of Politics* 13, no. 4 (October 1951).
34. The group was called the German Union and its founder was a theologian named Charles Frederick Bahrdt. It was basically a moneymaking scheme, and it did not last long.
35. For an argument that Illuminist ideas (as opposed to Illuminist agents taking orders from Adam Weishaupt) influenced revolutionaries in France and elsewhere, see James H. Billington, *Fire in the Minds of Men: Origins of the Revolutionary Faith* (Basic Books, 1980), 93–99. Billington notes that one way this influence was transmitted was through conservative conspiracy theories: "As the fears of the Right

became the fascination of the Left, Illuminism gained a paradoxical posthumous influence far greater than it had exercised as a living movement."

36. John Robison, *Proofs of a Conspiracy Against All the Religions and Governments of Europe, Carried on in the Secret Meetings of the Free Masons, Illuminati, and Reading Societies*, 4th ed. (George Forman, 1798), 14.
37. Jedidiah Morse, *A Sermon, Exhibiting the Present Dangers, and Consequent Duties of the Citizens of the United States of America* (Samuel Etheridge, 1799), 17. The sermon was originally delivered on May 9, 1798.
38. Ibid., 14.
39. Ibid., 15–16. Morse's son Samuel, the cocreator of Morse code and the inventor of an early telegraph, kept the family tradition of conspiracy hunting alive: He wrote a book alleging an Austro-papal plot to put the United States under the thumb of the Hapsburg Empire. See Brutus [Samuel Morse], *Foreign Conspiracy Against the Liberties of the United States* (Leavitt, Lord & Co., 1835).
40. Quoted in Vernon Stauffer, *New England and the Bavarian Illuminati* (Columbia University Press, 1918), 283.
41. Sally Sayward Wood, *Julia and the Illuminated Baron: The Critical Edition* (Library of Early Maine Literature, 2012 [1800]), 59.
42. Ibid., 207. Charles Brockden Brown, the preeminent novelist of the early republic, also drew on the Illuminati legend in his fiction, though he avoided the I-word. For more on Brown's interest in the Illuminati story and its influence on his writing, see Charles C. Bradshaw, "The New England Illuminati: Conspiracy and Causality in Charles Brockden Brown's *Wieland*," *The New England Quarterly* 76, no. 3 (September 2003).
43. The Declaration also accused the English of having "endeavoured to bring on the inhabitants of our frontiers, the merciless Indian Savages"—another alliance between the Enemy Above and the Enemy Outside.
44. Quoted in Harry Ammon, "The Richmond Junto, 1800–1824," *The Virginia Magazine of History and Biography* 61, no. 4 (October 1953).

45. Quoted in James M. Banner, Jr., *To the Hartford Convention: The Federalists and the Origins of Party Politics in Massachusetts, 1789–1815* (Alfred A. Knopf, 1970), 40–41.
46. Joseph Tufts, *An Oration, Pronounced Before the Federal Republicans of Charlestown, Massachusetts, July 4, 1814, Being the Anniversary of American Independence* (Samuel Etheridge, 1814), 9.
47. Banner, *To the Hartford Convention*, 44.
48. From the trial records: "[T]he prisoner . . . came to his house at dusk or dark where he was cutting wood, and asked him if he would join a free-mason society; this deponent replied no, because all free-masons would go to hell; upon this, the prisoner said it was not a free-mason society he wished him to join, but a society to fight the white people for their freedom." Quoted in Corey D. B. Walker, *A Noble Fight: African American Freemasonry and the Struggle for Democracy in America* (University of Illinois Press, 2008), 96.
49. The Anti-Masons were the first American political party to hold a nominating convention, assembling in Baltimore in 1831 to select a candidate for the following year's election. This was, in turn, the first nominating convention to sell out a party's principles: The nominee selected, former U.S. attorney general William Wirt, was a former Freemason—not an ex-Mason who had turned his back on the secret society but an ex-Mason who didn't really find the order objectionable at all. In a letter to the convention, Wirt denounced the men who had murdered Morgan but added that "in the quarter of the Union with which I am acquainted," Masonry included many "intelligent men of high and honourable character" who would never privilege their oaths to the order over "their duties to their God and their country." William Wirt, letter to the Anti-Masonic Party Convention, September 28, 1831, in *Memoirs of the Life of William Wirt, Attorney-General of the United States*, vol. 2, ed. John P. Kennedy (Blanchard and Lea, 1849), 355.
50. John Quincy Adams, *Memoirs of John Quincy Adams, Comprising Portions of His Diary from 1795 to 1848*, vol. 8, ed. Charles Francis Adams (J. B. Lippincott & Co., 1876), 368.

51. For a scholarly argument that some of those suspicions were justified, see Ronald P. Formisano with Kathleen Smith Kutolowski, "Antimasonry and Masonry: The Genesis of Protest, 1826–1827," *American Quarterly* 29, no. 2 (Summer 1977).
52. Kathleen Smith Kutolowski, "Freemasonry and Community in the Early Republic: The Case for Antimasonic Anxieties," *American Quarterly* 34, no. 5 (Winter 1982).
53. The fear of secret societies resembled many early Americans' fear of political parties. The fact that people were meeting in order to influence politics was itself seen as suspicious, and critics found it easy to slip from the word *faction* to *junto* and then *conspiracy*.
54. Andrew Jackson and Roger B. Taney, paper read to the cabinet, September 18, 1833, in *The Correspondence of Andrew Jackson*, vol. 5, ed. John Spencer Bassett (Carnegie Institution of Washington, 1931), 194.
55. Andrew Jackson, letter to Edward Livingston, June 27, 1834, ibid., 272.
56. Frederick Robinson, *An Oration Delivered Before the Trades Union of Boston and Vicinity, on Fort Hill, Boston, on the Fifty-Eighth Anniversary of American Independence* (Charles Douglas, 1834), 6, 18.
57. L. Frank Baum, *The Sea Fairies* (Reilly & Britton, 1911), 104–5.
58. The octopus turns up in Enemy Below and Enemy Outside literature as well—it's too powerful an image to be limited to just one form of fear. The social forces drawn or described as octopods over the years include capitalism, socialism, landlords, railroads, Harvard, the Pentagon, inflation, monopolies, drugs, Jews, Catholics, Mormons, organized crime, several different countries, several different corporations, and "the system."
59. Samuel Ajayi Crowther, quoted in Patricia A. Turner, *I Heard It Through the Grapevine: Rumor in African-American Culture* (University of California Press, 1993), 12.
60. Quoted in William D. Piersen, *Black Legacy: America's Hidden Heritage* (University of Massachusetts Press, 1993), 7.
61. William Piersen has suggested that African slave-traders did the same thing, spreading rumors of white cannibalism "to placate new cap-

tives by pointing out that their present situation was not so bad when compared to the fate they could suffer among alien masters." He also cited evidence that white slave-traders applied the same strategy—informing their prisoners that though *they* weren't cannibals, the pirates about to attack the ship were, so they had better join in the fight to defend the vessel. Ibid., 8–9.

62. J. L. S. Holloman, quoted in Gladys-Marie Fry, *Night Riders in Black Folk History* (University of Tennessee Press, 1975), 178.
63. Eva Francis Parker, quoted ibid., 184. In another D.C.-based version of the story, the experiments were conducted not in a hospital but at the Smithsonian.
64. Lucille Murdock, quoted ibid., 191.
65. Todd L. Savitt, "The Use of Blacks for Medical Experimentation and Demonstration in the Old South," *The Journal of Southern History* 48, no. 3 (August 1982).
66. Turner, *I Heard It Through the Grapevine*, 84.
67. James Daniel Tymes, quoted in Fry, *Night Riders in Black Folk History*, 192.
68. This story has been told in several places; for a good, short primer, read David Zucchino, "Sterilized by North Carolina, She Felt Raped Once More," *Los Angeles Times*, January 25, 2012.
69. Terry Ann Knopf, *Rumors, Race, and Riots* (Transaction Books, 1975), 143–44.
70. Ibid., 222.
71. Quoted in Daniel Pipes, *Conspiracy: How the Paranoid Style Flourishes and Where It Comes From* (Free Press, 1997), 117. For a critique of Pipes's book, see Jesse Walker, "Conspiracy," *The Independent Review*, Summer 1998.
72. *Register of Debates in Congress, Comprising the Leading Debates and Incidents of the First Session of the Twenty-Third Congress*, vol. 10 (Gales and Seaton, 1834), 1173.
73. *Register of Debates*, May 24, 1834. On the broader subject of suspicious rhetoric in the battle over the bank, see Major L. Wilson, "The 'Country' Versus the 'Court': A Republican Consensus and Party Debate

in the Bank War," *Journal of the Early Republic* 15, no. 4 (Winter 1995).

74. Quoted in Robert Churchill, *To Shake Their Guns in the Tyrant's Face: Libertarian Political Violence and the Origins of the Militia Movement* (University of Michigan Press, 2009), 117. Both sides feared the Enemy Below, too. Just as southerners fretted about insurrectionist slave conspiracies, northern Republicans accused propeace Democrats of organizing subversive secret societies. See Frank L. Klement, *Dark Lanterns: Secret Political Societies, Conspiracies, and Treason Trials in the Civil War* (Louisiana State University Press, 1984).

Chapter 6: Conspiracies of Angels

1. J. D. Salinger, *Raise High the Roof Beam, Carpenters and Seymour: An Introduction* (Little, Brown, 1963), 88.
2. Manly P. Hall, *The Secret Destiny of America* (Jeremy P. Tarcher/Penguin, 2008), 70. This edition includes not just the full text of *The Secret Destiny of America*, originally published in 1944, but also the follow-up book *America's Assignment with Destiny*, originally published in 1951.
3. Ibid., 57.
4. Ibid., 187.
5. Ibid., 92, 94.
6. Ibid., 120–21.
7. Quoted in Rob Brezsny, *Pronoia Is the Antidote for Paranoia: How the Whole World Is Conspiring to Shower You with Blessings* (Frog Books, 2005), 16.
8. "Fama fraternitatis, or, A Discovery of the Fraternity of the Most Laudable Order of the Rosy Cross" (1614), trans. Thomas Vaughan, reprinted as an appendix to Frances A. Yates, *The Rosicrucian Enlightenment* (Routledge, 2003 [1972]), 307.
9. Karl von Eckartshausen, *The Clouds upon the Sanctuary*, trans. Isabel de Steiger (Book Tree, 2006 [1802]), 16, 27.
10. A neo-Rosicrucian group in eighteenth-century Germany, the Order

of the Golden and Rosy Cross, became influential for a time, with one member, Friedrich Wilhelm II, ascending to the throne of Prussia. In a clash that must have been made in conspiracy-theory heaven, members of the order played a significant role in the campaign against Weishaupt's Illuminati. See Christopher McIntosh, *The Rose Cross and the Age of Reason: Eighteenth-Century Rosicrucianism in Central Europe and Its Relationship to the Enlightenment* (State University of New York Press, 2011 [1992]).

11. Quoted in Joscelyn Godwin, *The Theosophical Enlightenment* (State University of New York Press, 1994), 259.
12. Wallace, while serving as secretary of agriculture, persuaded President Franklin Roosevelt to add the eye-in-the-pyramid symbol to the country's currency, thus giving ammo to generations of conspiracists convinced that the Illuminati control the money supply.
13. Quoted in K. Paul Johnson, *The Masters Revealed: Madame Blavatsky and the Myth of the Great White Lodge* (State University of New York Press, 1994), 10. The full letter can be read at blavatskyarchives.com/blavatskyhartmann6.htm.
14. Shambhala, which the Theosophists borrowed from a Buddhist legend, inspired Shangri-la, the hidden utopia in the book and movie *Lost Horizon*. Yes, it also inspired that Three Dog Night song.
15. For a wonderful take on this sort of organization, read Charles Portis, *Masters of Atlantis* (Alfred A. Knopf, 1985). The hero of Portis's satiric novel is introduced to the fictional Gnomon Society by a con man, fails to realize that the contact was a swindle, and guilelessly builds a Gnomon order of his own.
16. H. Spencer Lewis, *Rosicrucian Questions & Answers* (Book Tree, 2006 [1929]), 63–64.
17. The only portion of the story at the beginning of this chapter that does not appear in those two books involves the Invisible Government of the World. Hall alluded to the Invisible Government in *America's Assignment with Destiny*, but he did not speculate about where it is located; that part of the story draws on other Benevolent Conspiracy texts.

18. Hall, *The Secret Destiny of America*, 44.
19. Even the British occultist Aleister Crowley fell prey to this, despite his antiauthoritarian reputation. Crowley, who had his own alleged encounters with the Secret Chiefs, was a radical individualist in many ways, famously proclaiming, "Every man and every woman is a star" and "Do what thou wilt shall be the whole of the law." But he was also able to propose a bizarre plan in which government-appointed experts would "work out, when need arises, the details of the True Will of every individual, and even that of every corporate body whether social or commercial, while a judiciary will arise to determine the equity in the case of apparently conflicting claims." Quoted in Brian Doherty, "Do What I Wilt," *Reason*, February 2001.
20. On the intersection between Populism and Theosophy, see Charles Postel, *The Populist Vision* (Oxford University Press, 2007), 263–65. The preeminent Theosophist in the Populist Party was Ignatius Donnelly of Minnesota, a former congressman who wrote the preamble to the party's 1892 platform and later ran for vice president on a Populist ticket. He was also the author of speculative books on Atlantis and on Francis Bacon's alleged authorship of William Shakespeare's plays.
21. On Glinka's relationship to Theosophy and the *Protocols*, see Norman Cohn, *Warrant for Genocide: The Myth of the Jewish World-Conspiracy and the Protocols of the Elders of Zion* (Harper & Row, 1967), 100–2.
22. William Dudley Pelley, *Seven Minutes in Eternity* (Kessinger Publishing, 2006 [1929]), 12.
23. Quoted in Jim Rodgers and Tim Kullman, *Facing Terror: The Government's Response to Contemporary Extremists in America* (University Press of America, 2002), 44.
24. Ferguson did allude in a foggy way to Rosicrucian legend, and that probably didn't help matters. "At first," she wrote, Aquarian "traditions were transmitted intimately, by alchemists, Gnostics, cabalists, and hermetics." Marilyn Ferguson, *The Aquarian Conspiracy: Personal and Social Transformation in the 1980s* (J. P. Tarcher, 1980), 46.
25. Constance Cumbey, *The Hidden Dangers of the Rainbow: The New Age*

Movement and Our Coming Age of Barbarism (Huntington House, 1983), 61.

26. Ibid., 53.
27. Godfré Ray King [Guy Ballard], *Unveiled Mysteries* (Saint Germain Press, 1934), x.
28. Ibid., 83. Robert Heinlein borrowed the concept of a Shasta-based Benevolent Conspiracy in his science fiction story "Lost Legacy," published two years after Ballard's death. Heinlein gave the idea a libertarian spin: In his tale, the secret order in the mountain is working to protect individual liberty and expand human potential. It is opposed by a Long Island–based psychic cabal that controls "the racketeers, the crooked political figures, the shysters, the dealers in phony religions, the sweat-shoppers, the petty authoritarians." Robert Heinlein, "Lost Legacy" (1941), in Robert Heinlein, *Assignment in Eternity* (Baen, 1987 [1953]), 224.
29. King, *Unveiled Mysteries*, 43. Pelley of the Silver Shirts also believed that the Benevolent Conspiracy was guiding the United States toward a special destiny, but in his case the idea was soaked in anti-Semitism. The United States, he proclaimed, was to be "a bright and shining light" that "cast a pattern visible to all races as the thing which all mankind can attain." Before we could get there, though, we would have to defeat the "megalomaniacal Jew." Quoted in Geoffrey S. Smith, *To Save a Nation: American "Extremism," the New Deal, and the Coming of World War II*, 2nd ed. (Ivan R. Dee, 1992), 80.
30. Quoted in Gerald Bryan, *Psychic Dictatorship in America* (Truth Research Publications, 1940), 193.
31. Ibid., 194.
32. Ibid., 21.
33. Ibid., 194.
34. Philip Jenkins has pointed out that the prosecution of the I AM leadership coincided not just with Bell's and Pelley's legal problems but with crackdowns on the Jehovah's Witnesses, the Nation of Islam, and various polygamist and snake-handling sects—a multifront war

on minority religions that Jenkins calls "the purge of the forties" and that we could classify as an attack on the Enemy Within. See Philip Jenkins, *Mystics and Messiahs: Cults and New Religions in American History* (Oxford University Press, 2000), 149–60.

35. "Interestingly," one historian has pointed out, "Swedenborg visits each planet known to exist in the 1750s on his way beyond the solar system to the starry heavens, but fails to note the existence of Uranus, Neptune, or Pluto." J. Gordon Melton, "The Contactees: A Survey," in *The Gods Have Landed: New Religions from Other Worlds*, ed. James R. Lewis (State University of New York Press, 1995), 4.
36. Perhaps I shouldn't call them *Ascended* Masters. The "theosophical components are still there," one scholar has noted, "but the highly evolved entity is not now understood to have originated on Earth and *ascended*, but rather to have originated on another planet and *descended*." Christopher Partridge, "Understanding UFO Religions and Abduction Spiritualities," in *UFO Religions*, ed. Christopher Partridge (Routledge, 2003), 36.
37. Nick Herbert, "Nick Meets the Galactic Telepaths," January 6, 2012, quantumtantra.blogspot.com/2012/01/nick-meets-galactic-telepaths.html.
38. Decades after his death, as witch hunts were raging, Dee's diary describing those contacts would be cited as evidence that he had been in league with the Devil. The Benevolent Conspiracy is always in danger of being recast as one of the Enemies.
39. The most famous of the ancient-astronauts books is Erich von Däniken, *Chariots of the Gods? Unsolved Mysteries of the Past*, trans. Michael Heron (G. P. Putnam's Sons, 1970). (First published in German in 1968.)
40. Sylvia Browne, *Sylvia Browne's Book of Angels* (Hay House, 2003), 14.
41. Gustav Davidson, *A Dictionary of Angels, Including the Fallen Angels* (Free Press, 1967); Peter Lamborn Wilson, *Angels* (Thames and Hudson, 1980); Hope MacDonald, *When Angels Appear* (Zondervan, 1982).
42. Sophy Burnham, *A Book of Angels: Reflections on Angels Past and Pres-*

ent, and True Stories of How They Touch Our Lives (Jeremy P. Tarcher/Penguin, 2011 [1990]), 72.

43. Author's interview with Sophy Burnham, March 6, 2012. All subsequent Burnham quotes are from this interview unless otherwise noted.
44. Burnham, *A Book of Angels*, 118.
45. Wilson is an anarchist and a mystic, and his copiously illustrated piece of cross-cultural scholarship ultimately paid more attention to Islam and paganism than to anything in the Bible. Any reader who bought it expecting a piece of pop Christianity was in for a surprise.
46. Joan Wester Anderson, *Where Angels Walk: True Stories of Heavenly Visitors* (Ballantine, 1992), ix.
47. Doreen Virtue, *Healing with the Angels: How the Angels Can Assist You in Every Area of Your Life* (Hay House, 1999), 155.
48. Bill Myers and David Wimbish, *The Dark Side of the Supernatural: What Is of God and What Isn't* (Zondervan, 2008 [1999]), 16–17.
49. Author's interview with Peter Lamborn Wilson, March 4, 2012.
50. Marie D. Jones and Larry Flaxman, "11:11—The Time Prompt Phenomenon and the Profound Nature of Numbers," *Phenomena*, November 2009.
51. "Do You See 11:11?" n.d., 1111angels.net.
52. George Mathieu Barnard, *The Search for 11:11: A Journey into the Spirit World* (11.11 Publishers, 2004 [2000]), ix.
53. "11:11: What Is It About? What Does It All Mean?" n.d., board.1111angels.com/viewtopic.php?t=345.
54. Jack Sarfatti, "Higher Intelligence Is Us in the Future," *Spit in the Ocean* 3 (1977).
55. Yates, *The Rosicrucian Enlightenment*, 278–79. Yates also made a speculative argument that the Rosicrucian pamphlets were intended as propaganda for one side in the struggles shaking the Holy Roman Empire.
56. Ronald Reagan, "Your America to Be Free" (1957), reagan2020.us/speeches/Your_America_to_be_Free.asp.
57. Mitch Horowitz, "Reagan and the Occult," April 20, 2010, voices.washingtonpost.com/political-bookworm/2010/04/reagan_and_the_occult.html.

58. Ronald Reagan, "Speech Announcing Presidential Candidacy" (1979), in *Tear Down This Wall: The Reagan Revolution*, ed. Editors of *National Review* (Continuum International Publishing Group, 2004), 17.

Chapter 7: The Water's Gate

1. Gil Scott-Heron, "H_2O Gate (Watergate) Blues," on *Winter in America*, LP, Strata-East Records, 1974.
2. San Diego special agent in charge, memorandum to FBI director, November 8, 1968. Declassified COINTELPRO files can be downloaded at vault.fbi.gov.
3. FBI director, memorandum to San Diego special agent in charge, November 26, 1968.
4. David Cunningham, *There's Something Happening Here: The New Left, the Klan, and FBI Counterintelligence* (University of California Press, 2004), 32. See also William W. Keller, *The Liberals and J. Edgar Hoover: Rise and Fall of a Domestic Intelligence State* (Princeton University Press, 1989), 72ff.
5. Baltimore special agent in charge, memorandum to FBI director, March 28, 1969.
6. Baltimore special agent in charge, memorandum to FBI director, August 26, 1969.
7. Philadelphia special agent in charge, memorandum to FBI director, November 21, 1968.
8. Los Angeles FBI Field Office report, July 24, 1967.
9. Select Committee to Study Governmental Operations with Respect to Intelligence Activities, United States Senate, *Supplementary Detailed Staff Reports on Intelligence Activities and the Rights of Americans* (U.S. Government Printing Office, 1976), 9.
10. On the deaths of Hampton and Clark, see Mike Royko, *Boss: Richard J. Daley of Chicago* (Signet, 1971), 209–13.
11. John Dean, "Dealing with Our Political Enemies" (1971), in *Watergate: A Brief History with Documents*, 2nd ed., ed. Stanley I. Kutler (Wiley-Blackwell, 2010), 30.

12. Doyle Niemann, "Watergate: Excuse Us for Bragging but We Told You So!" *The Great Speckled Bird*, July 9, 1973.
13. Quoted in Fred P. Graham, "F.B.I. Files of Surveillance of Students, Blacks, War Foes," *The New York Times*, March 25, 1971.
14. Kathryn S. Olmsted, *Challenging the Secret Government: The Post-Watergate Investigations of the CIA and FBI* (University of North Carolina Press, 1996), 17.
15. Quoted in Select Committee to Study Governmental Operations with Respect to Intelligence Activities, United States Senate, *Foreign and Military Intelligence* (U.S. Government Printing Office, 1976), 389.
16. Ibid., 391.
17. Lasky at one point received $20,000 from the Committee for the Re-Election of the President, which should put to rest any suspicion that he was an unbiased observer. For a balanced assessment of what his book got right and wrong, see Barton J. Bernstein, "Call It a Tradition," *Inquiry*, November 21, 1977.
18. Victor Lasky, *It Didn't Start with Watergate* (Dial Press, 1977), 220.
19. Nicholas B. Dirks, *The Scandal of Empire: India and the Creation of Imperial Britain* (Harvard University Press, 2006), 30.
20. For an account of Felt's actions and intentions during the Watergate scandal, see Max Holland, *Leak: Why Mark Felt Became Deep Throat* (University Press of Kansas, 2012).
21. For some problems with the idea that investigators were putting agents' lives at risk, see Jesse Walker, "Agee's Revenge," July 14, 2005, reason.com/archives/2005/07/14/agees-revenge.
22. On the use of the charge of McCarthyism against congressional and journalistic investigators, see Olmsted, *Challenging the Secret Government*, 126, 131–32, 138, 164.
23. *The Final Assassinations Report: Report of the Select Committee on Assassinations, U.S. House of Representatives* (Bantam Books, 1979), 100.
24. Roscoe Drummond, "Revived Theory of a 'Conspiracy' Still Resting on Tenuous Grounds," *Observer-Reporter* (Washington, Pa.), January 23, 1979.
25. I first encountered the Skeleton Key online in 1990 or so, on a proto-

Internet at the University of Michigan called the Michigan Terminal System. I got the impression even then that people had been forwarding it around cyberspace for a while already.

26. Robert Eringer, "Dossier on Conspiriologists: Mae Brussell & Peter Beter," *Critique* 5 (Autumn 1981). The conversation took place in late 1977 or early 1978. Eringer's article doesn't identify the publication that he telephoned, but he informed me, looking back more than three decades later, that he was "reasonably certain" it was a magazine called *It*. Robert Eringer, e-mail to the author, April 16, 2012.
27. Paul Krassner, *Confessions of a Raving, Unconfined Nut: Misadventures in the Counterculture*, 2nd ed. (New World Digital, 2010), 224.
28. Mae Brussell, "From Monterey Pop to Altamont—OPERATION CHAOS: The CIA's War Against the Sixties Counter-Culture" (1976), maebrussell.com/Mae%20Brussell%20Articles/Operation%20Chaos.html.
29. John Judge, "Why Everybody Is a Government Patsy" (1978), in New Yippie Book Collective, *Blacklisted News: Secret Histories from Chicago to 1984* (Bleecker Publishing, 1983), 546. Judge's article originally appeared in the *Yipster Times*.
30. Stephen Hall, "'Robot' Behavior of Ryan Murder Suspect," *San Francisco Chronicle*, November 28, 1978.
31. Mae Brussell, tape 365, December 1, 1978. A transcription of the tape can be found at maebrussell.com/Transcriptions/365.html.
32. Quoted ibid. Lane did not reply to a request to comment on the quote's accuracy.
33. Quoted in "'Crusader' Mark Lane," *The Lawrence Daily Journal-World*, November 29, 1978.
34. Brussell, tape 365.
35. That said, Brussellesque ideas could surface in surprising places. A popular biography of the rock star Jim Morrison, for example, included this passage:

> Still other theories claimed Jim was the victim of a political conspiracy aimed at discrediting and eliminating the hippie/New Left/counterculture lifestyle (actually this is supposed to have

> been a vast, pervasive, connected set of conspiracies that included the shootings at Kent State and Jackson State, the riots at Isla Vista, the Weathermen bombings, the stiff prison sentences given to Timothy Leary and the Chicago Eight, the Charlie Manson murders—not to mention the deaths of Hendrix and Joplin and more than two dozen Black Panthers).

Rather than mocking the theory, the authors commented that "Jim was certainly popular enough and, more threateningly, smart enough to cause the powers that be ample reason to take some sort of action to prevent his subversive influence." Jerry Hopkins and Danny Sugerman, *No One Here Gets Out Alive* (Warner Books, 1981), 372.

36. The code's commands started to lose their force in 1952, when the Supreme Court ruled that the First Amendment protects motion pictures. Movies gradually grew more adventurous, and the code finally died when a ratings system replaced it in 1968.
37. Interview at youtube.com/watch?v=fRiZtqVPJ9U.
38. Fredric Jameson, *The Geopolitical Aesthetic: Cinema and Space in the World System* (Indiana University Press, 1995), 55.
39. *The Parallax View*, directed by Alan J. Pakula, screenplay by David Giler and Lorenzo Semple, Jr., from a novel by Loren Singer, Paramount Pictures, 1974. *The Parallax View* is also notable for including one of the most chilling and bizarre brainwashing sequences ever set in celluloid.
40. Olmsted, *Challenging the Secret Government*, 102.
41. *Executive Action*, directed by David Miller, screenplay by Dalton Trumbo, from a story by Donald Freed and Mark Lane, National General Pictures, 1973. Freed's other notable contribution to conspiracy cinema was to coscript Robert Altman's Nixon movie, *Secret Honor* (1984).
42. *Scorpio*, directed by Michael Winner, screenplay by David W. Rintels and Gerald Wilson, MGM, 1973. Winner's previous film, *The Mechanic* (1972), had a similar story. In both pictures a professional assassin takes on an understudy who in turn tries to kill him. But *The Mechanic*'s protagonist works for a group called "the organization"—

presumably the Mafia, though that is never stated outright—and we never learn much about why his victims have been slated to die. *Scorpio* gave the story line an explicitly political edge.

43. *The Domino Principle*, directed by Stanley Kramer, screenplay by Adam Kennedy from his novel, AVCO, 1977.

44. *Network*, directed by Sidney Lumet, screenplay by Paddy Chayefsky, MGM/United Artists, 1975.

45. Another popular Spielberg film, *Close Encounters of the Third Kind* (1977), offered an alternative to the era's apprehensive atmosphere by imagining a Benevolent Conspiracy. *Two* benevolent conspiracies, actually: There are the aliens who want to welcome humanity to the larger cosmic community, and there are the government officials who plant disinformation and cover up important facts for the citizens' own good.

    In 1982, widely perceived as a time of greater faith in public institutions, Spielberg returned to the cinema of suspicion with *E.T.*, a sentimental but sometimes terrifying tale in which children have to hide a friendly extraterrestrial from the government. The agents of the American state are portrayed here as a fearsome squadron of secret police. The liberal pundit David Sirota later criticized *E.T.* for "depict[ing] the government as a faceless menace," arguing that this amounted to propaganda against intervention in the economy: "Yeah, we think, why should we let those jackbooted federal sentries from *E.T.* make our health care decisions?" David Sirota, *Back to Our Future: How the 1980s Explain the World We Live in Now—Our Culture, Our Politics, Our Everything* (Ballantine Books, 2011), 86, 93. For a critique of Sirota's book, see Jesse Walker, "That '80s Show," *Reason*, July 2011.

46. Ira Levin, *The Stepford Wives* (Random House, 1972), 50.

47. Betty Friedan, *The Feminine Mystique* (Dell, 1963), 234–35.

48. The *Stepford Wives* movie was the basis for three made-for-TV follow-ups. *Revenge of the Stepford Wives* (1980) changed the scenario somewhat: The town's women are drugged and brainwashed rather than replaced by robots, a sign that possession and imposture are close

enough in spirit for Hollywood to treat them as interchangeable. The story ends with two liberated women seizing the means of mind control and inducing a Stepford riot. In *The Stepford Children* (1987) the conspiracy is back to using androids, and with *The Stepford Husbands* (1996), predictably, the tables are turned.

The franchise returned to theaters in 2004, when a muddled *Stepford Wives* remake attempted to update Levin's story for an era when gender equality wasn't as controversial as it was in the seventies. That take on the tale features androids *and* mind control, as though the screenwriter couldn't quite make up his mind what was happening. Fittingly for a film in which people are reduced to puppets, the picture was directed by the veteran muppeteer Frank Oz.

49. Quoted in Judy Klemesrud, "Feminists Recoil at Film Designed to Relate to Them," *The New York Times*, February 26, 1975.
50. "Top Secret," *My Three Sons*, ABC, December 26, 1963.
51. "The Investigation," *Good Times*, CBS, January 27, 1976.
52. Clifton Daniel, "The Rockefeller Panel and Its C.I.A. Mission," *The New York Times*, January 20, 1975.
53. Quoted in Olmsted, *Challenging the Secret Government*, 61.

Chapter 8: The Legend of John Todd

1. Quoted in Robert M. Price, "With Strange Aeons: H. P. Lovecraft's Cthulhu Mythos as One Vast Narrative," in *Third Person: Authoring and Exploring Vast Narratives*, ed. Pat Harrigan and Noah Wardrip-Fruin (MIT Press, 2009), 242.
2. Todd's Chambersburg testimony is transcribed at textfiles.com/occult/jtc1.txt. A slightly different rendition appears in Christopher A. LaRock, *John Todd: Beyond the Legend* (Lulu, 2011). I have not always followed either transcriber's punctuation and capitalization.
3. The $1,000 estimate comes from Edward E. Plowman, "The Legend(s) of John Todd," *Christianity Today*, February 2, 1979. The same article claimed that about a thousand people attended Todd's talk, but the church's then pastor, Dino Pedrone, today estimates that the total

was four hundred or five hundred. It is possible that Pedrone's memory is playing tricks on him, but it is also possible that Plowman confused the number of people the auditorium could seat with the number it seated that day.

4. Quoted ibid.
5. Author's interview with Dino Pedrone, May 15, 2012.
6. Gary Chartier, e-mail to the author, June 28, 2012.
7. Recordings of Todd's talks have been posted on several websites; I downloaded them from kt70.com/~jtamesjpn/articles/john_todd_and_the_illuminati.htm. The quotes in this paragraph and the next two paragraphs come from the recording labeled tape 3A. None of the aforementioned sites list dates for the tapes, but a passage quoted from this speech is dated March 30, 1978, in Darryl E. Hicks and David A. Lewis, *The Todd Phenomenon: Ex–Grand Druid vs. the Illuminati, Fact or Fantasy?* (New Leaf Press, 1979), 23.
8. Todd, tape 1B. According to Hicks and Lewis, this one was recorded in Canoga Park, California, in the summer of 1977.
9. "Spellbound?" *The Crusaders* 10 (1978). This comic book was produced by Jack T. Chick with Todd's input. Todd himself appears as a character under the name Lance Collins, an alias he sometimes used; the quoted text is one of Collins's lines in the comic.
10. Todd, tape 3B. According to Hicks and Lewis, this was recorded in Philadelphia in February 1978. The quotation in the following paragraph comes from the same source.
11. Though Todd claimed that every president since Wilson had been in the Illuminati, he also claimed that the Illuminati had favored George McGovern in the 1972 election and that "Nixon defied the Illuminati when he made peace overtures to Red China," a country the conspiracy had "slated for total destruction." Quoted in Hicks and Lewis, *The Todd Phenomenon*, 43.
12. Todd, tape 1A.
13. Todd, tape 4A. According to Hicks and Lewis, this tape was recorded on March 31, 1978.

14. Quoted in Michael Saler, *As If: Modern Enchantment and the Literary Prehistory of Virtual Reality* (Oxford University Press, 2012), 146.
15. Todd, tape 3A. This may be the only time a Roger Corman production has been recommended as a guide to the external world.
16. *Donahue*, WGN-TV, January 1, 1979. The host went on to ask the questioner who the Illuminati were. She replied that they were "the international bankers, Rothschild, the Rockefellers, and all the Bilderbergers." Donahue took that to mean she thought Rand's ideas would lead to "capitalist control."
17. Hicks and Lewis, *The Todd Phenomenon*, 71–72.
18. Plowman, "The Legend(s) of John Todd."
19. Ibid.
20. P. E. I. Bonewits, "Official Report of the President to the Board of Directors on His Investigation of the John Todd/Lance Collins Affair in Dayton Ohio," *Green Egg*, March 1976.
21. FBI memorandum, Cincinnati, Ohio, March 1, 1976.
22. Bonewits, "Official Report of the President."
23. Ruth Tomczak and Elmer L. Towns, "Christian Teachers Deny John Todd: Fundamentalists Cautioned of Former Witch," *Journal Champion*, December 22, 1978.
24. "John Todd: Dividing the Brethren" (Christian Research Institute, 1978).
25. Hicks and Lewis, *The Todd Phenomenon*, 22.
26. Tomczak and Towns, "Christian Teachers Deny John Todd."
27. Quoted in Tom Nuget, "In Search of the Ultimate Conspiracy," *The Sun* (Baltimore), October 30, 1978.
28. Quoted in Plowman, "The Legend(s) of John Todd."
29. Nesta H. Webster, *World Revolution: The Plot Against Civilization* (Small, Maynard & Company, 1921), 313.
30. Ibid., 310–11.
31. Ibid., 306.
32. Winston Churchill, "Zionism Versus Bolshevism: A Struggle for the Soul of the Jewish People," *Illustrated Sunday Herald*, February 8, 1920.

33. William Guy Carr, *The Red Fog over America* (St. George Press, 1962 [1955]), 3–4.
34. The index to one of Carr's books includes the entry "Jewry, International, 48–168." Yes: 121 consecutive pages. William Guy Carr, *Pawns in the Game* (Omni Publications, n.d. [1955]), 187.
35. "I do not believe the Synagogue of Satan (S.O.S.) is Jewish, but, as Christ told us for a definite purpose, it is comprised of 'Them who say they are Jews . . . and are not . . . and do lie' (Rev. 2:9 and 3:9)." William Guy Carr, *Satan, Prince of This World* (Omni Publications, 1997), 6. (Written in 1959 and published posthumously.)
36. See Joseph W. Bendersky, *The "Jewish Threat": Anti-Semitic Politics of the U.S. Army* (Basic Books, 2000), 14.
37. Edith Starr Miller, *Occult Theocrasy*, vol. 2 (privately published, 1933), 564.
38. Gertrude M. Coogan, *Money Creators: Who Creates Money? Who Should Create It?* (Omni Publications, 1963 [1935]), 280.
39. Michael Barkun, *A Culture of Conspiracy: Apocalyptic Visions in Contemporary America* (University of California Press, 2003), 48.
40. G. Edward Griffin, *The Capitalist Conspiracy* (H. B. Patriots, 1982 [1971]), 58. Griffin's book consists largely of a transcript of a filmstrip of the same name. The filmstrip was released in 1969.
41. John Todd shared the Birchers' aversion to the idea of a Jewish conspiracy. Despite that, he denounced the John Birch Society as anti-Semitic, claiming in tape 4A that "its platform and the American Nazi platform and the Klan's platform are almost identical." Meanwhile, he was willing to share a platform with Colonel Curtis Dall of the Liberty Lobby, a group that really *was* anti-Semitic.

    Todd also on at least one occasion repeated Carr's and others' description of the Illuminati as "the Synagogue of Satan." Confusingly, he said this in the midst of an attack on anti-Semitism. Though you can take this as a sign of a hidden prejudice against Jews bubbling to the surface, it's more likely that he just hadn't thought hard about the implications of the fragments of conspiracy theory he had cobbled together.

42. Gary Allen with Larry Abraham, *None Dare Call It Conspiracy* (Concord Press, 1972), 39.
43. Marvin S. Antelman, *To Eliminate the Opiate* (Zionist Book Club, 1974), 143.
44. Sirhan himself scrawled the word "Illuminati" several times in his notebook. His interest was probably mystical rather than political: He also wrote the name "Master Kuthumi," a reference to one of Blavatsky's benevolent Masters, and he possessed a copy of Manly P. Hall's *The Secret Destiny of America*. Sirhan belonged to the Ancient Mystical Order of the Rosae Crucis, H. Spencer Lewis's fauxicrucian group, leading Los Angeles Mayor Sam Yorty to declare after the shooting that Sirhan "was a member of numerous Communist organizations, including the Rosicrucians."
45. Gale Thorne, "Eighteenth Century Dies Committee," *New Masses*, January 9, 1940.
46. Quoted in J. Hoberman, *An Army of Phantoms: American Movies and the Making of the Cold War* (New Press, 2011), 47.
47. *Ramparts*, September 1969. Jack Chick got in on the environmental doomsaying with a tract that discussed overpopulation, the dying oceans, and other green concerns before informing us that "*JESUS* predicted these problems." "Escape!" (Jack T. Chick, 1972).
48. Joseph McBride, *What Ever Happened to Orson Welles? A Portrait of an Independent Career* (University Press of Kentucky, 2006), 228.
49. Todd's earlier forecasts were even closer to Smith's: In his Phoenix days, he had predicted 1981 rather than 1980 as the year it all would end.
50. Key's book *Subliminal Seduction*, published in 1973, featured an introduction by the famed Canadian communication theorist Marshall McLuhan. McLuhan had his own history of conspiracy theorizing: For a period of his life he convinced himself that the Freemasons were to blame for the American Civil War, for Vatican II, and for several setbacks in the career of Professor Marshall McLuhan. For more on McLuhan's interest in Masonic (and Satanic) conspiracies, see Philip Marchand, *Marshall McLuhan: The Medium and the Messenger* (MIT Press, 1998 [1989]), 111–15.

51. Wilson Bryan Key, *Media Sexploitation* (Prentice Hall, 1976), 140. Allen's thoughts on "Hey Jude," and on popular music in general, can be found in Gary Allen, "That Music: There's More to It than Meets the Ear," *American Opinion*, February 1969. Allen's basic approach to rock criticism was to take "Back in the U.S.S.R." literally while assuming that everything else had a hidden meaning.
52. Key, *Media Sexploitation*, 146.
53. To see some attempts to read the *entire* backward recording of "Stairway to Heaven" as a long Satanic incantation, go to YouTube; several competing interpretations can be found there.
54. Quoted in Jon Trott and Mike Hertenstein, *Selling Satan: The Tragic History of Mike Warnke* (Cornerstone Press, 1993), 101.
55. Mike Warnke, "Foreword," in Hicks and Lewis, *The Todd Phenomenon*, 9.
56. Warnke was hit hard by the revelations of the early 1990s, but he continues to perform as a Christian standup comic today. He still insists that his story is essentially true, though he has admitted inventing some of the details.
57. Richard Hofstadter, *The Paranoid Style in American Politics and Other Essays* (Harvard University Press, 1965), 34–35.
58. "Angels?" (Jack T. Chick, 1986).
59. "Dark Dungeons" (Jack T. Chick, 1984).
60. "Bewitched?" (Jack T. Chick, 1972).
61. Quoted in David Waldron, "Role-Playing Games and the Christian Right: Community Formation in Response to a Moral Panic," *Journal of Religion and Popular Culture*, Spring 2005.
62. Quoted in Michael A. Stackpole, "The Pulling Report" (1990), rpgstudies.net/stackpole/pulling_report.html.
63. Tipper Gore, *Raising PG Kids in an X-Rated Society: What Parents Can Do to Protect Their Children from Sex and Violence in the Media* (Abingdon Press, 1987), 118.
64. Quoted in Nuget, "In Search of the Ultimate Conspiracy."
65. Quoted in Hicks and Lewis, *The Todd Phenomenon*, 93.

66. Sheila Todd's letter is reprinted online at holysmoke.org/jtcsheil.txt. According to Hicks and Lewis, Todd sometimes tried to pass off Sheila as his previous wife, Sharon. But they are not the same person.
67. The angry mail is mentioned in "John Todd's Record Confirmed," *Journal Champion*, February 9, 1979.
68. Quoted in "*Cornerstone*'s Near-Miss Interviews with Madalyn Murray O'Hair and John Todd," *Cornerstone* 48 (1979).
69. Quoted in Jess Walter, *Every Knee Shall Bow: The Truth and Tragedy of Ruby Ridge and the Randy Weaver Family* (Harper Paperbacks, 1996), 53. My description of Todd's behavior during the talk draws on Alan W. Bock, *Ambush at Ruby Ridge: How Government Agents Set Randy Weaver Up and Took His Family Down* (Dickens Press, 1995), 38.
70. Kerry Noble, *Tabernacle of Hate: Seduction into Right-Wing Extremism*, 2nd ed. (Syracuse University Press, 2010), 77, 81.
71. *Witchcraft and the Illuminati* (CPA Book Publisher, 1981), 42–43, 45, 78. The book was published anonymously, but Noble identified himself as its author in *Tabernacle of Hate*, 119.
72. Quoted in Jessica Stern, *Terror in the Name of God: Why Religious Militants Kill* (HarperCollins, 2003), 21.
73. Todd may have helped inspire another would-be terrorist in 1997, when a bank was robbed and an adult bookstore bombed in Damascus, Oregon. (No one was injured.) Fritz Springmeier, a conspiracy theorist heavily influenced by Todd, was among the people eventually charged with the crimes, and he served time from 2003 to 2011. Springmeier maintains that the Illuminati framed him.
74. For a balanced discussion of those early attempts to estimate the number of missing children in general and stranger abductions in particular, see Joel Best, "Missing Children, Misleading Statistics," *The Public Interest*, Summer 1988.
75. Jello Biafra, "Tales from the Trial," on *High Priest of Harmful Matter*, CD, Alternative Tentacles, 1989.
76. Debbie Nathan and Michael Snedeker, *Satan's Silence: Ritual Abuse and the Making of a Modern American Witch Hunt* (Basic Books, 1995), 86.

77. Quoted ibid., 88.
78. Quoted in Sam Howe Verhovek, "Death in Waco," *The New York Times*, April 20, 1993.
79. Joel Best, *Threatened Children: Rhetoric and Concern About Child-Victims* (University of Chicago Press, 1990), 2.
80. "The Devil Worshippers," *20/20*, ABC, May 16, 1985.
81. There is a hint of sophistication in the argument here: Though the filmmakers who shot *The Exorcist* wanted to make a Christian movie, it is certainly possible for someone who views it to ignore their intentions and identify with the Devil. Of course, if you accept this, you also have to accept the converse—that people who listen to a "Satanic" metal band don't necessarily take the lyrics at face value either.
82. This was a theme of the first comic book Todd made with Jack Chick. See "The Broken Cross," *The Crusaders* 2 (1974).
83. Quoted in David Alexander, "Giving the Devil More Than His Due," *The Humanist*, March–April 1990.
84. "Devil Worship: Exposing Satan's Underground," *The Geraldo Rivera Specials*, NBC, October 25, 1988.
85. Kenneth V. Lanning, "Satanic, Occult, Ritualistic Crime: A Law Enforcement Perspective," *The Police Chief*, October 1989.
86. holysmoke.org/wicca/wicca-letters-hoax.htm.
87. Quoted in Kurt Kuersteiner, *The Unofficial Guide to the Art of Jack T. Chick: Chick Tracts, Crusader Comics, and Battle Cry Newspapers* (Schiffer, 2004), 24.
88. Quoted in Danny C. Flanders, "Jury Deliberating John Wayne Todd's Fate in Rape Case," *The State*, January 22, 1988.
89. John Todd, "John Todd's Testimonial While in Prison," February 26, 1991, kt70.com/~jamesjpn/articles/john-todd-from-prison.html.
90. Quoted in Roy Livesey, "The Church *Versus* the New World Order: Examples from South Carolina Are Lessons for Us All," *New Age Bulletin*, July 1994.
91. *Kollyns v. Gintoli*, U.S. District Court, District of South Carolina, Columbia Division, August 12, 2005.

92. *Kollyns v. Hughes*, U.S. District Court, District of South Carolina, Columbia Division, September 22, 2006.
93. youtube.com/watch?v=qMYrSPuEYTk.

Chapter 9: Operation Mindfuck

1. Quoted in Scott Thill, "Grant Morrison Talks Brainy Comics, Sexy Apocalypse," March 19, 2009, wired.com/underwire/2009/03/mid-life-crisis/.
2. Paul Eberle, "The Minutemen," *The East Village Other*, July 23, 1969.
3. "Current Structure of Bavarian Illuminati Conspiracy and the Law of Fives," *The East Village Other*, June 4, 1969.
4. Thomas M. Disch, *The Dreams Our Stuff Is Made Of: How Science Fiction Conquered the World* (Touchstone, 1998), 29. In the same passage, Disch described an encounter with Robert Anton Wilson: "I saw him once, after a book signing in Los Angeles, gravely romancing a would-be true believer, throwing out dark hints, then lapsing into winks and giggles. Did he experience cognitive dissonance?"
5. Mark Dery, "Kraken Rising: How the Cephalopod Became Our Zeitgeist Mascot," May 24, 2010, hplusmagazine.com/2010/05/24/kraken-rising-how-cephalopod-became-our-zeitgeist-mascot.
6. Michael Kelly, "The Road to Paranoia," *The New Yorker*, June 19, 1995.
7. Charles Fort, *The Book of the Damned* (Boni and Liveright, 1919), 163.
8. Charles Fort, *Wild Talents* (Claude Kendall, 1932), 240.
9. John A. Keel, *Disneyland of the Gods* (Amok Press, 1988), 101–2.
10. John A. Keel, *The Mothman Prophecies* (I-Net, 1991 [1975]), 123–24.
11. This was a man, after all, who in the 1980s spoofed the UFO buffs with a poker-faced publication that claimed "the National Zoo and the Smithsonian have been lying to the press for years in their campaign to hide the fact that unicorns really exist." "The Great Unicorn Conspiracy," *The Unicorn Review*, n.d.
12. Quoted in John C. Sherwood, "Gray Barker's Book of Bunk: Mothman, Saucers, and MIB," *The Skeptical Inquirer* 26, no. 3 (May–June 2002).

13. Keel, *The Mothman Prophecies*, 173.
14. Ibid., 240–41.
15. Quoted in Sherwood, "Gray Barker's Book of Bunk."
16. Quoted ibid. Moseley described several of his UFO hoaxes in James W. Moseley and Karl T. Pflock, *Shockingly Close to the Truth! Confessions of a Grave-Robbing Ufologist* (Prometheus Books, 2002). Despite his hoaxing—and unlike Barker—Moseley did think that there might be something real to some saucer stories. Or at least he said he did; maybe he meant it, and maybe it was another gag. Once you start down that road, it's easy to get lost: At one point, Moseley wrote, he was temporarily taken in by a story that turned out to be an echo of one of his own pranks, thus ever so briefly hoaxing himself.
17. The letter is reprinted at johnkeel.com/?p=489.
18. Keel, *The Mothman Prophecies*, 55–56.
19. Some call this a prelude to the underground press. I call it a prelude to the Internet.
20. "Tricky Dick Rides Again," *The Realist*, Fall 1991.
21. Quoted in Paul Krassner, *Confessions of a Raving, Unconfined Nut: Misadventures in the Counterculture*, 2nd ed. (New World Digital, 2010), 150.
22. "The Parts That Were Left Out of the Kennedy Book," *The Realist*, May 1967.
23. "Why 'The Up Your Tenth Anniversary Issue of The Realist Editorial Giggy Trip' Will Be Two Years Late," *The Realist*, May–June 1970.
24. Reginald Dunsany [James Curry], "Final Solutions to the Assassination Question," *The Realist*, March 1968.
25. David K. Johnson, *The Lavender Scare: The Cold War Persecution of Gays and Lesbians in the Federal Government* (University of Chicago Press, 2004), 260. When I told Krassner a scholar had mistaken Curry's article for an earnest exposé, he replied, "[Y]ou just made my day."
26. Leonard C. Lewin, *Report from Iron Mountain on the Possibility and Desirability of Peace* (Dial Press, 1967), 3.
27. Ibid., 39, 41.
28. Ibid., 84.

29. "Report from Iron Mountain Lives On and On," podcast, February 22, 2010, bookpod.org/report-from-iron-mountain-lives-on/.
30. In the ensuing legal fight, which ended in 1994, the Liberty Lobby was represented by Mark Lane.
31. David Germain, "War Never Came, So Mine's Now Warehouse," *The Sunday Gazette* (Schenectady), July 21, 1990.
32. Stewart C. Best, "Conspiracy Briefing," Best Video Production, Christian Intelligence Alert, 1997.
33. The faith's birth date has been variously given as 1957, 1958, and 1959.
34. Malaclypse the Younger [Greg Hill], *Principia Discordia: How I Found Goddess and What I Did to Her When I Found Her* (IllumiNet Press, 1991 [1969]), 7–8.
35. Adam Gorightly, *The Prankster and the Conspiracy: The Story of Kerry Thornley and How He Met Oswald and Inspired the Counterculture* (Paraview Press, 2003), 27.
36. A friend of Thornley wrote that Oswald's role in the book gave it "a sort of eerie novelty, like the appearance of Fidel Castro as an extra in a Busby Berkeley film." Trevor Blake, "The Idle Warriors," *Ovo* 11 (September 1991).
37. Malaclypse the Younger [Greg Hill], *The Principia Discordia, or How the West Was Lost: Discordianism According to Malaclypse (The Younger), H.C., ande beeing the Officale Handebooke of The Discordian Societye ande A Beginning Introdyctun to the Erisian Misterees, Which Is Most Interesting* (privately published, 1965). This text overlaps with the 1969 *Principia*, but it is essentially a different book.
38. Malaclypse, *Principia Discordia: How I Found Goddess*, 54.
39. "Robert Anton Wilson Interview," *Conspiracy Digest*, Spring 1977.
40. Robert Anton Wilson, *The Illuminati Papers* (Sphere Books, 1982), 2.
41. Ibid., 47. "Vertebrate competition depends on knowing more than the opposition, monopolizing information along with territory, *hoarding* signals," he elaborated.
42. Robert Anton Wilson, *Cosmic Trigger II: Down to Earth*, 2nd ed. (New Falcon Press, 1996), 33–34.
43. Quoted ibid., 106.

44. Ibid., 49. Italics in the original.
45. Ibid., 132.
46. Many years later, Wilson and Shea satirized Rand in *Illuminatus!* as "Atlanta Hope," the crazed right-wing author of a mammoth novel called *Telemachus Sneezed*. Robert Shea and Robert Anton Wilson, *Illuminatus!* (Dell, 1988 [1975]).
47. Wilson reenacted this uneasy relationship with his uncle when he discovered the work of Ezra Pound. In addition to loving Pound's poetry, Wilson was attracted to some of the poet's economic ideas, but he was repelled by Pound's anti-Semitism and his sympathy for fascism. Wilson was pleased when he heard about Pound's comment to the Jewish poet Allen Ginsberg, a friend of Wilson: "The worst mistake I made was that stupid, suburban prejudice of anti-Semitism." Wilson was probably pleased as well with something Ginsberg told Pound during the same encounter: "[Y]our economics are *right*." Quoted in J. J. Wilhelm, *Ezra Pound: The Tragic Years, 1925–1972* (Pennsylvania State University Press, 1994), 344.
48. Robert Anton Wilson, "Left and Right: A Non-Euclidean Perspective," *Critique* 27 (1988).
49. Robert Anton Wilson, *Wilhelm Reich in Hell* (Falcon Press, 1987), 25.
50. Fredric Wertham, "Calling All Couriers," *The New Republic*, December 2, 1946.
51. Mildred Edie Brady, "The Strange Case of Wilhelm Reich," *The New Republic*, May 26, 1947. Brady also attacked Reich in an article mocking California's anarchist bohemians. See Mildred Edie Brady, "The New Cult of Sex and Anarchy," *Harper's*, April 1947.
52. See Landon R. Y. Storrs, *The Second Red Scare and the Unmaking of the New Deal Left* (Princeton University Press, 2013), 79–80.
53. Reich, in turn, could almost have passed for McCarthy himself if you snipped the right quote out of context. He referred to one psychiatrist who had written unkindly about him as "a well-used stooge of the American Red Fascist conspirators," for example. Not that he admired McCarthy. The educator A. S. Neill, concerned that the psychiatrist saw Stalinists behind everything bad, wrote to Reich that

surely McCarthy was an evil who "isn't inspired by red fascism." The psychiatrist reacted by scrawling in the margin, "HE IS." *Record of a Friendship: The Correspondence of Wilhelm Reich and A. S. Neill*, ed. Beverley R. Placzek (Farrar, Straus and Giroux, 1981), 389, 396.

54. A. Nonymous Hack [Robert Anton Wilson], "The Anatomy of Schlock," *The Realist*, September 1965. Wilson was identified as the article's author in *Best of* The Realist, ed. Paul Krassner (Running Press, 1984), 166.
55. A private alternative to the Post Office was also the subject of 1966's most enduring conspiracy novel, Thomas Pynchon's *The Crying of Lot 49*. In Pynchon's story it is never clear whether the underground post office, called Trystero, is a genuine ancient conspiracy, a practical joke, or a figment of the protagonist's imagination—an ambiguity that admirers of the ironic style should appreciate. Wilson and Shea later gave Trystero a cameo in *Illuminatus!*
56. "Repartee," *Innovator*, October 1967. Wilson used the pseudonym Simon Moon several times in this period. He eventually gave the name to a character in *Illuminatus!*
57. Author's interview with Christina Pearson, February 9, 2012.
58. Mark Frauenfelder and Carla Frauenfelder, "Boing Boing Interview: Robert Anton Wilson," *Boing Boing* 1 (1989).
59. Robert Anton Wilson, letter to Art Kleps, Paul Krassner, Franklin Rosemont, Bernard Marszalek, Mike Aldrich, Randy Wicker, and Eric West, November 8, 1968, scribd.com/doc/95686467/The-Principia-Discordia-or-How-the-West-Was-Lost-1st-Ed.
60. Rev. Charles Arthur Floyd II [Robert Anton Wilson], letter to Rev. David Noebel, n.d., at historiadiscordia.com/bavarians-beethoven-and-bloodshed-week-13-illuminatus-group-reading. Wilson later recalled a letter to the Christian Crusade, written on Illuminati stationery, claiming that "we've taken over the Rock Music business. But you're still so naïve. We took over the business in the 1800s. Beethoven was our first convert." This may be a separate letter, but it's more likely that Wilson simply misremembered the document's details. Quoted in Margot Adler, *Drawing Down the Moon: Witches,*

Druids, Goddess-Worshippers, and Other Pagans in America Today, 2nd ed. (Penguin Compass, 1986), 331.

61. Robert Anton Wilson, *Cosmic Trigger: Final Secret of the Illuminati* (Falcon Press, 1986 [1977]), 63.
62. Wilson wrote frequently for *rogerSPARK*, both under his own name and under a host of pseudonyms: Simon Moon, Mordecai Malignatus, Ronald Weston, the Reverend Brother Kevin O'Flaherty McCool. Arlen Riley Wilson and Kerry Thornley contributed to the paper as well.
63. *rogerSPARK*, February 3, 1969.
64. "Daley Linked with Illuminati," *rogerSPARK*, July 1969.
65. "The Playboy Advisor," *Playboy*, April 1969.
66. "We actually had a recognized student group at Cal called the Bavarian Illuminati," reported Sharon Presley, one of the Berkeley anarchists. She added that "the by-laws were a hoot; obviously no bureaucrat actually read them." Sharon Presley, e-mail to the author, October 20, 2012.

    Since the publication of *Illuminatus!* groups called the Illuminati have become a perennial gag, and not just on college campuses. In the 1980s, a prankster managed to get an alleged organization named the Libertarian Illuminati listed in the *Encyclopedia of Associations*. When a reporter called to ask about it, he replied by weaving an elaborate fake history for the group going back centuries.
67. Wilson, *Cosmic Trigger*, 64. This is a good place to note a proto-Mindfuck prank in 1967, when an unknown person or persons—Doug Skinner speculates that Gray Barker was responsible—sent John Keel and other UFO researchers some mysterious mail whose letterhead identified the authors as The International Bankers. "We are a very powerful organization Mr. Keel and can make things very uncomfortable for you and your friends who try to find out too much about Phase One, Three or any thing concerning other parts of the Universe," the alleged banking conspiracy wrote in one letter. "We are always watching Mr. Keel, we have eyes and ears that never sleep."

The entire document is reprinted at johnkeel.com/?p=1667. Barker, for the record, did periodically allude to the International Bankers in his published writing. In one book he described them as "shadowy terrorists," rumored to be based in the Orion galaxy, who "had even dared to mail letters, written on formal, engraved stationery, threatening the cleansing of Earth." Gray Barker, *The Silver Bridge: The Classic Mothman Tale* (Metadisc Books, 2008 [1970]), 91.

68. Quoted in Kerry Wendell Thornley, "Wonders of the Unseen World," *New Libertarian*, June 1985.
69. Robert Anton Wilson, "The Illuminatus Saga Stumbles Along," *Mystery Scene*, October 1990.
70. On the nature and extent of the cuts, see Tom Jackson, "The ILLUMINATUS! Cuts—How Substantial?," May 21, 2012 (rawillumination.net/2012/05/illuminatus-cuts-how-substantial.html) and the discussion in the blog post's comment thread. Wilson claimed that five hundred pages had been removed and subsequently lost. Other sources suggest that the excisions were more modest.
71. Alan Moore, "Robert Anton Wilson 10 : Alan Moore 2" (2007), youtube.com/watch?v=P8ah5VLztK4.
72. "Robert Anton Wilson Interview."
73. Quoted in "The Other Side," *LeFevre's Journal*, Winter 1976.
74. LaRouche and his followers were also known for a distinct style of over-the-top invective. This description, for example, appeared in a front-page article in a LaRouche paper: "Exhibiting the strong flavor of faggotry, the puffy-cheeked, baby-faced Moss combined the worst English pomposity with that exquisite, simpering quality that most Americans dislike about the British aristocracy." Robert Dreyfuss, "A Close Encounter with Robert Moss of MI-6," *New Solidarity*, May 5, 1980. The author of that passage would later leave the LaRouche orbit and become a frequent contributor to *Rolling Stone*.
75. "Anti-Semitism in Conspiracy Literature," *Conspiracy Digest*, Winter 1976.
76. "Apollo Hoax?" *Conspiracy Digest*, Winter 1977.

77. "Cover-Up Lowdown," *Cover-Up Lowdown* 1 (1977).
78. Author's interview with Jay Kinney, February 22, 2012. All Kinney quotes come from this interview unless otherwise noted.
79. "Passing the Buck," *Cover-Up Lowdown* 1 (1977).
80. Steve Jackson, "Illuminati Designer Article," n.d., sjgames.com/illuminati/designart.html.
81. Steve Jackson, e-mail to the author, January 12, 2012. All Jackson quotes come from this e-mail unless otherwise noted.
82. Wilson was not completely consistent here, since he elsewhere expressed his opposition to intellectual property laws. He would later enter the world of games on his own terms as the host of a role-playing game called *Conspiracy*.
83. Jay Kinney, "Backstage with 'Bob': Is the Church of the SubGenius the Ultimate Cult?" *Whole Earth Review*, Fall 1986.
84. William A. Covino, *Magic, Rhetoric, and Literacy: An Eccentric History of the Composing Imagination* (State University of New York, 1994), 140.
85. Author's interview with Ivan Stang, August 8, 2012. All Stang quotes come from this interview unless otherwise noted.
86. The church wasn't shy about turning its critique against itself. In a rant about the United States' "diabolically seductive brand of mindless consumerism," for instance, one SubGenius book invoked Amazonian tribespeople "walking around in Coca-Cola™ T-shirts, Aerosmith shirts, 'Bob' shirts." *Revelation X: The "Bob" Apocryphon—Hidden Teachings and Deuterocanonical Texts of J. R. "Bob" Dobbs*, ed. Ivan Stang and Paul Mavrides (Fireside, 1994), 21.
87. "SubGenius Pamphlet #1" (Church of the SubGenius, 1980).
88. *The Book of the SubGenius*, ed. Ivan Stang (McGraw-Hill Book Company, 1983), 93.
89. Kerry Thornley, "Introduction," in Malaclypse, *Principia Discordia: How I Found Goddess*, v.
90. *Arise! SubGenius Recruitment Film 16*, directed by Cordt Holland and Ivan Stang, screenplay by Stang, Paul Mavrides, and Harry S. Robins, SubGenius Foundation, 1991. An earlier version of this film started circulating around 1986.

91. *Tribulation 99* cinematographer Bill Daniel was the brother of *Slacker* cinematographer Lee Daniel. Incidentally, 1991 was a banner year for conspiracy cinema: Along with those two pictures, it saw the release of Oliver Stone's assassination flick *JFK*, the film that made the phrase "Oliver Stone movie" a lazy synonym for "conspiracy movie" even though most of Stone's films do not involve vast conspiracies.
92. Author's interview with Craig Baldwin, March 26, 2009.
93. *Tribulation 99: Alien Anomalies Under America*, written and directed by Craig Baldwin, Facets Multi-Media, 1991.
94. The boundary between Wilson's countercultural and Christian readers is more fluid than you might expect. In his study of a London millenarian church, the British journalist Damian Thompson spoke with a Christian who in his younger years "flirted with anarchism, punk rock, witchcraft, and Satanism." During that period, Thompson reported, the interviewee accepted *Illuminatus!* as "truth lightly clothed as fiction." When he was born again, he "carried out only minor adjustments to this narrative." Damian Thompson, *Waiting for Antichrist: Charisma and Apocalypse in a Pentecostal Church* (Oxford University Press, 2005), 103–4.
95. "Nardwuar vs. Robert Anton Wilson," November 8, 1996, nardwuar.com/vs/robert_anton_wilson/index.html.
96. Firesign Theatre was a quartet of comics whose dense, nonlinear audio plays drank from the same well as *Illuminatus!* At one point, in fact, they considered the idea of optioning Wilson and Shea's trilogy, though they never followed through. For more on their career, see Jesse Walker, *Rebels on the Air: An Alternative History of Radio in America* (New York University Press, 2001), 78–80.
97. Krassner, *Confessions of a Raving, Unconfined Nut*, 216.
98. Quoted ibid., 223.
99. Ibid., 247. Like Hoffman, Krassner was heavily involved with the Yippies—indeed, he was the one who gave the group its name.
100. Ibid., 254.
101. Author's interview with Paul Krassner, July 26, 2012. After Krassner moved to San Francisco, he, Kinney, and a few friends started a group

they initially called the Conspiracy Club. (Later, when it became clear that the refreshments deserved equal billing with the conversation, it became the Conspiracy Dessert Club.) Everyone would bring in clippings from the news that might seem to suggest a conspiracy, and the group would discuss the stories. Sometimes participants were serious, sometimes they were joking, and sometimes they hovered in between. "I think our approach and our sensibility was to question everything," Kinney told me, "including our own tendency to read into some of this material."

102. Krassner, *Confessions of a Raving, Unconfined Nut*, 320.
103. Quoted in Gorightly, *The Prankster and the Conspiracy*, 91.
104. Kerry Thornley, "A Bulletin to All 'Rightwing Anarchists' and Other Libertarians," *Free Trade*, July 1968.
105. Kerry Thornley, "Living On the Sea and Off the Land: A Suggestion," *Ocean Living* 1, no. 4 (1968).
106. Quoted in Gorightly, *The Prankster and the Conspiracy*, 194.
107. Thornley, "Wonders of the Unseen World."
108. Kerry Thornley, "How Our Movement Began: Extremism in the Defense of Liberty, Part II," *New Libertarian*, April 1985.
109. Kerry Thornley, letter to Doc Hambone, n.d., multistalkervictims.org/mcf/hambone/thornley.html.
110. Quoted in Gorightly, *The Prankster and the Conspiracy*, 193.
111. Quoted in Adler, *Drawing Down the Moon*, 336.

Chapter 10: The Ghost of Rambo

1. *Good Guys Wear Black*, directed by Ted Post, screenplay by Bruce Cohn and Mark Medoff, from a story by Joseph Fraley, Action One Film Partners, 1978.
2. Quoted in Rick Perlstein, "Ronald Reagan's Imaginary Bridges," *The Baffler* 19 (2012).
3. Thomas Frank, *The Wrecking Crew: How Conservatives Rule* (Metropolitan Books, 2008), 250. For a critique of Frank's book, see Jesse Walker, "What's the Matter with Libertarians?" *Reason*, December 2008.

4. David Morrell, *First Blood* (Warner Books, 2000 [1972]).
5. Morrell, "Rambo and Me," introduction to *First Blood*, xii. The first version of Morrell's essay appeared in *Playboy*, August 1988.
6. The relevant research was summarized in Peter Rowe, "Busting Vietnam Stereotypes," *The San Diego Union-Tribune*, November 11, 2005.
7. Morrell, "Rambo and Me," x.
8. Ibid., xii.
9. *First Blood*, directed by Ted Kotcheff, screenplay by Michael Kozoll, William Sackheim, and Sylvester Stallone, from a novel by David Morrell, Anabasis Investments, 1982.
10. Morrell, "Rambo and Me," ix–x.
11. Andrew Kopkind, "Red Dawn," *The Nation*, September 15, 1984.
12. *Red Dawn*, directed by John Milius, screenplay by Milius and Kevin Reynolds, MGM/UA, 1984.
13. Susan Faludi, *Stiffed: The Betrayal of the American Man* (Harper Perennial, 2000), 395.
14. On whether Cosmatos or Stallone deserves credit for directing *First Blood Part II*, see Henry Cabot Beck, "The 'Western' *Godfather*," *True West*, October 1, 2006.
15. *Rambo: First Blood Part II*, directed by George Cosmatos, screenplay by Sylvester Stallone and James Cameron, from a story by Kevin Jarre, Anabasis Investments, 1985.
16. Quoted in "Reagan Gets Ideas at 'Rambo' Showing," *The Milwaukee Sentinel*, July 1, 1985.
17. Gustav Hasford, "Vietnam Means Never Having to Say You're Sorry," *Penthouse*, June 1987.
18. There's a hint of another primal conspiracy myth too. When the Chuck Norris and Anne Archer characters are holed up at the Squaw Valley Inn, Norris looks out the window warily. "Any enemies out there?" Archer asks. Norris, who has started to suspect Archer of being part of the conspiracy, replies pointedly, "I'm just as worried about the enemy within."
19. For a thoughtful discussion of *Good Guys Wear Black*'s relationship to both the eighties POW/MIA rescue cycle and the colonial Indian

captivity narratives, see Louis J. Kern, "MIAs, Myth, and Macho Magic: Post-Apocalyptic Cinematic Visions of Vietnam," in *Search and Clear: Critical Responses to Selected Literature and Films of the Vietnam War*, ed. William J. Searle (Popular Press, 1988).

20. David Morrell, *Rambo: First Blood Part II* (Jove Books, 1985), 235. One of the POWs responds to the news about Reagan with the words "Holy fuck." Rambo replies, "Yes, I said that many times."
21. For a comparison of the POW/MIA films with certain westerns of the 1940s and '50s—many of them conspiracy-themed—see Nick Redfern, "The Military Metaphor of Government in the Cold War Western," April 16, 2009, nickredfern.wordpress.com/2009/04/16/the-military-metaphor-of-government-in-the-cold-war-western. Redfern linked *Rambo* to pictures whose anti-Washington attitude often reflected an authoritarian impulse, while I'm highlighting the picture's ties to the more antiauthoritarian movies of the 1970s. I see this less as a disagreement with Redfern than as a sign of the complexities and contradictions of our shared subject.
22. *Rambo III*, directed by Peter MacDonald, screenplay by Sylvester Stallone and Sheldon Lettich, Carolco Pictures, 1988.
23. Sometimes the comparisons between Waco and Wounded Knee were direct and overt. For an example, see S. Leon Felkins, "The 110th Anniversary of the Wounded Knee Massacre: Some Chilling Modern Parallels," December 28, 2000, lewrockwell.com/orig/felkins4.html.
24. On Posey's career, see J. M. Berger, "Patriot Games," *Foreign Policy*, April 18, 2012; R. M. Schneiderman, "My Life as a White Supremacist," *Newsweek*, November 11, 2011.
25. *Waco: The Rules of Engagement*, directed by William Gazecki, written by William Gazecki, Dan Gifford, and Michael McNulty, New Yorker Films, 1997.
26. Andrea Chase, "Rambo," n.d., killermoviereviews.com/main.php?nextlink=display&dId=959.
27. Gina Carbone, "'Rambo' Review: There Will Be Blood," *Seacoast Online*, January 26, 2008.
28. David Morrell, "David Morrell FAQ," n.d., at 66.241.209.129/faq.cfm.

29. Quoted in "Answering Questions Is as Easy as Breathing—Sly Answers Back! Day 1," January 14, 2008, aintitcool.com/node/35279.
30. I wouldn't have minded seeing some of the Afghan heroes of *Rambo III* return as villains in *Rambo IV*. But that might have pushed the franchise into areas that Stallone would rather leave alone.
31. Richard Slotkin, *Regeneration Through Violence: The Mythology of the American Frontier, 1600–1860* (University of Oklahoma Press, 1973), 94. Or you may remember it from chapter 2.
32. If *The Searchers* is the most notable recent incarnation of the Indian captivity narrative, the most notable recent incarnation of the white-slavery captivity tale is a movie that *The Searchers* directly inspired: *Taxi Driver*, a 1976 film scripted by Paul Schrader and directed by Martin Scorsese. Robert De Niro's version of the Wayne character is relentlessly unappealing—he is a murderer and a madman—but he becomes a folk hero after "rescuing" a prostitute in a bloody raid on a brothel.

    De Niro's character brushes against another archetype, the "lone nut" assassin, when he flirts with shooting a presidential candidate. A few years later, life imitated art when John Hinckley attempted to assassinate President Reagan. An obsessive fan of *Taxi Driver*, Hinckley hoped his act would impress the actress Jodie Foster, who played the prostitute in Scorsese's movie.
33. Slotkin, *Regeneration Through Violence*, 95.

Chapter 11: The Demonic Cafeteria

1. Philip Sandifer, "Pop Between Realities, Home in Time for Tea 39 (Prime Suspect, Cracker)," September 12, 2012, philipsandifer.com/2012/09/pop-between-realities-home-in-time-for_12.html.
2. For a twenty-first-century account of black prisoners using the sovereign citizens' legal arguments, see Kevin Carey, "Too Weird for *The Wire*," *The Washington Monthly*, May–July 2008. Carey identified one conveyer belt by which these concepts reached black hands—the prison system—but that was hardly the only one. People affiliated with

offshoots of the Moorish Science Temple had preached similar notions before the events at the core of Carey's article occurred. And in the 1990s, when I was writing a lot about pirate radio, I met several black radicals who defended their right to operate unlicensed stations using arguments essentially identical to those of the sovereign citizen crowd.

3. Michael Barkun, *A Culture of Conspiracy: Apocalyptic Visions in Contemporary America* (University of California Press, 2003), 11.
4. Robert Churchill, *To Shake Their Guns in the Tyrant's Face: Libertarian Political Violence and the Origins of the Militia Movement* (University of Michigan Press, 2009), 8.
5. Ibid.
6. Steven M. Chermak, *Searching for a Demon: The Media Construction of the Militia Movement* (Northeastern University Press, 2002), 235.
7. David Neiwert, *The Eliminationists: How Hate Talk Radicalized the American Right* (Paradigm Publishers, 2009), 35.
8. Churchill, *To Shake Their Guns in the Tyrant's Face*, 233.
9. Quoted ibid.
10. See Jonathan Karl, *The Right to Bear Arms: The Rise of America's New Militias* (Harper Paperbacks, 1995), 91, 133.
11. The Southern Poverty Law Center—not a group given to minimizing militia violence—keeps a running tally of post–Oklahoma City right-wing terror plots (militia-related and otherwise) at splcenter.org/get-informed/publications/terror-from-the-right.
12. Quoted in Michael Kelly, "The Road to Paranoia," *The New Yorker*, June 19, 1995.
13. Author's interview with Bob Banner, May 1, 2012. All Banner quotes come from this interview unless otherwise noted.
14. I contacted Livergood to ask him to comment on Banner's description of his group. After replying to my introductory e-mail, he did not answer the follow-up containing my questions. Subsequent attempts to elicit responses were equally unsuccessful.
15. "Introduction," *Critique* 1, no. 1 (Autumn 1980). Banner wrote the editorial, though it appeared unsigned; it was reprinted several times in subsequent editions of the journal.

16. "Doubles?" *Critique* 1, no. 2 (Winter 1980–81).
17. Samuel Edward Konkin III, "Special Review: The Project, Part II," *New Libertarian* 4, no. 17 (February–April 1987).
18. Tony Elias, "Interview with Mr. Martin," *Flatland Magazine* 16 (February 1999). "Perot" is a reference to Ross Perot, a Texas billionaire who ran for president in 1992 and 1996.
19. Anson Kennedy, "PhenomiCon 1991: A Recipe for Weirdness," January–February 1992, lysator.liu.se/skeptical/newsletters/Georgia_Skeptic/GS05-01.TXT.
20. The two PhenomiCons weren't the only attempts to put on a conspiracy-themed convention. Notably, an annual gathering called Conspiracy Con has been held in Santa Clara, California, since 2001.
21. Author's interview with Brian Redman, September 5, 2012.
22. "A couple of times he was right," *The Chicago Sun-Times* reported when Skolnick died. "But the other theories Mr. Skolnick scattered with his shotgun style of crying corruption made him the Chicken Little of tipsters, a media pariah in Chicago." Mark J. Konkol, "Conspiracy Theorist Helped Bring Down Ex-Gov," *The Chicago Sun-Times*, May 23, 2006.
23. I drew those figures from "Branch Davidians Who Died at Mt. Carmel," in *Armageddon in Waco: Critical Perspectives on the Branch Davidian Conflict*, ed. Stuart A. Wright (University of Chicago Press, 1995), 379–81.
24. I interviewed Bob Fletcher in 1995 for Jesse Walker, "The Populist Rainbow," *Chronicles*, March 1996. All Fletcher quotes come from this interview unless otherwise noted.
25. I interviewed Afrika Islam in 1995 for "The Populist Rainbow." All Islam quotes come from this interview.
26. Anthony J. Hilder, "Ordo Ab Chao," on *Amerika*, cassette, Anthony Music Corporation, 1994.
27. I interviewed Anthony Hilder in 1995 for "The Populist Rainbow." All Hilder quotes come from this interview unless otherwise noted.
28. I interviewed Michael Moor in 1995 for "The Populist Rainbow." All Moor quotes come from this interview.

29. Quoted in Brian McManus, "The Illuminati: Conspiracy Theory or New World Order?" *Philadelphia Weekly*, December 1, 2010.
30. Tony Brown, *Empower the People: Overthrowing the Conspiracy That Is Stealing Your Money and Freedom* (HarperCollins, 1998), 191.
31. Ibid., 186.
32. Ibid., xv. Brown's version of the Illuminati story cites some of the same sources you see in conspiracy tracts of the right, from Edith Starr Miller to William Guy Carr.
33. Daniel Levitas, *The Terrorist Next Door: The Militia Movement and the Radical Right* (Thomas Dunne Books, 2002), 318.
34. Quoted in Karl, *The Right to Bear Arms*, 112. Butler added, "I think they are a government-sponsored movement, maybe the CIA."
35. Department of Justice, "Good O' Boy Roundup Report," March 1996, justice.gov/oig/special/9603/exec.htm.
36. Kenneth S. Stern, *A Force upon the Plain: The American Militia Movement and the Politics of Hate* (Simon & Schuster, 1996), 247.
37. Ibid., 246.
38. Ibid., 219.
39. Dick Morris, *Behind the Oval Office: Getting Reelected Against All Odds*, 2nd ed. (Renaissance Books, 1999), 418. Morris today is a fierce critic of the Democrats, including his former colleagues in the Clinton White House. So it's worth noting that this book was written before he reinvented his public persona. It was generally friendly toward Bill Clinton and his administration, and its discussion of the "ricochet" plan did not treat it as a scandal. For a discussion of Morris's subsequent evolution, which culminated with the man borrowing the rhetoric of the very militias he had once targeted, see Jesse Walker, "The Cynicism of Dick Morris," January 18, 2013, reason.com/archives/2013/01/18/the-cynicism-of-dick-morris.
40. Quoted in Morris, *Behind the Oval Office*, 419–23.
41. Ibid., 210. Interestingly, Morris felt that the bombing served as a turning point that allowed Clinton to formulate a "values agenda" around such issues as smoking and TV violence. If so, it's an intriguing example of the transmutability of moral panics.

42. "The Pine Bluff Variant," *The X-Files*, Fox, May 3, 1998.
43. Paul Cantor, *Gilligan Unbound: Pop Culture in the Age of Globalization* (Rowman & Littlefield, 2001), 185.
44. "The Truth," *The X-Files*, Fox, May 19, 2002.
45. Chung's investigation of the alleged abduction resembles John Keel's investigation of the Mothman, and he is identified as the author of a thriller called *The Caligarian Candidate*.
46. Ventura, who later served as governor of Minnesota, would still later write several books about conspiracies and host a cable TV show called *Conspiracy Theory with Jesse Ventura*.
47. "Jose Chung's *From Outer Space*," *The X-Files*, Fox, April 12, 1996.
48. For an example, see Kenn Thomas, "Clinton Era Conspiracies! Was Gennifer Flowers on the Grassy Knoll? Probably Not, but Here Are Some Other Bizarre Theories for a New Political Age," *The Washington Post*, January 16, 1994. Thomas, as it happens, was the editor of *Steamshovel Press* and a sincere believer in several nonmainstream conspiracy theories. It isn't clear to what extent his ironic tone was the camouflage he adopted to write for the *Post* and to what extent it was imposed by editors who felt the style was the appropriate approach for discussing the subject.
49. Xandor Korzybski, letter to the editor, *Mondo 2000* 3 (Winter 1991).
50. R. U. Sirius, e-mail to the author, September 6, 2012, 5:19 P.M. Sirius would not reveal Korzybski's identity, but he reported that the writer is "actually sort of a credible person in tech journalism circles, in his real life."
51. R. U. Sirius, e-mail to the author, September 6, 2012, 6:15 P.M.

Chapter 12: Everything Is a Clue

1. "The Bottle Deposit," *Seinfeld*, NBC, May 2, 1996. The scene that this line of dialogue comes from, in which George and Jerry ponder the possibility that a message is encoded in the song "Downtown," is Exhibit A for my perhaps insane pet theory that *Seinfeld*, not *The X-Files*, was the most paranoid program of the 1990s.

2. For a useful overview of the 9/11 truth movement, see chapter 7 of Mark Fenster, *Conspiracy Theories: Secrecy and Power in American Culture*, 2nd ed. (University of Minnesota Press, 2008).
3. Michael Barkun, *Chasing Phantoms: Reality, Imagination, and Homeland Security Since 9/11* (University of North Carolina Press, 2011), 77. It's too international a story to fit into this America-centric book—Moriarty comes from England, Mabuse from Germany, Fantômas from France—but there's a fascinating study to be written on the history of the supervillain.
4. Author's interview with Joel Best, October 26, 2001.
5. The anthrax attacks, in which envelopes containing anthrax spores were mailed to various politicians and media outlets, were almost certainly perpetrated by someone who didn't have anything to do with 9/11. At the time, though, they were widely assumed to have been the brainchild of the same conspiracy. The White House reportedly pushed the FBI to prove that Al Qaeda was responsible for the anthrax mailings, but the Bureau didn't buy the theory. See James Gordon Meek, "FBI Was Told to Blame Anthrax Scare on Al Qaeda by White House Officials," *Daily News* (New York), August 2, 2008.
6. Quoted in "New Scare Diverts US Flight," October 11, 2001, news.bbc.co.uk/2/hi/americas/1592417.stm.
7. Gwen Shaffer, "Novel Security Measures," *Philadelphia City Paper*, October 18–25, 2001.
8. Quoted in "Two Plead Not Guilty to Boston Hoax Charges," February 2, 2007, web.archive.org/web/20070210181101/http://www.cnn.com/2007/US/02/01/boston.bombscare/index.html.
9. Richard Landes, *Heaven on Earth: The Varieties of the Millennial Experience* (Oxford University Press, 2011), 14.
10. Some e-mails told readers to enter Q33NY, allegedly the flight or tail number of one of the planes that struck the World Trade Center. The results:

In that case, the e-mail was a hoax: Neither plane was associated with the code Q33NY.

11. Conspiracy thinking played a role in the president's policies abroad as well as at home. Consider Bush's description of Iran, Iraq, and North Korea as an "axis of evil." Since an axis is an alliance, his formulation suggested that Iran and Iraq—parties to one of the most bitter international rivalries of the day—were secretly aligned.
12. Meg Stalcup and Joshua Craze, "How We Train Our Cops to Fear Islam," *The Washington Monthly*, March–April 2011. Sadly, Kharoba wasn't the worst alleged expert giving talks on Islamic terrorism. On the Christian circuit, self-proclaimed defectors from jihadist conspiracies told tales worthy of John Todd. For some examples, see Jorg Luyken, "The Palestinian 'Terrorist' Turned Zionist," *The Jerusalem Post*, March 20, 2008; Doug Howard, "Mixed Message," *Books & Culture*, May–June 2010; Tim Murphy, "An Ex-Terrorist Walks into a Conservative Conference . . . ," *Mother Jones*, September 15, 2012. For a report of such speakers addressing an air force audience, see Neil MacFarquhar, "Speakers at Academy Said to Make False Claims," *The New York Times*, February 7, 2008.
13. "MIAC Strategic Report: The Modern Militia Movement," Missouri Information Analysis Center, February 20, 2009, scribd.com/doc/13290698/The-Modern-Militia-MovementMissouri-MIAC-Strategic-Report-20Feb09.
14. "2009 Virginia Terrorism Threat Assessment," Virginia Fusion Center, March 2009, rawstory.com/images/other/vafusioncenterterrorassessment.pdf.
15. *North Central Texas Fusion System Prevention Awareness Bulletin*, February 19, 2009.
16. "A Cautionary Note for Law Enforcement," *Pennsylvania Actionable Intelligence Briefing*, November 13–15, 2009.
17. "Federal Support for and Involvement in State and Local Fusion Centers," United States Senate Permanent Subcommittee on Investigations, Committee on Homeland Security and Governmental Affairs, October 3, 2012.

18. Kathleen Tierney, "The Red Pill," June 11, 2006, understandingkatrina.ssrc.org/Tierney.
19. When a subsequent storm, Sandy, hit New York in 2012, some pranksters deliberately fed the rumor mill by creating a Twitter hashtag called #SANDYLOOTCREW and posting lists and pictures of the goods they had allegedly stolen: a laptop, a TV, a shirt, even a cat. Sometimes they added inflammatory messages, such as "WE NOT STEALIN, WE TAKIN BACK FROM DA WHITE MAN." Their hoax posts were repeated uncritically by the *Drudge Report*, the *Daily Mail*, and other outlets.
20. Lee Clarke and Caron Chess, "Elites and Panic: More to Fear Than Fear Itself," *Social Forces* 87, no. 2 (December 2008). Clarke and Chess didn't coin the term "elite panic"—they quoted a Kathleen Tierney article that used the phrase, and it is possible that other writers deployed it earlier as well. But Clarke and Chess gave the concept a more systematic treatment.
21. Sara Robinson, "Tragedy at the Holocaust Museum: Stand Up to Terror," June 11, 2009, blog.ourfuture.org/20090610/tragedy-at-the-holocaust-museum-stand-up-to-terrorism.
22. Bonnie Erbe, "Round Up Hate-Promoters Now, Before Any More Holocaust Museum Attacks," June 11, 2009, usnews.com/opinion/blogs/erbe/2009/06/11/round-up-hate-promoters-now-before-any-more-holocaust-museum-attacks.
23. Paul Krugman, "The Big Hate," *The New York Times*, June 11, 2009.
24. Bob Herbert, "A Threat We Can't Ignore," *The New York Times*, June 19, 2009.
25. Frank Rich, "The Obama Haters' Silent Enablers," *The New York Times*, June 13, 2009.
26. "Rightwing Extremism: Current Economic and Political Climate Fueling Resurgence in Radicalization and Recruitment," U.S. Department of Homeland Security, Office of Intelligence and Analysis, April 7, 2009, fas.org/irp/eprint/rightwing.pdf.
27. The paper's own author has had trouble explaining exactly what he meant. In his memoir, Johnson stressed that Homeland Security's con-

cern was with "violent antigovernment groups and potential terrorists," adding that in hindsight his "definition of right-wing extremist should have incorporated the aspects of supporting, endorsing, and conducting criminal acts and violence." But later in the book he related his long struggle with the department's Office of Civil Rights and Civil Liberties, which tried to add precisely that sort of language to the report before it was released. Rather than recognizing in retrospect that the office had a point, Johnson became defensive. "Extremism should not be limited to those groups or individuals solely involved in criminal, illegal, or violent activity," his book argued. "Extremism has a much broader definition, because it is the phase that precedes terrorism. Extremism involves ideologies that facilitate individuals and groups toward violence and terrorism." Daryl Johnson, *Right-Wing Resurgence: How a Domestic Terrorist Threat Is Being Ignored* (Rowman & Littlefield, 2012), 9, 236–37. For a critique of Johnson's book, see Jesse Walker, "Homeland Security Meets Office Politics," October 30, 2012, reason.com/archives/2012/10/30/homeland-security-meets-office-politics.

28. See "Leftwing Extremists Likely to Increase Use of Cyber Attacks over the Coming Decade," U.S. Department of Homeland Security, Office of Intelligence and Analysis, January 26, 2009, fas.org/irp/eprint/leftwing.pdf.
29. Michael German, "Soon, We'll All Be Radicals," April 16, 2009, aclu.org/blog/national-security-technology-and-liberty/soon-well-all-be-radicals.
30. Johnson, *Right-Wing Resurgence*, 266.
31. Allison Kilkenny, "Discussion of Dead Census Worker Highlights Right-Wing Paranoia," September 24, 2009, huffingtonpost.com/allison-kilkenny/discussion-of-dead-census_b_298534.html.
32. Rick Ungar, "Send the Body to Glenn Beck," September 24, 2009, trueslant.com/rickungar/2009/09/24/send-the-body-to-glenn-beck-kentucky-census-worker-hanged-fed-clay-county.
33. Josh Marshall, "Ideas Have Consequences," February 18, 2010, talkingpointsmemo.com/archives/2010/02/ideas_have_consequences.php.

34. *CNN Newsroom*, CNN, August 28, 2009.
35. For the original assertion, see Ronald Kessler, *In the President's Secret Service: Behind the Scenes with Agents in the Line of Fire and the Presidents They Protect* (Crown, 2009), 225.
36. Author's interview with Malcolm Wiley, March 30, 2010.
37. Quoted in Rachel Slajda, "Secret Service Director: Threats Against Obama Not Up," December 3, 2009, archive.is/Qpp7.
38. Martin Vaughan, "Threats Against IRS Employees on the Rise, Official Says," *The Wall Street Journal*, February 21, 2010.
39. I spoke with the official in April 2010.
40. Paul Krugman, "Climate of Hate," *The New York Times*, January 9, 2011. The report he's referring to is Erika Lovley, "Exclusive: FBI Details Surge in Death Threats Against Lawmakers," May 25, 2010, politico.com/news/stories/0510/37726.html.
41. Mark Potok, "Rage on the Right," *Intelligence Report*, Spring 2010.
42. "Active 'Patriot' Groups in the United States in 2009," *Intelligence Report*, Spring 2010.
43. Ibid.
44. Quoted in Alan Maimon, "Oath Keepers Pledges to Prevent Dictatorship in United States," *Las Vegas Review-Journal*, October 8, 2009.
45. Quoted in Jennifer Chambers and Doug Guthrie, "FBI Raids Mich.-Based Militia Group," *The Detroit News*, March 29, 2010.
46. David Neiwert, "FBI Busts of Michigan Militias' Hutaree Sect Once Again Rip the Facade Away from Patriots' Civil Pose," March 29, 2010, crooksandliars.com/david-neiwert/fbi-busts-michigan-militias-hutaree.
47. Author's interview with Amy Cooter, March 31, 2010.
48. Quoted in Mike Wilkinson, "Other Militias Told on Hutaree," *The Detroit News*, April 17, 2010.
49. Arie Perliger, "Challengers from the Sidelines: Understanding America's Violent Far-Right," Combating Terrorism Center at West Point, November 2012, ctc.usma.edu/wp-content/uploads/2013/01/ChallengersFromtheSidelines.pdf. All subsequent Perliger quotes come from this paper.

50. The 1996 campaign was an exception, Perliger hypothesized, because it featured "the least competitive elections of the last 22 years." He raised the possibility that "far-right groups and individuals are more inclined to engage in violence in a contentious political climate." Maybe.
51. I do not mean to suggest that the militias necessarily opposed the Minutemen's agenda and vice versa. Many militiamen wanted stronger border controls, and many Minutemen favored reducing government power in areas unrelated to immigration. But even where there was overlap, the emphasis was different.
52. Daryl Johnson's company, DT Analytics, includes the birthers among the groups it tracks, listing "Birthers, Truthers, Oath Keepers and Three Percenters" as examples of "anti-government extremists" on "the far right of the political spectrum." People who adopt such "extremist belief systems" have allowed a "poison" into their minds, the company's site says; they may be on "the path from extremist sympathizer to extremist activist to terrorist." "Radicalization and Mobilization," n.d., dtanalytics.org/help.php.
53. *The Lou Dobbs Show*, United Stations Radio Networks, July 15, 2009.
54. *Hardball*, MSNBC, July 23, 2009.
55. Gene Healy, *The Cult of the Presidency: America's Dangerous Devotion to Executive Power* (Cato Institute, 2008), 4.
56. Gary G. Kreep, "FAX All 50 State Attorneys General to Investigate Obama's Birthday Fraud," July 2009, scribd.com/doc/17682329/Why-Can-Obama-Keep-College-Papers-Hidden.
57. Bob Miller, "Got Birth Certificate?" July 15, 2009, unitedconservatives.blogspot.com/2009/07/got-birth-certificate.html.
58. "An Open Letter to Barack Obama," December 1, 2008, wethepeoplefoundation.org/UPDATE/misc2008/Obama-USA-TODAY-ad.htm.
59. Hugh McInnish, "Fire the Silver Bullet!" *The McInnish Newsletter*, May 21, 2009.
60. *On Point*, National Public Radio, July 27, 2009.
61. Markos Moulitsas (markos), "Mission Accomplished, Sarah Palin, http://is.gd/knNgl," tweet, January 8, 2011, 2:19 P.M. Moulitsas's link

went to a post at the liberal site Firedoglake that reprinted the Palin map under the headline "Sarah Palin's Hit List."

62. Michael Daly, "Rep. Gabrielle Giffords' Blood Is on Sarah Palin's Hands After Putting Cross Hair over District," *Daily News*, January 9, 2011.
63. Ed Pilkington, "Jared Lee Loughner: Erratic, Disturbed and Prone to Rightwing Rants," *The Guardian*, January 9, 2011.
64. Erad3 [Jared Lee Loughner], "Infinite Source of Currency!?!?" August 7, 2010, abovetopsecret.com/forum/thread591520/pg1.
65. Will Rahn, "Fellow Commenters at UFO Conspiracy Website Questioned Jared Lee Loughner's Sanity in Threads," January 11, 2011, dailycaller.com/2011/01/11/fellow-commenters-at-ufo-conspiracy-website-questioned-jared-lee-loughners-sanity-in-threads.
66. youtube.com/watch?v=nHoaZaLbqB4.
67. Mark Potok, "Who Is Jared Lee Loughner?" January 9, 2011, splcenter.org/blog/2011/01/09/who-is-jared-lee-loughner. Potok elaborated: "Miller claims that the government uses grammar to 'enslave' Americans and offers up his truly weird 'Truth-language' as an antidote. For example, he says that if you add colons and hyphens to your name in a certain way, you are no longer taxable." Loughner, meanwhile, wrote that the government was performing "mind control on the people by controlling grammar." QED.

    It could conceivably emerge that Loughner encountered Miller's ideas at some point. But it's worth noting some things that Loughner hasn't done. For one, he hasn't added any colons or hyphens to his name. Also, he hasn't declared that he isn't taxable. Miller's following, to the extent that he has one, consists of people who think his ideas will let them avoid penalties in court. Yet when Loughner was arraigned, a day after Potok published his speculations, he didn't invoke a single Millerism. And while Miller believes he has discovered a "correct language" (sorry, ":Correct-Language:") that everyone should use instead of the "bastardized" English imposed by elites, Loughner's YouTube channel raised the possibility of creating *new* languages. What exactly he meant by that is anyone's guess, but it sounds rather different from Miller's project.

68. Quoted in Nick Baumann, "Exclusive: Loughner Friend Explains Alleged Gunman's Grudge Against Giffords," January 10, 2011, motherjones.com/politics/2011/01/jared-lee-loughner-friend-voicemail-phone-message.
69. *Harsh Realm* was created by Chris Carter, the man behind *The X-Files*.
70. My fantasy for how the trilogy should have concluded: After learning that every level of reality is just another matrix, Neo shrugs his shoulders and walks off the film set. A digital camera follows him across the street to a lecture hall, where a professor is denouncing metafiction and declaring postmodernism a literary dead end. Keanu's cell rings: It's his agent. We hear them chatting about how much they're making from *Matrix* merchandise. Then the wall collapses and the cast of *Blazing Saddles* falls into the classroom, throwing pies.
71. Philip K. Dick, "How to Build a Universe That Doesn't Fall Apart Two Days Later" (1978), in *The Shifting Realities of Philip K. Dick: Selected Literary and Philosophical Writings*, ed. Lawrence Sutin (Vintage Books, 1995), 262.
72. After a series of mystical experiences in the 1970s, Dick began to believe this was happening in his life as well as his stories. In one of the theories he conceived to explain what he had gone through, he suggested that the world we seem to live in is a *Matrix*-like "Black Iron Prison." (This idea worked its way into one of his last and best novels, the autobiographical *VALIS*.) He also played with the idea of a Benevolent Conspiracy. At one point he told an interviewer that "the Illuminati are doing for Bob Wilson and me what God is doing for everybody else. Running the world very well, and doing a great job of it." Quoted in Gregg Rickman, *Philip K. Dick: The Last Testament* (Fragments West/Valentine Press, 1985), 42.
73. wikipedia.org/w/index.php?title=Jamie_Kane&diff=528503901&oldid=20854738.
74. Fraser M, "Jamie Kane Dead," *Top of the Pops*, April 6, 2005.
75. *The Beast* had precursors, of course. For an overview of ARGs' antecedents, see Bryan Alexander, *The New Digital Storytelling: Creating Narratives with New Media* (Praeger, 2011), 153–55.

76. Jane McGonigal, "'This Is Not a Game': Immersive Aesthetics and Collective Play," *Digital Arts & Culture 2003 Conference Proceedings*, May 2003.
77. Quoted ibid.
78. Quoted ibid.
79. Quoted in Cory Doctorow, "BBC: Wikipedia Is Not a Viral Marketing Tool," August 15, 2005, boingboing.net/2005/08/15/bbc-wikipedia-is-not.html.
80. Bryan Alexander, "ARG vs Wikipedia vs Blogosphere," August 16, 2005, infocult.typepad.com/infocult/2005/08/arg_vs_wikipedi.html.
81. Quoted in Robert Anton Wilson, "Timothy Leary and His Psychological H-Bomb," *The Realist*, August 1964.
82. Quoted in Xeni Jardin, "BBC Punks Wikipedia in Game Marketing Ploy?" August 13, 2005, boingboing.net/2005/08/13/bbc-punks-wikipedia.html.
83. youtube.com/watch?v=ESguSeFQzzk. In another throwback to the seventies, Dollins devoted a portion of the lecture to describing the movie *Telefon*. He suggested that the film's army of Manchurian candidates actually exists and that it is capable of carrying out attacks on U.S. soil.
84. In 1990, half a decade before those cards were published, the Secret Service raided Steve Jackson's offices because an agent suspected that hackers were using an electronic bulletin board the company ran. The bulletin board was called Illuminati, and its tongue-in-cheek welcome message may have played a role in unleashing the raid. As District Judge Sam Sparks wrote, a federal agent "reviewed a printout of Illuminati on February 25, 1990, which read, 'Greetings, Mortal! You have entered the secret computer system of the Illuminati, the on-line home of the world's oldest and largest secret conspiracy . . . fronted by Steve Jackson Games, Incorporated. Fnord.' The evidence in this case strongly suggests Agent Foley, without any further investigation, misconstrued this information to believe the Illuminati bulletin board was similar in purpose to [a different] bulletin board, which provided information to and was used by 'hackers.'" *Steve Jackson Games v.*

United States Secret Service, U.S. District Court, W.D. Texas, Austin Division, March 12, 1993. Years later, naturally, a story spread that the raid had been intended to stop the distribution of the *Illuminati* cards.

85. Jonah Weiner, "Is Lady Gaga a Satanist Illuminati Slave?" November 21, 2011, slate.com/articles/arts/culturebox/2011/11/lady_gaga_kanye_west_jay_z_the_conspiracy_theories_that_say_pop_stars_are_illuminati_pawns.html.
86. godlikeproductions.com/forum1/message1871717/pg1.
87. Dr. Dre, "Been There, Done That," on *The Aftermath*, CD, Aftermath Entertainment, 1996.
88. Raekwon, Pusha T, Common, 2 Chainz, Cyhi the Prynce, Kid Cudi, and D'banj, "The Morning," on *G.O.O.D. Music: Cruel Summer*, CD, G.O.O.D. Music/Def Jam, 2012.
89. Prodigy, "Illuminati," on *H.N.I.C. Pt. 2*, CD, AAO Music, 2008. Prodigy was heavily influenced by Malachi York, a figure whose worldview mixed black nationalism, ufology, and the legal theories of the sovereign citizens. In the lead-up to the 2012 presidential primaries, Prodigy endorsed the race's most vocal critic of the New World Order, the constitutionalist libertarian Ron Paul.
90. *Jonesy in the Morning*, WUSL, November 3, 2009.
91. Rick Ross featuring Jay-Z, "Free Mason," on *Teflon Don*, CD, Def Jam/Maybach Music/Slip N Slide, 2010.
92. That was in the Marvel Comics universe. Marvel's chief rival, DC, had already featured an evil order called the Illuminati in *Time Masters*, a 1990 miniseries written by Bob Wayne and Lewis Shiner. Shiner was a vocal fan of *Illuminatus!*, and Wayne used that interest to get him involved with the comic: "When Bob first pitched the *Time Masters* series to me, he put the Illuminati in there specifically to hook me." Lewis Shiner, e-mail to the author, April 4, 2013.
93. *Holy Blood, Holy Grail* also contributed a conspiracy theory to one of Robert Anton Wilson's prequels to the *Illuminatus!* trilogy. See Robert Anton Wilson, *The Widow's Son* (Bluejay, 1985).
94. Dan Brown, *The Da Vinci Code* (Anchor Books, 2006), 273.
95. The sculpture, Jim Sanborn's *Kryptos*, itself contains a coded message,

which amateurs and CIA analysts alike have been attempting to solve since the artwork was erected in 1990.

96. The conspiracy text that took the everything-is-a-clue mind-set further than any other just might be "King-Kill/33°" (1987), James Shelby Downard's samizdat essay on the JFK assassination. Downard analyzed the external world with techniques more akin to literary criticism, searching for symbolism and attributing it to a Masonic hidden hand. Here is a typical passage:

> Let us take as an example the "Mason Road" in Texas that connects to the "Mason No El Bar" the Texas-New Mexico ("The Land of Enchantment") border. This connecting line is on the 32nd degree. The thirty-second degree in Masonry of the Scottish Rite is the next to the highest degree awarded. . . .
>
> When this thirty-second degree line is traced some little distance farther west, into Arizona, it crosses an old trail which meandered north of what is now another ghost town but which at one time was the town of "Ruby." . . . [T]he Ruby road twists north into the area of two mountain peaks that are known as the Kennedy and Johnson Mountains.

Downard's document was produced with the assistance of Michael A. Hoffman II, a Fortean anti-Semite who has staked out what may be a unique position on the intellectual spectrum: He believes that the Holocaust didn't exist but fairies do.

97. lysistrata, "He Let Them Down. He Ran Around and Hurt Them," June 25, 2008, metafilter.com/72804/He-let-them-down-He-ran-around-and-hurt-them.

Epilogue: The Monster at the End of This Book

1. David Hume, *The Natural History of Religion* (A. and H. Bradlaugh Bonner, 1889 [1757]), 11.
2. Mark Phillips, *Satan in the Smoke? A Photojournalist's 9/11 Story* (South Brooklyn Internet, 2011), e-book.

3. "Devil Face in Smoke of 911 at the WTC," n.d., at christianmedia.us/devil-face.html.
4. Texe Marrs, "Face of the Devil," n.d., at texemarrs.com/102001/face_of_devil.htm.
5. Quoted in "Faces in the Cloud," April 23, 2008, snopes.com/rumors/wtcface.asp.
6. "Allah's Edict Against Terrorism," n.d., devilsmokemessageforum.blogspot.com/2012/06/comments.html.
7. Sadly, the bird goes unmentioned in *The Da Vinci Code*.
8. "Dali Gives His Theories on Painting," *The Hartford Courant*, December 19, 1935.
9. Rob MacDougall, "Pastplay," May 5, 2010, www.robmacdougall.org/blog/2010/05/pastplay. The game was partly inspired by Umberto Eco's 1988 novel *Foucault's Pendulum*.
10. Quoted in "Tim Powers Rewrites the Cold War," October 10, 2006, powells.com/blog/interviews/tim-powers-rewrites-the-cold-war-by-dave.
11. Paul Krassner, *Confessions of a Raving, Unconfined Nut*, 2nd ed. (New World Digital, 2010), 213.
12. "Paranoia seems to require being imitated to be understood, and it, in turn, seems to understand only by imitation." Eve Kosofsky Sedgwick, *Touching Feeling: Affect, Pedagogy, Performativity* (Duke University Press, 2003), 131.
13. Michael Shermer, *The Believing Brain: From Ghosts and Gods to Politics and Conspiracies—How We Construct Beliefs and Reinforce Them as Truths* (Times Books, 2011), 87. Shermer applied the idea of agenticity to conspiracy theories on 207–27.

Afterword

1. Quoted in Marisa Taylor and Jonathan S. Landay, "Obama's crackdown views leaks as aiding enemies of U.S.," June 20, 2013, mcclatchydc.com/2013/06/20/194513/obamas-crackdown-views-leaks-as.html.

2. "INSIDER THREATS: Combating the ENEMY within your organization," Defense Security Service.
3. "Examples of Behavior of Potential Security Concern," dm.usda.gov/ocpm/Security%20Guide/S3stndrd/Examples.htm.
4. Bruce Schneier, "WikiLeaks," December 9, 2010, schneier.com/blog/archives/2010/12/wikileaks_1.html.
5. Robert Anton Wilson, *Prometheus Rising* (New Falcon Publications, 1997 [1983]), 222.
6. Julian Assange, "The non-linear effects of leaks on unjust systems of governance," December 31, 2006, web.archive.org/web/20071020051936/http:/iq.org/#Thenonlineareffectsofleaksonunjustsystemsofgovernance.
7. zunguzungu [Aaron Bady], "Julian Assange and the Computer Conspiracy; 'To destroy this invisible government,'" zunguzungu.wordpress.com/2010/11/29/julian-assange-and-the-computer-conspiracy-"to-destroy-this-invisible-government".
8. Quoted in Sara Yin, "U.S. Military BANNED From Viewing WikiLeaks," August 5, 2010, huffingtonpost.com/2010/08/05/us-military-banned-from-v_n_671967.html.
9. Quoted in Benjamin Wittes, "DoD to Troops: Lawfare=Wikileaks," December 3, 2010, lawfareblog.com/2010/12/dod-to-troops-lawfare wikileaks.
10. Phillip Molnar, "Restricted web access to *The Guardian* is Armywide, officials say," *The Monterey Herald*, June 27, 2013.
11. Stuart Stevens, "As WikiLeaks Takes on the Roles of a State, America Must Treat It as One," June 24, 2013, thedailybeast.com/articles/2013/06/24/as-wikileaks-takes-on-the-roles-of-a-state-america-must-treat-it-as-one.html.
12. James F. Moore, "The Second Superpower Rears Its Beautiful Head," March 31, 2003, web.archive.org/web/20030603201941/http://cyber.law.harvard.edu/people/jmoore/secondsuperpower.html.
13. This was partly the result of a WikiLeaks statement that said Snowden was "being escorted by diplomats and legal advisers from WikiLeaks." Stevens misread that as meaning the diplomats, not just the legal advisors, were from WikiLeaks, and he concluded that this meant

WikiLeaks was "acting like some kind of faux state that welcomes immigrants bearing secrets."

14. Quoted in Daniel Dombey, "Erdogan says same forces behind Brazil and Turkey protests," *Financial Times*, June 23, 2013.
15. Patrícia Fachin, "Brazilian Revolt: An Interview with Giuseppe Cocco," June 28, 2013, viewpointmag.com/2013/06/28/brazilian-revolt-an-interview-with-giuseppe-cocco.
16. For an interesting exploration of conspiracy fears around the world—though of course it can only scratch the surface of the subject—see *Transparency and Conspiracy: Ethnographies of Suspicion in the New World Order*, ed. Harry G. West and Todd Sanders, Duke University Press, 2003. For a globe-spanning (or at least West-spanning) look at conspiracy narratives in fiction and drama, covering such topics as the secret-society-focused "lodge novels" that emerged in eighteenth-century Germany, see Theodore Ziolkowski, *Lure of the Arcane: The Literature of Cult and Conspiracy*, The Johns Hopkins University Press, 2013.
17. I discuss those anti-Gypsy conspiracy stories in Jesse Walker, "The Legend of the Child-Snatching Gypsies," October 30, 2013, reason.com/archives/2013/10/30/the-legend-of-the-child-snatching. For a taste of that strange Nigerian saga, see "Charly Boy Threatens to Sue over Gay and Illuminati Story," May 28, 2012, africanspotlight.com/2012/05/28/charly-boy-threatens-to-sue-over-gay-and-illuminati-story.

INDEX

Note: Page numbers in *italics* refer to illustrations.

ABOUT THE AUTHOR

Jesse Walker is books editor at *Reason* magazine and the author of *Rebels on the Air: An Alternative History of Radio in America.* He lives in Baltimore with his wife and their two daughters.